Güvenç Koçkaya – Albert Wertheimer

Pharmaceutical
Market Access
in Developed Markets

SEEd

Editors

Güvenç Koçkaya
CarthaGenetics, Pully, Switzerland

Albert Wertheimer
College of Pharmacy, Nova Southeastern University, Ft. Lauderdale, FL, USA

First edition
January 2018

ISBN 978-88-97419-73-0
https://doi.org/10.7175/747

Summary

Preface

In the good old days, pharmaceutical companies used to develop a new molecule and launch it without any resistance, except those regarding clinical effectiveness, safety, and quality assessment. The main assessment was conducted on the basis of science-driven, evidence-based characteristics. However, in the last decades, market access has become the most important element for the pharmaceutical industry, with a primary focus on pricing and reimbursement, which are political and economic-driven characteristics.

Depending on specific health policies, some medicines are favored over others in the market access process, because the reflexes in the community for politics are different in each country, depending on demographics and the community perceptions. For example, elderly patients are more considered in the developed countries, due to health policies focusing on late-life diseases. But children are more considered in the emerging countries, due to health policies focusing on early-life diseases.

In this political and economic-driven environment, market access is getting harder than ever for all countries, especially the developed ones. After the financial crisis in 2008, developed countries have been under pressure due to a lack of cash and budget deficits. This situation is more important in government-based reimbursement countries, like France and United Kingdom, rather than private-based insurance countries, like the United States and Germany.

The pharmaceutical market access in the emerging markets has been thoroughly reviewed in the book "Pharmaceutical Market Access in Emerging Markets", published in 2016. The perception of readers was amazing. The book had been listed among Amazon's top 100 hot books for nearly three months. After such "literary" success, we decided to start a new project, focusing on the developed countries. This book focuses on the developed markets, with the aim of helping students, academics, industry employees and government decision-makers understand the environment in the developed markets. Hopefully, it will be helpful to all who want to understand market access, which is rock and roll compared to the evidence-based and science-driven decision process.

I would like to extend my thanks to my beloved wife, Dr. Pınar Daylan Kockaya, and my son, Uras Kockaya, of whom I am proud, for enduring my lack of presence in their life; my dearest lecturer and supporter Prof. Dr. Albert I. Wertheimer, for supporting me without any questions in any situation, and the authors and reviewers of the book, for supporting this project.

Dr. Güvenç Koçkaya, MD, MSc, PhD

https://doi.org/10.7175/747.ch1

1. Introduction to the Market Access

Mondher Toumi[1], Szymon Jarosławski[1]

[1] *Public Health Department – Research Unit EA 3279. Aix – Marseille University, Marseille, France*

1.1 Origin of the Market Access Term

Market Access for Goods

The Market Access (MA) term was first introduced by the World Trade Organization (WTO) to define the competing relation between the domestic and the imported products of a country.

The WTO defines MA as a set of conditions, tariff and non-tariff measures, agreed by WTO members for the entry of specific goods into their markets, that is to say, the government policies regarding trade-barriers in general, and specifically the issues of import substitution (to promote local production) and free competition.

Healthcare Market Specifics

In spite of many similarities between healthcare products and other goods in a free market economy, the healthcare market challenges the traditional economic paradigm. There are four features that clearly differentiate the healthcare market from other markets.

1. **The price is not determined by supply and demand**. In a traditional market economy context, the price is determined by supply and demand. In the healthcare market, however, the prices are determined by payers through negotiation or are simply notified by the manufacturer. Further, in the traditional market, a single entity assumes the functions of the buyer, the payer, and the consumer. In the healthcare market, however, the buyer is the physician who prescribes the treatment, the payer is the health insurance provider, and the consumer is the patient. The three parties do not necessarily have convergent views on the value of healthcare goods.
2. **Payers are committed to purchasing health for the society**. The healthcare payers' intent is to provide health for the patient. When payers fund medicine they wish to fund health production. However, they can only buy a proxy of health through the purchase of medicine and healthcare services. The actual outcome in terms of health improvement remains uncertain.
3. **Health is specific to each individual.** Unlike food or technology, health cannot be shared or traded between individuals. The outcome of a treatment procedure also depends on individual characteristics of the patient. The patients' characteristics may be not fully known *a priori* because of the lack of appropriate tools. This repertoire of

medical tools is evolving and changes our understanding of the disease and our approach to therapies.

4. **Externality of health.** Medicines can have a positive impact on the health of people, other than the ones who consume it. This is particularly the case for vaccinations and antibiotics. The treatment and prevention of contagious diseases at the level of an individual can protect the global population from a potential epidemic. Therefore, i) restricting access to health care for a population's subgroup can have dramatic impact on that population health status, ii) poor health care in a population's subgroup will affect the health of the remaining part of the population that has good access to health care. This is one of the main reasons for the creation of national health care systems. Illustratively, it has been iteratively reported that, despite the highest *per capita* healthcare expenditure, the US does not have the best population health status, notably because of the wide disparity in access to health care.

1.2 Healthcare Market Access Definition

The concept of MA is complex to define, depending on whether we are dealing with a private, public or mixed health care system. MA is the process by which a healthcare goods company gets its product available on the market after having obtained a Marketing Authorization (MAu) from a regulatory agency and by which the product becomes available/affordable for all patients for whom it is indicated as per its MAu.

The following definition will be used in this chapter:

MA for pharmaceuticals defines the ability for a drug to achieve through a health insurance system a reimbursed price and a favorable recommendation for medical prescriptions.

It covers a group of activities intended to provide access to the appropriate medicine for the appropriate group of patients and at the appropriate price.

For the manufacturers, the ideal outcome of the MA process is to achieve the optimal price with maximum reimbursement for the approved target population with no limitation on prescription or funding procedures. However, in practice the company needs to strike a trade-off between:

- Price and reimbursement conditions;
- Target patient population selection;
- Prescription and funding procedures.

Therefore, MA can be also seen as activities that support the management of potential barriers, such as non-optimal price and reimbursement level, the restriction of the scope of prescription for a drug or complicated prescription or funding procedures.

The scope of these activities encompasses the management of pricing and reimbursement, Health Technology Assessment (HTA) and formularies. The formularies are the lists of medicines that may be prescribed at the expense of the institutionalized payer.

MAu from a regulatory agency, which could be the Food and Drug Administration (FDA) in the US or the European Medicines Agency (EMA) in the EU, is issued based on consideration of the product's safety, efficacy, and quality in the highly controlled conditions of Randomised Clinical Trials (RCT). In the case of UE, national agencies are responsible for the implementation of this authorization in their local settings. Once a medicine is approved for marketing, HTA bodies are responsible for assessing its real-life efficacy (i.e. effectiveness), cost-effectiveness, relative efficacy, related medical need, budget impact and other evidence that will be later used by payers for pricing and reimbursement (P&R) decisions, as well as formulary listing and prescription guidelines.

Institutionalized healthcare payers (such as the national health funds, health insurers, etc.) themselves are typically not qualified to evaluate those criteria, so they delegate these activities to independent groups of experts which elaborate the HTA evidence. HTA evaluations aim to inform payers' decisions and help them set the appropriate P&R conditions.

Finally, MA is not and should not be confused with the following activities: obtaining regulatory approval (license, MAu), medical marketing and sales (e.g. medical representatives getting access to doctors or pharmacists), distribution (access to pharmacy shelves), choosing the right channel to promote product (e.g. marketing, direct-to-customer advertising etc.).

1.3 Market Access Key Concepts

If we consider the WTO definition, obtaining MA should be the ability to access the whole market in a given country, sell the product and achieve revenue from the market without obstacles. In the case of pharmaceuticals, these obstacles are: obtaining MAu, P&R levels, logistics (storage and supply conditions), the drug surveillance (follow up on potential and actual product adverse effects), etc. In practice, however, the pharmaceutical industry has become proficient in addressing all those hurdles except P&R. Thus, MA for the industry has become equivalent to the addressing the hurdle of achieving optimal P&R levels.

Measuring Value

MA is related to the concept of 'value for money' from a payer's point of view. As a result, the primary objective of MA studies is to define and measure the value of health services and products.

In economics, the value is a concept that refers to two different theories. The first one is an objective theory, or the intrinsic theory of value, where the value of an object, good or service, corresponds to the cost of the production that is the cost of raw material and human work needed.

The second one is a subjective theory and is more consistent with the idea of value as perceived in the healthcare market. According to this theory, the value of a good is neither determined by any inherent property of the good, nor by the amount of labor required to produce the good, but is determined by the importance of acting individual place on a good for the achievement of their desired outcome. The price offered is therefore not a measure of the subjective value; it is just a means of communication between the buyer (healthcare payer) and the seller (the manufacturer).

As far as healthcare and MA are concerned, this last definition is the most relevant and should be used. In MA, the value of a drug or a health service depends on the institutionalized payers' subjective perception of a particular medical need in the society and how the product addresses that need.

This assessment of value made by payers is subjective, yet based on scientific evidence, such as clinical trials, epidemiology, cost-effectiveness or other HTA studies. Most institutionalized payers formally require drug manufacturers and healthcare providers to submit evidence that corroborates the value of their product in terms of clinical outcomes and/or the cost of achieving such outcomes. Achieving a positive coverage decision at an optimal price depends on the ability of the pharmaceutical industry to submit pertinent evidence. If they succeed, this translates into successful MA for the concerned product. This calls for a thorough understanding of this evidence-based concept of value on the part of this industry.

The kind of evidence required by the payers for the assessment of a product differs from one country to another and covers a wide array of indicators, such as proof of clinical and economic value and more specific considerations of ethics, equity and/or politics. The set of evidence generated and presented by the manufacturer for the payer is called the value proposition. The development of such proposition is the ultimate aim of MA activities from an industrial perspective.

However, from a payer's perspective, the objective is to relate the drug's value to its price considering all available evidence. This is one of the most debated issues at the moment among healthcare actors and is often called value-based pricing.

Market Access and the Structure of Healthcare Markets

Pharmaceutical markets can have a varying degree of fragmentation, from countries with a single national insurer to countries with multiple private insurers or a mix of both. In the latter two cases, securing MA is the ability to systematically gain access at optimal conditions in each and every geographic area with each and every insurer. Depending on the type of healthcare market organization (e.g. centralized vs. decentralized or fully fragmented) the MA strategy may focus on different aspects as described below.

Publicly-funded health care systems

Within publicly funded national health insurance in Europe, Australia and Canada, the government defines the overall public health goals and the corresponding budget. Then, the rules of access to the public healthcare market by the industry are laid out by a central agency or agencies. These rules involve the kinds of evidence which are required for the value assessment of health products and the criteria for making the funding decision. In principle, the public healthcare payers represent the society's interest and try to integrate the societal perspective when making the funding decisions.

Mixed or private health care systems

The US is an example of a country where health insurance is fragmented and largely private. There is no unified framework which regulates the conditions of obtaining MA in the US and the public, as well as each of the private insurers, follow their own pathway. In this setting, for-profit private healthcare payers engage in independent negotiations with the industry. This can be seen a negotiation between two business entities that are looking to maximize their profits. However, in the US, the public payers (the Centers for Medicare & Medicaid Services – CMS, e.g., Medicare, Medicaid, and the Children's Health Insurance Program – CHIP) represent an increasing proportion of the healthcare budget that is almost nearing the commercial insurance sector. The CMS pathway resembles that of many European countries, Australia or Canada, except that formal health-economic analysis or HTA is not compulsory in the US, excluding very rare cases. Further, unlike in some European countries, the high cost of a product should not be a cause for a negative reimbursement advice by the CMS.

Centralized and regional market access

A trend towards decentralization is emerging in the public healthcare settings, as policy-making is increasingly devolved from the central, national bodies to local health authorities. As healthcare payers are compelled to restrain their pharmaceutical budgets, in a context of the economic recession, local policy makers are faced with funding decisions. However, these responsibilities are not always matched with competencies at the regional level. In many countries, the regional authorities accountable for medicine spending are seldom prepared to negotiate the costs of the drugs or to assess their value.

This trend is blurring the traditional division between countries with decentralized healthcare systems, such as Spain, Italy, Sweden or Germany and countries with more

	France	Germany	UK
Objective	Secure access to all new products, but at the right price	Obtain savings on drug spending with no detriment to safety/efficacy	Obtain rational allocation of resources
Process	Driver: Public health relevance of benefit compared to the next best alternative Method: Single/double-blind randomised clinical trial Effect size	Driver: Same effect – same price (e.g. jumbo groups) Method: Meta-analysis Efficiency frontier as a backup	Driver: Maximization of efficiency of the health care output Method: Cost-utility threshold is 30000 £/QALY
Impact	Gate-keeper for market entry	Reimbursement level	Recommendation for prescriber Formulary listing

Table 1. Cultural differences between countries regarding the objective, the process and the impact of HTA evaluation in MA

Northern Europe (UK, Scandinavia, The Netherlands)
- **Prescribers** follow guidelines and recommendations from National Health Insurance and are willing to accept cost containment measures
- **Payers** use cost-effectiveness to support decisions and prefer restriction of drug recommendation to subpopulations of patients

Southern Europe (France, Italy, Spain)
- **Prescribers** behavior is difficult to control by National Health Insurance
- **Payers** use efficacy to support decisions and prefer to negotiate the lower price with manufacturer rather than restrict drug use to subpopulations of patients

Figure 1. The cultural differences among prescribers and payers in Europe

centralized ones, like France or England. E.g. in England, where strategic decisions affecting the National Health System remain in the authority of the national Department of Health, the power of execution is assigned to a large number of Primary Care Trusts (PCTs). This means that, apart from the national bodies, the pharmaceutical industry has to engage directly with PCTs, in order to access the regional markets in England.

1.4 Cultural Specificities of Market Access

Any MA strategy needs to be culturally-sensitive. For instance, European countries that employ formal HTA in the funding decision framework can still substantially differ in the objective, the process and the impact of the HTA in MA (Table 1).

Finally, in Europe, there is a geographical dichotomy between medicine prescribers and payers in the Northern and Southern European countries. The former countries are typically more centralized and reluctant to price negotiation than the latter ones (Figure 1).

1.5 Market Access from Payers' Perspective

The Payers of Healthcare

In healthcare markets, payers are generally entities that finance or reimburse the cost of health services. In the health care market, payers always act as gatekeepers for MA.

In most European countries, there is one main payer in each country, corresponding to the national public health insurance. Sometimes, there are additional payers at a regional level or a mix of national and fragmented private payers as in the US. Importantly, each payer can have different objectives, perspectives, and processes.

Payers should not be considered as a homogeneous audience, but rather as a complex and heterogeneous one. The arguments accepted by one payer may be counterproductive for another payer within the same country.

Payers' Tools to Control Drug Expenditure

Despite an increasing proportion of health care products that have cheaper, generic versions, the pharmaceutical market value continues to grow. To tackle this growth, payers have employed a variety of cost containment measures since the late '90. Nevertheless, they have failed to control the growth of the expenditure. In the Organization for Economic Co-operation and Development (OECD) countries, excluding the US, healthcare spending has almost doubled its share of Gross Domestic Product (GDP) over the last 10 years. The demographic changes (population aging) and the expected future healthcare innovations are expected to generate a disruptive pressure on healthcare budgets unless an appropriate action is taken. Pharmaceutical spending growth is a lot more significant than the healthcare spending growth and accounts for as high as 20% in many developed countries.

The most common regulation of drug expenditure is price control. This tool means that the institutionalized payer, rather than the manufacturer, decides on the appropriate price for a medicine. This decision is often preceded by a negotiation with the MAu holder. Only two developed countries still enjoy the free (uncontrolled) pricing process: the US and the UK. However, the two countries have put in place a number of regulatory processes that indirectly regulate prices. For instance, if a drug is thought to be overpriced by the national payer in the UK, the access to the market can be narrowed by means of the so-called negative list recommendations. Further, free pricing in the UK was supposed to be replaced by a controlled pricing process, following the recommendation of the UK's Office of Fair Trading (OTC). Although the initiative of value based pricing failed, the UK Department of Health is now routinely accepting very high discounts that remain confidential but are often above 50% of the list price of many costly medicines.

Other pharmaceutical cost-containment measures developed by payers include general price cuts, reference pricing or exceptional taxes on turnover and profit.

During the 90s, the pricing regulation in Europe was often based on the health authorities' subjective perception of what the right price was. In order to dissolve political pressure around patients' access to new medicines and incentives for the industry to innovate, the authorities needed to implement more clear and objective rules for establishing prices. This resulted in two key developments:

- The creation of national Health Technology Assessment (HTA) bodies across EU countries, Australia and Canada that assess evidence supporting the benefit of new medicines and other health technologies.
- The creation of reference pricing within the therapeutic class and across EU countries.

This trend is also seen in the US where The American Recovery and Reinvestment Act (ARRA) provided $ 1.1 billion for comparative effectiveness research.

The Value Assessment by Payers

Given the limited financial resources, payers wish to contain drug expenditure and invest in products that can create best health outcomes for the insured. In this endeavor, they need to assess the uncertainty about the drug's potential health benefits, as well as the potential costs related to funding it. This process is referred to as the value assessment framework.

The process of assessing the value for money of a medicine is broadly a four-step assessment:

1. **Comparative efficacy from clinical trials of the medicine** (as compared to alternative treatments for the same condition).The quality of the data is scrutinized, as to the clinical trial design, the inclusion/exclusion criteria, the randomization procedure etc.

2. **Comparative effectiveness from real-life data on use of the medicine**. If an added benefit is observed in clinical trials, it may or may not be pertinent to real-life medical practice. The following conditions are scrutinized: i) the statistical effect size of the additional benefit of the medicine showed in a clinical trial (i.e. is the effect sufficient to be clinically important or does it present a significant improvement for the patients?), ii) the transferability of the clinical trial data across jurisdictions or regions, and iii) the transferability from a clinical trial model to real life. If a medicine doesn't show significant benefit after these two steps, the value will be considered equal or lower than that of the comparator treatment. If it is so, no premium price can be granted. However, if the benefit is shown, value for money can be further assessed by comparing the extra benefits to the extra costs of the new medicine.

3. **Cost-effectiveness**. This method compares the drug's effectiveness benefit against the cost consequences of using the drug (e.g. cost per Life Year Saved, per Quality Adjusted Life Year (QALY), per success, per relapse avoided etc.). Cost per QALY has been increasingly adopted by most HTA organizations over the recent years. Because the (real-life) effectiveness of a new intervention is often unknown at its market launch, this approach remains quite theoretical. Nevertheless, it is commonly considered rational to set a maximal threshold for the Incremental Cost-Effectiveness Ratio

---

Box 1. The Importance of Affordability

In the US, payers pay for certain oncology products $ 80,0000 to increase life expectancy by 1.2 months. By simple extrapolation, survival gain of 1 year would be valued at $ 800,000. In the country, 550,000 patients die from cancer annually. If new drugs are developed that extend life by one year, $ 440 billion would be needed to purchase this drug for all patients. This amount seems unaffordable, even for the richest countries. Therefore, it seems that beyond assessing what is the value of the additional health benefit a new medicine, we need to be concerned about what is the affordability of the payer to fund this new medicine.

(ICER) per QALY gained for funded interventions. However, this approach may lack consideration for the payer's affordability (Box 1).

4. **Budget Impact**. This stage determines if the intervention is affordable in the current budget and if not, what is the additional budget needed to reimburse this new drug or what actions should be undertaken to make it affordable. Some countries do not consider budget impact as they believe it is redundant with the efficiency assessment, as the ICER threshold is expected to reflect/be adjusted on the country's affordability. This remains debatable. Following the exemplary value assessment framework presented above, the payers may wish to estimate what is the right price for the medicine in question. In the institutionalised health care payer settings, the value-based pricing is currently considered to be the most promising model, but the methodology is only emerging and it remains to be seen if it will be implemented successfully.

The Link Between HTA and Pricing & Reimbursement Conditions

Negative HTA recommendation for use of a medicine translates into sub-optimal MA in various ways. The impact on price can be through direct reduction of the price by the payer, price-volume agreements or co-payments (e.g. in Germany). The impact on reimbursement is by reducing the maximum percentage of reimbursement (e.g. in France).

Further, restrictions can be applied on the scope of prescription of a drug. Partial restriction consists in defining a population of patients or an indication that is narrowed as compared to the MAu of a drug. The full restriction means that a drug will not be included in formularies or in guidelines (e.g. in Canada, UK). Pre-authorization of prescription for a medicine by the payer or by a specialist medical center are further means of ensuring that the drug is only prescribed to the patient population strictly defined by the payer. Finally, Market Access Agreements discussed in section 7 are contracts between the manufacturers and the payers that aim at obscuring the real medicine price or that allow a temporary premium price until stronger evidence on drug's effectiveness or safety is developed.

Non-HTA Tools That Affect Drug Pricing

HTA is a laborious process and it's often unclear how to link HTA recommendations to the price of a medicine. Reference pricing is a benchmarking model of setting prices of medicines by comparing them to the prices of the same medicine in other countries or by comparing them to prices of existing medicines in the same therapeutic area or with a similar mechanism of action in the same country. These methods are described below.

External Reference Pricing

External Reference Pricing (ERP) (also referred to as "External Price Referencing", "International Price Benchmark", "External Price Benchmark", "External Price Linkage" or else "International Price Linkage") has rapidly become a widespread cost-containment tool. It is used among European countries, as well as by other countries such as Brazil,

Jordan, South Africa, Japan, Turkey, Canada and Australia that refer to the European drug prices in order to establish their own.

The WHO Collaborating Centre for Pricing and Reimbursement Policies defines ERP as «the practice of using the price(s) of a medicine in one or several countries in order to derive a benchmark or reference price for the purposes of setting or negotiating the price of the product in a given country». Consequently, the change of price for a given product in one country affects the price in other countries.

Altogether, ERP methods and rulings are outlined with different levels of accuracy within the national pricing regulations. Portugal and Austria are examples of countries in which the legislation provides ample details on the use of ERP. German and Estonian laws provide much less guidance on the matter. On one extreme, Luxembourg resorts to ERP to determine the price of all newly marketed drugs. In contrast, Estonia, France and Germany resort to ERP in the case of innovative and publicly reimbursed medicines only.

Internal Reference Pricing

Benchmarking prices of existing medicines in the same therapeutic area or with a similar mechanism of action in the same country is used by some countries to set prices of new drugs. E.g. in Germany, when no additional benefit has been established in HTA of a newly approved medicine, it is allocated to a reference price group with pharmacologically and therapeutically comparable pharmaceuticals. All pharmaceuticals in this group will have the same price. In many European countries, an internal reference pricing system is in place for reimbursed generics, that is all products that contain the same off-patent molecule are priced at the same level.

1.6 Market Access Agreements

Definition

The high cost of novel treatments is a common cause of negative or restricted reimbursement decisions by healthcare payers. Such decisions can reduce or even eliminate MA for new products. Therefore, both the payers and the industry seek compromise in achieving MA for novel products.

The outcome of such negotiations can be called Market Access Agreements (MAA). MAA can be defined as "an agreement between two or more parties, who agree to the terms and conditions under which a product will get access to the market". MAA specify, often in a confidential manner, the conditions under which a concerned treatment will be priced and reimbursed in a given population of patients.

Taxonomy

To simplify the nomenclature and taxonomy, MAA can be generally grouped into financial (Commercial Agreements, CA) or outcomes-based (Payment for Performance

Agreements (P4P) or Coverage with Evidence Development (CED): financial agreements are CA between two or more parties entering into a deal for goods acquisition; outcome-based agreements are part of an insurance or warranty facility: the payer agrees to a price under the insurance that the product will deliver a predefined health outcome in a given patient. This regroups two kinds of MAA: P4P and CED.

These two types of MAA are subdivided into two categories, MAA at the population level (certain types of CA, such as price-volume agreements, CED) and MAA at the individual patient level (certain types of CA, such as price cap per patient, free drug supply after a pre-defined treatment duration etc., P4P).

P4P are agreed by payers to avoid expenditure on treating patients who do not respond to a drug and who cannot be identified *ex ante*, by permanently linking the payment to drug's performance in individual patients. P4P is set to pay only for patients who achieve a pre-specified response to a drug.

In contrast, CED are temporary MAA where the payers agree to finance the new technology as a part of a well-designed study, in order to generate real-life evidence that will enable final price and reimbursement decisions. Such evidence may not be available at the time of drug launch because data from clinical trials do not reflect the real-life use, health outcome, dosage or duration of treatment, actual targeted patient population or the impact of the medicine in question on the use of other health care resources.

Finally, MAA can be a mix of two types of agreements, e.g. a simple price discount (CA) is often an element of P4P.

The Future of MAA

CA and P4P ensure drug cost reductions to payers while maintaining high list prices. The importance of high list prices for the industry pertains from the use of ERP globally. Therefore, maintaining high visible prices in the major pharmaceutical markets can help manufacturers ensure high prices in countries that use those countries to set prices of new drugs. In the future, the complex and burdensome P4P will likely be replaced by CA when payers need to reduce the cost or by CED when they wish to reduce uncertainty about drug's performance.

1.7 Market Access for Orphan Drugs

Definitions of Orphan Drugs

Orphan medicinal products, or "orphan drugs", constitute a class of drugs that have been developed specifically to treat a rare medical condition generally referred to as "orphan disease". As the name suggests, rare diseases occur in a very small population. Therefore, making orphan drugs profitable for the industry may require obtaining high prices for a low number of users. At present, there is no universal definition of rare disease and it differs among countries.

In the US, an orphan drug is defined in the *Orphan Drug Act* as: «Orphan drugs are used in diseases or circumstances which occur so infrequently in the USA, that there is no reasonable expectation that the cost of developing and making available in the USA a drug for such disease or condition will be recovered from sales in the USA for such drugs».

The limit of prevalence for a rare condition in the US is defined as the absolute number of 200,000 people in the population. In 1985 and 1990 the definition of orphan drugs was extended to products other than drugs like biologics, medical devices, and medical foods.

The EU orphan drugs regulation was implemented almost 20 years after the US regulation. As defined by the regulation EC No 141/2000, a product can be designated as orphan drug, if it is intended for the treatment, prevention or diagnosis of a disease that is life threatening or chronically debilitating; the prevalence of the condition in the EU is not more than 5 in 10,000 or it must be unlikely that marketing of the medicine would generate sufficient returns to justify the investment needed for its development; no satisfactory method of diagnosis, prevention or treatment of the condition concerned can be authorized, or, if such a method exists, the medicine is of significant benefit to those affected by the condition.

In 2005, France was the first EU country that established a national plan for orphan drugs that also included funding provisions. France hosts several European organisations that work in the field of orphan diseases, such as Eurordis, Orphanet portal, and the Orphanet Journal of Rare Diseases.

Spain was the second European country that published a national strategy for rare diseases in 2008. Some regions like Andalucía, Extremadura and Catalonia have created their own rare disease plans.

Further, the UK's National Institute for Health and Care Excellence (NICE) is developing new methodology to evaluate the so called ultra-orphan drugs, called Highly Specialised Technologies (HST). The use of the term ultra-orphan drug is restricted to drugs used to treat conditions with a prevalence of less than one case per 50,000 population.

The HTA Frameworks for Orphan Drugs and Ultra-Orphan Drugs

Different European jurisdictions focus on various HTA criteria for the evaluation of orphan drugs, such as cost-effectiveness, budget impact, disease severity, therapeutic need, social benefits etc. There is no universal HTA decision framework and the existing approaches are facing many challenges.

Standard HTA approaches that require data from RCTs are often relaxed when applied to orphan drugs. This is because there may be little data available, or the data may be of low validity or quality, even if the drug in question has been licensed for use. Because of the high unmet needs, despite the data paucity, higher levels of uncertainty on clinical efficacy, safety, incremental cost-effectiveness and budgetary impact may be allowed by decision makers and these drugs are reimbursed in certain countries.

These various approaches result in disparities in access to orphan drugs among countries. Interestingly, France and Italy focus on criteria such as proven clinical value, evidence from cohort studies, and the degree of innovation, but do not require a formal cost-effectiveness analysis for regular and orphan drugs.

In contrast, in England and Wales, a threshold of ICER per QALY is the benchmark of medicine funding recommendations by NICE. For instance, one study showed that NICE gave only two positive recommendations on 43 EMA-approved orphan drugs, 69% of them were reimbursed in Sweden and 94% and 100% of them were reimbursed in Italy and France respectively. However, for ultra-orphan drugs, NICE would like to operate as a "broker" putting together all the stakeholders around the same table and looking for a reasonable price that would satisfy all parties, which should allow greater patient access to such products.

This illustrates a trend where countries that require standard cost-effectiveness analysis typically have a lower coverage of orphan drugs than countries that do not. Consequently, patients with rare diseases in countries which employ solely the cost-effectiveness approach may be deprived of access to orphan drugs.

As shown before, ICER-based decision making that focuses on the allocation of limited resources in order to maximize the health value generated may not be compatible with the pursuit of social equity. However, incorporating social values into the HTA framework requires more empirical research that measures the social preferences in a given society. For instance, people can share two notions of equity: horizontal equity (equal treatment of equals, implying that everyone in the society is equal by birth and spending health care budget on rare diseases is unfair) and vertical equity (unequal treatment of unequals, implying that people in the society are not equal by birth (e.g. in terms of their genetic make-up) and therefore are entitled to special treatments). From the utilitarian perspective of allocation of limited resources, funding of orphan drugs must support the vertical equity.

However, many orphan drugs would not be recommended for reimbursement even if societal perspectives were incorporated into funding decisions, because of their very high prices.

In the US, there are no formal HTA frameworks to assess the value of orphan drugs and the prices are unregulated. The high cost of orphan drugs is driven by the perceived need for a return on investment from a smaller than usual population of patients, lack of alternative treatments and the severity of the rare disease.

Further, pricing of orphan drugs has been described as obscure and the prices of orphan drugs in the US do not seem to correlate with the patient population sizes.

Therefore, more transparent pricing methods, such as 'cost-plus' or 'rate of return', could be considered when pricing orphan drugs. However, it's complex to assess objectively what is the cost of developing a drug and how to account for the cost of unsuccessful candidate molecules that had to be discontinued without financial return to manufacturers.

Conclusion

Orphan drug incentives have stimulated the pharmaceutical industries to the development of research into diseases with significant unmet medical need. The revenue-generating potential of orphan drugs is similar for non-orphan drugs, even though patient populations for rare diseases are significantly smaller. Moreover, orphan drugs may be more profitable, when considered in the full context of developmental drivers including government financial incentives, smaller clinical trial sizes, shorter clinical trial times and higher rates of regulatory success. However, current orphan drug policies are unlikely to be sustainable, because they have led to high prices of orphan drugs and to limited coverage and restricted patient access when cost-effectiveness is the sole decision-making criterion. This calls for policy changes which are unavoidable in order to ensure sustainability of the health care systems.

1.8 Early Advice

Medicine manufacturers have an opportunity to consult regulators and HTA bodies, early in the development process of a medicine as a part of specific early advice schemes. The authorities concerned by these schemes use various terms, such as "early dialogue" or "scientific advice".

Such advice can help pharmaceutical companies establish what evidence these authorities will need in order to determine a medicine's benefit-risk balance (in the marketing authorization process) and its "value-for-money" in real-life use (in the HTA process).

For instance, manufacturers can apply for parallel scientific advice from EMA and national HTA bodies at any stage of development of a medicine, whether the medicine is eligible for the centralized authorization procedure in the EU or not.

Further, the so called adaptive pathway is an accelerated scientific advice pathway of EMA for therapies indicated for serious conditions with high unmet needs. It requires that there is an iterative development with use of real-life data. It provides to the possibility to engage various stakeholders including regulators, HTA bodies and patient representatives in multiple discussions along the development pathway.

EMA has also developed a scheme for priority medicines called PRIME, in order to optimize the development and accelerated assessment of medicines of major public health interest. PRIME reinforces early dialogue and builds on regulatory processes such as scientific advice to optimize the generation of robust data and the accelerated assessment procedure to improve timely access for patients to priority medicines.

Further, individual EU countries have also implemented similar programs. The company needs to identify the appropriate timing to seek early advice. For instance, very early in the drug development (non-clinical/proof of concept stage), the company may seek clarifications/adjustments of general clinical trial design but limited patient data. They are likely to obtain a general response with a less specific advice. In contrast, later in the drug development (prior to phase III) the company can obtain more precise responses regarding clinical trial design and pharmacoeconomic questions. When phase III plans have been finalised, advice can still help to adjust design/statistical analysis plan of phase IIIb/IV studies.

Overall, the advice should be sought early enough to ensure that the company can integrate the advice in all phases of the development. However, if the advice is sought too early, population(s) and indication(s) may be dramatically affected by the advice from the HTA agencies. Therefore, end of phase IIb should be a reasonable time to request the advice.

In summary, the main goal of the early HTA advice is to achieve consensus between HTA bodies and the EMA (when relevant) on the global drug clinical development plan. Simultaneous feedback from HTA bodies and regulators can help companies to identify key areas of consensus and divergence between these different stakeholders.

1.9 Early Access Programs

Early Access Programs (EAPs) are country-specific regulatory processes which grant MA to unlicensed medical drugs to specific patients, under specific terms, provided that they fulfil specific criteria.

The EU, through the European Regulation 726/2004/EC, defines Compassionate Use as a treatment option that allows the use of an unauthorized medicine for patients who either have a disease for which no satisfactory authorized therapies exist or who cannot enter a clinical trial.

In the US, FDA regulations have allowed patients access to investigational drugs and biologics through Expanded Access since 1987. Expanded Access is a regulation that makes promising drugs and devices available to patients with serious or immediately life-threatening diseases. The FDA currently approves Expanded Access, on a case-by-case basis for an individual patient, for intermediate-size groups of patients with similar treatment needs who otherwise do not qualify to participate in a clinical trial, or for large groups of patients who do not have other treatment options available and sufficient information is known about the safety and potential effectiveness of a drug from ongoing or completed clinical trials.

EAPs can be divided into two main types of programs:

- **Nominative or named-patient EAPs** are typically initiated by physicians for an individual patient in great need of a medicinal product, which will be administered under the physician's responsibility. Companies usually have little influence on this type of EAP. However, companies can try to anticipate these demands and define in advance a set of criteria allowing safe access and administration to patients.
- **Cohort EAPs** are usually initiated by the manufacturer to allow access for a group of patients to an unauthorized medicinal product.

The different countries may refer to them differently but all the programs fall within this binary classification. The regulatory requirements for each programmer also vary.

Global EAP Trends

The majority of countries have both nominative and cohort EAPs (France, Italy, Spain, Denmark, Norway, Brazil, and South Korea). UK, Switzerland, Australia, Israel, and Turkey have nominative programs only and only Germany has a cohort programmer only. All the programs are under the remit of relevant government health authorities. Commercial provision of drugs/devices in EAP is possible in most of the programs and the price is usually set freely. In the remaining cases, the price is negotiated with relevant authorities. Reimbursement is usually conditional. Full reimbursement is only possible in France, Italy, Spain, and in the License Procedure in Sweden.

There is currently no evidence that these programs expedite the speed at which medicines receive market authorization. Similarly, EAPs do not guarantee market authorization and there is currently no aggregate evidence showing that EAPs will guarantee reimbursement/coverage after marketing authorization.

1.10 **To Know More**

Market Access Definitions

- Center for International Development at Harvard University. Available at http://www.cid.harvard.edu/cidtrade/issues/marketaccess.html
- Menger C. Principles of Economics. Auburn, Ala: Ludwig von Mises Institute, 2007
- Robinson SW. Market Access – The Definition Depends on the Viewpoint. Evidence Matters 2010; 16. Available at http://www.paramountcommunication.com/ubc/pdf/01_Market_Access_The_Definition.pdf
- HTA and value assessment frameworks
- Claxton K, Briggs A, Buxton MJ, et al. Value based pricing for NHS drugs: an opportunity not to be missed. *BMJ* 2008; 336: 251-4
- Garattini L, Cornago D, De Compadri P. Pricing and reimbursement of in-patent drugs in seven European countries: A comparative analysis. *Health Policy* 2007; 82: 330-9
- Kristensen FB, Sigmund H. Health Technology Assessment Handbook. Copenhagen: Danish Centre for Health Technology Assessment, National Board of Health, 2007
- Market access for Pharma: pulling in the same direction? – a UK perspective from Alan Crofts. Available at http://www.thepharmaletter.com/file/79052/market-access-for-pharma-pulling-in-the-same-direction-a-uk-perspective-from-alancrofts.html
- Sackett DL, Rosenberg WM, Gray JA et al. Evidence based medicine: what it is and what it isn't. *BMJ* 1996; 312: 71-2
- Surveying, Assessing and Analysing the Pharmaceutical Sector in the 25 EU Member States. Commissioned by European Commission – DG Competition,

2006. Available at http://ec.europa.eu/competition/mergers/studies_reports/oebig.pdf

- Toumi M, Michel M. Define Access Agreements. PMlive, 2011. Available at http://www.pmlive.com/pharma_news/define_access_agreements_283271#

Market Access Agreements

- Jarosławski S, Toumi M. Design of patient access schemes in the UK: influence of health technology assessment by the National Institute for Health and Clinical Excellence. *Appl Health Econ Health Policy* 2011; 9: 209-15
- Jarosławski S, Toumi M. Market access agreements for pharmaceuticals in Europe: diversity of approaches and underlying concepts. *BMC Health Serv Res* 2011; 11: 259

Orphan Drugs

- Jarosławski S, Auquier P, Toumi M. No correlation between the prices of oncology orphan drugs in the US and their patient population sizes. *J Cancer Policy* 2017; 14: 1-4
- Drummond M, Towse A. Orphan drugs policies: a suitable case for treatment. *Eur J Health Econ* 2014; 15: 335-40
- Eurordis – Rare Diseases Europe. Available at www.eurordis.org
- Orphanet. Available at www.orpha.net
- Orphanet Journal of Rare Diseases. Available at www.ojrd.com

This is an updated version of the chapter Toumi M, Jarosławski S.
Introduction to the Market Access. In: Kockaya G, Wertheimer A (eds).
Pharmaceutical Market Access in Emerging Markets. Turin: SEEd, 2016

https://doi.org/10.7175/747.ch2

2. Market Access in Germany

Anke-Peggy Holtorf[1]
[1] *Health Outcomes Strategies GmbH, CH 4055 Basel, Switzerland*

2.1 General Outlook of Healthcare System and Health Policies

The Environment

Being initiated under Chancellor Bismarck in 1883, Germany's social statutory insurance is one of the earliest systems offering formal healthcare coverage for employed people as a part of a social security system.

Since then, ever-changing environmental factors put continuous pressure on the functioning of the system:

1. the population grew to today approximately 82 million inhabitants,
2. scientific and medical progress has allowed the growth of an active healthcare industry, which today is an important pillar of the German economy,
3. better access to healthcare has increased longevity to a life expectancy at birth of 83.1 for women and 78.2 for men [1],
4. many otherwise deadly diseases can now be cured or controlled as chronic diseases, and
5. at the same time, the birth rate went down to currently about 1.5 children per woman (2015) [1] and therefore, a decreasing number of younger working people have to bear the increasing bill of total social security cost.

Due to all these developments, healthcare expenditure has been continuously increasing to today about 11.3% of the German Gross Domestic Product (GDP) [2] and throughout the ongoing dynamics, the German healthcare system has experienced many revisions and changes over the years.

Particular events were the split of Germany into two politically and economically strictly separated parts in 1949 and the reunification into the current Nation with the capital of Berlin in 1990. During these 50 years, the eastern part (about 1/3 of the territory; today 5 states plus Berlin) as "German Democratic Republic" was under the rule of the socialist Union of Soviet Socialist Republics (USSR) and the Western part (Federal Republic of Germany with 10 states) under temporary control of the 3 other victorious powers (USA, UK, France) favoring a democratic political system of social market economy. The reunification of the two healthcare systems after 1990 was driven by the social statutory insurance system established in the West. Figure 1 summarized facts and numbers about Germany.

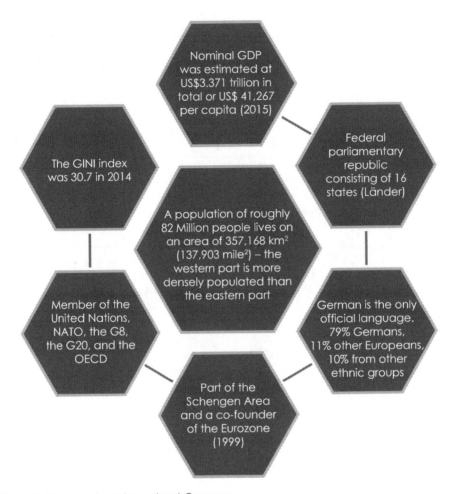

Figure 1. Facts and numbers about Germany

The Healthcare System

German citizens finance and access their healthcare through two insurance options, the public health insurance scheme (89% of the population) or private health insurance (11%) (Figure 2), through their tax contributions and through out-of-pocket expenditure. Total healthcare expenditure in 2016 was the 5th highest among the OECD countries after the USA, Switzerland, Luxembourg and Norway with USD 5,551/capita of which USD 23/capita were out-of-pocket costs [3].

The entitlements, rights and responsibilities of insured individuals are defined in the German social legal code (*Sozialgesetzbuch* – SGB), most importantly in part V (SGB-V), which establishes the regulatory framework for the Statutory Health Insurance (SHI) system. The aims of the German Statutory Health Insurance are summarized in Figure 3.

With an expenditure on pharmaceuticals of USD 678 per capita (USD PPP), Germany is one of the highest pharmaceutical spenders among OECD countries (OECD average USD 515 PPP) [4].

The latest major reform was introduced in 2011 with the Act on the Reform of the Market for Medicinal Products (*Arzneimittelmarktneuordnungsgesetz* – AMNOG), which regulates the processes for pricing and reimbursement of newly authorized pharmaceuticals.

More adaptations can be expected in future since the challenges continue to grow due to continuing dynamics and external pressures such as EU pressures around cross boarder healthcare or the influx of a considerable refugee population from economically and politically unstable regions in Asia, the Middle East and Africa.

Statutory (public) Health Insurance	Private Health Insurance
Based on the principle of solidarity	*Risk based: the insurance tariff depends on income, state of health, age and gender*
• Every employee pays together with the employer the same percentage of his income for his or her membership (currently 14.6% on average without risk adjustment) up to a fixed maximum contribution to one of the around 130 public non-profit "sickness funds". • Publicly insured persons receive medical care services, whereby each state determines the scope. • With statutory health insurance, insuring children and spouses is free within a family insurance plan.	• Can only be used by people with an income above a defined threshold (e.g. 57,600 €/year in 2017). • The scope is not regulated by the state and is often more extensive than statutory insurance. • Privately insured generally have more choice of providers and preferred access due to higher tariffs paid to the providers. • Insurance fees are individual and per person.

Since a few years, publicly insured people can also bridge the gap between public and private insurance by selecting a supplementary insurance plan.

Figure 2. Public and private health insurance in Germany

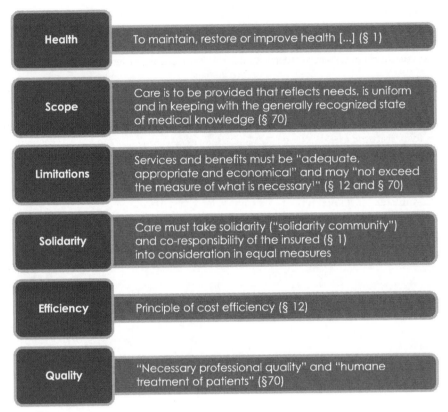

Figure 3. Aims and frame of the German Statutory Health Insurance System as defined in the social legal code (SGB-V)

[1] The 'necessity' needs to be proven by evidence; there is no right for access to a therapy if the evidence is missing [6]

In addition, there is still room for improvement. A recent study comparing 195 health-care systems worldwide through a Healthcare Access and Quality Index based on the Global Burden of Disease Study 2015 ranked Germany on place 20 after many other European countries and Australia [5].

2.2 Pathways of Market Access (Regulation, Pricing, and Reimbursement)

Market Authorization

The licensing of pharmaceutical products mostly follows EU laws and regulations, which were adopted to the German National Law. The admission of pharmaceuticals for humans on to the market is the responsibility of the Paul Ehrlich Institute (blood, blood products, sera and vaccines) and the Federal Institute for Pharmaceuticals and Medical Devices (all other products) [6]. National regulation applies for those substances which have not yet undergone regulatory assessment by the European Medicines Agency (EMA).

Coverage and Reimbursement of Pharmaceutical Products

Germany does not have a "positive list" of pharmaceuticals reimbursed (covered) by the German statutory health insurance (*Gesetzliche Krankenversicherung* – GKV). However, drugs which are not effective for the desired purpose or where the effect cannot be evaluated with certainty, can be excluded from reimbursement under SGB-V rules. Since 2004, the decision on reimbursement of drugs is under the responsibility of the Federal Joint Committee. Their decisions are legally binding and may also limit the prescription of drugs to certain indications, or determine the therapeutic steps in specific diseases.

On 11 November 2010, the German parliament passed the law called AMNOG which regulates pricing processes for newly authorized pharmaceuticals and their reimbursement by statutory health insurance providers. The core of this law is the benefit assessment in accordance with the German Social Code, Book Five (SGB-V), section 35a. The Federal Joint Committee (*Gemeinsamer Bundesausschuss* – G-BA) was charged with the implementation and with the activities of benefit assessment with the support of the Institute for Quality and Efficiency in Health Care (*Institut für Qualität und Wirtschaftlichkeit im Gesundheitswesen* – IQWiG). Pharmaceutical companies are obliged to submit a dossier on product benefit for all products newly launched on the German market or authorized for new indications.

Act on the Reform of the Market for Medicinal Products (AMNOG)

The AMNOG defined a new way to assess the value of patented medicines and the reimbursement category at the time of launch. This was intended to counteract increasing prices of newly launched pharmaceuticals and to reduce the time until a fair price was determined.

Steps to benefit assessment

Figure 4 summarizes the 6-month process of deciding on the reimbursement price following the AMNOG.

1. At the time of launch of a new active substance or a new indication, the company submits an evidence dossier to the G-BA who, in most cases, will charge IQWiG with an evidence review for assessing the additional benefit relative to a comparator (standard of care as defined by G-BA). During the time of the assessment and decision process the product can be marketed at a price set by the company.
2. The strongest driver for the extent and probability of additional benefit are the results of the relevant randomized clinical trials. The G-BA will publish the results on the website based on the IQWiG report and potential additional considerations. The

extent of benefit is categorized as major, considerable, minor, non-quantifiable, or worse while the probability can be described as no prove, hint, indication, or prove.

3. The company or other stakeholders can comment during a hearing
4. The G-BA will elaborate a resolution based on the assessment and the hearing

The same product can be rated with different results for different patient sub-populations. The results of G-BA decisions over the years 2011-2016 are summarized in Figure 5. Only few applications have been considered to have proof for considerable added benefit. Between 2011 and 2014, IQWiG had submitted 60 assessment reports on non-orphan therapies to the G-BA. Of these, 32 (53%) stated no additional benefit, and 28

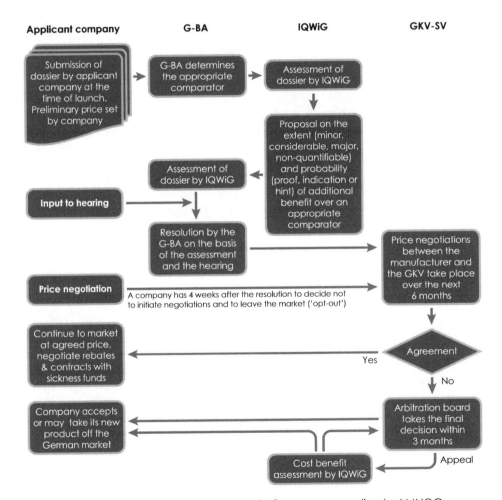

Figure 4. Pricing and reimbursement process in Germany according to AMNOG
G-BA = Federal Joint Committee; GKV-SV = National Association of Statutory Health Insurance Funds; IQWiG = Institute for Quality and Efficiency in Health Care

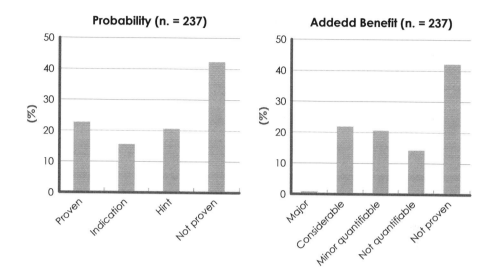

Figure 5. G-BA extent of additional benefit for pharmaceuticals and stated probability in the period 2011–2016 (based on data from the G-BA website)

found additional benefit (47%) classified as major in 6 cases, considerable in 12 cases, minor in 8 cases, and not quantifiable in 2 cases [7].

Orphan Drugs

A special legal framework allows the automatic recognition of additional benefit with an abbreviated submission dossier for drugs with European orphan drug designation [8] without additional benefit assessment in comparison to the current standard of care if the GKV expenses stay below € 50 million per 12 months [9]. Because of the legal link of orphan drug designation to the market authorization a large number of the assessments cannot conclude a quantifiable additional benefit due to lack of relevant evidence, and they are rated as 'non-quantifiable additional benefit'. The G-BA may define a time limit for its resolutions to allow further assessment after a period of post-marketing experience. If the 12-month sales exceed the limit of € 50 million, IQWiG will be charged by the G-BA with conducting a full assessment versus an appropriate comparator. A few case studies have been summarized by Bouslouk and colleagues in 2016 (Box 1) [9].

Like with non-orphan drugs, the manufacturer of orphan drugs must negotiate the price with the GKV-SV. Although all negotiation up to now could be concluded successfully, this may be a challenge because of the lack of comparators or comparative data [9].

The AMNOG process had to be adapted for orphan drugs to compromise between the strict German requirements for high-quality evidence and the strive for faster market access for break-through therapies pushed by the EU and EMA. Similar adaptations may

---

Box 1. Orphan Drugs. A Case Study

In 2013, the Vertex Pharmaceuticals cystic fibrosis drug Kalydeco (ivacaftor) has been given a high additional benefit rating in one group (12 years and older), and a low one in another (children between 6 and 11 years) for the treatment of cystic fibrosis (CF) in patients with the G551D mutation. Although Kalydeco had received European orphan status and Vertex had calculated that the annual cost of treatment in Germany with Kalydeco would be € 45 million (which was below the threshold of € 50 million for orphan drugs in Germany), it had to undergo the assessment of the benefit because the German Institute for Quality and Effectiveness in Healthcare (IQWiG) estimated that the actual figure will be about € 53 million [9].

---

happen in future but the political and institutional pressure for the AMNOG pathway in Germany will continue to be strong. Therefore, we will continue to see disputes such as a current example of Crizotinib in the treatment of lung cancer. G-BA decided that there is no prove for additional benefit, the medical professional societies however, see a major advancement for the 300-400 patients with lung cancer and the ROS1-gene mutation and recommend the product as first line treatment [10]. The discrepancy is caused by the limited evidence from randomized controlled trials, a consequence of a low number of patients and the ethical challenges.

Pharmaceutical Care Strengthening Act (*Arzneimittelversorgungsstärkungsgesetz – AMVSG*)

Recently, a new law AMVSG (Figure 6) has been approved to complement AMNOG by strengthening and adapting the provision of healthcare, especially to special populations (rare diseases, pediatric diseases etc.) [11]. A key objective is again to further control the cost of pharmaceuticals and avoid overspending throughout the period of free pricing in the first year between launch and completion of the price negotiations with the GKV-SV.

The Role of the G-BA

The Joint Federal Committee (*Gemeinsamer Bundesausschuss – G-BA*) is the highest decision-making body of the joint self-governance of physicians, dentists, psychotherapists, hospitals, and health insurances in Germany. The G-BA "issues directives for the benefit catalogue of the statutory health insurance funds (GKV) for more than 70 million insured persons and thus specifies which services in medical care are reimbursed by the GKV" and "specifies measures for quality assurance in inpatient and outpatient areas of the health care system" [12].

The leading umbrella organizations of the self-governing German healthcare system form the G-BA: the providers (Physicians, Dentists, Hospitals) and the insurances (GKV-

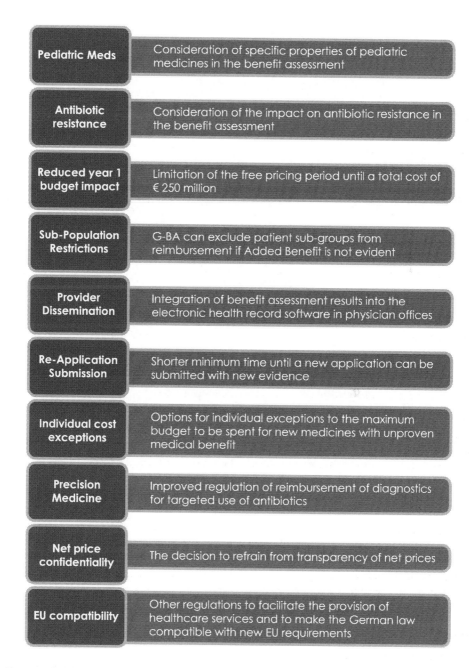

Figure 6. Constituents of the *Arzneimittelversorgungsstärkungsgesetz* (AMVSG) to be introduced in 2017 [11]

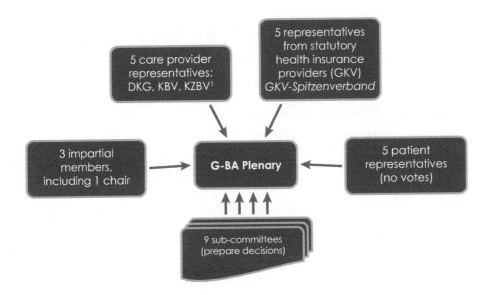

Figure 7. Composition of the G-BA [12]
[1] Care providers are entitled to vote only on issues affecting their area of expertise
GKV-Spitzenverband = National Association of Statutory Health Insurance Funds; DKG = German Hospital Federation; KBV = National Association of Statutory Health Insurance Physicians; KZBV = National Association of Statutory Health Insurance Dentists

SV). Patient representatives also participate in all sessions; they are entitled to put topics on the agenda, but not to vote.

The plenary decision body is composed of 13 voting members and 5 non-voting members (Figure 7).

The Role of IQWiG

The Institute for Quality and Efficiency in Healthcare (*Institut für Qualität und Wirtschaftlichkeit im Gesundheitswesen* – IQWiG) was founded in 2004 with the mission to produce independent evidence based expert reports on the quality and efficiency of therapies in the German healthcare system, comprising pharmaceutical and non-pharmaceutical methods, clinical guidelines, and disease management programs. IQWiG will only analyze and assess existing data without having decision power or own research capacities.

IQWiG can be commissioned by the G-BA or the Ministry of Health (*Bundesministerium für Gesundheit*) or can conduct assessments on own imitative. Since 2016, additional assessments will be generated on selected therapies proposed by patients [13].

G-BA will consider the evidence review produced by IQWiG but will not always follow the recommendations. Between 2011 and 2015, G-BA deviated from IQWiG's recommendations in 32% of all judgements [14]. While IQWiG aims to follow a strict scientific analytical process, G-BA may see a broader picture of health policy and modulate its recommendations around the needs and input or various stakeholders in healthcare [15].

Methodological Requirements for Early Benefit Assessment in Germany

The main source for the assessment is the dossier provided by the applicant. The dossier to be submitted in German language has a defined structure and format including the technical standards and documentations. The template and guidance for completing the dossier can be downloaded from the G-BA website. The completeness of the dossier can be controlled using a standardized checklist (also available from the G-BA website). A normal dossier can have around 300 pages plus supporting documentation of about 1000 pages. A comprehensive and in depth description of the requirements can be found in a review by Ivandic et al [16].

Impact of G-BA Decisions on Pricing and Reimbursement

During the 4 weeks after the resolution of the G-BA (see Figure 4), the company can decide to 'opt out' and discontinue to market the product in Germany. Otherwise, the published resolution of G-BA will inform the National Association of Statutory Health Insurances (*Spitzenverband der gesetzlichen Krankenversicherungen* – GKV-SV) for the price negotiations during the following 6 months. If a drug has been categorized differently for different patient sub-populations, the health insurers will aim to negotiate an average price which reflects the added benefit and number of qualifying patients in each of the sub-populations.

The manufacturer can continue to market the product in Germany after the agreement. Without agreement, an arbitration board will make the final decision within 3 months. An in-depth cost-benefit assessment by IQWiG may be requested. In the end, the manufacturer must accept the final decision on the reimbursement price or leave the market.

If no added benefit was proven by the submitted evidence, the health insurers will aim to fix the price in relation to the price of the comparator treatment, which may be a low-cost treatment. In most cases (about 80%) between 2011 and 2016, the negotiations between the GKV-SV ended with an agreed reimbursement which up to now, was rarely fixed to a reference group (about 2%). In about 13% of cases, an arbitration board had to make the final decision on the reimbursement. Some manufacturers (< 10%) decided after a negative outcome of the G-BA decision to opt-out and to not market their product in Germany; another 10% decided to withdraw the product from the market (mostly products for chronic diseases with low-cost comparators).

The rating will be the base for the reimbursement discussions, but the resulting price is influenced by additional factors such as added benefit in different subgroups, the choice of comparator on subgroup level, or even by political or contextual healthcare considerations [15]. Price premiums are driven by health gain, the share of patients benefiting from a pharmaceutical, European price levels, and whether comparators are generic [17].

2.3 Mapping and Structure of Decision Makers (Reimbursement/HTA)

Healthcare Policy

Healthcare related decision making is shared by the states (*Bundesländer*), the federal government and institutionalized civil organizations.

Key players with impact on healthcare on the **federal level** are the Federal Assembly (*Bundestag*), The Federal Council (*Bundesrat*), and the Federal Ministry of Health (*Bundesministerium für Gesundheit*). The Ministry supervises a few agencies including the Federal Institute for Pharmaceuticals and Medical Devices (*Bundesinstitut für Arzneimittel und Medizinprodukte*), which authorizes pharmaceuticals or medical devices and supervises their safety, the Paul Ehrlich Institute (Federal Institute for Vaccines and Biomedicines) organizing licensing of vaccines and biomedicines, the German Institute for Medical Documentation and Information (*Deutsches Institut für Medizinische Dokumentation und Information* – DIMDI) charged with information services around medicines, medical devices, life sciences, and healthcare and with publishing the German versions of classification systems such as the International Classification of Diseases (ICD-10-GM), the International Classification of Functioning, Disability and Health (ICF) and the German Procedure Classification (*Operationen- und Prozedurenschlüssel*).

Payers

As mentioned above, about 72 million people in Germany are insured in one of the 113 sickness funds (status of 1. January 2017) [18]. Since 2008, all sickness funds are represented on a federal level by the Federal Association of Sickness Funds (GKV-*Spitzenverband*) in all non-competing matters and negotiations. Leading sickness funds are the Techniker Krankenkasse (7.4 million members, 9.9 million insured in 2017), the Barmer GEK (7.5 million members, 9.4 insured), and the Deutsche Angestellten Krankenkasse (4.7 million members, 5.8 insured) [19]. The Federal Association of Sickness Funds delegates 5 members to the Joint Federal Committee (G-BA) and thus, strongly influences the key decisions in healthcare.

Private health insurance companies have formed an own association (*Verband der privaten Krankenversicherungen*) through which they lobby for their interests.

2.4 Organizations/Physician or Patient Organizations

A few quasi-public **institutionalized civil organizations** represent key stakeholders in the healthcare system. Physicians and dentists must be registered members in regional and federal physician associations (*Kassenärztliche Vereinigungen*), with representation at federal level by the Federal Association of GKV Physicians (*Kassenärztliche Bundesvereinigung*). All healthcare providers must also be members of their respective professional chambers (physicians, pharmacists, psychologists, etc.) and adhere to their educational and ethical standards. In addition, there are many medical or scientific professional organizations which are either engaged in lobbying activities or have scientific-medical objectives.

Over the last years, patients have gained more visibility and influence on healthcare decisions. There are an uncounted number of local self-help organizations and patient counselling groups, some of them are semi-organized on the federal level by taking part in the forum for the Chronically Ill and Disabled (*Forum chronisch kranker und behinderter Menschen*) or by participating in the Association of Independent Voluntary Welfare Organizations, or the Federal Alliance for the Support of the Disabled (*Bundesarbeitsgemeinschaft Selbsthilfe von Menschen mit Behinderung und chronischer Erkrankung und ihren Angehörigen*) or the German Disability Council (*Deutscher Behindertenrat*) for lobbying activities.

Hospitals are also members of self-governing organizations such as the German Hospital Federation which is also represented in the G-BA.

The pharmacists are members in the regional chambers and, for the majority, in the German Organization of Pharmacists (*Deutscher Apothekerverband*) with a high lobbying profile.

Germany is home to many pharmaceutical companies. Their network organizations differ from each other by the type of member companies (e.g., the Association of Research-based Pharmaceutical Companies – *Verband forschender Arzneimittel-Hersteller*, VFA) represents the companies with strong research arms, the Federal Association of the Pharmaceutical Industry (*Bundesverband der Pharmazeutischen Industrie*) represents small and medium-sized companies, the Federal Association of Pharmaceutical Manufacturers (*Bundesfachverband der Arzneimittel-Hersteller*) lobbies for manufacturers of over-the-counter (OTC) pharmaceuticals, and the German Generics Association (*Deutscher Generikaverband*) and Pro-Generics for generics manufacturers. In addition, there are associations for medical device manufacturers or for other healthcare technologies.

2.5 Challenges and Catalyzers for Market Access

While the G-BA considers the implementation of AMNOG and the supporting processes mostly a success story, there are also critical voices from other stakeholders such as medical societies or the pharmaceutical industry. Some of the challenges or potential catalyzers are discussed in more detail below.

Comparison to Other Countries

An international comparison of decisions for comparable patient groups resulting from health benefit assessment of pharmaceuticals during the 4 years of 2011 to 2014 in Germany versus the UK National Institute for Health and Care Excellence (NICE), the Scottish Medicines Consortium (SMC) and the Australian Pharmaceutical Benefits Advisory Committee (PBAC) revealed astonishing disagreements [20]. Only 40% of the final G-BA decisions were in line with those of NICE, 47.6% with SMC, and 48.7% with those of Australia's PBAC. The differences start already with the definition of the comparator. The agency's conclusions on comparative effectiveness only overlapped slightly more: G-BA agreed with NICE in 52.7%, with SMC in 64.5%, and with PBAC in 69.7% of patient subgroups.

Categorization into 'No Prove for Additional Benefit'

Often, the reason for the classification of 'added benefit not proven' is not the lack of evidence but rather that the submited evidence was disqualified during the process [21].

Patient Subgroup Analysis and Subgroup Exclusion

G-BA has always insisted in the analyses of subgroups with the clinical trial data ("slicing of data"), which has strongly influenced the categorization of the result [21]. With the new Pharmaceutical Care Strengthening law (AMVSG) introduced in 2017 G-BA can decide to exclude patient sub-groups from reimbursement if the Added Benefit is not evident and thereby, G-BA will limit the treatment choice of physicians. Sub-group analysis may require higher patient numbers and IQWiG may rate studies low if a patient subgroup fails due to low patient numbers and the exclusion of patient sub-groups from reimbursement limits the treatment choices available to the physicians and patients. For companies submitting dossiers for new pharmaceuticals in Germany, it will be important to anticipate the extensive sub-group analysis and to be prepared for contingencies with limited reimbursement [22].

Additional Turnover Threshold for the First-Year Sales

Estimates are that the newly introduced first-year budget impact threshold of € 250 million will hit about 50% of all new agents. Manufacturers must anticipate the Net Present Value impact of crossing the € 250 million threshold and develop appropriate contingency plans [22].

Selection of Comparator

The selection of the comparator by the G-BA is strongly driven by the organizations represented in this decision board and is often not aligned with the clinical guidelines or clinical expertise of medical societies. The cost-effective comparative therapies are often generic drugs or "best supportive care" and this comparator will also be used by the GKV-SV to negotiate the price. A 2013 revision of AMNOG permits G-BA to name several comparators. This allows companies to submit studies which are using any of these comparators and hence, increase the flexibility for evidence submission. However, there is still a perception, that the selection of the comparator often does not follow medical-clinical criteria but more the need for a subsequent low-cost negotiation base [21].

Initiating specific studies for Germany to improve the rating is often not justifiable due to the extra-cost of development. Hence, some manufacturers decided to not market a product in Germany, when the discussion about the choice of comparator could not be resolved.

Patient Relevant Endpoints

The AMNOG requires the comparison of impact on patient relevant clinical endpoints, namely measures like morbidity, mortality, and quality of life, as opposed to surrogate endpoints. This limitation causes heated discussion between the decision-making body, the pharmaceutical companies, and the clinical community (Box 2). For example, Progression Free Survival (PFS), which is used as a key endpoint by the clinical community, is often not accepted as endpoint for comparison because it combines mortality and morbidity.

Early Advice by G-BA

The G-BA offers non-binding early advice for pharmaceutical companies planning to access the German market with a new therapeutic. The best time for such interaction is when the company has formed a clear position on the expected value proposition and evidence generation strategy and study protocols have been designed but can still be modified.

The formal request for the process to G-BA must use a standard template and include a summary of the study design, the questions, and the own standpoint what the answers to these questions will be (in German language). G-BA has 8 weeks to prepare the response. A face to face meeting lasting between 20 and 120 minutes will take place with G-BA ex-

---

Box 2. Patient Relevant Endpoint. An Example

In the case of the hepatitis drugs Victrelis (boceprevir) and Incivek (telaprevir), IQWiG refused to recognize sustained viral response (SVR) as patient relevant endpoints and consequently the clinical evidence measuring SVR was rated as not relevant and therefore, no proof for added benefit was recognized. However, after heated discussions with the other stakeholders, G-BA deviated from IQWiG's recommendation and rated the products as "benefit not quantifiable", which allowed to negotiate a reimbursement price with the insurers.

perts but not with the actual current decision makers. Therefore, there is no room for including additional information, data, or arguments. The request should already include all material of interest.

Two weeks after this meeting, the G-BA will provide written minutes, to which the company can provide written comments.

Coverage with Evidence Development

An option for new treatment alternatives with insufficient evidence was introduced in 2013 with the law for improvement of the health service structure (§137e SGB-V). If the potential of the new therapy is recognized after review of the evidence base or manufacturers propose such a solution, G-BA can now allow access to a new therapy under the condition that additional evidence will be developed in a clinical study which has been designed in agreement with the G-BA. For the applicant, this allows early access to promising new therapies and for G-BA it is now possible to design a subsequent study of high relevance for G-BA (Box 3).

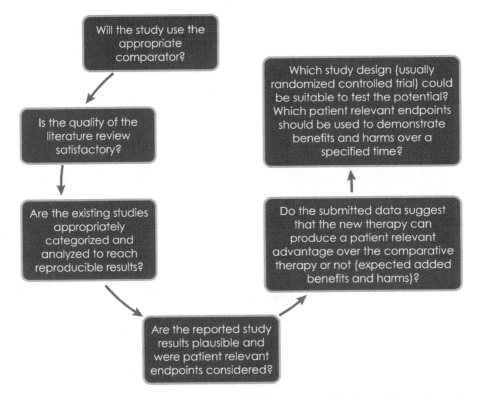

Figure 8. IQWiG's 6 steps for assessing the potential for improving the evidence base for a new therapy [23]

Box 3. Coverage with Evidence Development. An Example

In May 2017, Germany's Federal Joint Committee (G-BA) issued its assessment of Lartruvo (olaratumab; Eli Lilly, United States) in the treatment of adult patients with advanced soft-tissue sarcoma, in combination with doxorubicin, in the case of patients who cannot undergo surgery or radiotherapy and who have not previously been treated with doxorubicin. Because of the orphan drug status, the G-BA assessed its additional benefit based on a Phase 2 study in which Lartruvo in combination with doxorubicin was compared with doxorubicin in monotherapy on a conditional base (pending more data). According to the G-BA, Lartruvo demonstrated a considerable improvement in overall survival of on average 11.8 months. Because data for the assessment of health-related quality of life and disease-specific symptoms were missing, the G-BA restricted the duration of the validity of its decision on Lartruvo's added benefit for 3 years expecting the results from a Phase 3 clinical trial.

IQWiG will assess the potential of the product to be a new and necessary treatment alternative based on the mode of action and the existing evidence base as documented in the application. The review follows 6 key steps (Figure 8) and a recommendation must be given within 6 weeks of the application [23].

Adaptive Pathways

In August 2016, IQWiG took a critical position against the report of the European Medicines Agency on the pilot study for adaptive pathways. The use of real world data to produce evidence on benefits and harms after the market authorization was not seen as a sufficiently resilient procedure.

Uptake of Products after Positive G-BA Decision and Conclusion of Price Negotiations

The uptake of innovative products even after a positive G-BA decision and conclusion of price negotiations may remain limited due to demand regulations on the prescriber side, which prevent doctors to make full use of new medications and patients from having access [21].

2.6 Key Success Factors for Market Access in Germany

While the final reimbursement price cannot be predicted from the outset of the evidence analysis and price setting process, there are a few key items that should be considered when planning to market a product in Germany:

- Using the opportunity for early guidance by G-BA will improve the understanding of the data and endpoints needs and the appropriate comparator in the target population or some of the expected sub-groups.
- Follow the rules, use the dossier template and instructions, and fulfill the requirements for data, endpoints, and the choice of comparator in the clinical trial design.
- Anticipate the need for subgroup analysis and its potential impact on the perceived benefit of the therapeutic.
- Understand the stakeholder roles as decision makers or influencers including the clinical community, the patient advocates, the payers, or health policy.
- Understand G-BA and the health insurers to build your negotiation "tool box".

Finally, the cost of meeting all the requirements of the German decision bodies may be high. It will be important to manage and monitor the risks connected with the German submission.

2.7 Look-out for Near Future

Comparing prices for pharmaceuticals between countries is generally difficult due to a lack of price transparency and variable components of retail prices. Yet, Germany is frequently counted among the countries with comparably high prices for new patented drugs such as for treatment of cancer or rare diseases [4]. Some of these new medicines may bring great benefits to patients, but others may provide only marginal or even no improvements. The proliferation of high-cost specialty medicines and increasing patient pressure for access to these medicines will continue to be a major challenge to the efficiency of pharmaceutical spending in Germany. Therefore, cost-containment measures are applied frequently, including the freeze on the prices of medicines not included in reference-pricing groups and mandatory discounts, which all have a negative effect on producers' profitability. It can be expected that the German health policy makers will continue to support initiatives aiming at prescription and consumption of lower-price generics or biosimilars, applying value-based pricing models centered around added benefit of new medicines, and increasing the transparency of reimbursement prices, e.g., through publication of net prices [24].

Further reforms may also be expected concerning the German dualistic health insurance system. For example, the model of a citizen insurance has been discussed in order to ensure future financing and improved equity in German healthcare [25]. However, the focus of the German health policy will for the next years remain more efficient use of resources, strengthening primary care, reducing pharmaceutical spending, and reducing risk factors such as harmful alcohol consumption.

2.8 Acknowledgements

The chapter has been contributed and reviewed by Alric Ruether & Hans Peter Dauben.

2.9 **References**

1. Statistisches Bundesamt (Destatis). 2015. Available at https://www.destatis.de (last accessed May 2017)
2. Worldbank. Health expenditure in Germany. 2014. Available at http://data.worldbank.org/indicator/SH.XPD.TOTL.ZS?locations=DE (last accessed May 2017)
3. OECD. Health resources - Health spending. OECD Data, 2016. Available at http://data.oecd.org/healthres/health-spending.htm (last accessed July 2017)
4. OECD. Health policy in Germany. OECD Data, 2016. Available at https://data.oecd.org/chart/50uo (last accessed November 2017)
5. GBD 2015 Healthcare Access and Quality Collaborators. Healthcare Access and Quality Index based on mortality from causes amenable to personal health care in 195 countries and territories, 1990-2015: a novel analysis from the Global Burden of Disease Study 2015. *Lancet* 2017; 390: 231-66
6. Busse R, Blümel M. Germany: Health system review. *Health Syst Transit* 2014; 16: 1-296, xxi
7. IQWiG. AMNOG seit 2011. Available at https://www.iqwig.de/de/ueber-uns/10-jahre-iqwig/amnog-seit-2011.6333.html (last accessed May 2017)
8. European Medicines Agency - Orphan designation. Available at http://www.ema.europa.eu/ema/index.jsp?curl=pages/regulation/general/general_content_000029.jsp&mid=WC0b01ac0580b18a41 (last accessed May 2017)
9. Bouslouk M. G-BA benefit assessment of new orphan drugs in Germany: the first five years. *Expert Opin Orphan Drugs* 2016; 4: 453-5
10. Pharma Fakten: News und Informationen zu Arzneimitteln. April 4, 2017. Available at https://www.pharma-fakten.de/news/details/482-nutzenbewertung-fuer-arzneimittel-medizinischer-nutzen-prallt-auf-regulatorisches-korsett/ (last accessed May 2017)
11. Bundesministerium für Gesundheit. Bundesgesundheitsminister Hermann Gröhe: 'Hochwertige, innovative und finanzierbare Arzneimittelversorgung auch für die Zukunft sichern'. Bundesgesundheitsministerium. 12 Oktober 2016. Available at https://www.bundesgesundheitsministerium.de/presse/pressemitteilungen/2016/4-quartal/amvsg-kabinett.html (last accessed May 2017)
12. G-BA. Federal Joint Committee. Available at: http://www.english.g-ba.de/ (last accessed May 2017)
13. IQWiG. Auftraggeber und Finanzierung des IQWiG. 2004. Available at: https://www.iqwig.de/de/ueber-uns/aufgaben-und-ziele/auftraggeber-und-finanzierung.2951.html (last accessed May 2017)
14. Pharma Fakten: News und Informationen zu Arzneimitteln. November 15, 2016. Available at: https://www.pharma-fakten.de/news/details/445-amnog-nutzenbewertung-so-streng-urteilt-deutschlands-g-ba/ (last accessed May 2017)

15. Sieler S, Rudolph T, Brinkmann-Sass C, et al. AMNOG Revisited: How has German health reform impacted pharma pricing and market access, and what can the industry learn from the experience? *McKinsey and Co.* originally published in PharmaTimes May 2015. Available at http://www.mckinsey.com/industries/pharmaceuticals-and-medical-products/our-insights/amnog-revisited (last accessed November 2017)

16. Ivandic V. Requirements for benefit assessment in Germany and England – overview and comparison. *Health Econ Rev* 2014; 4: 12

17. Lauenroth VD, Stargardt T. Pharmaceutical Pricing in Germany: How Is Value Determined within the Scope of AMNOG? *Value Health* 2017; 20: 927-35

18. Verband der Ersatzkassen. Daten zum Gesundheitswesen: Versicherte. 2017. Available at https://www.vdek.com/presse/daten/b_versicherte.html (last accessed May 2017)

19. Krankenkassennetz.de GmbH. Mitglieder und Versicherte je Krankenkasse. 2017. Available at http://www.krankenkasseninfo.de/zahlen-fakten/mitgliederzahlen/ (last accessed May 2017)

20. Fischer KE, Heisser T, Stargardt T. Health benefit assessment of pharmaceuticals: An international comparison of decisions from Germany, England, Scotland and Australia. *Health Policy* 2016; 120: 1115-22

21. VFA. Das AMNOG im vierten Jahr. 2014. Available at https://www.vfa.de/embed/amnog-4tes-jahr-lang.pdf (last accessed November 2017)

22. Eye for Pharma. AMNOG and the German Reforms: What Will Change? 2016. Available at http://social.eyeforpharma.com/column/amnog-and-german-reforms-what-will-change (last accessed May 2017)

23. IQWiG. Potenzial vorhanden? Der Medizinprodukte-Check. 2013. Available at https://www.iqwig.de/de/ueber-uns/10-jahre-iqwig/potenzial-vorhanden.6334.html (last accessed May 2017)

24. Belloni A, Morgan D, Paris V. Pharmaceutical Expenditure And Policies: Past Trends And Future Challenges. *OECD Health Working Papers* Paris: OECD Publishing, 2016

25. Gerlinger T, Burkhardt W. Gesundheitswesen im Überblick. Bundeszentrale für politische Bildung. 2012. Available at https://www.bpb.de/politik/innenpolitik/gesundheitspolitik/72547/gesundheitswesen-im-ueberblick (last accessed May 2017)

https://doi.org/10.7175/747.ch3

3. Market Access in the UK

Fatma Betul Yenilmez [1]

[1] *Akil Consultancy, New Malden, UK*

3.1 Introduction

The UK healthcare system is primarily governed by the National Health Service (NHS), a body that commissions services such as general practitioners (GPs), pharmacists and medicines as per the needs of the UK population, for effective healthcare provision. NHS successfully provides good healthcare services in the UK, assisting all stakeholders in meeting their goals. Due to lack of regulation, until 2009 the pharmaceutical companies would negotiate with the government on a particular price, and provided medicines to the patients at that price. However, after the Pharmaceutical Price Regulation Scheme (PPRS) of 2009, healthcare delivery in the UK changed drastically. Currently, the NHS has divided the decision-making power as well as healthcare budgets of the United Kingdom into regional and local levels, to take care of the unique unmet medical needs of the different regions. Therefore, the healthcare market has changed, leading to differentiated markets for every drug, forcing companies to come up with differentiated market access strategies for their drugs. Thus, the price regulation and reimbursement landscape of a medicine after its approval is segmented, and pharmaceutical companies face several challenges in negotiating with different payers, healthcare organizations and decision makers in order for the value of their product at a given price to be recognized. The scenario of pricing and market access in the UK is discussed in the following sections.

3.2 General Outlook of Healthcare System and Health Policies

The United Kingdom consists of England, Wales, Scotland and Ireland, and all regions have different healthcare policies in terms of value decision-making, as well as medicine reimbursement schemes. In 2015, the government financed £ 147.1 billion of healthcare expenditure, with a total healthcare expenditure in the UK accounting for 9.9% of the total GDP. However, the extension of therapeutic networks and hospital formularies remain the same. The UK healthcare budget is spread across 211 Clinical Commissioning Groups (CCGs), which are NHS organizations responsible for planning and commissioning of healthcare services for the needs of patients in a particular geographical area. The healthcare system in the UK is publicly funded. The NHS has a well-established constitution, published in 2011 by the Department of Health. Besides the constitution, the Health and Social Care Act of 2012, under which the Clinically Commissioning Groups were established, regulates the NHS budget. The NHS provides assistance to these CCGs through Commissioning Support Units (CSUs), in addition to providing clinicians, as well as payers, an outlook on which practices are good for a particular therapeutic area.

The Act also brought about significant legal changes, such as the implementation of the Healthwatch network, to reinforce the voice of the consumer, and the Public Health England, to protect and improve the nation's health and wellbeing, and reduce health inequalities. This act also oriented the competition in the healthcare market towards the interest of the patients, by establishing Monitor, which issues licenses to regulate providers of NHS services. Now in the UK pharmaceutical companies have to operate alongside many local groups, each with different unmet needs and value definitions. Thus, companies need to first understand the needs of the stakeholders and deliver healthcare solutions to the population of that area accordingly.

The NHS is not only concerned with price regulation, but also with the health insurance system of the region. Healthcare is covered by the NHS for the majority of the population, entirely funded by taxes. Besides the government-funded public healthcare insurance, certain private companies, which hold minor sectors, also cover residents, offering additional benefits. In order to involve local health councils and authorities to join the NHS and contribute to the enhancement of social welfare and healthcare, in 2015 the UK government allocated £ 2.7 billion and £ 200 million, respectively, to these bodies. The government also established Integrated Care and Support Exchange (ICASE), which is aimed at bringing expertise from different parts of the nation to contribute to the goal of developing integrated models of care and support in different places, to enhance the degree of public healthcare in the respective locations.

3.3 Pathways of Market Access

As seen above, the UK government exercises control over healthcare, insurance, and pharmaceuticals to a great extent, ensuring and safeguarding the interest of consumers and patients alike. The market access of pharmaceutical companies in the UK involves several processes, but it is mainly related to government regulations, pricing and reimbursement strategies. Figure 1 shows the common steps involved in enabling market access on the part of any pharmaceutical company within the UK.

Pharmaceutical Regulation

The Medicines and Healthcare products Regulatory Agency (MHRA) is an executive agency of the Department of Health. The MHRA has three centres: 1) the Clinical Practice Research Datalink (CPRD), which is a data research service that provide anonymized

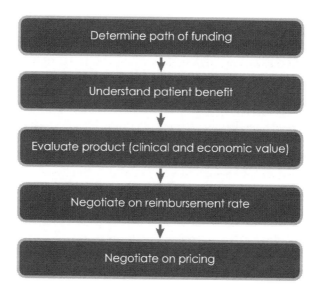

Figure 1. Market Access Process within the UK pharmaceutical sector

NHS clinical data, 2) the National Institute for Biological Standards and Control (NIB-SC), which has been established to standardize and control biological medicines, and 3) the MHAR, which regulates medicines, medical devices and blood components for transfusion, according to the standards set to ensure their safety, efficacy and quality. The degree of control to be exercised over the supply of a medicinal product depends on the legal classification the latter falls into. There are three such categories, namely: 1) Prescription, which includes the drugs that must be dispensed only by a licensed facility, and upon a prescription written by a health professional, 2) Pharmacy, which includes the drugs that can be bought under the supervision of a pharmacist, and 3) General sales list, which includes the drugs available at retail stores.

Besides the need of an appropriate license for the distribution of medicines, drugs must meet the minimum production standards, as determined by the Good Manufacturing Practices (GMP). The MHRA is responsible for carrying out the inspection in the manufacturing and distribution sites, to ensure the adherence to GMP guidelines, and for issuing GMP ratings, depending upon the compliance report, the information regarding the previous inspection history, and any changes in the organization. MHRA works alongside the EMA (European Medicine Agency) to provide recommendations for the various medicines that are submitted for approval. However, Brexit has changed the dynamics between EMA and MHRA, and this might lead to a different process of drug approval and access in the UK. Furthermore, the agency aims at ensuring that the applicable standards are met. The regulatory dilemma arisen post-Brexit poses implications of serious nature on the UK pharmaceutical industry, since UK lost EMA, and the influence of MHRA is also perceived as decreasing.

Pharmaceutical Pricing

Pharmaceutical pricing has changed since 2009, after the Pharmaceutical Price Regulation Scheme (PPRS) was enforced by the NHS. In the UK, the NHS is the main buyer of pharmaceutical products, either branded, innovative drugs/biologics or generic drugs/biosimilars. To finalize the price of these prescription drugs, the manufacturers discuss matters with the government, and these discussions are different for innovative and generic drugs. The price of branded drugs is controlled by PRRS, which was brought into effect by an agreement between the pharmaceutical industry and the government. The payment percentage of PPRS is also set by an agreement between the pharmaceutical industry and the government, to bring stability to the stakeholders – to plan investment strategies – and to support NHS funding, in order to provide health services, respectively. The PPRS for 2017 has been revised and set at 4.75%. The scheme regulates the profits pharmaceutical companies can make on the sales of their drugs to the NHS, and includes a clause for a renegotiation to be implemented every 5 years. NICE assesses the clinical efficacy and cost-effectiveness of each drug on behalf of the NHS for England, Wales, and Ireland, and then recommends a fair price to the NHS. Since the budget allocation with the NHS for healthcare is fixed, the price of new treatments comes at the expense of other treatments. Thus, the NHS is always looking for effective and safe generics and biosimilars for the treatment of various diseases.

Pharmaceutical Reimbursement

The healthcare system in the UK is largely public, with around 80% of funds sourced from taxes, 12% from insurance, and the rest from miscellaneous charges and sources as depicted in Figure 2.

In terms of reimbursement, the process in the UK is quite different from the other European countries. The country has little direct pricing control, since the originator drug price is set by the PPRS and the drug price is reimbursed by the NHS to the contractors under the Community Pharmacy Contractual Framework. However, the reimbursement prices to be dispensed by the NHS are determined by the Secretary of the State, with the reimbursements being issued in the form of a combinations of allowances, medicine margins, and fees. The medicine margin, as achieved by a contractor, is assessed by the Department of Health and Pharmaceutical Services Negotiating Committee. Apart from the price set, there is a matter of spending through patient co-payment as a form of prescription charges, which is a claw-back system operated by the UK government for government hospitals and community pharmacies [15].

3.4 Mapping and Structure of Decision Makers

The Code of Practice for Pharmaceutical Industry was laid out by the Association of the British Pharmaceutical Industry (ABPI), to ensure the appropriate promotion of drugs to

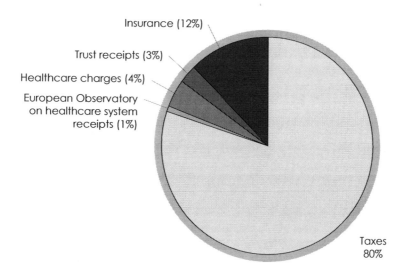

Figure 2. NHS healthcare funding

health professionals and other decision makers. The code incorporates the principles set out in the codes of different organizations around the world (i.e., IFPMA – International Federation of Pharmaceutical Manufacturers and Associations, EFPIA – European Federation of Pharmaceutical Industries and Associations, WHO, etc.). The code of practice is administered by the Prescription Medicines Code of Practice Authority (PMCPA), which monitors the activities and provides guidance.

In terms of assessing value through Health Technology Assessment (HTA), The National Institute of Health Research (NIHR) in the UK runs various programs. The most

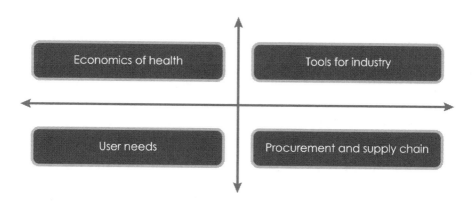

Figure 3. The four themes assessed by the MATCH

prominent is NIHR Health Technology Assessment Programme, which assesses drugs through conventional HTAs through evidence synthesis and modeling, and generates evidence of effectiveness through cohort studies. Apart from this organization, the Multidisciplinary Assessment of Technology Centre for Healthcare (MATCH) also plays a HTA role, in collaboration with the NHS, to assess various industrial partners. The main four themes that MATCH organizes for assessment are shown in Figure 3.

The PPRS is a voluntary agreement between the Government and the pharmaceutical industry. The current scheme runs for five years from January 2014. Companies that choose not to join the PPRS are covered by the Statutory Scheme for Pricing of Branded Medicines. In this scheme, a 15% cut is applied on the NICE list price, and is subject to revision. The scheme does not include the companies that have sales lower than € 5 million and the products which have been launched after December 2013 are not allowed for discounts.

3.5 Challenges and Catalyzers for Market Access

Challenges

Marketing consultant PharmaBase surveyed 27 European pharmaceutical companies (while the UK was still a part of the Community), which included 5 top Pharma companies of the region, and the results suggested that the greatest challenge for an effective market access strategy was local decision making, something that would change with changing territory. Another challenge revealed by the survey concerned the NHS's constant drive to increase cost-savings in the healthcare sector, driving up negotiations on discounts and reimbursement. QALY was also seen as a hurdle, since it was considered a blunt tool to measure the value of a drug. Even though QALY measures cost-effectiveness through clinical benefit for the patient, it fails to look into the impact the drug might have on caregivers and family members, as well as on the wider social costs and benefits for the general population or the NHS. For example, four of AstraZeneca's drugs were voted as being cost-effective for moderate to severe Alzheimer, but not so effective for mild Alzheimer. However, many argue that providing drugs in a mild setting helps slow the progression to a moderate and severe condition, and helps increase the quality of life of the patient, as well as being beneficial from the caregiver's perspective.

Catalysts

The main processes that prove to be a driving force for an effective market access strategy include an effective pricing strategy, accurate health outcomes/health technology assessments (HTAs), as well as an efficient milestone management of drug candidates by the companies. Additionally, stakeholder mapping, the issues regarding the preparation for market access and patient advocacy are also factors that help create a successful market strategy in the pharmaceutical sector.

Successful Market Access Strategies

AstraZeneca developed an innovative drug – osimertinib – to treat patients suffering from a type of lung cancer characterized by high unmet medical needs. Using the Early Access to Medicine Scheme (EAMS), AstraZeneca could enter the market sooner. The scheme directly helped 22 UK patients benefit from this decision, and the marketing approval was granted to the drug only eight months after its submission to EMA for authorization. The drug, thus, reached the patients only 3 years after it was first tested on humans, providing a great example of an effective development and marketing strategy by AstraZeneca.

Similarly, Abbvie's drug glecaprevir/pibrentasvir (G/P), was the first treatment for HCV to be approved through EAMS. The approval was granted in May 2017, and UK patients would have early access to the drug while it is being reviewed by EMA for potential authorizations in other countries of the European Union and the European Economic Area.

Another non-cancer drug to be approved through EAMS is dupixent by Sanofi, for the treatment of atopic dermatitis. Through EAMS, Sanofi received the NICE recommendation and MHRA approval in 30 days, instead of the standard 3-month procedure. These are two examples of successful strategies to gain pre-authorization approval and accelerated pricing and reimbursement approval. These were possible because the company had decided to develop therapies that had a high unmet medical need in the UK.

3.6 Advances in the Near Future

The challenges and drivers, along with the processes and organizational policies in the UK pharmaceutical industry, suggested that there is no 'one-size-fits-all' process that a company can undertake to implement price and reimbursement schemes for their different products. The highly localized and customizable processes for any drug in different setting urged the companies to develop their market access strategies in order to examine every process in detail beforehand, and be ready for any consequences from any stakeholder. The market access management has become a great need for the future, and the companies need to implement market access strategies, in order to create better prospects. Moreover, they have to increase their engagement with government bodies as well as patient organizations, GPs, chief pharmacists and patients. Companies also need to create robust methodologies, have transparent testing systems, implement post-launch trials and improve their patient-awareness processes, to promote their products among each stakeholder, in order to increase sales and profit, keeping in mind the fact that drug development and manufacturing require huge R&D expenses.

3.7 **Bibliography**

- AbbVie Press Release. Early Access to Medicines Scheme (EAMS) Granted to AbbVie's Investigational Pan- genotypic Regimen for Chronic Hepatitis C – the First EAMS in HCV. May 2017
- Accelerated Access Review: Final Report. Review of innovative medicines and medical technologies. An independently chaired report, supported by the Wellcome Trust. October 2016. Available at https://www.gov.uk/government/uploads/system/uploads/attachment_data/file/565072/AAR_final.pdf (last accessed July 2017)
- Ainge D, Aitken S, Corbett M, et al. Global Access Programs: A Collaborative Approach for Effective Implementation and Management. *Pharmaceut Med* 2015; 29: 79-85
- Carlson JJ, Gries KS, Yeung K, et al. Current status and trends in performance-based risk-sharing arrangements between healthcare payers and medical product manufacturers. *Appl Health Econ Health Policy* 2014; 12: 231-8
- Castle G, Bogaert P. Impact of Brexit on Pharmaceutical Regulations and Structures. Covington, June 2016
- Ciani O, Jommi C. The role of health technology assessment bodies in shaping drug development. *Drug Des Devel Ther* 2014; 8: 2273-81
- Chang J, Peysakhovich F, Wang W. The UK Health Care System. New York: Columbia University, 2015. Available at http://assets.ce.columbia.edu/pdf/actu/actu-uk.pdf (last accessed July 2017)
- Danzon P, Keuffel E. Regulation of the pharmaceutical-biotechnology industry. In: Economic Regulation and Its Reform: What Have We Learned? Chicago: University of Chicago Press, 2014
- Dawson S, Rosen E. Market Access in practice: do you have a strategy? PharmaField 2008
- Department of Health. Integrated Care: Our Shared Commitment. Gov.UK, May 2013. Available at https://www.gov.uk/government/publications/integrated-care (last accessed July 2017)
- Department of Health. PPRS: payment percentage 2017. December 2016. Available at https://www.gov.uk/government/publications/pprs-payment-percentage-2017 (last accessed July 2017)
- Devlin N, Dakin H, Rice N, et al. NICE's cost effectiveness threshold revisited: new evidence on the influence of cost effectiveness and other factors on NICE decisions. European Conference on Health Economics. Helsinki, July 2010
- Garattini L, Curto A, Freemantle N. Pharmaceutical Price Schemes in Europe: Time for a 'Continental' One? *Pharmacoeconomics* 2016; 34: 423-6
- Gautam A, Pan X. The changing model of big pharma: impact of key trends. *Drug Discov Today* 2016; 21: 379-84
- Hannah L, Phillips J. Is the Current UK System of Pharmaceutical Price Regulation Working? Lexology, February 2017

- Hill CA, Harries M. The Uk Pharmaceutical Price Regulation Scheme (Pprs) - Considerations of Voluntary Versus Statutory Regulations and How to Negotiate Pricing. *Value Health* 2015; 18: A520
- Macaulay R. The Future Of Uk Drug Pricing: The 2014 Pprs (An Interim Review). *Value Health* 2016; 19: A447
- Medicines and Healthcare products Regulatory Agency. Medicines: reclassify your product. Gov.uk, December 2014. Available at https://www.gov.uk/guidance/medicines-reclassify-your-product (last accessed July 2017)
- Medicines and Healthcare products Regulatory Agency and Department of Health. Good manufacturing practice and good distribution practice. Gov.uk, December 2014. Available at https://www.gov.uk/guidance/good-manufacturing-practice-and-good-distribution-practice (last accessed July 2017)
- Murteira S, Millier A, Ghezaiel Z, et al. Drug reformulations and repositioning in the pharmaceutical industry and their impact on market access: regulatory implications. *J Mark Access Health Policy* 2014: 2
- NHS England. Medicines reimbursement prices. Available at https://www.england.nhs.uk/commissioning/primary-care/pharmacy/meds-reimbursement/ (last accessed July 2017)
- NHS England. Understanding the new NHS. A guide for everyone working and training within the NHS. NHS England, 2014
- Prescription Medicines Code of Practice Authority. Code of practice for the pharmaceutical industry. 2016. Available at http://www.pmcpa.org.uk/thecode/Documents/Code%20of%20Practice%202016%20.pdf (last accessed July 2017)
- Owen L, Morgan A, Fischer A, et al. The cost-effectiveness of public health interventions. *J Public Health* 2012; 34: 37-45
- Rowland B. UK: Pricing and Reimbursement- The Basics. Lexology, December 2015
- Shkopiak T, Epping M, Schultes R. To what extent are pharmaceuticals prices controlled? TaylorWessing 2015. Available at https://united-kingdom.taylorwessing.com/synapse/regulatory_pricecontrol.html (last accessed July 2017)
- Song C. Understanding the aftermath of Brexit: implications for the pharmaceutical industry. *Pharmaceutical Medicine* 2016; 30: 253-6

https://doi.org/10.7175/747.ch4

4. Market Access in France

Haythem Ammar [1]

[1] *European Pricing & Reimbursement Manager, Carthagenetics, Paris, France*

4.1 General Outlook of Healthcare System

National health insurance coverage is mandatory for all residents in France for more than three months (Statutory Health Insurance – SHI). Health care in France is characterized by a national health insurance (*Sécurité Sociale*), where universal access is ensured by schemes for people on low incomes and/or with chronic conditions. The state manages entirely the healthcare system, which is financed by both employee and employer payroll contributions, and earmarked taxes. However, treatments are not free at the point of use and patients contribute with up-front payments, which are partially reimbursed by the government.

The rate of SHI coverage varies across goods and services, but some patients – such as those with chronic conditions (diabetes and AIDS), pregnant women after the fifth month, disabled children, and war pensioners – are exempt from co-payments [1].

However, patients may opt for a private Voluntary Health Insurance (VHI) and they could be reimbursed for most of the out-of-pocket payments that are known as the *ticket moderateur*. For this reason, the compulsory government scheme is accompanied by a significant voluntary private insurance sector, which covers the costs that are not covered by SHI.

Some of the co-payments are not reimbursed by either national or private health insurance systems, in order to improve patient cost-consciousness without causing great financial strain. These co-payments are limited to an annual ceiling of € 50 and include: € 1 per doctor visit, € 0.50 per prescription drug, and € 18 for hospital treatment above € 120 [2].

Approximately 90% of the population has joined a private plan and this number has been increasing over the years. For this reason, the VHI sector is increasingly making up for shortages in SHI funding, through taxes on its increasing income. This in exchange for a bigger involvement in the management of the healthcare provision.

Although the healthcare management and financing comes mainly from public sources, the provision of healthcare is more mixed: providers of outpatient care are largely private, whilst approximately three-quarters of hospital beds are provided by public or non-profit hospitals [3].

4.2 Pathways of Market Access (Regulation, Pricing and Reimbursement)

In France, due to economic downturns and the growing healthcare needs of an aging population, budget and cost controls have become key issues, as in most other developed countries. Over the past twenty years, authorities faced large deficits and the government focused on driving down healthcare costs to ensure sustainability.

In order to decrease the government-sponsored reimbursement rates for some types of treatment and population, the authorities implemented several reforms, leaving some patients with higher co-payments and co-insurance. The reimbursement, through private insurance, of certain types of co-payments (some drugs, doctor visits, and ambulance transport) has recently been discontinued, despite the fact that more than 90% of the country's population has a prominent voluntary private health insurance [4,5].

The French Government regulates the healthcare spending through several mechanisms, such as decreased reimbursement, removal of more than six hundred drugs from public reimbursement, reduction in the number of acute-care hospital beds, monitoring and sanctioning of medical practitioners for prescribing too many drugs, and promotion of the uptake of generics and over-the-counter medicines.

With these mechanisms, in addition to the changes to its health technology assessment (HTA) process, the French Government aims to cut an additional € 10 billion over the next three years [6].

In France, after the marketing approval, the manufacturer can ask for the reimbursement, and therefore the price is regulated. For non-reimbursed drugs, the manufacturer freely defines the price.

The Transparency Commission (*Commission de la Transparence* – TC) decides whether a drug is reimbursed or not by the SHI, by determining the comparative evidence-based value.

Among other factors, the Transparency Commission takes in consideration the level of innovation the drug brings to the market, and how important it is for the health of the population. It assigns a score from 1 to 5 to determine the drug's improvement of medical benefit (*Amelioration du Service Medical Rendu* – ASMR) compared to the current standard of care [7,8]. The ASMR answers the question: Does the drug improve the patients' clinical situation vs. existing therapies? The consequences of ASMR rating and price level are listed below.

- ASMR V: no improvement. The drug can be listed only if the cost is lower than the comparators. Discounted pricing for the new drug is typical.
- ASMR IV: minor improvement. The drug can be listed if the cost is not higher than the comparators. The price of the new drug can be higher if it has a better effect in a more restricted population.
- ASMR III: moderate improvement.
- ASMR II: important improvement.

- ASMR I: major improvement. This is reserved for the few drugs that have demonstrated a substantial effect on mortality in a severe disease.
- ASMR I, II, III, and IV: the drug can have a higher price than the comparators.

Actual benefit (SMR)	Reimbursement rate (%)	
	Illness usually benign	Serious illness
Important	35	65
Moderate	30	30
Mild	15	15
Insufficient	0 (not included in the positive list/not reimbursed)	0 (not included in the positive list/not reimbursed)

Table 1. Reimbursement rates according to the severity of the disease and evaluation of the SMR (2014). Modified from [8]

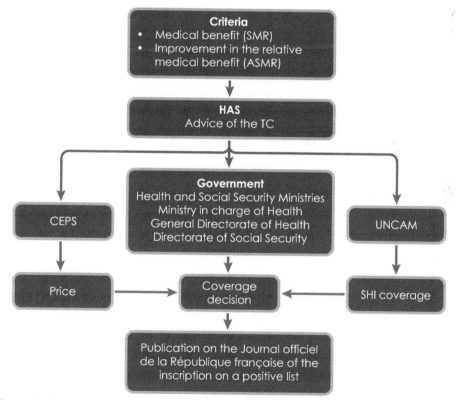

Figure 1. Pricing and reimbursement process. Modified from [8]
CEPS = Economic Committee on Health Care Products; HAS = French National Authority for Health; SHI = Statutory Health Insurance; TC = Transparency Commission; UNCAM = National Union of Health Insurance Funds

- ASMR I, II or III: faster access (price notification instead of negotiation) and price consistent with the lowest price within the ones defined in Germany, UK, Spain, and Italy [7,8].

In addition to the ASMR, the Transparency Commission also determines the the product's medical benefit (*Service Medical Rendu* – SMR) by answering the question: Should the drug be reimbursed? Is the drug clinically differentiated (interesting)? The SMR takes into account five criteria:

- Severity and impact on morbidity and mortality of the disease.
- Clinical efficacy/effectiveness and safety of the drug.
- Aim of the drug (preventive, symptomatic or curative).
- Position, as regards to comparator, within the treatment strategy.
- Public health considerations (burden of disease, health impact at community level, transposability of clinical trial results, etc.) [7,8].

Based on the SMR and the severity of the disease, a reimbursement rate is then attributed (Table 1).

The *Comité Economique des Produits de Santé* (CEPS), after considering the ASMR and SMR ratings, negotiates the reimbursement price and rate of the drug with the manufacturer. Both the ASMR level and the expected annual sales volume (partly defined based on the estimation of the target population by the TC) are key considerations for the CEPS when establishing the price.

For drugs that are not covered by the French reimbursement system, pricing is free [8].

In France, most of the hospital-only products are not subject to assessment by CEPS, since they are reimbursed from the budget allocated to the hospital. Therefore, manufacturers are free to negotiate prices directly with the hospitals that purchase the drugs, through a competitive bid process.

Since 2004, payment for innovative and expensive hospital drugs has been financed through the Diagnosis Related Group (DRG) flat rate (*Tarification à l'Activité* – T2A) payment and costs are completely reimbursed by the health insurance system [9].

Figure 1 summarizes the pricing and reimbursement process.

4.3 Mapping and Structure of Decision Makers

French National Authority for Health (*Haute Autorité de Santé* – HAS)

In order to improve the quality of patient care and to guarantee equity within the healthcare system, in August 2004 the French government created the HAS (*Haute Autorité de Santé*) or French National Authority for Health. HAS brings together several activities, from the assessment of drugs and medical devices, to the accreditation of healthcare organizations and certification of doctors.

HAS has been built on three founding principles: a very broad field of action, a high degree of scientific rigor, and independence.

Despite not being a government body, HAS liaises closely with government health agencies, healthcare professional unions, national health insurance funds, patients' representatives, and research organization [10].

Transparency Commission (*Commission d'Evaluation des Médicaments* – TC)

The purpose of the Transparency Commission (TC), which is the Commission for drug and health technology assessment, is to provide scientific opinions concerning the usefulness, interest and good use of drugs. It is the body responsible for the assessment of the medical service provided by a new drug, as well as the improvement of this medical service subsequent to its use. This opinion will be used in the price negotiation and for the establishment of the reimbursement rate applied by the social security organizations [11].

National Agency for Medicines and Health Products Safety (*Agence Nationale de Sécurité du Médicament et des Produits de Santé* – ANSM)

The National Agency for Medicines and Health Products Safety (ANSM) was created by Law 29 December 2011 on reinforcing the safety of medicines and health products. The ANSM, entrusted with new responsibilities and missions, replaced the French Agency for the sanitary safety of medicines and health products (Afssaps) on 1 May 2012. ANSM has two central missions: providing equitable access to innovation for all patients and ensuring the safety of health products throughout their life cycle, from initial trials to post-marketing surveillance [12].

Furthermore, ANSM develops several activities in France and on behalf of the European Union:

- Scientific and technical evaluation of the quality, efficacy and safety of drugs and biological products.
- Ongoing monitoring of predictable or unexpected adverse effects of health products.
- Inspection of facilities engaged in manufacturing activities;
- Importation, distribution, pharmacovigilance and expertise of clinical trials.
- Laboratory control for the release of batches of vaccines and medicines on the market, control of products on the market, samples taken during inspections, seizures by judicial authorities or customs [12].

Organizations Who Determine the Reimbursement

1. Health and Social Security Ministers: Ministry in charge of Health, General Directorate of Health, and Directorate of Social Security determine whether a drug is included in the refundable list [11].
2. National Union of Health Insurance Funds (*Union Nationale des* Caisses *d'Assurance Maladie* – UNCAM): it was created following the reform law of 12 August 2004. It has

two main roles, which are to obtain a better health insurance management by coordinating the three mandatory disease funds and linking with complementary scheme and with healthcare professionals, and to attend the negotiation of agreements with medical professionals regarding the decisions on drug prescription and healthcare reimbursement procedures [11].

3. Economic Committee on Health Care Products (*Comité Economique des Produits de Santé* – CEPS): after negotiation with the manufacturer, CEPS fixes the drug price [11].

4.4 Challenges and Catalyzers for Market Access in France

In France, almost 80% of the total expenditure on health is publicly funded.

Health spending is one of the most important item, when compared with the OECD average, however, is still below the health expenditure of Germany and Switzerland [15].

After the economic crisis in 2008, many reforms have been implemented to contain health expenditure and to decrease the cost supported by the government. These reforms include strict accounting cost-containment policies, which are mainly focused on reducing the size of the profit benefit basket and levels of coverage, and medical-based cost-containment policies, which are mainly focused on reducing the loss of money and quality due to medical practice changes and aim to improve medical practice as a whole [13].

4.5 Acknowledgements

The chapter has been contributed and reviewed by Ann Dandon.

4.6 References

1. Duriez M, Lancry PJ, Lequet-Slama D, et al. Le Système de Santé en France. Paris: Universitaires de France, 1996

2. HOPE - European Hospital and Healthcare Federation. Out-of-pocket payments In healthcare systems in the European Union. Brussels: HOPE Publications, 2015

3. The Commonwealth Fund. International Profiles of Health Care Systems, 2011. New York: The Commonwealth Fund, 2011. Available at http://www.commonwealthfund.org/~/media/Files/Publications/Fund%20Report/2011/Nov/1562_Squires_Intl_Profiles_2011_11_10.pdf (last accessed December 2017)

4. Cabral M, Mahoney N. Externalities And Taxation Of Supplemental Insurance: A Study Of Medicare And Medigap. NBER Working Paper No. 19787. January 2014. Available at http://www.nber.org/papers/w19787 (last accessed December 2017)

5. The Commonwealth Fund. International Profiles Of Health Care Systems, 2014. New York: The Commonwealth Fund, 2015. Available at http://www. commonwealthfund.org/~/media/files/publications/fund-report/2015/jan/1802_ mossialos_intl_profiles_2014_v7.pdf (last accessed December 2017)
6. The Local. The key reforms of France's healthcare bill. March 2015. Available at https://www.thelocal.fr/20150331/five-things-to-know-about-frances-healthcare-law (last accessed December 2017)
7. GlobalHealthPR. Reimbursography – France. Available at http://www. globalhealthpr.com/services/france/ (last accessed December 2017)
8. Chevreul K, Berg Brigham K, Durand-Zaleski I, et al. France. Health system review. *Health Systems in Transition* 2015; 17. Available at http://www.euro.who.int/__ data/assets/pdf_file/0011/297938/France-HiT.pdf (last accessed December 2017)
9. Mihailovic N, Kocic S, Jakovljevic M. Review of Diagnosis-Related Group-Based Financing of Hospital Care. *Health Serv Res Manag Epidemiol* 2016; 3: 2333392816647892
10. HAS – Haute Autorité de santé. Available at https://www.has-sante.fr/portail/ jcms/c_415964/en/has-profile?portal=c_2567632 (last accessed December 2017)
11. ISPOR Global Health Care System Road Map. France – Pharmaceuticals. 2009. Available at https://www.ispor.org/HTARoadMaps/France.asp (last accessed December 2017)
12. ANSM – *Agence Nationale de Sécurité du Médicament et des Produits de Santé*. Available at http://ansm.sante.fr/L-ANSM/Une-agence-d-expertise/L-ANSM-agence-d-evaluation-d-expertise-et-de-decision/(offset)/0 (last accessed December 2017)
13. FraviMed. A modification of the French "SMR / ASMR" system is necessary, but is not urgent. March 2015. Available at http://www.fravimed.com/news/a-modification-of-the-french-smr-asmr-system-is-necessary-but-is-not-urgent/ (last accessed December 2017)

https://doi.org/10.7175/747.ch5

5. Market Access in Italy

Lorenzo Pradelli[1], **Marco Bellone**[1]

[1] AdRes HE&OR, Turin, Italy

5.1 General Outlook of National Health Service and Health Policies

The Italian National Health Service (*Servizio Sanitario Nazionale* – SSN) – established with the law 833/1978 [1] – is a network of structures and facilities to guarantee health services access to all the citizens, as stated by Article 32 of the Italian Constitution [2]. The SSN operates under the direction and responsibility of the Ministry of Health (MH), which determines general healthcare policies, while the "retail sale" is planned, coordinated and managed at regional level, as a consequence of the process of devolution from State to Regions, regulated by the Constitution title V reform in 2001 [3].

The Italian Government as warrantor of health rights (article 32) [2], through MH, determines the essential levels of care (*Livelli Essenziali di Assistenza* – LEAs) that every region has to be able to provide in the public setting.

Every Region autonomously defines its strategic planning, especially in terms of financial resources and distribution on regional territory of Local Health Units (*Aziende Sanitarie Locali* – ASLs) and Hospital Units (*Aziende Ospedaliere* – AOs), as well as act as supervisors of granting procedure of private health units. ASLs and AOs operate autonomously to guarantee the organization of local health care and supply of healthcare services.

The collaboration between the various governments of SSN, i.e. State, Regions, ASLs and AOs, is a fundamental principle for ensuring uniform health conditions and guarantees throughout the national territory acceptable and appropriate levels of health services for all citizens.

The cooperation between the State, on one side, and the nineteen Regions plus the autonomous provinces of Trento and Bolzano, on the other, is promoted through *Conferenza Permanente Stato Regioni* that represents the policy place in which politic negotiation between central administration and regional autonomies occurs. It was established with the law of 12 October 1983 4].

Long-time planning is a qualifying element of SSN: the MH, as delegate of the central Government, with the cooperation of Regions establishes the National Health Plan (*Piano Sanitario Nazionale* – PSN). It describes the general targets and elements that must be reached in health matter on the national territory, taking into account the financial, demographical and epidemiological contexts, as well as new scientific and technological innovations. It has three-year validity, but it may be revised *in itinere* if needed. The PSN defines the line that all health care stakeholders must follow for guaranteeing LEAs, and how funding must be broken down by levels of care.

The LEAs are all the health services and benefits – included some pharmaceuticals – that the SSN supplies to all citizens free of charge or on payment of a prescription charge, which is independent of income or residency. The LEAs have been defined at the national level with the law of the President of the Council of Ministers of 29 November 2001 [5]. The reform of title V of the Constitution [3] has also provided for the regions the chance to use their own resources to supply additional services and benefits, but never less than those included in LEAs. This implies that LEAs could be different from region to region, provided that those defined nationally are guaranteed all over the regional territory.

The financial resources available for supporting the SSN are annually allocated by Italian Government. The national health care fund is financed by earnings deriving from prescription charge for health services, taxation (VAT, for example), and State budget. The resources are allocated to each Region and autonomous provinces for capitation share and specific criteria negotiated in occasion of *Conferenza Permanente Stato-Regioni*. The Regions assign the funding to ASLs, AOs and private health care units for warranting the essential health care services defined by LEAs [5], and further resources on the basis of out-patient and in-patient health services supplied – through the payment of tariffs decided by national government and integrated with regional ones for extra health care services provided. ASLs play the double role of provider and buyer of healthcare services, whilst AOs and private health units work to reach as many patients as possible (competition) and receive reimbursements by ASL for the health services performed.

The financial crisis that has struck Italy and the consequent need to rationalize public spending has constrained legislators to review the organization of the SSN. Government and Regions signed a three-year financial and programmatic agreement on SSN expenditure and programming, which aims to improve and promote the quality and the appropriateness of the health services (*Patto della Salute* 2014-2016) [6]. According to *Patto della Salute*, the State commits to the intended funds allocation to the Regions at the beginning of the three-year period, basing on which they may initiate their mid-term planning, relying on resource certainty, and struggle the wastefulness, with the purpose to allocate the savings to improve quality of care services. In case of health over exceeding the budget allocated, regions have the task of compensating for the debt through taxation. Pharmaceuticals (may) fall within the LEAs and follow a specific regulation: the Italian Medicines Agency (*Agenzia Italiana del Farmaco* – AIFA) is the authority under direction of MH responsible for drugs regulation and guarantees access to medicines all over the national territory, ensuring unity of the national pharmaceutical system in agreement with the regional authorities, pharmaceutical industries and distributors.

5.2 Pathways of Market Access

Pricing and Reimbursement of Pharmaceuticals

Classification of drugs by supply and reimbursement regimen

Medical products in Italy are pooled in two main categories, i.e. medicinal products and medical devices.

The first ones are regulated by the law 219/2006 [7] (and successive modifications), whilst medical devices follow the law 37/2010 [8], as implementation of the Directive 2007/47/CE of European Parliament and Council. Medical devices, managed directly by Minister of Health, consist in any instrument, material or other article used alone or in combination with the purpose of diagnosis, prevention, monitoring, treatment or alleviation of either disease, any injury or handicap, or a physiological process.

Medicinal products, i.e. "any substance or combination of substances presented as having proprieties for treating or preventing disease in human being", are managed by AIFA [7].

According to the law 219/2016 [7], at the time of Marketing Authorization (MA) issue, medicinal products are classified for the prescription and supply rules (Table 1).
- Drugs subjected to medical prescription:
  - Medicinal products on renewable (RR) (not more than 10 times in 6 months) or non-renewable medical prescription (RNR).
  - Medicinal products subjected to special medical prescription (e.g. a narcotic or if there is a risk of medicinal abuse).
  - Medicinal products on restricted medical prescription, reserved for use in certain specialized areas (e.g. in a hospital environment [OSP] or prescription of a specialist [RLR and RLNR]).
- Drugs not subjected to medical prescription:
  - Over the counter (OTC).
  - Other medicinal products not subjected to medical prescription (SOP).

In general, pharmaceuticals are subjected to medical prescription when they are either administered via parenteral route, or associated to particular adverse events or when the risk of incorrect use with associated patient health risk exists. Moreover, some pharmaceuticals are administered in hospital environment or by specialist, due to high risks associated to administration, for safeguarding public health or for the innovative nature of medicinal products that require supervision by medical personnel during or immediately after administration.

Prescription type	Specification
Renewable (RR)	Not more than 10 times in 6 months
Non-renewable (RNR)	Repeated each time
Triple copy (TPC)	Prescription for narcotic drugs
Renewable w/ limitation (RRL)	For drugs prescribed only by specialist
Non-renewable w/ limitation (RNRL)	For drugs prescribed only by specialist and repeated each time
Hospital (OSP)	For drugs allowed in hospital environment only
Used by specialist limitation (USPL)	For drugs that can be used only by a specialist

Table 1. Prescription classes of medicinal products in Italy

The SSN guarantees pharmacological therapy for all citizens with acute and chronic severe diseases according to LEAs as reported in the law of the President of the Council of Ministers of 29 November 2001 [5]. Medicinal products are classified according to reimbursement regimen in drug reimbursed by SSN and drug not reimbursed by SSN.

Drug reimbursed by SSN, and listed in the National Pharmaceutical Handbook (*Prontuario Farmaceutico Nazionale* – PFN), the positive list of drugs.

- Class A: drugs dispensed by SSN for their approved therapeutic indications, as reported in the Summary of Product Characteristics (SPC), through territorial pharmacies. Regions may demand prescription charge, except for some categories of patients (e.g. low income, veterans), or decide to reimburse them only when used for specific therapeutic indications – defined by a legal act by AIFA (nota AIFA).

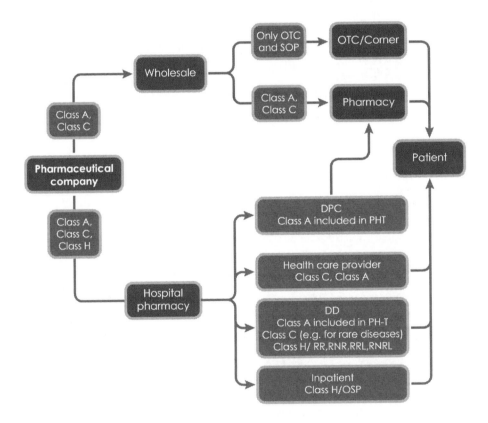

Figure 1. Drug flow based on supply and reimbursement regimen

DD = *Distribuzione Diretta* (drugs distributed directly through hospital pharmacies);
DPC = *Distribuzione Per Conto* (drugs distributed by territorial pharmacies); OSP = hospital
prescription; OTC = Over The Counter; PH-T = *Prontuario Ospedale Territorio*; RNR = non-renewable
prescription; RNRL = non-renewable w/ limitation prescription; RR = renewable prescription;
RRL = renewable w/limitation prescription

- Class H: drugs that are dispensed by SSN and distributed through public structures. These drugs may only be used in hospital, or in a structure similar to it, when prescribed with OSP prescription. If prescription occurs through either RR, RNR, RRL or RNRL prescription, the distribution takes place directly from the public structure on the order of treatment plan issued by the authorized center.

In 2004 the *Prontuario Ospedale Territorio* (PH-T) [9] was introduced. It contains a list of class A drugs for which normally the first administration began during hospital stay or in secondary care facilities. Each Region has to supply medicinal products included into the PH-T directly through hospital pharmacies (*Distribuzione Diretta* – DD) or by territorial pharmacies (*Distribuzione per conto* – DPC), under special reduction of distribution costs, in order to guarantee the therapeutic continuity from hospital to home and govern the pharmaceutical expenditure. Drugs with authorized off-label use(s), innovative and very costly drugs classified in class A are also integrated in the PH-T.

Drug not reimbursed by SSN.

- Class C: drugs that do not fall within the above classes; they are considered useful but not essential and are totally paid by patients (or by health care providers when used within a LEA). OTCs and SOPs are integrated as subcategory of class C, dispensed without prescription (class C-bis).

Figure 1 summarizes the Italian drug flow based on supply and reimbursement regimen.

Applying for Reimbursement of a New Drug: the Procedure

Determination of pricing and reimbursement (P&R) class is the unique activity regarding drugs that is not regulated at the European level, but is managed by national regulatory agencies.

The price of drugs reimbursed by the SSN is determined through negotiation between AIFA and pharmaceutical companies (according to law 326/03 [10]) on the basis of the procedures and criteria set out in Interministerial Committee for Economic Planning (CIPE) deliberation of February 2001 [11]. Marketing authorization (*Autorizzazione Immissione in Commercio* – AIC) and P&R application are procedures that have to be presented separately according to the law 189/2012 [12].

In general, the pharmaceutical companies may present the P&R application for new medicinal products only after publication of the marketing authorization on the Italian Official Gazette (GU): approved drugs are provisionally classified in the new Class Cnn – it contains all medicinal products with AIC but not yet negotiated (nn) from AIFA for the purpose of reimbursement– and may be distributed through private market or by reaching an agreement directly with Regions as long as P&R application is not evaluated and approved by AIFA. The manufacturer has to communicate to AIFA the ex-factory and retail price. This procedure is not adopted for orphan drugs, medicinal products with exceptional therapeutic relevance and drugs for exclusive hospital use (supplied through OSP prescription) for which the P&R application may occur simultaneously with the AIFA marketing authorization process.

In detail, within 60 days from publication on the European Official Gazette (GUEU) of a marketing authorization of a drug authorized through centralized procedure (via European Medicines Agency – EMA), AIFA publishes on the Italian GU a law provision, including drug details, supply class – determined after CTS (Technical-Scientific Committee) consultation – and classification in the provisional Cnn class. The manufacturer may present the P&R application to AIFA immediately after publication on GUEU of EMA drug approval. For the other registration procedures (mutual recognition, decentralized and national), the marketing authorization holder may present P&R application only after the publication on GU of decisions on marketing authorization and classification for supply. In both registration procedures, pharmaceutical company has to present an application to change reimbursement class (from Cnn to either A or H).

Figure 2 summarizes the P&R procedures for centralized, mutual recognition, decentralized and national MA application in Italy.

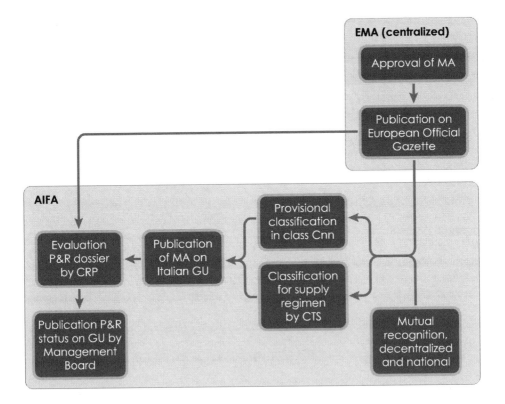

Figure 2. The P&R procedures for centralized, mutual recognition, decentralized and national MA application (modified from [13])
CRP = prices and reimbursement committee; CTS = technical-scientific committee;
GU = Official Gazette; MA = Marketing Authorization; P&R = Price and Reimbursement

Initiation of the application

As first step, the pharmaceutical company has to present the P&R application, which shows either:

- a positive cost-effectiveness ratio – for medicinal products that are either innovative or provide a more appropriate response than drugs already available for the same therapeutic indications, or
- a better risk-benefit ratio compared to other drugs already available for the same indication, or
- other elements of interest for the SSN (read lower cost), if the new drugs do not present a significant clinical superiority compared to medicinal products already available but is of at least equal effectiveness and safety.

The negotiation process

AIFA, through the Prices and Reimbursement Committee (CPR), reviews reimbursement requests, also supported by consumer and spending data provided by Medicines Utilization Monitoring Centre (OSMED), an instrument for collecting data on General Practitioner (GP) prescriptions and sales data from territorial and hospital pharmacies and monitoring the prevalence of use, and expenditure for pharmaceuticals.

In particular, the criteria to define reimbursement class and price of the new drug rely on:

- Target disease and place in therapy;
- Added therapeutic value and competitor prices;
- Budget impact on SSN expenditure (the new medicinal product integrates the armamentarium or take drugs' place in the market);
- Prices in other European community countries.

The negotiation begins taking into account the daily cost of medicinal products having the same indications. A "premium price" – financed through a fund established by the Italian authorities in order to support research and development of innovative drugs – is allowed for very innovative or orphan drugs. In case of no therapeutic advantage, a lower or the same price as the cheapest drug in the same therapeutic category is fixed (therapeutic reference pricing).

The contract and publication on Italian Official Gazette

The price and reimbursement class, resulting from CPR and pharmaceutical company negotiation, have to be ratified by CTS; the final step consists in Management Board approval, followed by publication of ex-factory price with reimbursement class on Italian Official Gazette.

The price determined at the end of the negotiation procedure has 24 months of validity, save different contractual clauses. Upon expiration, the contract is renewed automatically, if pharmaceutical company or AIFA do not make request of amendments to the original contract within 90 days before expiration date.

Pricing

Containment policy of pharmaceutical expenditure

For limiting pharmaceutical spending and make resources available to promote innovation and assure SSN sustainability, the Italian Governments and AIFA (since 2004), consistent with the *Conferenza Permanente Stato-Regioni*, introduced several measures in the last 20 years. In detail, the law 405/2001 [14] established a territorial ceiling pharmaceutical expenditure (i.e. deriving from outpatients only) that had not to exceed 13% of overall health expenditure both at national and regional level. Every Region and autonomous province is responsible of spending control and corrective interventions: a fixed fee paid by patient (copayment) for prescribed and reimbursed drugs is adopted in many Regions. Furthermore, for supporting Regions to control pharmaceutical expenditure, central Government implements a reference price for drugs not covered by patent and mandatory discounts – proportional to the retail price – that every pharmacy has to apply to SSN (the payer). In 2004, the amount of pharmaceutical expenditure ceiling was incremented to 16% of the overall health expenditure and included both inpatient and outpatient pharmaceutical spending [10]. In the same year, as first responders from establishment, AIFA updates the PFN, and adopts the PH-T to guarantee prescription persistence and govern the pharmaceutical expenditure: drugs included in PH-T are bought by the SSN directly from the pharmaceutical industry at the hospital price (ex-factory price, net of mandatory and hidden discounts), and distribution costs are totally abolished or reduced. Each Region has to supply medicinal products included into the PH-T directly through hospital pharmacies (*Distribuzione Diretta* – DD) or by territorial pharmacies (*Distribuzione Per Conto* – DPC: it consists in a measure to acquire medicinal products at hospital price and deliver to the patients through the territorial pharmacies, establishing a lower distribution margin for the pharmacy). In 2005, with the aim to balance annual pharmaceutical overspending, AIFA applies a reduction of 4.4% to all refundable pharmaceuticals (i.e. classified as A and H), save blood products, vaccines, and drugs covered by patent with retail price lower than 5 euros [15]. In July 2006, AIFA increases the mandatory discount to 5%, and in September of the same year establishes a further discount of 5%, in view of overruns 2006 pharmaceutical budget [16]. The financial plan for 2007 [17], presented in December 2006, introduces the payback as alternative to the reduction of drug prices provided for by September determination. The payback consists in a direct payment to Regions equivalent to the amount deriving from the price cut: it is currently still in force. Every year pharmaceutical companies may decide to employ payback mechanism to its products on the basis of market and financial strategies.

General reform of pharmaceutical policy is in force with the law 222/2007 and promotes a synergy between Minister of Health, Minister of Economy and Finance, AIFA and Regions, and pharmaceutical companies, with the aim of regulating and developing the pharmaceutical system [18]. The outpatient pharmaceutical budget, including products supplies through direct distribution (both DD and DPC), was set at 14%, both at national and regional level, and split from inpatient pharmaceutical expenditure. The overspending of outpatient expenditure at national level is covered by manufacturers and supply chain through measures *ad hoc* determined by AIFA, as a direct payment to Regions, with the payback mechanism, and increment of mandatory discount. Regions are stimulated at control of their own spending since they balance the overspending due to outpatient expenditure only in that case exceed locally and not at national level. Whereas inpatient pharmaceutical expenditure could not exceed 2.4% of the overall healthcare expenditure: Regions are responsible for respect of ceiling, and refund any overspending through reduction of hospital and overall healthcare resources. Moreover, for controlling the pharmaceutical expenditure, a maximum budget ceiling, based on volumes and pricing data during the previous year, is assigned to every manufacturer. It represents the amount that SSN is available to reimburse and is allocated according to resources of the national healthcare fund for pharmaceutical expenditure (determined every year with financial law), which is increased with a part (maximum of 60%) of the amount made available by savings originating drug patent expiration. Companies may increase budget allocated, within any specific therapeutic class, gaining market shares. Innovative drugs are excluded from payback procedure and have a specific fund (20% of medicine fund, increased with expired drug patent) to promote the innovation and support the companies committed to research and development. In case of overspending of this amount, all companies have to participate in the fund, in proportion of market share.

In 2010 according to disposition provided for by law 222/2007, the overspending of outpatient expenditure constrain AIFA to introduce further and provisional discounts for class A drug prices to pharmacists – in the amount of 1.82% – and companies – 1.83%, which companies remit through payback mechanism [19].

The pharmaceutical expenditure ceilings currently in force are established by law 95/2012 [20]: the outpatient expenditure limit is set at 11.35% of total healthcare expenditure, while the inpatient expenditure is not allowed to exceed 3.5%. In case of exceeding of expenditure ceilings, measures adopted remain in effect, except for the deficit of the inpatient pharmaceutical expenditure that is financed for 50% by Regions, and the remaining 50% by pharmaceutical companies, via the payback mechanism.

Price definition process: the basics

The prices of drugs classified in class C are directly determined by the pharmaceutical companies and may be increased in January of any odd year (the increment has not to exceed the annual inflation), whilst the reduction price may be performed anytime. The publication in GU is not requested, but the retail price has to be communicated to AIFA by manufacturer.

For drugs reimbursed by SSN, the prices and the margins for pharmaceutical companies, pharmacists and wholesalers are fixed by law. Ex-factory price is the 66.65% of retail price, at net of VAT (in Italy this tax for basic goods amounts to 10%), and represents the maximum hammer price paid by SSN public administrations, such as ASLs and AOs [7]. For drugs supplied through territorial pharmacies, SSN (via ASL) reimburses the retail price, which includes the margins for pharmacist and wholesaler (33.35% of retail price at net of VAT). According to the law 39/2009 [21], the ex-factory price of products never covered by a patent, is set at 58.65% of the net public price, for increasing the margin for the distribution channel (up to 41.35%), with the aim to extend generic drug market. Drugs in class H and directly sold to the public administrations (class A included in PH-T) are privately negotiated between pharmaceutical company and hospital pharmacy, based on budget allocated for that specific pathology.

Reference pricing and alternative strategies

Italian pharmaceutical policy works for containing pharmaceutical expenditure through price negotiation, prescription monitoring, and reference pricing. The latter measure limits the pharmaceutical expenditure by fixing the maximum SSN reimbursement price to all off-patent drugs having the same active pharmaceutical ingredient, pharmaceutical form, administration route, release mode, and unit dose (generic drug). The pricing of generic drugs has a price reduction at least equal to 20 per cent relative to originator drug (with expired patent); the price of other generic products will be equal or lower to the reference price established by negotiation. The policy of reference pricing is used also for some drugs sharing therapeutic indications with equivalent efficacy and safety. This procedure is common at the regional level, where ASLs and AOs may launch tenders for pharmaceutical products in the same therapeutic area, conform to AIFA [20].

The prescription monitoring occurs via AIFA notes and therapeutic plans. AIFA notes are a regulatory tool aimed at improving the appropriateness of the drug prescription, limiting the class A drug reimbursement only for specific indications, essentially chronic diseases: for other indications, drugs remain at patient charge. Therapeutic plans, established with the law 537/1993 [22], are other instruments for limiting prescription and reimbursement only to those indications for which clinical evidence is reported, and for guaranteeing patient therapeutic adherence and appropriateness of use. AIFA lists the drugs needing therapeutic plan, which may be only delivered by specialized centers identified in each Region. Since 2007, AIFA implements AIFA Registers to verify appropriateness in prescribing: they are placed in the early phases after MA of new drugs, and in some cases for the authorized off label use, with the purpose to value real world data on safety and effectiveness – bridge a gap on clinical evidence due to poor clinical data available – apply and manage the negotiation conditions – i.e. Managed Entry Agreements (MEAs) – and consequently govern the public expenditure.

Negotiation based on future events by MEAs is a further strategy for containing SSN pharmaceutical expenditure. MEAs are arrangements between manufacturers and payers that enable the reimbursement of a medicine with specific conditions for reducing impact of uncertainty relating to clinical benefit, cost-effectiveness, and expenditure.

They may consider responding patients (outcome based) or sales volume (price/volume based). Some measures are:
- Payment by results: payback of costs for not responder patients during the first efficacy evaluation;
- Risk-sharing: discount on price (averagely 50%) for no responder patients during first evaluation of efficacy;
- Success fee: reimbursement on responder patients;

- Cost-sharing: discount on price (up to 100%) for the first course of eligible patients;
- Capping: payback of costs for overrun the budgets.

If the benefits obtained are lower then those expected, AIFA may initiate a process of re-negotiation with manufacturer, in order to reduce economic impact.

Financial Flows After the Reimbursement Decision

After publication on GU of P&R approbation, medicinal products may be delivered to the patient, according to supply regimen granted by AIFA. SSN reimburses the price of the medicinal products of class A and H at net of mandatory (and potentially hidden) discounts to the supply chain.

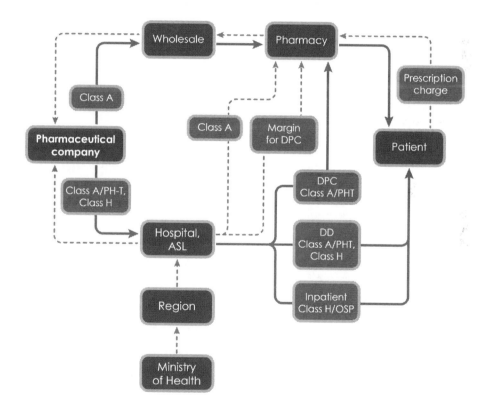

Figure 3. Financial flows for reimbursement of drug classified in class A and H. Dashed lines show the money flow for reimbursing the pharmaceutical company. Continuous lines show the flow of medicinal products based on supply and reimbursement classification

ASL = Local Health Unit; DD = *Distribuzione Diretta* (drugs distributed directly through hospital pharmacies); DPC = *Distribuzione Per Conto* (drugs distributed by territorial pharmacies); OSP = hospital prescription; PH-T = *Prontuario Ospedale Territorio*

The medicinal products sold by territorial pharmacies are reimbursed directly by ASL, which pays the reference price withholding mandatory discounts for the pharmacies and wholesales (and prescription charge paid by patient for in-patent drugs). Moreover, the ASL pays to the territorial pharmacies a margin for the distribution service of drug delivery in DPC regimen.

Pharmaceutical companies receive the reimbursement for class A and H drugs directly by hospital pharmacies (located in each ASL and AO), which acquire at hospital price (i.e. at net of mandatory and hidden discounts) both the medicinal products that are delivered via hospital and via DD and DPC.

Figure 3 summarizes the financial flows for reimbursement of drug classified in class A and H.

5.3 Mapping and Structure of Decision Makers

Minister of Health

It was established in 1958 and it is the core of SSN. It decides the policy line for warranting the health to all citizens.

The duties of the MH are focused for:

- Guaranteeing quality, transparency, equity and efficiency of SSN through appropriate communication to population;
- Resolving disparity and inequity;
- Collaborating with regions to increase the efficiency of SSN;
- Taking and drawing a line in case of emergency for public health.

Secretary of MH trusts on three departments:

- *Dipartimento sanità pubblica e innovazione*, which coordinates and monitors health conditions and safety of persons at work, promotion and development of research, funding and supervision of IRCCS and other national bodies;
- *Dipartimento della programmazione e dell'ordinamento del SSN*, which coordinates and monitors activities of healthcare planning, administrative organs that assurances the SSN quality, Italian health care abroad, information and statistical systems of SSN, trainings of SSN staff, territorial organization of pharmaceutical assistance and clinical risk;
- *Dipartimento di sanità pubblica veterinaria, sicurezza alimentare e organi collegiali per la tutela della salute*, which coordinates and monitors on veterinary medicine, nutrition and alimentary safety.

Moreover, MH avail oneself of technical and scientific consultation of authorities, as:

- AIFA that decides on pharmaceutical field;
- *Consiglio Superiore di Sanità* (CSS) that provides opinions on health field (i.g. during epidemic);
- *Istituto Superiore di Sanità* (ISS) that provides opinions to MH carrying out research, monitor, documentation and training to SSN administrations.

AIFA

AIFA was established with the law n. 326 of 24/11/2003 (article 48) [1]: it is a public body having legal position and administrative, organizational, patrimonial, financial and management autonomy, under the direction of the Ministry of Health and under the vigilance of the Ministry of Health and the Ministry of Economy. According to the law 245/2004 [2], the management of AIFA consist of a General Director, a Management Board and a College of Auditors of Account. General Director is the Agency's legal representative: he is designated by Minister of Health with the State-Regions Conference support, with a 5-years mandate, that is renewable. Management Board, in charge for 5 years, consists of 1 chairman, appointed by the Ministry of Health together with State-Regions Conference, and 4 members, 2 appointed by Ministry of Health and 2 by State-Regions Conference. College of Auditors of Accounts, in charge for 5 years too, is formed by 3 members: 1 chairman appointed by the Ministry of Health, 1 by the Ministry of Economy and 1 by the State-Regions Conference.

The AIFA is subdivided in 6 functional Areas, 5 technical and 1 with administrative tasks:

- Pre Authorization: competences on clinical trials of medicines, Good Clinical Practice (GCP), independent research funded by AIFA;
- Registration: responsibilities on registration process of medicinal products for human use, according to official regulations at national and European level (Mutual Recognition, Decentralized Procedure);
- Post-Marketing Surveillance: responsibilities on drugs safety after their commercialization;
- Pharmaceutical Strategy and Policy: competences on price and reimbursement of medicines, supervision on pharmaceutical expenditure at national and regional level, through the OSMED; it studies the national and international scenario in the field of pharmaceutical policy and may suggest new models and procedures to foster the development of the sector;
- Inspections and certification: tasks of control activities, inspection and issuing of permits for the production of medicines, medicinal gases and raw materials;
- Administrative Affairs: tasks of ensuring the unity and integrity of administrative, legal, regulatory and business affairs of regulatory agency.

AIFA is supported by four technical-scientific committees' activities [3], constituted by experts having documented knowledge in their field.

- Technical-Scientific Committee (CTS) evaluates and gives consultative opinions on national and communitarian applications; it classifies medicinal products for reimbursement and gives technical-scientific advice. CTS is set up by a Ministry of Health decree and it is constituted by 10 members, i.e. General Director of Agency, ISS's chairman and by 8 experts, appointed by Ministry of Health (3 members), Ministry of Economy (1 member) and State-Regions Conference (4 members). The 8 members stay in charge for 3 years.
- Prices and Reimbursement Committee (CPR) performs negotiation activities with pharmaceutical companies in order to define the price of medicinal products that are reimbursed by National Healthcare System (SSN). CPR is set up by a Ministry of

Health decree and it is constituted by the AIFA General Director, ISS's chairman and 8 experts appointed by Ministry of Health, State-Regions Conference and Ministry of economy. As for CTS, the members of CPR, excluding AIFA General Director and chairman of ISS, are in charge for 3 years.

- Agency-Regions Liaison Center assures a close collaboration between AIFA and the Regions. It analyses the pharmaceutical expenditure trend at a national level, promotes generic drugs and analyses the drug distribution and reimbursement at regional level. It is constituted by 10 members, appointed every 5 years.
- Research and development promotion Committee promotes public scientific research in the welfare strategic sections and supports private investments on the national territory. It is constituted by 10 members in charge for 5 years.

The main AIFA tasks are:

- to authorize marketing of medicinal products by national or European procedures according to quality, safety, and efficacy criteria;
- to continuously monitor adverse reactions using the national pharmacovigilance network that links together all the pharmacovigilance services in Health Local Units (ASL), hospitals (AO), Regions and pharmaceutical companies;
- to inspect pharmaceutical companies manufacture sites in order to guarantee the medicinal products and starting materials manufacturing quality (GMP);
- to verify the enforcement of GCP during clinical trials.

Regions: ASLs and AOs

Above it has been presented who guarantees the public health and determines the essential levels of care, MH, and who regulates the pharmaceutical market, AIFA. The nineteen Regions and autonomous provinces of Trento and Bolzano are the public administrations that decide the local health politics inside its jurisdiction, establishing legislative and administrative functions: they autonomously plan the *Piano Sanitario Regionale* (PSR), following the indication of PSN promulgated by MH, and govern the resources obtained by national and local taxation, allocating to ASLs, AOs and private health units for pharmaceutical, ambulatory, rehabilitative and hospital assistance (i.e. LEAs). AOs are hospital chosen by region with a high level of specialization, financial and administrative autonomy and provide healthcare services to patients regardless of regional provenance: patient residence ASL pays by tariff the health care service supplied by AO. MH defines maximum tariffs, but every region may decide to integrate the health supply based on financial availability.

5.4 Challenges and Catalyzers for Market Access

Health and Pharmaceutical Expenditure and New Health Policy

An Italian study observed that 13% of patients use 55-60% of health resources [23]: these patients had an age between 60 and 85 years and were simultaneously interested by 1-4 chronic diseases. In the next future (about 25-35 years), the population with more than 60 years old will increase at least of 10%, with consequently increment of patients that need more health resources. The control of health expenditure is fundamental for the sustainability of Italian SSN. In 2015, the pharmaceutical expenditure, which included drugs reimbursed by SSN and these payed by patients, was of 28.9 billions of Euros (1,9% of Italian GDP), of which 76% at the expense of SSN, due to innovative medicines, in particular for treating hepatitis C [24]. In 2016, the overall health spending was estimated to € 113 billions, about 6.8% of Italian GDP, with a rise expectation in the short and mid term, and simultaneously with a minor impact on PIL, which is expected to grow according to the latest forecasts [24]. The pharmaceutical expenditure exceeded the allocated budget, both for inpatient and outpatient: in particular, inpatient expenditure overcame the ceiling of 3.5% in all regions, and reached 5.1% at national level, with an extra expenditure that amount at 1.2 billions of Euros. Outpatient expenditure was about 0.6% over the ceiling of 11.35%: innovative drugs via PH-T were the main responsible, with an increment of 23% versus the same period of 2015. The overall healthcare expenditure will increase, driven by pharmaceutical expenditure, but with a minor impact on GDP: this scenario may allow to free resources for improving the healthcare.

5.5 **References**

1. Legge del 23 dicembre 1978, n. 833. Istituzione del servizio sanitario nazionale (GU n. 360 del 28 dicembre 1978)
2. Costituzione della Repubblica Italiana. Available at http://www.quirinale.it/qrnw/costituzione/pdf/costituzione.pdf (last accessed April 2017)
3. Legge Costituzionale 18 ottobre 2001, n. 3. Modifiche al titolo V della parte seconda della Costituzione. GU n. 248 del 24-10-2001
4. Decreto del Presidente del Consiglio dei Ministri del 12 ottobre 1983. Istituzione della Conferenza Stato Regioni. GU n. 300 2 novembre 1983
5. Decreto del Presidente del Consiglio dei Ministri del 29 novembre 2001. Definizione dei livelli essenziali di assistenza. GU Serie Generale n.33 del 8-2-2002 - Suppl. Ordinario n. 26
6. Presidenza del Consiglio dei Ministri. Conferenza Permanente per i Rapporto tra lo Stato, le Regioni e le Provincie Autonome di Trento e Bolzano. Patto della Salute 2014-2016. Available at www.salute.gov.it (last accessed April 2017)
7. Decreto Legislativo 24 aprile 2006, n. 219. Attuazione della direttiva 2001/83/CE (e successive direttive di modifica) relativa a un codice comunitario concernente i medicinali per uso umano, nonché della direttiva 2003/94/CE. GU Serie Generale n.142 del 21-6-2006 - Suppl. Ordinario n. 153
8. Decreto Legislativo 25 gennaio 2010, n. 37 Attuazione della direttiva 2007/47/CE che modifica le direttive 90/385/CEE per il ravvicinamento delle legislazioni degli stati membri relative ai dispositivi medici impiantabili attivi, 93/42/CE

concernente i dispositivi medici e 98/8/CE relativa all'immissione sul mercato dei biocidi. GU Serie Generale n.60 del 13-3-2010

9. Determinazione 29 ottobre 2004. Note AIFA 2004 (Revisione delle note CUF). GU Serie Generale n.259 del 4-11-2004 - Suppl. Ordinario n. 162

10. Legge 24 novembre 2003, n. 326. Conversione in legge, con modificazioni, del decreto-legge 30 settembre 2003, n. 269, recante disposizioni urgenti per favorire lo sviluppo e per la correzione dell'andamento dei conti pubblici. GU Serie Generale n.274 del 25-11-2003 - Suppl. Ordinario n. 181

11. Deliberazione 1 febbraio 2001. Individuazione dei criteri per la contrattazione del prezzo dei farmaci. GU Serie Generale n.73 del 28-3-2001

12. Testo Coordinato Del Decreto-Legge 13 settembre 2012, n. 158. Disposizioni urgenti per promuovere lo sviluppo del Paese mediante un più alto livello di tutela della salute. GU Serie Generale n.263 del 10-11-2012 - Suppl. Ordinario n. 201

13. AIFA – Agenzia Italiana del Farmaco. Available at www.aifa.gov.it (last accessed April 2017)

14. Legge 16 novembre 2001, n. 405. Conversione in legge, con modificazioni, del decreto-legge 18 settembre 2001, n. 347, recante interventi urgenti in materia di spesa sanitaria. GU n.268 del 17-11-2001

15. Determinazione 30 dicembre 2005. Misure di ripiano della spesa farmaceutica convenzionata e non convenzionata per l'anno 2005. GU Serie Generale n. 2 del 3-1-2006

16. Determinazione 3 luglio 2006. Elenco dei medicinali di classe a) rimborsabili dal Servizio sanitario nazionale (SSN) ai sensi dell'articolo 48, comma 5, lettera c), del decreto-legge 30 settembre 2003, n. 269, convertito, con modificazioni, nella legge 24 novembre 2006, n. 326. Prontuario farmaceutico nazionale 2006. GU Serie Generale n.156 del 07-07-2006 - Suppl. Ordinario n. 161

17. Legge 27 dicembre 2006, n. 296. Disposizioni per la formazione del bilancio annuale e pluriennale dello Stato (legge finanziaria 2007). GU n.299 del 27-12-2006 – Suppl. Ordinario n. 244

18. Legge 29 novembre 2007, n. 222. Conversione in legge, con modificazioni, del decreto legge 1° ottobre 2007, n. 159, recante interventi urgenti in materia economicofinanziaria, per lo sviluppo e l'equità sociale. GU n.279 del 30-11-2007 - Suppl. Ordinario n. 249/L

19. Decreto-Legge 31 maggio 2010, n. 78. Misure urgenti in materia di stabilizzazione finanziaria e di competitività economica. GU Serie Generale n.125 del 31-05-2010 - Suppl. Ordinario n. 114 convertito con modificazioni dalla L. 30 luglio 2010, n. 122

20. Decreto Legge 6 luglio 2012, n. 95. Disposizioni urgenti per la revisione della spesa pubblica con invarianza dei servizi ai cittadini. GU Serie Generale n.156 del 06-07-2012 - Suppl. Ordinario n. 141 convertito con modificazioni dalla L. 7 agosto 2012, n. 135

21. Decreto-Legge 28 aprile 2009, n. 39. Interventi urgenti in favore delle popolazioni colpite dagli eventi sismici nella regione Abruzzo nel mese di aprile 2009 e

ulteriori interventi urgenti di protezione civile. GU Serie Generale n.97 del 28-4-2009

22. Legge 24 dicembre 1993, n. 537. Interventi correttivi di finanza pubblica. GU Serie Generale n.303 del 28-12-1993 - Suppl. Ordinario n. 121

23. Madotto F, Riva MA, Fornari C, Scalone L, et al. Administrative databases as tool for identifying healthcare demand and costs in an over-one million population. *Epidemiology Biostatistics and Public Health* 2013; 10: 8840-11

24. Magnano R. AIFA presenta il report Osmed 2015: spesa farmaceutica a 28,9 mld (+8,6%), consumi stabili. Territoriale a +8,9%.Strutture pubbliche a+24,5%. Boom innovativi. E il cittadino paga di più: +2,9% sul 2014. Il Sole 24 ore, 24 giugno 2016

https://doi.org/10.7175/747.ch6

6. Market Access in Spain

Carme Pinyol [1]**, Natividad Calvente** [2]**, Cristina Espinosa** [3]**, Toni Gilabert** [4]**,
Carlos Martin** [5] **(from the ISPOR Regional Spain Chapter)**

[1] Head of Pricing and Market Access Southern Europe at Pierre Fabre; President of the
    ISPOR Regional Spain Chapter
[2] Associate Director, Policy Department at MSD Spain; Vice-President of the ISPOR
    Regional Spain Chapter
[3] Corporate Director Market Access & Health Economics at Ferrer; Secretary of the
    ISPOR Regional Spain Chapter
[4] Director of Pharmacy and Medicines at Catalan Health and Social Care Consortium;
    Assistant Professor in Clinical Pharmacy and Pharmacotherapy at Barcelona
    University
[5] Health Technology Assessment Unit at Universidad Francisco de Vitoria; Treasurer of
    the ISPOR Regional Spain Chapter

6.1 General Outlook of Healthcare System and Health Policies

The Environment

Spain has been a parliamentary monarchy since 1978. Political devolution to regional governments has been incrementally implemented over the last 30 years. Thus, the political organization of the Spanish state is made up of the central state and 17 highly decentralized regions (termed *Comunidades Autónomas*, that is, Autonomous Communities) with their respective governments and parliaments (Figure 1). With a population of 46,468,102 (December 2016), Spain covers 505,370 km^2 and has the third largest surface area in Western Europe (Table 1).

The fertility rate is one of the lowest in the EU (1.27 children per woman in 2014). The inflow of migrant population, especially in the last decade, has had a demographic impact in rejuvenating a population that is otherwise rapidly ageing. Life expectancy in Spain is one of the highest in Europe: 85.5 for women and 82.8 for men in 2015.

The top three causes of death in Spain since 1970 have been: cardiovascular diseases, cancer and respiratory diseases, albeit there has been a steady decrease in the actual mortality rates from these causes. Still, mortality rates for these causes are among the lowest in the WHO European Region. Maternal and child health indicators (neonatal, perinatal and maternal mortality rates) have experienced a dramatic improvement, current rates scoring below European averages.

Regarding lifestyle factors affecting health status, the proportion of daily smokers has been declining, though regular alcohol consumption is quite widespread and hazardous drinking affects some 7% of men and 3% of women. Obesity and overweight is increasing, doubling the 1987 rate for adult population to reach 15.6%.

Figure 1. Territorial organization of Spain: Regions

Capital	Madrid
Language	Spain has an official language for the entire State (Spanish) and four co-official languages in six of its 17 Regions (Galician, Basque, Catalan and Aranese).
Government	Parliamentary Monarchy
Area	505,370 Km²
Population	46,468,102 Hab. [Census December 2016, INE]
GDP (PPP)	$ 34,727.1 [2015 World Bank]
Per capita	€ 23,700 [2016 provisional, EUROSTATS]
Per capita	$ 26,609 [FMI 2016]
GDP (nominal)	$ 304.9 [December 2016, OCDE]
Currency	Euro

Table 1. Spain: an overview

The Healthcare System

In Spain, according to the principle of decentralization promulgated by the Constitution, and after the dissolution of INSALUD in 2002, healthcare competence was transferred to each of the 17 regions. The central government only provides this service directly in Ceuta and Melilla and carries out general and basic coordination work between the different regions.

The Ministry of Health, Social Services and Equity develops the Government's policy on health, planning and health care and consumption, as well as it has the competences for the General State Administration to ensure to the citizens their right to health protection.

The Inter-Territorial Council of the National Health System (NHS) of Spain is the organ of cooperation and intercommunication of the health services of the regions with each other and with the State administration to give cohesion to the system and guarantee citizens' rights throughout the territory. In Law 16/2003, of May 28, on cohesion and quality of the NHS, the article 69 reflects its current composition and functions.

The State, through the general taxes collected, finances all health benefits and percentage of pharmaceutical benefits; but this budget is distributed among the different regions according to several criteria of distribution, since the regions are responsible for healthcare in their respective territories.

Public expenditure on healthcare in Spain increased by € 2,031.4 million in 2015, or 13.91%, to € 68,007.1 million, accounting for 14.5% of the total public expenditure. This figures assumes that public spending on healthcare in 2015 reached 6.29% of GDP, a drop of 0.05 points compared to 2014, when spending was 6.34% of GDP.

Pharmaceutical expenditure accounts for approximately one third of the total health expenditure. Pharmaceutical expenditure on prescriptions among all regions grew by 4.08% in 2016 compared to 2015, while hospital spending fell by 6.22% in the same period, which together results in a flat growth of the total pharmaceutical expenditure (-0.06%).

However, this growth has not been homogenous in all segments of the pharmaceutical market. Public expenditure on innovative drugs has fallen by 41.6% between May 2011 and December 2016. In contrast, generic drugs units have increased and their average price has increased as well. Currently, the market at generic prices accounts for more than half of the Spanish market on prescription drugs in values and about 80% of the market in dispensed units.

Andalusia, Catalonia, Valencian Community and Madrid are the regions that present a higher level of public expenditure on drugs, and represent 55% of the total pharmaceutical expenditure.

The NHS is organized in two environments or levels of care: Primary Care and Specialized Care, in which the spontaneous access of citizens and technologies complexity are in inverse relation.

Given their disposition in the community framework, Primary Care is entrusted with the tasks of health promotion and disease prevention. As a maximum expression of accessibility and equity in access.

Specialized care is provided in the specialty centres and hospitals, on an outpatient basis or hospitalized. After the care process, the patient and the corresponding clinical information are returned to the Primary Care physician who, by having all the data in his/her clinic history, guarantees the overall clinical and therapeutic vision. This allows continuity of care to continue to be characterized by equity, regardless of the place of residence and the individual circumstances of the region, since healthcare reaches the patient's own home.

The Basic Services Catalogue of the NHS was established in Law 16/2003, of May 28, on cohesion and quality of the NHS and in the Royal Decree 1030/2006, of September 15, by which regulates the Common Catalogue of Services of the NHS and the procedures for its updating. Subsequently, the Health System reform established by the Royal Decree-Law 16/2012, of April, on urgent measures to ensure the sustainability of the NHS and improve the quality and safety of its services, modifies the Common Catalogue of Services of the NHS including the following modalities:

- Common Basic Catalogue of Services of the NHS. Includes all the assistance activities of prevention, diagnosis, treatment and rehabilitation carried out in health centres or socio-health centres, as well as urgent health transportation.
- Common Supplementary Catalogue of Services of the NHS. Includes Pharmaceutical services, Orthopedic services, dietary products and non-urgent medical transportation subject to medical prescription for clinical reasons.
- Common Ancillary Catalogue of Services of the NHS. Includes all activities, services and technical procedures that are not considered essential and/or which are adjuvant or a support for the improvement of a chronic pathology.
- Complementary Catalogue of Services of the Regions. Regions, within the scope of their competences, may incorporate a technique, technology or procedure not included in the Common Basic, Supplementary or Ancillary Catalogues of Services of the NHS, for which they will stablish the necessary additional resources, informing, in a motivated manner, the Inter-Territorial Council.

The pharmaceutical supply includes medicines and medical devices and the set of actions aimed at patients receiving them adequately and their clinical needs, in the precise dosages, according to their individual requirements, during the appropriate period and at the lowest possible cost for them and for the community, to promote the rational use of the drug.

Patient's prescriptions include those drugs that have been authorized and registered by the Spanish Agency of Medicines and Health Products, masterful formulas and the official preparations made by the pharmacy offices as established in the National Formulary, and the vaccines.

The public funding of drugs is subject to the system of reference pricing and to mechanisms of selected prices as instruments of savings in the pharmaceutical spending, enhancing the use of generic drugs and adapting the packaging of the medicines to the duration of treatments.

The reform included in the Royal-Decree-Law 16/2012 modifies the system of user contributions in pharmacy that previously existed, establishing different levels of contribution for the co-payment of drugs and/or medical devices reimbursed by the Social Security.

Drugs dispensed at hospital level have no co-payment. The ambulatory pharmaceutical supply of drugs and/or medical devices that are dispensed to the patient through a community pharmacy are subject to a user's contribution at the time of dispensing. For pensioners, monthly maximum limits of contribution are established as a function of income.

The Drugs' Law 29/2006, of July 26, devotes its VII title to regulate the public funding of drugs and medical devices. Article 89 of the aforementioned law established the procedure to decide, once a drug has been authorized and registered, to include it in the pharmaceutical supply of the NHS. Specifically, the inclusion of medicinal products in the reimbursement of the NHS is made possible through a "selective and non-indiscriminate funding", considering, among others, the criteria of "therapeutic and social usefulness of the medicinal product" and "the rationalization of public expenditure for pharmaceutical provision". According to the same article, the decision on public funding of new drugs corresponds exclusively to the Ministry of Health, Social Services and Equity.

The Royal-Decree-Law 9/2011, modified articles 89 and 90 of the Law 29/2006. Some of these modifications would be ephemeral, since, Royal-Decree-Law 16/2012 would change those same articles again. However, the new criteria introduced by Royal-Decree-Law 9/2011 for the inclusion of drugs and medical devices in the pharmaceutical supply are still present, so that instead of "therapeutic and social use of drugs", the "therapeutic and social value of the drug and the incremental clinical benefit thereof considering its cost-effectiveness". In addition to the "rationalization of public spending for pharmaceutical provision", the "budget impact for the NHS" should also be considered.

Thus, Royal-Decree-Law 16/2012 adds a new article, 89 bis, to Law 29/2006, which explicitly stated that the cost-effectiveness and the budget impact analyses, as well as the innovation component for indisputable therapeutic advances, would be considered for the decision of reimbursement of new drugs, if it contributes positively to the GDP.

Spain has 21,937 community pharmacies where 48,424 pharmacist work. At present in Spain, there are on average 2.2 pharmacists per pharmacy and there is one for every 2,125 inhabitants.

The pharmaceutical industry is one of the leading sectors of the Spanish investments in R&D. The pharmaceutical industry is the first Spanish sector by intensity in R&D.

On the other hand, it is worth noting the promising future of biotechnology companies, since it is an emerging science, with a long way to go. Although Spain joined the sector a little later in reference to other more competitive countries in research such as the USA, England, Germany, France or Canada, in recent years an extraordinary effort has been made that could gradually translate into levelling with the most scientifically potent countries.

The pharmaceutical industry exported drugs made in Spain worth € 11,084.3 million in 2015. Foreign sales grew by 7.9% in 2015, more than double the total of the country's foreign market (+3.8%), which means that they already represent 4.4% of the total Spanish exports.

Spain is the fifth largest pharmaceutical market in Europe by volume of sales and employment generation (behind Germany, France, Italy and the United Kingdom) and the sixth European market in terms of production (after the four previously countries and Ireland).

In 2015, in this market have been introduced 91 new drugs, of which 43 were generics, 5 biosimilars and 20 components correspond to new active principles, the latter concentrated in the antineoplastic and antiviral areas. From them, 4 new drugs have been marketed as "orphan".

6.2 Pricing and Reimbursement

As we mentioned before, the Spanish Ministry of Health (MoH) oversees the pharmaceutical policy. Specifically, the General Direction of Basic Health Services and Pharmacy (*Dirección General de Cartera Basica y Farmacia* – DGCBSF) is the department which designs, develops and implements these policies in relation to medicines and medical devices.

The most important functions of this entity in relation to Pricing and Reimbursement (P&R) procedure are the following:

- Decide if a medicine or a medical device has public funding for the whole indications or for some of the approved indications for this product.
- Determine the conditions for the prescription and dispensation for the Health National System.
- Coordinate with regional governments all the decisions taken in relation to medicines and medical devices through the Sectorial Health Conference.
- Support a specific intersectoral commission, *Comisión Interministerial de Precios* (CIPM), which has the competence of approving the P&R proposals for medicines and medical devices.
- Capture and analyze data about the pharmaceutical expenditure in retail and in hospitals. They are also in charge of making the annual Spanish pharmaceutical expenditure report.
- Maintain updated all the databases of medicines and medical devices funded by the public system.
- Establish distribution margins and retail sales.

The DGCBSF has a Sub-directorate which oversees the implementation of all these activities, *Subdirección General de Calidad de Medicamentos y Productos Sanitarios* (SGCMPS). This Sub-directorate has two different sections, the first one in charge of the P&R procedure and the funding of medicines and medical devices, the other section has the responsibility for the databases of medicines and medical devices and to analyze the pharmaceutical expenditure.

Moreover, this Sub-directorate has three different advisor Committees.

1. *Comité Permanente de Farmacia del Consejo Interterritorial de Salud* (CPF): The MoH and all regional governments have representatives in it. Their main task is the coordination of pharmaceutical policies at national and regional level.

2. *Comisión Interministerial de Precios* (CIPM): This Committee has an intersectoral character. Four different ministries are part of it, MoH, Ministry of Industry, Ministry of Economy and Ministry of Finances, and regions are represented. Its main task is to approve the price of the drugs.

3. *Comité Asesor para la Financiación de la Prestación Farmacéutica del Sistema Nacional de Salud*: This Committee would be integrated by experts in Pharmaeconomy and Outcomes Research to advise about those topics to the Sub-directorate. This Committee has not been set up yet.

Pricing and Reimbursement Procedure

In Spain, the funding of medicines is selective, not all the approved medicines have to be funded and have reimbursement by the NHS, not even all the indications of the same medicine should be funded by the NHS.

The national regulation establishes several criteria for reimbursement:

- The severity of the disease.
- The duration and the sequela of the pathology.
- The added value of the drug.
- The unmet need.
- The cost-effectiveness ratio.
- The alternatives in the market.
- The degree of innovation.

As we mentioned previously, the CIPM decides if a new medicine or a new indication should be funded and reimbursed by the NHS and establishes at the same time the price of this medicinal product considering the cost-effectiveness data and the budget impact.

If these medicines are not funded or cannot be funded by the public system, they would be commercialized after a communication of the price to the Sub-directorate to assure that this is in line with the pharmaceutical policies of the MoH.

When a new medicine is authorized, the Spanish Medicines Agency send a communication to the SCMPS to start the procedure of P&R. First, the SGCMPS checks up on if this product is included in one of the ATC (Anatomical Therapeutic Chemical) groups funded by the MoH. Otherwise, they do not initiate any procedure. As we stated before, in this case the company should communicate the price to de SGCMPS.

If the new product can be funded, the SGCPM initiates the procedure of P&R (Figure 2) and requests the company the documentation for assessing this new product. So, they start the evaluation considering the dossier from the company which contains data related to clinical data, pharmacoeconomic issues, budget impact and added value (the most relevant aspect is the budget impact). After the assessment, the evaluators begin the negotiations about the price and the type of reimbursement with the company. After that, the SGCMPS includes this agreement in the following meeting of the CIPM for decision. If the decision is positive the SGCMPS communicates the approved price and the reimbursement conditions to the company and to the regional governments. If the deci-

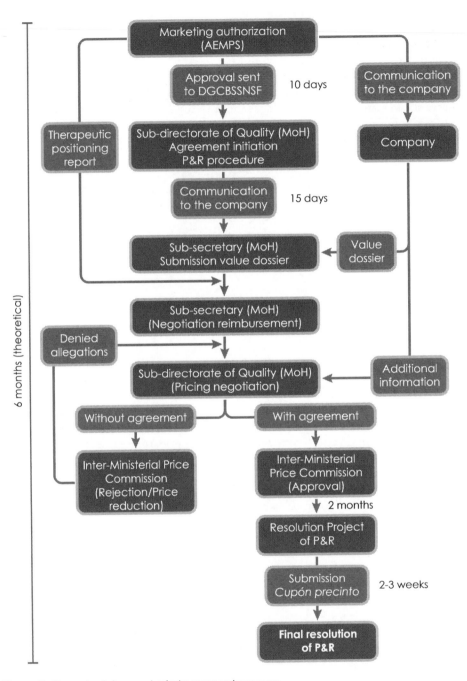

Figure 2. Current pricing and reimbursement process

sion is negative the company can submit more documentation taking into account, the objections proposed by the CIPM.

In case of generic products, there is no need to be reviewed by the CIPM because there is a specific policy for this type of drugs which we will comment afterwards.

This price agreed by the CIPM is not the final official price; some specific margins (distribution, pharmacies) and taxes (VAT) should be added.

As we stated formerly, it is mandatory that all new drugs with a new active ingredient and those authorized but with a new indication should be assessed by the SGCMPS and by the CIPM.

Control of Prices and Pharmaceutical Expenditure

Reference Price System and Homogenous Groups System

As commented before, the P&R procedure is decided by the MoH. There is a 10-year protection period for new medicines. After this period, they are included in specific price systems: Reference Price System (RPS) and/or Homogeneous Groups System.

A RPS is composed by different groups of drugs with the same active ingredient and the same route of administration. Each group must include at least two different presentations with the same active ingredient, one of them should be the original drug and the other one must be a generic or biosimilar medicine or another drug with the same active ingredient but different to the original one. The price of each group is established taking into consideration the lowest cost/treatment/day and the number of daily doses that has each package. This reference price system establishes the maximum price for each group. All drugs included in every group have the same price per unit. All prices are reviewed every year and the groups are updated considering the expiration of patents during the on-going year.

The Homogeneous Groups System is an extension mechanism of the RPS and establishes different groups. These are composed by drugs that have the same active ingredient related to dose, pharmaceutical form, quantity and method of administration. The price of each group is based on the minimum price of any of these drugs on the market when the group is created. Companies can request to be entitle to lower prices and this reduction is applied to the other drugs of the group. These prices are reviewed every three months.

In summary, both systems are complementary; the RPS is based on the application of the maximum price of each group reviewed annually and the Homogeneous Groups System is based in the minimum price of each group reviewed every three months.

Deductions

In 2010 due to the crisis, the Spanish MoH establishes general discounts for all innovative drugs. Both, retail and hospital drugs, have a general deduction of 7.5%. This discount is different for orphan drugs, 4%. For those medicinal products that do not have generic or biosimilar products but have lost exclusivity, this discount is 15%.

CAP

There is another specific mechanism at national level, the CAPs. This mechanism establishes the maximum budget that the NHS can spend in a specific drug. The companies should periodically report to the MoH the sales to the NHS to know when the CAP is reached.

There are three different models of CAP in Spain:

- CAP based on the maximum number of units supplied to the System. Once achieved the maximum, the remaining units are free for the System.
- CAP based on the maximum cost of the treatment per patient. This model stablished the number of packages per treatment. The exceeded packages are free for the System.
- CAP based on both models

National Tendering

There is a new mechanism for lowering the pharmaceutical expenditure, the National Tendering. The *Instituto de Gestión Sanitaria* (INGESA) oversees this entity. They publish the conditions for a national tendering for drugs and medical devices. The implementation of this agreement is done at regional level by the Regional Government. Hospital medicines, vaccines and invasive medical devices are included in these tendering. These agreements have a duration of two years.

6.3 Mapping and Structure of Decision Makers (Reimbursement/HTA)

Autonomous Communities (Regions)

Regarding the health system, starting in 1981 in Catalonia and finalized in 2002, the implementation of the roadmap been established by the 2003 NHS Cohesion and Quality Act. The Quality Act foresees that the MoH at national level will no longer has executive capacity over the running 17 regional systems. It has evolved to a role of guarantor of rights and entitlements.

One of the consequences of that Law was the creation of regional health ministries (17 in total all over Spain) in addition to the national one. This decision represents a division of competences at national and regional level as well as the necessity of establishing a coordination body: The NHS Inter-Territorial Council (CISNS) and the development of coordination and cohesion tools in a mature system. One key objective is to guarantee equity across the country.

The coordination body (CISNS) meets regularly with the National Ministry and the 17 Regional Ministries of health. This coordination body includes different *ad-hoc* commissions, committees and taskforces for discussing more in depth any relevant matters. Specific groups have been established to discuss related topics such as pharmaceutical policy, public health, benefits basket etc. Decisions in the CISNS must be adopted by consensus, but in those matters, that have been transferred to the Regions; they can only take the form of recommendations. Thus, regions are free to implement the recommendations issued by the CISNS but signed agreements or regulations have more binding effect and may become mandatory for regions.

Nowadays, the Spanish NHS is in a complex equilibrium facing major challenges in terms of sustainability, equity among regions and obtaining major benefits from the decentralization.

During this decentralization process, the key factors have been:
- The creation of governing bodies at national and regional level.
- Allocation of funds to national and regional administration.
- Definition of the common benefits package at health level.
- Development of the information system allowing interconnection among regions.
- Development of tools to track performance and resources distribution.

At regional level the health systems (*Consejerías de Sanidad*) consists of a Regional Ministry holding health policy and health care regulation and planning responsibilities, and one or more regional health care providers.

In the regions, the ministry of health is responsible for the territorial organization of health services within its jurisdiction. Usually, the most frequent model consists of two separate executive organizations, one for primary and one for specialist care (ambulatory and hospitals) and a pharmacy division is also created at a high organogram level in the organization. Drugs are seen as major expenses in the regions and in consequence ad-hoc structures have been created, mainly, to keep under control the drug expenditure.

In terms of drugs, the P&R process has been described in the previous chapter but since regions are fully responsible for pharmaceutical management and modulation of the consumption, additional measures have been put in place.

Retail Drugs Evaluation Committees

Since 2003 some regions have organized to perform joint drugs evaluation. The aim was to share methodology, findings and maximize resources. Under the name of Joint Committee for the Evaluation of New Medicines (CENM), Andalusia (CADIME), Aragon, Catalonia (CANM), Balearic Islands, Navarra, Bask Country and Castile and Leon are running evaluations. The aim is to share results and maximize resources by distributing the work among the different regions.

All reports are public as well as the methodology applied. It is mainly addressed to new innovative drugs but it also evaluates new pharmaceutical forms, presentations, and combinations etc. of already existing drugs.

Comparisons are made with already existing alternatives in terms of efficacy, safety and cost. No formal pharmacoeconomic evaluation is included and cost comparison is mainly based in terms of cost per defined daily dose (DDD) since most drugs are considered alternatives. Drugs are rated in five categories based on their relative innovation value: no added value, minor, moderate or significant added value and non-assessable due to insufficient information. More than 80% of evaluations performed are considering that drugs do not add any value to current alternatives available or there is insufficient information to evaluate and in consequence do not recommend the new alternative.

Other Regions have their own evaluation committees or although not being a formal part of the CENM take into consideration their recommendations available at websites.

In practice, those classifications play a variable role in the Regions. Some of them use incentives based on prescriptions recommendations and selection of drugs with high therapeutic benefit and try to avoid those with low benefit according to the evaluation of their committees.

The more the electronic prescribing and recording of medical records evolves, the more the Regions implement prescribing control systems under which an IT programme may select the most efficient drug, advice on those not recommended and include follow-up systems to track deviations according to the forecast.

The degree of implementation varies among Regions and meanwhile in some of them it has an impact on physician's prescribing choices, in some others stay as recommendations.

Hospital Drugs Evaluation Committees

At hospital level, the Commission of Therapeutic and Pharmacy (CFT) is the entity that decides on the therapeutic arsenal available in each hospital.

The commission has representatives from the hospital management, physicians, pharmacist etc. As within any evaluation, the elements considered for incorporating a product into the hospital are quality, safety, relative efficacy and cost.

Physicians can prescribe drugs not listed on the hospital's formulary, if they obtain previous authorization by the CFT and medical director.

The rational use of medicines is also monitored by the CFT and in some cases internal mechanisms for validation of prescriptions are put in place prior to dispensation.

In Spain, it is also very common to reach price-volume agreements and obtain discounts at hospitals level products. In some regions, especially in Catalonia there are also experiences in risk-sharing agreements with some specific products.

There has been a considerable budget impact increase in the hospital innovative drugs. Therefore, many regions have created commissions for the evaluation of these high impact, high price drugs at regional level. The details may vary from region to region but the major worry is how to cope with an increasing budget due to higher prevalence figures and the incorporation of high priced new drugs in this setting.

In practice, in some Regions the decision of incorporation of a medicine at the hospital is not taken at hospital level but at regional level. Thus, some hospital formularies may vary from region to region and even within the same region. Equity among Spanish citizens is questioned by most of Pharma companies.

The Spanish Society of Hospitals Pharmacist (SEFH) constituted a working group in the earlies 2000 with the objective of developing an evaluation guideline for hospital products. The group was named GENESIS group. The objective of this group was to develop a tool to support the evaluation of the therapeutic options at hospital level. The methodology is standardized and has been agreed by the members of the working group. In addition, the collaboration among the pharmacy departments of different hospitals is aimed to increase the efficiency, quality, speed and independency in the evaluation process. The methodology is publicly available and the reports performed by the participant's hospitals as well. This initiative is recognized by the Ministry of Health as well as by the Regions and considered as a best practice.

In November 2016, has been published a Guideline for the economic evaluation and budget impact of the products that has been integrated into the already in place evaluation guideline for hospital products created by the GENESIS group. This is a clear recognition not only of the relevance of the economic part of the reports but of the requirements of improving its economic evaluation. The Guideline is accessible at the web page of the scientific society. Among other recommendations, it has been established a threshold of € 21,000/QALY with a range varying between € 11,000 and € 50,000/QALY. A follow up of this guideline and its implementation should be carefully considered by all stakeholders.

Evaluation Agencies of Health Technology

The Spanish Network of Agencies for Evaluation of Health Technologies of the NHS is made up of agencies or evaluation units of the general administration of the state and the Regions, which work in a coordinated way, with a common methodology under the principle of mutual recognition and cooperation.

The Spanish Network is created by the NHS Inter-Territorial Council in 2012, to promote quality, efficiency and sustainability in health technology assessment in the NHS.

The Network's mission is to generate, disseminate and facilitate the implementation of information aimed at informing decision making in the NHS, contributing to the increase of quality, equity, efficiency and cohesion in the NHS.

The General Directorate for Public Health, Quality and Innovation is responsible for the management, financing, monitoring and dissemination of reports and products produced within the framework of the Network, in collaboration with the DGCBSF. Major focus of these institutions is on health technologies and the cooperation for the evaluation of drugs varies from Region to Region.

The institutions assigned are ISCIII (at national level), AQUAS (Catalonia); Avalia-t (Galicia); AETSA (Andalusia); Osteba (Bask Country); UETS (Madrid); SECS (Canary Islands) and IACS (Aragon).

Other Regional Prescribing Control Measures

Some Regions use prescribing incentives for generics and biosimilars. Some others have adopted a very strict approach for international non-proprietary name (INN) prescription being mandatory such as in Andalusia. The wide use of electronic prescribing systems has facilitated this type of measures.

Tenders at the retail market are another initiative with Andalusia playing a leading role. A lot of controversy has been generated. A series of tenders have been implemented since 2012 in the retail market for out-patented products such as: statins, antihypertensive, gastro-protectants, analgesics etc. Although all controversy generated, the process is not only still in place but also incrementing the type of products included in those tenders.

6.4 Challenges and Catalyzers for Market Access

Challenges

One of the important challenges for market Access in Spain, seems to be the methodology used for price regulation. Shifting from the current method to a value based pricing system appears to be the future although major changes in the current structure should be done e.g. strong HTA evaluation system, develop of the cost-effectiveness committee. Along with the methodology, the lack of transparency through the price regulation process appears to be a major issue because makes that the final decisions are quite a bit unpredictable. Within the lack of transparency there is an ignorance of real prices mainly in the hospital setting which concentrate an elevated proportion of high price drugs. Official list of prices exists but does not reflect real ones due to confidential discounts offered by the pharmaceutical companies and not included in any public document. This situation is sustained by some pharmaceutical companies but not all of them.

Other recognized challenge is related to the policy of generic drugs which it should be widely introduced but results in a modest impact.

A proposal for a change in Spain, should focus on fixing the price of those medicines protected by exclusive Intellectual Property Rights and not in those in the generic competition.

Price regulation based on criteria of international reference prices can be an appropriate option for other kind of countries but it does not seem to be a feasible option for Spain. Value based pricing appears to be the best option although not in the short term because the aforementioned need of a new Health Technology Assessment structure and more rigorous evaluations of every of the new technologies.

Catalysts

As a facilitator to change the situation and overcome the described challenges, emerge a new legislation that promote a new framework transparent and predictable along with a replicable methodology that provide clear guideline to companies to regulate prices adequately. This would avoid the ambiguous legislation around the current criteria for price regulation. New legislation should also develop a value based pricing system, what is demanded by experts from all areas.

A new structure to record use of resources, expenditure and prices could contribute to the development of an information system that helps government and companies to deal with innovative contracting and agreement formulas which facilitate the quick introduction of innovative medication based on equity criteria.

6.5 Innovative Mechanisms for Funding, Purchasing and Paying for Drugs

In Spain, the responsibilities for funding, buying and paying for drugs within the public health system are spread among the different levels of health administration. On the one hand, the decision of public funding and fixing the price is a competence of the Central Government. On the other hand, the Regional Governments should face the purchase and payment of these drugs with their budgets.

This is a system that largely transfers the pressure of funding the drugs to the Regional Governments that can influence little in the decisions of supply and pricing but who then have to prioritize and manage the existing resources to pay the pharmaceutical bill.

The payment of the prescription drugs is made directly from the health services of the Regional Governments to the community pharmacies based on the products dispensed each month. The payment of hospital drugs occurs in two stages: The payment that Regional Government makes to hospitals and the payment of hospitals to pharmaceutical companies through the purchase.

In relation to the purchase, it is usually done directly by hospitals or hospital groups in the case of hospital drugs, or by community pharmacies concerted with the public sector for prescription medicines. In the first case, the price set is a maximum price on which hospitals or groups of hospitals try to reduce by multiple mechanisms according to the product and the purchasing capacity. In the second case, it is a fixed price that incorporates the price of the pharmaceutical company and the margins of the wholesaler distribution and the community pharmacy.

The models of payment to the hospitals by the different Regional Governments are usually made through a payment by global annual budget or directly by the payment for dispensed product.

The payment by budget transfers the risk directly to the hospitals that with the amount allocated have to face the costs incurred. In the case of payment for dispensed product, this is not unlimited. For this, maximum limits of invoicing are established, from which the hospital has to face costs that exceed the limit. Most hospitals establish indicators and incentives for clinical services and physicians to stay within these limits.

In the case of the payment of prescription drugs, the Regional Governments pay directly to the community pharmacies through contracts with the Pharmaceutical Association of each Region. These contracts establish the payment of the drug dispensed at the official price established by the central Government. This payment includes the cost of the drug at the price set by the central government plus the margins of distribution (wholesaler) and dispensing (community pharmacy).

In recent years, in the traditional funding, purchasing and payment systems have been incorporating new mechanisms linked to the concepts of financial agreements, agreements based on the value of the drug and incentives for clinical and purchasing management. As innovative payment models, we also highlight some of the initiatives that have been recently developed that go beyond the established traditional payment. Specifically, we emphasize the payment by rate/patient/month in hospitals and the payment for pharmaceutical services, both in hospitals and in community pharmacies

The following section includes some more detailed information of the different innovative mechanisms adopted at each stage.

Funding of Drugs

The funding of drugs has traditionally been established through a central pricing system by the central government where, apart from the criteria established in the law, a fundamental element is the comparison of the price with other countries.

Two prices are established, one general price and the one for the National Health Service. The central government advertises the general price but not the price for the NHS which remains not visible outside the public health system.

Once fixed the price this can be revised periodically, either by a particular form or by a systematic form, as is the case of the RPS. Specifically, the RPS generates an automatic review of drugs when patents expire and the first generic appears.

Undoubtedly, the RPS is the pricing mechanism that has brought more returns to the sustainability of the system. It is a system more like a selective reimbursement model than a reference price in the strict sense. At the first stages of its implementation there was a maximum price to be paid by the public health system and the citizen had to cover the difference between the maximum price and the price of chosen drug. Over time, the system evolved to a model where the reference price became the price above which no product is publicly funded.

The central government has recently developed new pricing and reimbursement scenarios to try to finance new treatments with dynamic price mechanisms and minimizing budgetary risk. Specifically, we highlight the system of spending ceilings, price/volume agreements and maximum prices per treatment.

Spending ceilings

Spending ceilings are used to insure a maximum outlay for a drug or group of drugs. From a certain amount established as a ceiling, the pharmaceutical company should run with the costs that are generated above it. These ceilings try to minimize the uncertainty of the budgetary impact, so that without modifying the unit price of the product this is conditioned to the overcoming or not of the established ceiling.

Specifically, the central government has established spending ceilings for different molecules such as new antivirals for hepatitis C or some cancer treatments. The system has proved to be a safeguard to the budgetary deviation but its success has been conditioned by the difficulties of managing these ceilings from the central Government. The difficulty lies in being able to add in time and form all the necessary information, as well as the procedure of compensation by the companies to hospitals for the amounts paid above the ceiling.

Price/volume agreements

The price/volume agreements have recently been used by the central government to decide the reimbursement of some drugs. This has been the case for the new antivirals for the treatment of hepatitis C. Specifically, for the different active principles price ranges were established according to the number of patients treated at a global level and by regions. When the estimated volume of sales is reached to move from one range at national level to the next one where the price is reduced. Those regions that have contributed to comply with their regional range can benefit from the price reduction of the drug.

As in the case of spending ceilings, the main difficulty is the complexity of managing the price cuts for each range of sales volume. This is due to the time difference between the date when the agreed volume is reached and the date when this information is received at central level. Thus, the system requires complex invoicing regularizations with hospitals for drugs purchased at the price of the previous range from the day it is officially established that the range has been exceeded and the date on which it is notified.

Maximum cost per treatment

The maximum costs per treatment have also been used in the case of the new treatments for hepatitis C. They consist of setting a maximum cost for the treatment of a patient regardless of the duration of treatment. In this way, the company should pay the additional costs of those patients that exceed the established cost.

Payment by rate/patient/month

This system has been implemented at the hospital setting and consists in establishing a fixed monthly payment to the health provider for the pharmacological treatment of a patient with a certain pathology, independently of the drug or drugs administered.

This system has been implemented mainly in Catalonia for certain pathologies such as treatment of HIV, hepatitis C, rheumatoid arthritis, psoriasis and Chron's disease, growth hormone deficiency, and recently the treatment of cholesterol with the new monoclonal antibodies inhibitors PCSK9.

This payment model aims to encourage the hospital to develop not only purchase management mechanisms but also clinical management, selecting for each patient the most efficient drug for their clinical condition, the best therapeutic regimen and the use of doses and vials, explicitly implicating physicians in this task.

In addition, with this system, the Regional Government can periodically set and modify fees based on the appearance of new medicines for pathology and adapt the economic value of the therapeutic mix regardless of the prices of each drug. With this system, the pharmaceutical companies should adapt their offers according to the rate assigned to each pathology, thus gaining some control over the costs outside of the prices.

The Government of Catalonia has obtained significant efficiency advantages thanks to the implementation of this model compared to the traditional system of paying for each drug dispensed and administered. In addition, clinical hospital management and companies have been encouraged to compete in the market to offer purchase conditions to hospitals that facilitate compliance with these rates.

Payment for pharmaceutical services

In Hospitals: There are, in some cases, payments to hospitals for the pharmaceutical services associated with the preparation and dispensing of drugs. Specifically, in the region of Catalonia there is a program called "pharmaceutical care program" provided with funds from the efficiency obtained in the purchase of drugs that is distributed among different hospitals through a payment mechanism based on so-called pharmaceutical care units (Unidades de Atención Farmacéutica – UAF). These UAFs are calculated based on the workload that the hospital must perform to prepare, dispense, and administrate the treatment to a patient.

In Community Pharmacies: In the case of community pharmacies, several regions have established payment programs that are not linked to the dispensing of drugs. These programs establish payments for services such as the treatment of methadone withdrawal to patients addicted to parenteral drugs and the screening activities of colon cancer and HIV infection. In all of them, a fee is established per patient treated or test performed. There are currently several pilot trials underway to study new forms of payment linked to the development of customized dispensing systems based on unit doses and for the pharmacotherapeutic follow-up of chronic polymedicates patients.

Purchase of Drugs

The purchase of drugs in hospitals is done by tenders, generally for products that are adjudicated to those companies that offer the best conditions for each public offering, or by negotiation without competition in the case of exclusive products.

In the case of prescription drugs that are dispensed in the community pharmacies the purchase is made by pharmacies who then submit the invoice to the regional health service for reimbursement according to the prices set by the central government.

Lately, there are many experiences that are being carried out, both by hospitals and at regional level, of different and innovative models of purchasing with the objective of obtaining better prices or to introduce the concept of value in the acquisition. Specifically, we highlight the auction system in the field of prescription drugs and the models of aggregated purchase, purchase by results, purchase of complete processes and innovative public purchase for hospital drugs.

Drug auctions on prescription drugs

Drug auctions consist of adjudicating the supply of prescription drugs through a public tender. With the auctions the best offer is selected, thus setting the price to pay for a drug by the health service to the pharmacy offices, regardless of the prescribed brand. Thus, the laboratory that offers the lowest price takes the grant of a certain active principle.

This system has been implemented by the region of Andalusia that periodically publishes an auction in which it includes all the medicines that have generic. This system that seeks to achieve price reductions in those medicines that by the traditional system would not go down in price.

This mechanism, although foreseen in the Spanish Law under the heading of "selected prices", has not yet been developed at the central level. The auction model has reported price reductions on some drugs, generally not exempt of some controversy with some pharmaceutical companies as well as Farmaindustria (National Trade Association of the Spanish based Pharmaceutical Industry).

Aggregated purchases

There are several experiences of aggregated purchasing in our country, both at the central level and at regional level. Many regions like in Madrid, Galicia, Andalusia, Bask Country, etc. have a central purchasing office for tendering for all hospitals. Recently the central government has also set up a purchasing center to which some regions have joined. In some regions, there are several platforms of purchasing which recently are also conducting tenders jointly for all hospitals, like the joint platform of the Catalan Health Institute (ICS) and the Catalan Health and Social Care Consortium (CSC) in Catalonia.

Usually, tenders are addressed to pharmaceutical product but there are some experiences where the tender is by therapeutic indication. These tenders consider that the products are similar for the same indication and do not have, objectively, differences among them.

Purchase of complete processes

In some cases, such as for oxygen therapy or dialysis, there are tenders not just for drugs but for the entire service, including administration devices, tracking and monitoring mechanisms, distribution and home delivery services.

Payment by results

In some hospitals, payment by results is being introduced into the purchase contracts. That is, to pay to the pharmaceutical companies based on the results obtained instead of on the units sold. In that cases, only those units of product that have achieved the therapeutic goal previously agreed are paid. At regional level this is generally given in Catalonia where drugs for the treatment in some oncological indications like lung and colon cancer, among others, are already paid in this way.

The payment linked to results, apart from the difficulties inherent to its implementation, have proved to be a good way to align the objectives of public sector, mainly hospitals, and pharma companies in favor of health outcomes, while reducing costs to pay from the hospitals and accelerates the development of programs for registration and measurement of outcomes as a key and pivotal element of a health system. Measuring outcomes in real life settings may justify that the resources used and drug costs are an investment and have a clear return in the form of improvements in the health of the people.

Public Innovative Purchasing (PIP)

The PIP is a contract that is put out to tender for a solution for an existing problem or unmet need. In consequence, the product or system that does not exist at that time, but can probably be developed in a reasonable period. That is, the tender requests the development of new or improved technology to be able to meet the requirements demanded by the buyer.

Most of the existing experiences have been made with medical devices and services where what is bought is not an existing product but a system that responds to a health goal.

Although there is little experience in this type of procedure and it seems that drugs are not candidates for a PIP (due to its regulation through controlled clinical trials and authorizations related to them), they will surely be involved in this type of tenders in which there is a global solution that does not exist in which the drug can be a part of it.

6.6 Look-out for Near Future

The evolution of scientific knowledge especially in the health field is opening an exciting new era in this area. This will allow changes that will transform the rules of standard care moving towards more personalized and targeted drug technologies therefore enabling improvements in patients. Moreover, a change in the model of care is now necessary. The current health systems were designed to save lives and to treat acute diseases. At present the real challenge is to adapt new models due to patients live longer with chronic or degenerative conditions. So, we should design new future models that should consider this new condition of patients, chronification of pathologies, and not only based on acute situations. This implies that there will be a problem for the public system because they should face these new situations not only related to medicines or technologies but also to a new approach. It is necessary to treat or cure patients maintaining the sustainability and the affordability of public systems and providing early access of these innovations to patients.

The main characteristics of new models should:

1. **Guarantee sustainability and affordability.** These new models should ensure both principles through efficient allocation of resources and should stimulate at the same time innovation and promote a competitive environment.
2. **Provide Add value.** These new approaches should encourage the innovation of new medicines and technologies that really change the evolution of the diseases.
3. **Promote the Access**. These new proposals should make sure that patients get timely and equitable access to new medicines and technologies to obtain the benefits from these new therapies.
4. **Be Flexible.** These new proposed models should be designed with sufficient flexibility to reach new future challenges which mean that changes can be performed in the current models.
5. **Have different perspectives.** New approaches are needed to be done not only based on price and budget impact but on added value of medicines or technologies including a more holistic health and social care systems approach.

Traditional models are based on economic results, (rebates, price/volume agreement, etc.) without considering health outcomes. Now the perspective is changing and we are designing new agreement models which consider these health outcomes (partial response or total response, rebates for sub-optimal responses, reimbursement if clinically significant improvement is achieved etc.).

However, different and more efficient models will be needed in the future improving the existing ones. These models must include different perspectives by all the stakeholders and should be robust and with at least 3-5 years' perspective.

The future situation in Spain looks very complex. Our regulation on P&R was designed in the early nineties and the government has made two attempts in the last three years to pass a new one.

This new legislation should promote new principles in P&R procedures, transparency, robust assessment and multidisciplinary approach to this process. The system should be updated and adapted to the XXI century challenges.

We need to establish clear procedures to assess these new technologies with an appropriate methodology and to promote clear criteria for decision making. This new approach must include the regional perspective because Regional Governments are the real payers of these innovations. On the other hand, early dialogue with the different stakeholders are needed to have some predictability in the decision-making process. It is essential to harmonize all these criteria and the type of assessment at European level either by EU-netHTA or by the EMA to have the same European principles.

In conclusion, a holistic value-based approach is required. There is a need to change the current systems based only on price to systems based on health results and added value. The governance of this procedure at the UE level is very relevant and should be clarified in future. In Spain, the regulation should be reviewed, updated and aligned with the European principles. All these changes are to be based on two basic principles, to assure the sustainability of the systems guaranteeing the access of the innovation to patients.

6.7 Bibliography

- Agencia de evaluación de tecnologías sanitarias. Instituto de Salud Carlos III. Organización y funcionamiento de los Comités Autonómicos de Evaluación de Medicamentos. Madrid, 2014. Available at http://gesdoc.isciii.es/gesdoccontroller ?action=download&id=02/10/2014-4a73cebe24 (last accessed June 2017)
- Asociación de Economía de la Salud. Sistema Nacional de Salud: diagnóstico y propuesta de avance. Barcelona, November, 2013
- Boletín Oficial del Estado. Ley 16/2003, de 28 de mayo, de cohesión y calidad del Sistema Nacional de Salud. BOE num. 128 de 29/05/2003
- Boletín Oficial del Estado. Real Decreto Legislativo por el que se aprueba el Texto Refundido de la Ley de garantías y uso racional de los medicamentos y productos sanitarios. BOE num. 177, de 25 de julio de 2015
- Boletín Oficial del Estado. Real Decreto-ley 16/2012 de 20 de abril, de medidas urgentes para garantizar la sostenibilidad del Sistema Nacional de Salud y mejorar la calidad y seguridad de sus prestaciones. BOE num. 98 de 4/4/2012

- Boletín Oficial del Estado. Real Decreto-ley 9/2011, de 19 de agosto, de medidas para la mejora de la calidad y cohesión del sistema nacional de salud, de contribución a la consolidación fiscal, y de elevación del importe máximo de los avales del Estado para 2011. BOE num. 200 de 20/8/2011
- Comités evaluación nuevos medicamentos en atención primaria. CEVIME atención primaria. Available at http://www.osakidetza.euskadi.eus/r85-pkcevi02/es/contenidos/informacion/cevime_atencion_primaria/es_cevime/nuevos_medicamentos.html (last accessed June 2017)
- Diez temas candentes de la sanidad española. Available at https://www.pwc.es/es/publicaciones/sector-publico/assets/diez-temas-candentes-sanidad-2013.pdf (last accessed June 2017)
- Farmaindustria. Análisis de la evolución del gasto farmacéutico público en España. February 2017. Available at http://www.farmaindustria.es/web/indicador/analisis-de-la-evolucion-del-gasto-farmaceutico-publico-en-espana-mes-mes-2/ (last accessed June 2017)
- Farmaindustria. Comités de evaluación de medicamentos de las CCAA. http://www.farmaindustria.es/idc/groups/public/documents/observatorioccaa/farma_131389.pdf (last accessed June 2017)
- García-Armesto S, Begoña Abadía-Taira M, Durán A, et al. Spain: Health system review. *Health Syst Transit* 2010; 12: 1-295
- Guía de evaluación económica e impacto presupuestario en los informes de evaluación de medicamentos. Génesis. Sociedad española de Farmacia Hospitalaria. Noviembre 2016. Available at http://gruposdetrabajo.sefh.es/genesis/genesis/Documents/Introduccion_A_Ortega.pdf (last accessed June 2017)
- IMS Pharmaceutical Pricing &Reimbursement Concise Guide. Spain. 2015
- Joan Rovira Forns JR, Pajuelo PG, del Llano Señarís J. La regulación del precio de los medicamentos en base al valor. Madrid: Fundación Gaspar Casal, para la investigación y el desarrollo de la salud, 2012
- Memoria Annual Farmaindustria 2015. Available at: http://www.codigofarmaindustria.org/servlet/sarfi/docs/PRODF113025.pdf (last accessed June 2017)
- Ministry of Health, Social Services and Equality. NHS of Spain, 2012. Available at www.msssi.gob.es (last accessed June 2017)

https://doi.org/10.7175/747.ch7

7. Market Access in Portugal

Nuno Silverio [1]

[1] *Market Access and Governmental Affairs, Merck, Algés, Portugal*

7.1 **Introduction**

The Country: Portugal

An independent kingdom since 1143, Portugal is one of the oldest nations in Europe.

A former world power during the XV and XVI centuries, Portugal lost much of its wealth, power and status following the destruction of Lisbon in a 1755 earthquake, the occupation during the Napoleonic Wars, and the independence of Brazil in 1822 [1,2]. In 1910, a revolution deposed the monarchy, leading to the 1st Republic, which lasted until 1926 and was followed by the subsequent four decades of the repressive governments of the 2nd Republic, which lasted until 1974 [3].

Figure 1. Portugal

On the 25th of April of 1974, a left-wing military coup installed democratic reforms, which led to the independence of all African colonies. Since 1974, the country has had a democratic regimen – the 3rd Republic – and has seen remarkable human, social and economic development, embodied by the membership of the European Community in 1986, and the Euro Zone in 1999 [4].

Following the military coup, Portugal adopted a new Constitution in 1976, which established a democratic republic after 48 years of dictatorship. The main institutions are the President of the Republic, who is elected by direct universal suffrage for a period of four year, the Parliament, which has 230 members elected by universal suffrage for a period of four years, the government, and the courts. The President appoints the Prime Minister, based on election results and following consultations with all political parties with parliamentary seats, and the other members of the government, who are recommended by the Prime Minister [4].

The Parliament holds the legislative power, while the government develops and guides policy implementation [4].

Portugal is a unitary state, respecting the autonomous regimen of the Azores and Madeira regions, which have their own regional governments and Parliaments [4].

Portugal is located in the south-west of Europe (Figure 1) and it comprises the mainland, which has one land border with Spain to the north and east, and a long coastline with the Atlantic Ocean to the west and south; two archipelagos lying in the Atlantic Ocean, the Azores, with a total of nine islands, and Madeira, with two main islands – Madeira and Porto Santo. Two additional small islands, Desertas and Selvagens, are also part of Portugal [4].

The climate is temperate maritime, with hot summers and wet winters, affected by Atlantic, Continental and Mediterranean influences.

In Portugal, the first social security law was enacted in 1946. It provided healthcare for the employees and their families through social security and sickness funds, financed by compulsory contributions from both employees and employers [4].

After the revolution of 1974, a process of restructuring the health services began. It culminated in 1979 with the establishment of the National Health Service (*Serviço Nacional de Saúde* – SNS), a universal tax-financed system [4].

Currently, the Portuguese health system is characterized by three co-existing and overlapping systems: the universal SNS, the health subsystems – which are special health insurance schemes for certain professions or sectors (e.g. civil servants – ADSE, employees at banks and insurance companies), and private health insurance [4].

Demography

According to recent estimates for 2017, Portugal has a total of 10.3 million inhabitants [5]. Since the last census in 2011, the resident population in Portugal has decreased by 1.9% [5].

In Portugal, the distribution of the population is highly unbalanced, and this unbalance has increased over the years, due to migration to the metropolitan areas of Lisbon and Oporto and the coast, with the population of the interior decreasing. This trend has been accompanied by a gradual aging of the population, due to the increasing life expectancy and the steady decrease of birth rate [4].

According to Eurostat, in 2013, Portugal had the lowest fertility rate among the European Union (EU) Member States (1.2 total fertility rate, compared with an estimated rate of 1.5 in the EU). An increase in life expectancy and the decline in fertility rates are causing in Portugal a "double aging" effect, which will pose major challenges to the Portuguese health system in the coming years [4].

The Economic Crisis and the Bailout

The international financial crisis that started in 2008 had a major impact in Europe, and Portugal was no exception. Following several years of weak economic growth (an average gross domestic product – GDP – growth of 0.8% between 2001 and 2010), the Portuguese economy experienced recession in 2009, 2011 and 2012 [4].

The economic slowdown was coupled with a steady rise in unemployment and by a public debt crisis. The economic downturn and the turmoil that followed the Greek and Irish bailouts led to an increased difficulty in Portugal accessing the financial markets [4]. In this context, Portugal was unable to refinance its debt, which led the country to request financial assistance from the EU, the European Central Bank and the International Monetary Fund (also known as the "troika"). In May 2011, Portugal signed the Memorandum of Understanding in exchange for a total loan of 78 billion Euros [4].

The agreed Economic and Financial Adjustment Program included 34 measures aimed at increasing cost-containment, improving efficiency and increasing regulation in the health sector. Reforms implemented since 2011 by the Ministry of Health included the rebalancing of the pharmaceutical market through new rules for price setting, the reduction in the prices of pharmaceuticals and the increase in the use of generic drugs [4].

For this reason, since then Portugal has been subjected to several legal changes, that over the years pushed the prices down in both the retail and hospital sectors.

In the hospital market, values decreased for the first time in 2013, due to several cost-containment measures introduced throughout 2013, including severe restrictions in access to innovation and the first annual price review done on the hospital sector, using as reference the lowest price in the reference basket instead of the average used in the price of other medicines. This trend continued in 2014, although with a less accentuated slope. However, in 2015 and 2016 the marked started going up again, even in spite of severe limitations to the inclusion of new innovative drugs [6].

In the retail sector, values decreased between 2010 and 2013, the years of the intervention of the "troika" in Portugal, and since then have remained relatively flat, with a slight growth tendency in the last year. This was caused by pressure on the prices and mandatory price cuts, changes to distribution margins and also the strong promotion of generics by government authorities [6].

Total health expenditure in Portugal has risen steadily from 7.5% of GDP in 1995 to 10.4% of GDP in 2010, above the EU average of 9.8% in 2010. In 2011 the economic recession and the austerity measures required by the Economic and Financial Adjustment Program reversed this trend, with the total health expenditure decreasing to 9.5% of GDP in 2014 [4].

In 2015 the total health expenditure as a quota of the GDP in Portugal was 8.9% of GDP, well below the EU average of 9.9% [7].

OECD data from 2014 show that, when compared with the EU27 average of 402 € PPP, Portugal has a low pharmaceutical expenditure, with only 297 € PPP per capita [7].

Also, Portugal has always had a large level of out-of-pocket co-payments, currently at a level of 28% of the overall health expenditure [7].

7.2 Healthcare System and Subsystems in Portugal

SNS: The Portuguese NHS

The Portuguese health system is characterized by three co-existing and overlapping systems: the SNS; the health subsystems (i.e. special public and private insurance schemes); and private health insurance.

The health care delivery system in Portugal consists of a network of public and private health care providers; each of them is connected to the Ministry of Health and to the patients in its own way.

All the people residing in Portugal have access to the health care provided by the SNS, which is financed mainly through general taxes.

Out-of-pocket payments have been increasing over time, not only in terms of co-payments, but also in terms of direct payments for private outpatient consultations, examinations and pharmaceuticals [4].

The level of cost-sharing is at its highest for the pharmaceutical products, since many medicines are not reimbursed or have high patient co-payments (up to 85% of their price).

Between one-fifth and one-quarter of the population has a second (or more) layer of health insurance coverage through health subsystems (for specific sectors or occupations) and private health insurance [4].

The central government, through the Ministry of Health, is responsible for developing health policy, and overseeing and evaluating its implementation. The policy-making process takes place within the government. It is frequent that government rulings go to institutional partners for consultation, but the final resolutions are always issued at Governmental level with seldom cases of intervention by the Parliament [4].

Other Subsystems

In Portugal there are several health subsystems in place, both State-owned and private.

Among all, ADSE (*Assistência na Doença aos Servidores Civis do Estado* or Assistance in Disease to Civil Public Servants) stands as the most prominent subsystem serving the gross majority of public employees and their families. Overall, it covers more than 10% of the total Portuguese population, with more than 1 million insured. The financing of the system is done by a 3.5% tax on salaries of public employees, which gives them access to a system that allows both treatments at the SNS, but also at private sector entities that have agreements with ADSE.Other subsystems in place cover the military, the police, and Justice employees, among others.

In the private sector, the biggest and better known system is the SAMS (*Serviços de Assistência Médico Social* or Medic and Social Assistance Services), which covers bank employees and their families [8].

Private Systems

Several large private systems exist in Portugal, which provide coverage to a part of the population that has private insurance schemes and also to the subsystems that have agreements with these private providers.

This system is mainly used for small interventions, with the majority of the population still using the SNS when disease costs become catastrophic.

7.3 Pathways to Market Access

The Marketing Authorization

Marketing authorization (MA) for new medicines is granted in accordance with Decree-Law 176/2006, which establishes the legal framework regarding the marketing authorization and its changes, and the manufacture, import, export, marketing, labelling and information, advertising, pharmacovigilance and use of medicinal products for human use (including homeopathic medicinal products, radiopharmaceutical medicinal products and traditional herbal medicinal products) and their inspection [9].

MA can be granted through one of four possible procedures, namely, the national procedure, the mutual recognition procedure, the decentralized procedure, and finally, the centralized community procedure handled by EMA and the European Commission [9].

After MA approval, and regardless of the type of process used, the Marketing Authorization Holder (MAH) must request that Infarmed issues local country code numbers for each individual type of package that will be available [9].

Following the release of local country codes and their inclusion in the packages, the medicines can be introduced into the market, provided that they comply with the pricing rules set for the type of medicines in question (hospital, retail, prescription-free) [9].

Obtaining Medicines

Pharmaceuticals requiring prescription can only be sold to the public in a pharmacy.

Prescriptions can be obtained by individuals either in the private sector or the public one, either from an SNS doctor in a primary care unit or from the outpatient department of a hospital.

Under special circumstances, individuals may also obtain medicines directly from hospital pharmacies, when the medicines in question are not supposed to be available in retail pharmacies.

Regarding non-prescription medicines (over-the-counter or OTC), two types of OTC medicines exist, those that can only be sold at a pharmacy without a medical prescription and those that can be sold in specialized stores.

Primary care centers provide and administer vaccines that are part of the National Immunization Program, and are supplied for free.

Price of medicines

In Portugal, there are currently several types of prices, as can be seen in Figure 2.

Pricing in Portugal is mainly ruled by the Decree-Law 97/2015 [10] and subsequent Decree-Orders implementing the several types of prices [11-14].

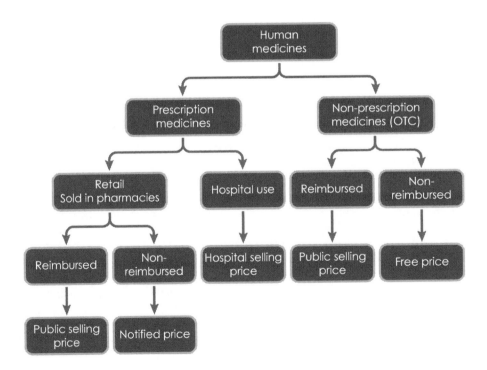

Figure 2. Types of drug prices in Portugal

Free prices

The prices of the OTCs, which require no prescription, are free, unless they are reimbursed (a rare situation), in which case they follow the same rules as a normally prescribed and reimbursed product.

Price and margins are defined by each individual pharmacy or store licensed by Infarmed to sell OTCs.

Hospital Selling Price – PVH

"Hospital use only" medicines have no official public selling price, since they cannot be sold to the public.

For these medicines, price is set as PVH (Hospital Selling Price or *Preço de Venda Hospitalar*), which is the value charged by the MAH (PVA) plus a 0.4% tax and 6% VAT.

For products that are not limited to the hospital environment but for which the MAH intends only to sell to hospitals, the price rules are basically the same as for "Hospital use only" medicines, although these products may or may not have an official public selling price (PVP). If they do have a public selling price, then they comply with the rules set out for the price setting of prescription products.

For purely private hospitals, these medicines can be purchased immediately after the approval of the national country codes, at the price set by the MAH.

For SNS hospitals, or hospitals that are in some way related to the SNS, this was also true until 2006, when the Government introduced new legislation requiring that all new hospital medicines or new indications for current ones should undergo HTA assessment by Infarmed [15].

Since then, hospitals are allowed to purchase new medicines only after they have been evaluated by Infarmed in a process known as *Avaliação Prévia* or Prior Assessment. Initial official timelines for such a procedure were 60 business days, but this has been increased to 180 calendar days under the current SiNATS legislation [10,11,15].

In this HTA process run by Infarmed, authorities negotiate with the MAH the conditions for the product to be made available at hospitals, namely its price (which can remain unpublished and thus confidential) and the number of patients to be treated (translated into the maximum expenditure incurred by the Government with such use). Additional conditions can also be agreed, such as risk-sharing, new data development, and price review conditions [10].

Public Selling Price – PVP

For prescription products, following marketing authorization and obtaining of the local country codes per pack, an international reference pricing system is applied to define the maximum market price for each presentation [10,12].

The international reference pricing system uses a basket of several EU countries, which can be changed every year by the Government (usually before November 15th).

For 2018, the basket is composed of France, Italy and Spain, but in recent years countries such as Slovenia and Slovakia have been used for reference [16].

For retail medicines, the ex-factory price, or PVA, cannot be higher than the average of the price in the reference countries. If the exact same medicine does not exist, a similar one is used (similar dosage and pharmaceutical dosage form). If the price is not available, the price of a similar product on the Portugal market or the price at point of origin may be used.

The public selling price of medicines in Portugal is the sum of several components:

$$PVP = (PVA + MgA + feeA + MgF + feeF + Inf\ Tax) \bullet 1.06$$

Where:
PVP = the Public Selling Price with VAT;
PVA = the MAH price to wholesalers, also known as ex-factory;
MgA = the margin gained by the wholesalers;
feeA = the fixed fee gained by wholesalers;
MgF = the margin gained by the pharmacists;
feeF = the fixed fee gained by pharmacies;
Inf Tax = the tax retained by the MAH and paid to Infarmed.

Values for each individual parameter depend on the PVA/PVP as can be seen in Table 1, with the sole exception of *Inf Tax* which is 0.4% of PVP without VAT (VAT equal to 6%) [12].

Application for price approval is performed online on the SIATS website [17]. Following application, price must be approved by Infarmed in no more than 15 business days, after which the price is considered tacitly approved [12].

This price is set as the maximum price that the medicine can have. However, the MAH may unilaterally decide to lower the price temporarily provided that it notifies Infarmed within adequate timeframes.

Once a year there is a price review, in which a price recalculation takes place, taking into consideration the current basket. After this review, prices can decrease but so far never increased.

PVA (€)	MgA (%)	feeA (€)	MgF (%)	feeF (€)
< 5.00	2.24	0.25	5.58	0.63
5.01-7.00	2.17	0.52	5.51	1.31
7.01-10.00	2.12	0.71	5.36	1.79
10.01-20.00	2.00	1.12	5.05	2.80
20.01-50.00	1.84	2.20	4.49	5.32
> 50.00	1.18	3.68	2.66	8.28

Table 1. Values for each individual parameter that compose the public selling price of medicines in Portugal

feeA = the fixed fee gained by wholesalers; feeF = the fixed fee gained by pharmacies; MgA = the margin gained by the wholesalers; MgF = the margin gained by the pharmacists; PVA = the MAH price to wholesalers, also known as ex-factory

Public Selling Price for generics

The maximum PVP of the generic medicine must be at least 50% lower than the maximum PVP of the reference medicinal product, of equal dosage, or if it does not exist, with the closest dosage and in the same pharmaceutical form [12].

If all PVA prices for all presentations of a specific medicine are below 10 €, then the maximum PVP for the generic must be, at least, 25% lower than the maximum PVP of the reference medicinal product with the closest dosage and in the same pharmaceutical form [12].

Public Selling Price for parallel import medicines

The maximum PVP of parallel-imported medicines should be, at least, 5% lower than the maximum PVP charged for identical or essentially similar medicinal products with a marketing authorization in Portugal [12]. If the concerned medicinal product has no approved price in Portugal, a PVP is calculated for that medicinal product and then the 5% reduction is applied [12].

Notified price

Since 2016 a new system has been implemented by the Government to allow greater flexibility in the pricing of prescription medicines that are neither reimbursed nor reimbursable [12-14].

For these products MAH can request price increases yearly, provided that these price increases follow the rules below:

- The increase of the PVP is not greater than 10%;
- The increase of the PVP is not greater than 2.50 €.

These increases have different margin rules than the normal price setting [12-14].

Infarmed may or may not accept the price increase request, however since no impact exists for the State budget, the tendency is to allow MAH to raise prices [12-14].

SiNATS: The National System for HTA

In 2015 the Portuguese government approved a new law revoking previous ones regarding the access to market of medicines and medical devices [10].

Decree-law 97/2015, June 1st, created the SiNATS (**Si**stema Nacional de **A**valiação de **T**ecnologias de **S**aúde or National System for Health Technologies Assessment), a system which was introduced with the following stated objectives:

1. Maximizing health gains and citizens' quality of life;
2. Contributing to the sustainability of the National Health Service;
3. Guaranteeing the efficient use of health public resources;
4. Monitoring the use and effectiveness of technologies;
5. Reducing waste and inefficiencies;
6. Promoting and awarding relevant innovation development;
7. Promoting equal access to technologies.

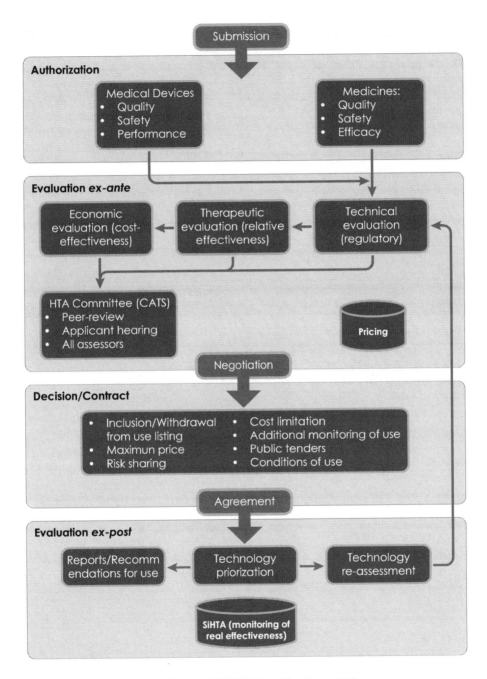

Figure 3. The National System for HTA (SiNATS). Modified from [18]

SiNATS covers all public and private institutions that produce, commercialize or use health technologies. Also, the assessment performed by SiNATS covers all health technologies.

When seen against the previous system, SiNATS has expanded Infarmed's reach in the following way (**bold denotes new areas**):

1. Health Technology Assessment National System
2. Technology:
   - Medicines + **Medical Devices**

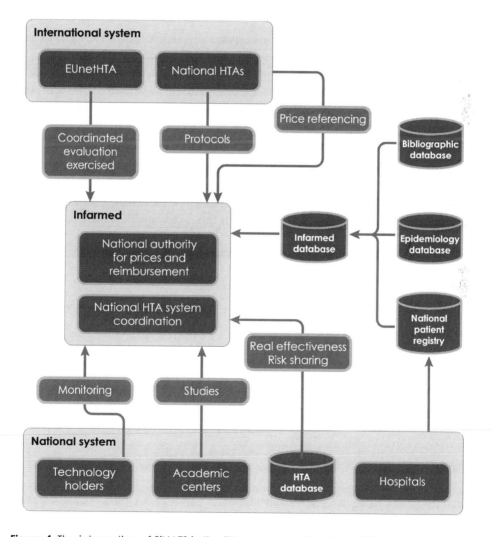

Figure 4. The integration of SiNATS in the EU system. Modified from [18]

3. Assessment:
   - Relative efficacy (Added value)
   - Cost-effectiveness (Economic value)
4. Decisions:
   - Price
   - Financing/Reimbursement
   - Control and cost containment
   - Risk Sharing
   - Additional use monitoring
5. **Reassessment of technologies on the market (*ex-post* evaluation)**
6. **Participation in the European model**

View of the intended structure of SiNATS and its integration in the EU system under EUnetHTA can be seen in Figure 3 and Figure 4 [18].

According to the Government SiNATS is expected to be able to subject health technologies to both assessment and reassessment with contracting with the MAH being its main way of regulation. The system which was created is supposed to be in line with the best European practices, and was considered to be an important step towards the improvement of the operations of the National Health Service [10].

When fully implemented, SiNATS will allow the technical, therapeutic and economic assessment of the technologies supported by an information system which collects and provides information to all entities interested in it. For these purposes, SiNATS will be supported by technical bodies such as the Health Technology Assessment Commission (CATS), which validate the information and assess the application of the health technologies.

One of the important aspects of the new system is the clear indication that the marketing approval and use of a health technology is a necessary, but not a sufficient condition for its financing by the SNS. As a matter of fact, the decision to authorize the use, within the SNS, of a certain health technology depends not only on the quality, safety and efficacy, which are behind the marketing authorization decision, but also on efficiency and effectiveness. These assessments allow to show that public resources are properly allocated and produce significant health gains [10].

Although fully approved in 2015, the SiNATS system had however several setbacks in its implementation, especially for what concerns the information system that should be used for the *ex-post* reassessment of health technologies, and also the full operationalization of the CATS, which has been so far slow in providing timely assessment of new medicines.

Reimbursement and Funding

Access to market funded by the SNS can mainly occur in two ways, either by reimbursement or by prior assessment.

Although frequently undistinguished by the majority of the public, both systems have substantial legal differences.

Reimbursement is mandatory by law, which means that all patients covered by the reimbursement (whole population, or special subgroups in the case of special reimbursements) have access to the reimbursement conditions within the entire SNS. This translates into an obligation for SNS hospitals to provide the medicines included in the reimbursement lists.

Prior assessment, on the other hand, is not mandatory by law, as it is only a condition that must be implemented before hospitals can freely buy these products. Therefore, hospitals may choose if they want to provide these medicines to their patients, having no legal obligation to do so. Under most circumstances, hospitals do provide medicines free of charge to patients when these are medicines that are technically restricted to the hospital setting.

Reimbursement

Following the approval of its price, or at the time of price application, MAH can apply for the inclusion of its medicine on the reimbursement list.

Overall, there are four normal levels of reimbursement by the State, 90%, 69%, 37% and 15%, with the patients having to support the remaining cost.

Under the normal reimbursement law, the level of reimbursement is determined by the type of product/seriousness of disease, with more serious diseases having a higher reimbursement by the State. For example, antidiabetic drugs are reimbursed at 90%, where antihypertensive drugs are reimbursed at 69%.

Life-saving drugs, such as insulins, are fully reimbursed by the State, with no patient co-payment [19].

Overall the process of reimbursement can be defined in the following steps:
1. MAH submits application to Infarmed;
2. Infarmed validates information and sends information to CATS;
3. CATS defines group of experts for the evaluation of the medicine and proposes an evaluation protocol that is sent to Infarmed;
4. Infarmed sends the proposed protocol to the MAH;
5. The MAH discusses and approves the proposed protocol. The MAH may submit additional information at this time;
6. CATS performs the clinical assessment of the medicine and issues a report on the existence or absence of added therapeutic value vs a specific comparator technology/medicine;
7. Infarmed sends the report on added therapeutic value to the MAH who may challenge it;
8. Following clarification of the added therapeutic value in question, CATS performs an economic assessment of the medicine;
9. After the end of the economic assessment of the medicine, CATS issues a final proposal regarding the inclusion/non-inclusion of the medicine from the reimbursed list;
10. Final proposal from CATS is communicated to Infarmed and then subsequently to the MAH;

11. Infarmed negotiates with the MAH the final contracting conditions for the reimbursement of the medicine;
12. Infarmed and the MAH reach an agreement and a final reimbursement proposal is sent to the member of the government responsible for its approval;
13. The member of the government approves the reimbursement and sends the documentation back to Infarmed, which notifies the MAH;
14. The MAH notifies Infarmed of the date when it will begin the commercialization under reimbursement;
15. The product reaches the market.

The overall timeframe for the above mentioned process for new indications or medicines is 180 days, with new dosages and new presentations of already approved products being reviewed in 75 days and generics and biosimilars being reviewed in 30 days. However, it should be noted that Infarmed in the past very rarely has been able to comply with these timeframes, with current average reimbursements tending to take more than one year, sometimes closer to two.

Special reimbursement

The current law also allows for the reimbursement of specific drugs for specific diseases or specific patient groups, taking into account, namely, the beneficiaries' income, the prevalence of the diseases and the public health targets.

Through a Ministerial order, the member of the Government responsible for the health sector may establish reimbursements specific to:
- Certain pathologies or special groups of beneficiaries;
- Certain therapeutic indications;
- Integrated management systems of diseases.

The approval process is similar to the one observed for the normal reimbursement of medicines with the sole difference that the reimbursement needs to be officially published.

These special reimbursements either reimburse drugs that are not reimbursed for the public in general or change the reimbursement level, usually to a lower patient co-payment level.

Examples of such circumstances are:
- Immunomodulators;
- Cystic fibrosis treatment;
- Chronic kidney failure treatment;
- Treatment for transplant rejection;
- Amyotrophic lateral sclerosis;
- Growth and anti-diuretic hormones;
- Specific drugs for hemodialysis;
- Hemophilia treatments;
- Antivirals for hepatitis C;
- Antiretrovirals for HIV.

Prior assessment

Prior assessment is in many ways similar to the reimbursement procedure. The steps taken are the same, with a few exceptions at the end of the process, which are specific for the hospital sector.

Steps in market access through prior assessment:

1. MAH submits application to Infarmed;
2. Infarmed validates information and sends information to CATS;
3. CATS defines group of experts for the evaluation of the medicine and proposes an evaluation protocol that is sent to Infarmed;
4. Infarmed sends the proposed protocol to the MAH;
5. The MAH discusses and approves proposed protocol. The MAH may submit additional information at this time;
6. CATS performs the clinical assessment of the medicine and issues a report on the existence or absence of added therapeutic value vs a specific comparator technology/medicine;
7. Infarmed sends the report on added therapeutic value to the MAH, who may challenge it;
8. Following clarification of the added therapeutic value in question, CATS performs an economic assessment of the medicine;
9. After the end of the economic assessment of the medicine, CATS issues a final proposal regarding the positive or negative assessment of the medicine for use within hospitals of the SNS;
10. Final proposal from CATS is communicated to Infarmed and then subsequently to the MAH;
11. Infarmed negotiates with the MAH the final contracting conditions for the assessment to the hospital SNS market;
12. Infarmed and the MAH reach an agreement and a final positive assessment proposal is sent to the member of the government responsible for its approval;
13. The member of the government approves the positive assessment and sends the documentation back to Infarmed, which notifies the MAH;
14. Infarmed notified hospitals within the SNS of the positive prior assessment and the conditions agreed for the acquisition of the medicine;
15. Infarmed published online the assessment report for the prior assessment;
16. The MAH notifies Infarmed of the date when it will begin the commercialization;
17. The MAH negotiates with each single hospital the inclusion of the medicine in the hospital formulary;
18. The product reaches the market.

As for the reimbursement, the overall timeframe for the above-mentioned process is supposed to be equal to the reimbursement one, 180 days for new products or indications, 75 days for new dosages or formulations and 30 days for generics and biosimilars. However, just like in the reimbursement situation, Infarmed very rarely is able to comply with these times. On average, prior assessments tend to take more than one year, sometimes closer to two.

Guidelines

The assessment of a health technology by CATS is ruled by specific guidelines, which define the procedures for both the clinical and the economic assessment of the new technology [20,21].

Guidelines for clinical assessment of healthcare technologies

In November 2016 the CATS issued some guidelines on their main procedures while evaluating the clinical added therapeutic value of any new technology [20].

The guidelines, which are comprehensive, adopt a methodology similar to GRADE.

Among other important elements, these guidelines define the rules used for defining the comparator against which the new medicine (or health technology) will be compared.

According to this, the comparator must:

1. Be commonly used in clinical practice;
2. Have data that validates its efficacy and safety for the said indication;
3. If more than one comparator exists that complies with the above, then the cheapest one must be selected;
4. Be chosen in a dosage regimen that is in accordance with its Summary of Product Characteristics (SPC);
5. Be funded by the SNS.

Economic guidelines for the assessment of medicines

Portugal does not have a tradition of health technology assessment, except for pharmaceutical products, in which it was a pioneer in the last years of the former century.

Although access to pharmaceuticals was facilitated through the existence of several insurance schemes, the real access to most of the population came about after the implementation of the Constitution in 1976 and the creation of the SNS in 1979.

Since then many laws over the years have governed the co-payment of drugs by the Government for patients in the SNS.

In 1992 a new law implemented the rules for reimbursement of medicines in Portugal, having been modified in 1998 to implement two important changes, the possibility of differential reimbursement for different patient populations and the possibility for the Government to request a health technology assessment during the reimbursement request assessment [22,23].

Also, in 2000, the possibility of specific contracting and the periodic re-assessment of reimbursed medicines was incorporated into the law [24].

Regarding HTA, Portugal was among the first countries in Europe to have Guidelines for implementing the assessment of HTA, having approved them in 1999. These guidelines – although considerably outdated – are currently still in force without a change, after more than 18 years [21].

Since the beginning of the millennium, the HTA in Portugal has slowly progressed, becoming mandatory in all situations in which a premium price is sought by the marketing authorization holder.

The currently existing guidelines present some challenges when viewed together with the ones used for the clinical assessment, since both were written at very different points in time and have considerable differences, for example, in the type of comparator that should be selected for an evaluation.

It is expected that with the implementation of SiNATS and CATS, new updated guidelines will have to be published in the foreseeable future.

Contracting

As already mentioned, contracting has been established under SiNATS as the preferred way to rule the relationship between MAH and Infarmed/Government in all that relates to the access to market of medicines.

The contracts used for both reimbursement and prior assessment conditions may rule a large number of parameters, including (non-exhaustive):

1. The presentations, strengths or pharmaceutical forms to be funded;
2. The maximum price deemed to be suitable for the concerned medicine;
3. The maximum amount of expenses to be borne by the State in the SNS based on a specific number of patients and the respective guarantee mechanisms;
4. The consequences of exceeding the previously agreed amounts;
5. The inclusion of targets to be met after the implementation of the health technology for the purposes of reassessing the latter;
6. The statement of all actions required for the creation and management of information which enables the assessment of the compliance with the targets set out for the medicine;
7. The monitoring mechanisms;
8. A clear and precise definition of the responsibilities of the different intervening parties;
9. The entities entitled to use the medicine in question;
10. Setting out restrictions to the use of the medicine;
11. The mechanisms of risk sharing regarding the use of the medicine.

An important issue to bear in mind when contracting with the Government is the fact that, according to the law, the MAH takes on the risk inherent not only to the possible non-compliance with the targets set out in the contract, but also the possible risk inherent to not getting sufficient information regarding the implementation of that technology, as well as the consequent uncertainty as to the greater claimed relative effectiveness.

In the area of contracting the current SiNATS law provides Infarmed with broad powers that include the following:

1. Contracts may be amended or terminated when facts which represent a change of the requirements for its signature occur or become known, including the reassessment of the State's priorities when allocating financial resources;
2. Termination of the effects of the reimbursement and prior assessment contracts may occur due to a unilateral decision from Infarmed, whenever causes for the exclusion of the reimbursement occur.

SIATS: The Information System for HTA

Alongside the approval of SiNATS, in 2015 the Government also approved the creation of an information system that would allow SiNATS to operate and to gather real-world data that would allow for the ex-post assessment of funded medicines.

Under its powers, Infarmed may request from all departments or bodies and individuals or legal persons intervening in the health system (including MAH) to convey any elements necessary for the operation of SIATS (*Sistema de Informação para a Avaliação das Tecnologias de Saúde*) [10].

Although several databases have been created for obtaining real-world data in some diseases, these have so far been limited to very few diseases, thus staying very short of the original objective initially proposed in 2015.

The SIATS system is currently mainly used to manage the application of price and HTA requests, and it's not to be expected that in the near future it will be able to gain the complexity that was originally planned during the approval of the whole SiNATS system.

Orphan Drugs

In Portugal, no special rules exist for the access of orphan drugs. From a technical point of view, orphan medicines are reviewed and assessed in the same way as other medicines.

Access to orphan medicines is either done at hospital level free of charge (and medicines are reviewed under the prior assessment process) or they are reimbursed under special conditions, solely for that specific population (special reimbursement), usually free of charge.

Although no real difference exists with other medicines, orphan drugs tend to see higher cost-effectiveness thresholds approved than their non-orphan counterparts.

7.4 Mapping of Stakeholders

In order to properly access the market, the MAH has to engage a series of stakeholders whose influence in the overall outcome of the process may vary from none to substantial.

Below are listed some of the stakeholders that must be taken into account when considering the application of any type of public funding for a medicine in Portugal.

Ministry of Health

At the Ministry of Health, only one member is usually responsible for the approval of the reimbursement and prior assessment of medicines. By law the role falls under the supervision of the Minister himself. However, he/she tends to delegate the function to the Health Secretary of State.

Infarmed

At Infarmed, the interaction for pricing and reimbursement or prior assessment of a medicine may occur mainly at three levels:

Executive Board

The Executive Board of Infarmed has a total of three members appointed by the Government. Overall there is a President, a Vice-president and an additional third Member. At the Executive Board one or more members may be responsible for the final negotiation of the market access conditions of the medicines. However, this may change with each executive team, and thus no proper rule exists. Currently, both the President and the Vice-President are actively involved in the negotiation of both reimbursement and prior assessment decisions.

DATS (Direcção de Avaliação das Tecnologias de Saúde)

This is the department within Infarmed responsible for managing the whole SiNATS, including the interaction between the MAH, the CATS and also the Executive Board of Infarmed.

CATS (Comissão de Avaliação de Tecnologias de Saúde)

The Commission for HTA is a pool of experts that are responsible for the assessment of the clinical and economic value of new health technologies, including medicines. The commission is managed by a President and two Vice-Presidents. The full list of the members of the CATS can be found online [25].

CNFT (National Commission of Pharmaceutical Products)

In 2013 the Ministry of Health created a National Commission of Pharmaceutical Products (*Comissão Nacional de Farmácia e Terapêutica*) in order to define a national list of pharmaceutical products and guidelines for their use. This commission works under the supervision of Infarmed and its members are appointed by the Minister. In a conceptual way, medicines approved for reimbursement or prior assessment should automatically be included in the formulary list. The most current list of members can be found at the Infarmed website [26].

Hospital Administrations and Hospital Therapeutic Commissions

Hospital administrations and Hospital Therapeutic Commissions assume a relevant importance in the case of products that are to be sold to hospitals.

Because the final decision by Infarmed is not binding when positive, hospitals can still refuse to use certain drugs in their environment, if they choose to do so.

Being so, the MAH's negotiation with hospitals for the inclusion of the medicine in the local formulary is an additional step after obtaining the positive prior assessment.

Patients Associations

Patient associations do not have any formal saying in the HTA process or the reimbursement/prior assessment process. However, they may have a political influence, which may influence all decision makers in the process, both at the Infarmed and the Ministry level.

7.5 **Major hurdles**

Having started in 2015, SiNATS currently suffers from issues that have been transferred from the previous system and which have so far not been properly solved.

Of all the hurdles in place, a few stand out as the most relevant.

Timelines

Although timelines are always established by the law, the truth is that Infarmed and the Government have always had absolutely no respect for them, thus not complying with the law.

Current official timelines for the review and approval of a reimbursement/prior assessment decision have been increased in September 2017 and currently vary between 30 and 180 days, depending on the type of product (new product, new dosage, generic), with an additional 30 business days for negotiation. However, data from the trade association, APIFARMA, show that currently approved medicines needed an average of 18.6 months to get approved, with a median of 16.1 months [27]. Of these products, approved between 2011 and 2016, only 5.9% were approved in less than 6 months, with 27.6% having taken more than 2 years to get approved [27].

Of the currently under evaluation medicines, the values seem to be similar, with an average waiting time so far of 19.7 months and with 23% of the products have been waiting for approval for more than 2 years [27].

Last, important differences seem to exist between the type of product under evaluation, with oncologic drugs (average 28.2 months) taking far more time to be approved than Hepatitis C or HIV drugs (12.8 and 12.4 months, respectively) [27]. Overall, these extremely long and unpredictable timeframes make market access in Portugal a substantial challenge for all MAHs operating in the country.

Lack of Transparency

Transparency is another important aspect of the market access system implemented under SiNATS.

With a strong pressure of the Government to reduce the total overall expenditure with medicines in the country, Infarmed and its structures have, over the years, become extremely biased in the type of evaluations performed. The tendency is to rarely grant any status of additional added value, thus forcing new medicines to have prices similar or cheaper than the ones already on the market.

The lack of full transparency on the reviewer's positions during the assessment and the lack of appeal mechanisms, when confronted with biased evaluation, are major challenges for MAHs.

Under this scheme, cost-minimization has become more frequent than cost-effectiveness, and budget impact has become determinant for the overall result of the assessment.

Lack of Data

Finally, one last hurdle exists which makes market access quite challenging in Portugal, which is the lack of good data. Portugal lacks availability of statistical and cost data at all levels, with information being sparse and usually limited to specific settings.

National databases are not the norm, and epidemiologic data is often not available.

Although the implementation of SiNATS has come with the promise of the implementation of SIATS and the broad availability of data on costs and effectiveness, the practice is far from the one expected, with serious challenges still existing in obtaining both clinical and economic data.

7.6 **References**

1. Oliveira Marques AH. História de Portugal – Volume I. Das Origens ao Renascimento. 14th Edition. Barcarena, Portugal: Editorial Presença
2. Oliveira Marques AH. História de Portugal – Volume II. Do Renascimento às Revoluções Liberais. 13th Edition. Barcarena, Portugal: Editorial Presença
3. Oliveira Marques AH. História de Portugal – Volume III. Das Revoluções Liberais aos Nossos Dias. 13th Edition. Barcarena, Portugal: Editorial Presença
4. Simões J, Augusto GF, Fronteira I, et al. Portugal: Health system review. *Health Systems in Transition* 2017; 19: 1-184
5. Instituto Nacional de Estatstica. Statistics Portugal. INE Statistics. Available at www.ine.pt (last accessed June 2017)
6. Infarmed. Market statistics reports from 2010 until 2016. Available at www.infarmed.pt (last accessed June 2017)
7. OECD. Health at a glance: Europe 2016. State of Health in the EU cycle. OECD Publications, Paris
8. Serviços de Assistência Médico Social – SAMS. Available at https://www.sbsi.pt/SAMS/servicos/Pages/default.aspx (last accessed June 2017)
9. Decree-Law number 176/2006. Diário da República n.º 167/2006, Série I de 2006-08-30

10. Decree-Law number 97/2015. Diário da República n.º 105/2015, Série I de 2015-06-01, updated by Decree-Law number 115/2017, Diário da República n.º 173/2017, Série I de 2017-09-07

11. Decree-Order number 195-A/2015. Diário da República n.º 125/2015, 1º Suplemento, Série I de 2015-06-30, updated by Decree-Order number 270/2017, Diário da República n.º 176/2017, Série I de 2017-09-12

12. Decree-Order number 195-C/2015. Diário da República n.º 125/2015, 1º Suplemento, Série I de 2015-06-30

13. Decree-Order number 154/2016. Diário da República n.º 102/2016, Série I de 2016-05-27

14. Decree-Order number 290-A/2016. Diário da República n.º 219/2016, 1º Suplemento, Série I de 2016-11-15

15. Decree-Law number 195/2006. Diário da República n.º 191/2006, Série I de 2006-10-03

16. Decree-Order number 359/2017. Diário da República n.º 223/2017, Série I de 2017-11-15

17. Sistema de Informação para a Avaliação das Tecnologias de Saúde – SIATS. Available at https://siats.infarmed.pt/Login.aspx (last accessed June 2017)

18. Martins JC. SINATS: Create the future.*Rev Port Farmacoter* 2017; 9: 222-42

19. Decree-Order number 195-D/2015. Diário da República n.º 125/2015, 1º Suplemento, Série I de 2015-06-30

20. CATS. Metodologia para Avaliação Farmacoterapêutica. Version 2.0. November, 2016

21. da Silva EA, Pinto CG, Sampaio C, et al. Orientações Metodológicas para Estudos de Avaliação Económica de Medicamentos. Infarmed, 1998. Available at https://www.ispor.org/PEguidelines/source/Orien_Metodologicas_EAEM.pdf (last accessed June 2017)

22. Decree-Law number 118/92. Diário da República n.º 144/1992, Série I-A de 1992-06-25

23. Decree-Law number 305/98. Diário da República n.º 231/1998, Série I-A de 1998-10-07

24. Decree-Law number 205/2000. Diário da República n.º 202/2000, Série I-A de 2000-09-01

25. Infarmed. Members of the CATS. Available at http://www.infarmed.pt/web/infarmed/institucional/estrutura-e-organizacao/comissoes-tecnicas-especializadas/comissao-de-avaliacao-de-tecnologias-de-saude (last accessed June 2017)

26. Infarmed. Members of the CNFT. Available at http://www.infarmed.pt/web/infarmed/institucional/estrutura-e-organizacao/comissoes-tecnicas-especializadas/comissao_nacional_de_farmacia_terapeutica (last accessed June 2017)

27. Apifarma. APIFARMA – Associação Portuguesa da Indústria Farmacêutica. Acesso à Inovação. Available at http://www.apifarma.pt (last accessed June 2017)

https://doi.org/10.7175/747.ch8

8. Pharmaceutical Market Access in Denmark, Sweden, and The Netherlands: an Overview

Amir Sharaf [1]

[1] *CarthaGenetics, Carthage, Tunisia*

8.1 Denmark

General Outlook of Healthcare System and Health Policies

Denmark has a public decentralized healthcare system that slightly varies among its regions. The healthcare legal framework and services are managed by each region, which owns the corresponding hospitals and employs and pays the healthcare personnel.

Healthcare expenditure – that in 2014 peaked at 102,569 billion DKK – is mainly funded through taxes, with a specific tax for healthcare [1]. Each region covers more or less totally its expenditure, in accordance with the overall national policy regulated by the Danish National Health Act, which covers all the citizens of the country. While the healthcare system appears to be strongly decentralized, the government still keeps control of the definition of the general directions of healthcare with minor choices of specific target health projects.

Private health practices are equally reimbursed by the regions, provided that they have set a prior agreement with the corresponding region, based on the number of physician per 1000 inhabitants [2].

On a more global scale, Denmark takes into consideration the European directives, not least for the pharmaceutical products' authorization. However, pricing and reimbursement, in addition to distribution, are rather assessed and discussed at national level [3].

Stakeholders

In addition to the Ministry of Health and the Danish Parliament, the Danish Health and Medicines Authority has a pivotal role in the healthcare system, with specific regard to pharmaceuticals' assessment, pricing and reimbursement. In 2015 this authority was divided into three independent yet complementary bodies: The Danish Health Authority, The Danish Medicines Agency, and the Danish Patient Safety Authority. These divisions are rather central and directly under the control of the Danish Ministry of Health (MoH). They are responsible for implementing the MoH directives, but also for reporting on the overall healthcare and pharmaceutical industry and consumption activities from the regions, with the elaboration of corresponding advisory opinions for the MoH. Once a year, the latter establishes the limits for the reimbursement of the approved pharmaceuticals [4].

The Danish Medicines Agency

The Danish Medicines Agency has responsibilities that are more targeted to the approval, reimbursement and distribution of medicinal products in the country. Specifically, it follows the EU regulations and monitors EU central and local decisions for pharmaceuticals, before dealing with them at national level. The Agency decides then which pharmaceuticals to approve, license and reimburse within the Danish market, then closely follows up their consumption and adverse events. The agency is also responsible for the pharmacy structure and operations, and supervises sales and retailers. It also authorizes clinical trials and monitors their operations. The agency performs similar activities for medical devices [5].

Reimbursement Committee

For the reimbursement of pharmaceuticals occurring at local level, the Danish Medicines Agency takes its primary decisions with respect to the regional landscape for the global and/or individual reimbursement of pharmaceuticals. For this, the Danish Medicines Agency receives continual advice from the Reimbursement Committee on the applications for reimbursement by the pharmaceutical companies, as well as reimbursement decision criteria, reimbursement schemes (single reimbursement, terminally ill, etc.) and final expert-based decisions, taken by the committee's expert groups [6].

Payer Stakeholders

Pharmaceuticals in Denmark are paid by the patient and the region the patient belongs to; such co-payment varies, but is always partially reimbursed by the region, as long as the drug is approved for reimbursement at central level [7].

Health Insurance

There are two categories of national health insurance in Denmark, called "Group 1" and "Group 2". The former – the main choice of Danish citizens – covers up to 97% of Danes. Members of this group visit general practitioners (GPs) and specialists for free, provided that the visit with the latter is subject to a referral from the former. Otherwise, patients join "Group 2", if they prefer to freely choose a GP and/or a specialist, without the need for a referral from the GP. While "Group 1" costs are fully covered by the state, those for "Group 2" are only partially covered by the regions [4].

Pathways of Market Access

Regulatory Process

Denmark closely follows the EU directives for the marketing authorization of medicinal products. The decisions regarding the pricing and reimbursement of pharmaceuticals remain rather an internal concern. As for manufacturers, they need to inform the Danish Medicines Agency of their Pharmacy Purchasing Price (PPP) as a first step to enter the market. Health Technology Assessment (HTA) follows later, to determine the eligibility for reimbursement from the national perspective [4].

Pricing

Pricing in Denmark is free and the Danish Medicines Agency has no influence in determining the manufacturer's price. Prices are fixed for 14-day period and the companies must report changes in price to the Danish Medicines Agency every two weeks. Any change is reported to pharmacies and patients through the "medicinpriser.dk" portal. A given drug has then the same price across all pharmacies.

It being free, pricing can drive the pharmaceuticals' costs to high levels. Furthermore, some medicines may not be exposed to a great competition and the original drugs are protected against competition from generics. These situations would further raise the prices. The Danish Medicines Agency decided to issue requirements about the number of medicine packages that each manufacturer could provide prior to entering the market. This requirement is based on the cheapest reimbursable drug, since this is the most demanded. Thanks to this measure, Denmark is able to offer the lowest-priced generic drugs in Europe [8]. Denmark shifted its reference pricing policy from external (EU) to internal (domestic) in 2005. Since then, retail prices have been falling (-26%) along with patient and government expenditures (reduction of 3.0% and 5.6%, respectively). On the other hand, revenues for pharmaceutical companies decreased by 5% [3].

Reimbursement

The Reimbursement Committee, part of the Danish Medicines Agency, along with the pharmacies, oversees the applications that companies submit to the Danish Medicines Agency for the reimbursement of their drug. They take into account different criteria, among which the drug's efficacy, safety, and additional value compared to what exists on the market and/or the standard of care for a given indication. Health economic evaluation also contributes to the decision of reimbursement, and price comparison with other alternatives is a key information. For this, the Danish Medicines Agency provides a pharmacoeconomic analysis guideline, which allows the companies to understand the key information required and to thus provide it accordingly, even though this is not mandatory [9]. Once a drug is approved for reimbursement in a given Danish region, the reimbursement is automatically deducted from the drug's price on retail, at pharmacy level. Some special rules are available for specific cases of prescription-only medicines that are still not yet approved in the country [10].

Health Technology Assessment

Health technology assessment (HTA) is applied to all levels of healthcare services, with the objective to have a rationale-(evidence)-based decision. HTA begins among all the healthcare providers who identify and seek national decision-making projects. Despite this high interest in evaluating healthcare interventions, there still are no HTA regulating policies or administrative procedures in Denmark, and often the outcomes of HTA studies are ignored, because of political or healthcare priorities. One main reason behind this is the time-consuming HTA process, which therefore cannot be adapted to the political processes offering and/or discussing short-term decisions for more or less immediate interventions [4].

Nordic Collaboration

The Nordic Council of Ministers oversees various healthcare issues for the Nordic Countries. In 2015, the Danish Minister of Health proposed a plan to gather all regulatory and pricing policies, as a first step to increase the sharing of information for a better management of healthcare costs. This step is among the first to harmonize decisions and ensure a comparative healthcare standard across the Nordic region.

8.2 **Sweden**

General Outlook of Healthcare System and Health Policies

The Swedish national healthcare system offers health services to all citizens and operates thanks to the funding from taxes collected at regional levels and from municipalities, along with state subsidies [11].

The system has three levels: central, regional (county councils) and local (municipalities). The county councils and regions are the main responsible for ensuring healthcare and pharmaceutical treatment coverage to the relevant citizens. Patients bear co-payment charges when using healthcare services, with a maximum of 2200 SEK (€ 232) per year for pharmaceuticals consumption in outpatient settings. Cost for pharmaceuticals in the benefits scheme are covered by a national grant [12].

Stakeholder	Abbreviation	Description
Medical Products Agency	MPA	National authority responsible for pharmaceuticals from regulation to development, manufacturing and sale
Dental and Pharmaceutical Benefits Agency	TLV	National authority responsible for pricing and reimbursement decisions
County councils	-	Self-governing local authorities responsible for financing and delivering health services
The Council on Technology Assessment in Healthcare	SBU	Organization responsible for Health Technology Assessment

Table I. Main stakeholders for the Swedish pharmaceutical market access

The Swedish healthcare system underwent a gradual shift from the responsibility on the part of physicians in choosing the best available treatment for their patients to a choice that is made more by county councils, thereby adding a politicized note to the decision-making process [13]. This process features independent budgets from one county to another, and led to gaps in the equality of healthcare service delivery across the country [14].

Stakeholders

Table I reports the main stakeholders for the Swedish pharmaceutical market access.

The Medical Products Agency (MPA)

The Medical Products Agency (*Läkemedelsverket* – MPA) is the national body that issues regulations and monitors the development of pharmaceuticals from manufacturing to sales. In addition, MPA issues drug monographs, reporting about safety and effectiveness. MPA is not involved in the pricing and reimbursement decision-making, nor the prescription and use of medicinal products [15].

The Dental and Pharmaceutical Benefits Agency (TLV)

The Dental and Pharmaceutical Benefits Agency (*Tandvårds-och läkemedelsförmånsverket* – TLV) is the main body responsible for the pricing and reimbursement process and decides which products and/or interventions should be covered by the pharmaceutical benefits scheme [16]. Final decision for new medicines is taken by the Pharmaceutical Benefits Boards, a separate expert board within the agency which consists of seven members from county councils, health economic centers and patients organizations [12].

While TLV decides on the reimbursement, it only validates the price which should be proposed by the manufacturer. TLV has, in fact, no involvement in price negotiations, but rather deals with the decision for reimbursement. TLV's decisions are binding at both national and local level (county councils). However, given the variability of the counties' budget, not all counties strictly follow the TLV's recommendations. For this, budget studies and cost-effectiveness modelling are having a growing importance, and pharmaceutical companies are more aware of their importance in applying for reimbursement at local levels, since this is another possibility which runs in parallel with TLV applications. Still, to ensure the reimbursement at national level, the TLV must approve the drug and recommends its reimbursement.

The Council on Technology Assessment in Healthcare (SBU)

The Council on Technology Assessment in Healthcare (*Statens beredning för medicinsk utvärdering* – SBU) looks for evidence to assess healthcare technologies on different levels, not least including medical and economic perspectives, in addition to ethical considerations and social impact. SBU issues guidelines and spreads data on new healthcare interventions without any intention to influence the pricing of pharmaceuticals, the reimbursement decisions nor the prescription or consumption of drugs.

Pathways of Market Access

Regulatory Process

To access the Swedish market, a drug has first to gain approval either at European level or from the MPA, according to the Medicinal Products Act (*Läkemedelslag* 2015:315) [12]. Manufacturers can first apply to the European Medicines Agency (EMA) and gain approval at EU level. It is possible to begin the national assessment in parallel to the European processes, which would allow early considerations and discussions about the pricing and reimbursement issues at national level. Pharmaceuticals are characterized by two sub-pathways at national level, depending on their primary target (in- or outpatient settings), even though there is no clear distinction between the two subgroups and the processes are quite similar.

Pricing and reimbursement

The pharmaceutical company submits an application for including a medicine in the reimbursement system.

According to the Act on Pharmaceutical Benefits (SFS 2002:160) pricing and reimbursement decisions must take into account three fundamental principles: the human principle (equity), the need and solidarity principle – prioritizing more severe conditions over mild ones, and the cost-effective principle (the requested price is reasonable from a medical, humanitarian and social-economic perspective) [12].

Generally, the TLV delivers its decisions within 180 days from the submission. If a drug is denied reimbursement, it is still possible for a company to reapply and submit new data and/or a new price and the process starts all over. Even if the TLV rejects a drug, it is still possible to have it reimbursed at local level, provided that some conditions are fulfilled, like unmet needs, number of patients who would benefit from the drug and – above all – cost-effectiveness [12].

TLV sets the pharmacy retail margin (difference between pharmacy purchasing price and pharmacy retail price) and regulates the substitution of medicines at the pharmacies, knowing that generic substitution is mandatory, unless the patients request the original brand, and therefore are ready to pay the difference out of their pocket. As for the drugs for hospital use, they are directly funded by counties' hospitals, with discounts [11].

Health Technology Assessment

A TLV assessment of a new drug is a closed process, and only its conclusions are made available to the public. TLV issues guidelines helping the manufacturers to submit their application and comply with the TLV's assessment criteria. The cost-effectiveness rationale is a key piece of information and should be supported by a health economic model. TLV seriously consider all cost aspects, including direct and indirect costs to patients and society [11]. The importance of cost-effectiveness has increased so much that all drugs previously reimbursed before 2002 are being closely re-examined by the TLV.

Challenges and Catalyzers for Market Access

Sweden's healthcare system features many challenges caused by the decentralized healthcare system across the country, which makes it difficult to coordinate between healthcare centers and local authorities [17]. The system remains fragmented, with many gaps in the funding, and therefore in the quality of the delivered services. For the pharmaceutical industry, the regionalized landscape makes it challenging to gain access to the whole country, which is not guaranteed by TLV approval but still requires efforts to secure reimbursement at each county level. Sweden is currently undertaking new measures for having the TLV decision making more transparent and to reduce market access gaps between regions, by focusing more on health economics and cost-effectiveness criteria in addition to managed and early access programs for the patients in need. Sweden has created a special commission of inquiry (SOU) to review the current system of financing, pricing and reimbursement of pharmaceuticals, with a final report to be made public in December 2018 [12].

8.3 The Netherlands

General Outlook of Healthcare System and Health Policies

The Dutch healthcare system is based on a social health insurance system. Since 2006, a mandatory health insurance is required for every person who lives or works in the Netherlands. Adults pay a monthly premium, plus an income-related contribution, for the basic insurance covers most healthcare services, as care provided by GP, hospital treatment, prescription drugs, etc.

Although the Dutch health system is among the most expensive in Europe, in the last years it has enjoyed a prestigious position among the 35 European healthcare systems, according to the Euro Health Consumer Index (EHCI). This is not surprising, since the Netherlands' healthcare has continually searched for innovation and reforms, in partnership with the industry, with the aim of reaching and implementing a sustainable system, in order to promote translational medicine and public-private partnership [18].

Stakeholders

Medicines Evaluation Board (CBG)

The Medicines Evaluation Board (*College ter Beoordeling van Geneesmiddelen* – CBG) is an independent body that is responsible for marketing authorization. It also assesses and monitors the efficacy, risks and quality of medicines [19]

The Ministry of Health, Welfare and Sports (VWS)

The Ministry of Health, Welfare and Sports (VWS) is responsible for including drugs and healthcare services in the benefit package, negotiating lower drug prices with pharmaceutical companies, and setting maximum allowable prices for medicines in accordance with the Medicine Prices Act (*Wet geneesmiddelenprijzen* – WGP) [20].

The National Health Care Institute (ZIN)

The National Health Care Institute (*Zorginstituut Nederland* – ZIN; formerly *College voor Zorgverzekeringen* – CVZ) is an independent body that oversees and ensures the quality, accessibility and affordability of healthcare services across the country. It is responsible for advising the VWS on the content of the basic health insurance package, improving healthcare services' quality, and managing contribution funds distributing them over the health insurers

Within the National Health Care Institute, the Scientific Advisory Board (*Wetenschappelijke Adviesraad* – WAR; formerly *Commissie Farmaceutische Hulp* – CFH) and the Appraisal Committee (*Adviescommissie Pakket* – ACP) are involved in the assessment of pharmaceuticals for the inclusion in the Medicines Reimbursement System (GVS) and thus for reimbursement [21].

Health Insurers

Every person who resides or works in the Netherlands is insured under the Health Insurance Act (*Zorgverzekeringswet* – ZVW), which covers basic medical expenses, and the Long-term Care Act (*Wet Langdurige Zorg* – Wlz), which covers long-term nursing and care treatment (i.e. patients with dementia or other severe mental, physical and sensory impairments) [20]. The health insurance is compulsory and is funded by a monthly premium set by each insurer (people on a low-income may be eligible for a government contribution), an income-related contribution, and a government grant for children under 18. The content of the benefit package is defined by The Ministry of Health, Welfare and Sports (VWS) and includes basic medical care, hospital treatment, dental age up to 18 years, maternity care, prescription drugs, etc. Health insurers must offer the same insurance package to each insured and must accept all applicants, regardless of age or state of health.

In addition to this compulsory scheme, voluntary health insurance allows to cover for other benefits that do not figure in the mandatory insurance, as dental care for adults, physiotherapy, glasses and contact lenses, and homeopathic or other alternative medical products.

Pathways of Market Access

Pricing and reimbursement

Manufacturers who seek the reimbursement approval submit a request to the Ministry of Health, Welfare and Sports (VWS). The ZIN prepares an assessment report based on four criteria: necessity, effectiveness, cost-effectiveness, and feasibility. Finally, the ZIN incorporates the advices of the WAR and the ACP and forward the final advice to Ministry of Health, Welfare and Sports (VWS) who makes the reimbursement decision [20,21]. Figure 1 shows the procedure for reimbursement application in the Netherlands.

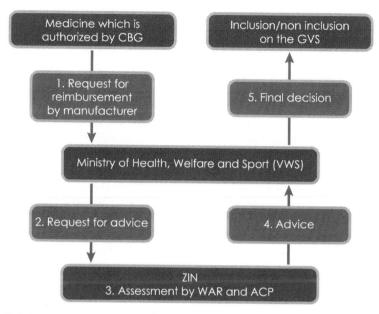

Figure 1. Dutch procedure for the reimbursement application

ACP = Appraisal Committee; CBG = Medicines Evaluation Board; GVS = Medicines Reimbursement System; WAR = Scientific Advisory Board; ZIN = National Health Care Institute

Once a medicine is included on the GVS it is eligible for reimbursement and belongs either to List 1A, which collects therapeutically interchangeable drugs reimbursed according to the reference price system (reimbursement limit), or List 1B, which collects drugs with added therapeutic value that can not be reimbursed according to the reference price system (no reimbursement limit). Finally, List 2 includes specialist drugs that are only reimbursed under specific circumstances. A health economic evaluation is only required for application for List 1B and List 2.

The Medicine Prices Act (*Wet Geneesmiddelenprijzen* – WGP) is the legal framework regulating the pricing of pharmaceuticals in the Netherlands. According to this Act, the Ministry of Health, Welfare and Sport sets maximum prices for specific medicines and pharmacies are not allow to purchase medicines exceeding these prices. These prices are subject to revision every six months, according to the drug prices in reference countries and to exchange rates. The countries of reference are Belgium, France, the UK and Germany [20].

8.4 References

1.   Danmarks Statistik. Available at http://www.statistikbanken.dk/ (last accessed December 2017)

2. The Department of Civil Affairs of Denmark. Official law database. February 2017. Available at https://www.retsinformation.dk/ (last accessed December 2017)

3. Kaiser U, Mendez SJ, Rønde T, et al. Regulation of pharmaceutical prices: Evidence from a reference price reform in Denmark. *J Health Econ* 2014; 36: 174-87

4. ISPOR Global Health Care System Road Map. Denmark – Pharmaceutical. December 2015. Available at https://www.ispor.org/HTARoadMaps/Denmark.asp (last accessed December 2017)

5. The Danish Medicines Agency (*Lægemiddelstyrelsen*). Available at https://laegemiddelstyrelsen.dk/en/about/ (last accessed December 2017)

6. The Danish Medicines Agency (*Lægemiddelstyrelsen*). The Reimbursement Committee. Available at https://laegemiddelstyrelsen.dk/en/reimbursement/reimbursement-committee/ (last accessed December 2017)

7. GLOBAL HealthPR. Denmark – Reimbursography. Available at http://www.globalhealthpr.com/services/denmark/ (last accessed December 2017)

8. The Danish Medicines Agency (*Lægemiddelstyrelsen*). Prices of medicines. Available at https://laegemiddelstyrelsen.dk/en/reimbursement/prices/ (last accessed December 2017)

9. Pricing and Reimbursement Questions. European lawyers' conference on Pharmaceuticals and Health Care Affairs. Conférence bleue 2016. Available at http://www.arthurcox.com/wp-content/uploads/2015/06/Pricing-and-Reimbursement-Questions.pdf (last accessed December 2017)

10. The Danish Health and Medicines Agency. Guidelines for application for general reimbursement of medicinal products. Available at https://laegemiddelstyrelsen.dk/en/reimbursement/general-reimbursement/reassessment/guidelines/guidelines-for-application-for-general-reimbursement-of-medicinal-products/ (last accessed December 2017)

11. ISPOR Global Health Care System Road Map. Sweden – Pharmaceutical. May 2009. Available at https://www.ispor.org/HTARoadMaps/Sweden.asp (last accessed December 2017)

12. Dental and Pharmaceutical Benefits Agency. PPRI Pharma Profile 2017. Available at https://www.tlv.se/Upload/English/PPRI_Pharma_Profile_Sweden_2017.pdf (last accessed December 2017)

13. Antonov K. Flera bedömningsnivåer ger inte patienterna snabbare tillgång till ny behandling. LIFe-time.se February, 2013. Available at https://www.life-time.se/ledare/flera-bedomningsnivaer-ger-inte-patienterna-snabbare-tillgang-till-ny-behandling/ (last accessed December 2017)

14. Dennier A, Podolskaya Y. The Complexities of Introducing New Pharmaceuticals to the Swedish Market. How Do Pharmaceutical Companies In the Swedish Market Handle Uncertainty? A Case Research Study of Seven Pharmaceutical Companies. Stockholm School Of Economics. Department of Management and Organisation 6180 International Business Case Research Thesis. May 2015. Available at https://www.lif.se/contentassets/46a62b3ac56141ffb1280ba230a6fd05/case-research-

thesis-how-do-pharmaceutical-companies-in-the-swedish.pdf (last accessed December 2017)

15. The Medical Products Agency, MPA (*Lakemedelsverket*). Available at https://lakemedelsverket.se/english/ (last accessed December 2017))

16. The Dental and Pharmaceutical Benefits Agency, TLV (Tandvårds- och läkemedelsförmånsverket). Available at https://www.tlv.se/in-english.html (last accessed December 2017)

17. Priya Wahal V. Market Access Challenges in 2017: Changing Healthcare Scenarios in Sweden. DRG – Decision Resources Group, 2017. Available at https://decisionresourcesgroup.com/drg-blog/market-access-challenges-2017-changing-healthcare-scenarios-sweden/ (last accessed December 2017)

18. Pharmaceutical Executive Editors. Country Report: The Netherlands. Pharmaceutical Executive 2016 ; 36. Available at http://www.pharmexec.com/country-report-netherlands (last accessed December 2017)

19. The Medicines Evaluation Board, CBG (*College ter Beoordeling van Geneesmiddelen*). Available at https://english.cbg-meb.nl/ (last accessed December 2017)

20. The Ministry of Health, Welfare and Sports, VWS. Available at https://www.government.nl/ministries/ministry-of-health-welfare-and-sport (last accessed December 2017)

21. The National Health Care Institute, ZIN (*Zorginstituut Nederland*) Available at https://english.zorginstituutnederland.nl/ (last accessed December 2017)

https://doi.org/10.7175/747.ch9

9. Market Access in Japan

Kally Wong [1]

[1] Senior Manager Commercial Insight and Sales Planning, EMEAC, Alexion Pharmaceuticals, Zurich, Switzerland

9.1 Market Background

In 1961, Japan was the first country to implement universal healthcare coverage in Asia.

Japan has also been consistently ranked as one of the nations with the longest life expectancy. In 2016, with an average expectancy of 85 years, a male life expectancy of 81.7 and a female life expectancy of 88.5 Japan had the second highest life expectancy at birth in the world. Similarly, infant mortality rate is one of the lowest in the world, recorded at 2.1 deaths per 1,000 live births in 2014. Other health data also indicated another positive aspect of the Japanese healthcare. It has a very low obese prevalence among the OECD Countries. An example is that in 2015, only 3.7% of the total adult population (aged 15 or above) was considered obese.

All in all, the aforementioned key health indicators reflect the quality of healthcare in Japan, which is ranked as one of the best in the world. The affluence of the country, built with several decades of strong economic development, provided the basis of a better health for its population. On the other hand, this achievement is now being tested by a diminishing replacement rate of the population, as well as a growing elderly population.

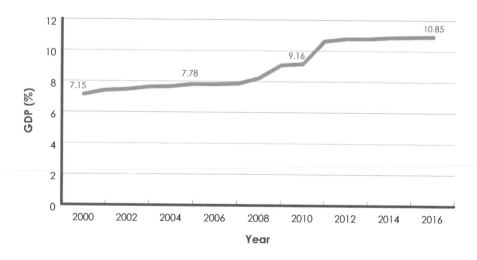

Figure 1. Japan healthcare spending % GDP 2000-2016 [OECD Health Statistics]

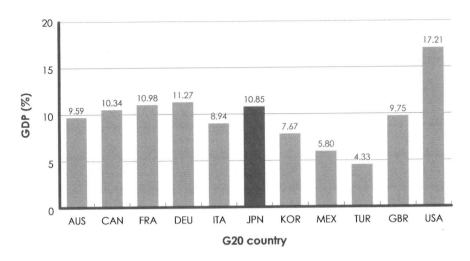

Figure 2. G20 Countries healthcare spending in 2016 [OECD Health Statistics]

	Healthcare spending 2015 (% GDP)	
	Public	Private
France	79	21
Germany	84	16
Italy	75	25
U. K.	80	20
Japan	84	16
South Korea	56	44

Table 1. Healthcare spending by public and private sectors 2015 [OECD Health Statistics]

Effectively, it requires the allocation of a hefty amount of public resources. The Japanese government increased its healthcare spending from 7.15% of GDP in 2000 to 10.89% of GDP in 2015, i. e. USD 343.5 billion to USD 527.3 billion (Figure 1). Figure 2 and Table 1 show healthcare spending in some G20 Countries.

9.2 General Outlook of Healthcare System and Health Policies

The present status of the healthcare system in Japan is closely tied to two factors; the economic situation and the demographics of the population. Japan has entered into a chronic economic stagnation since the 1990s. Its fiscal deficit, which is projected to be

JPY 11.3 trillion (USD 103 billion), or 1.9% of GDP for the fiscal year 2018, has become a perpetual cause for concern for its fiscal policy. While the country is diving into a deeper deficit, healthcare spending is surging in another direction; from USD 1,501 per capita in 1996 to USD 4,519 per capita in 2016. This three-fold increase of healthcare spending is mostly borne by the government, which is always the major payer for healthcare services in Japan. The public sector is responsible for 84% of the payment for the total healthcare expenditure in 2016, which was almost at the same level in 1996, which was 80.1%. Nevertheless, due to a declining birth rate, a decrease in the working population and a sluggish economic recovery, all these factors contribute to a diminishing base for social contributions. This is in contrast with the healthcare budget, which is continuously driven up by an aging population who demands more medical attention. All these factors form the cradle of needs for the search of an effective solution to relieve the financial pressure on the healthcare system.

As the Japanese Ministry Health Labour & Welfare (MHLW) pointed out, the change in the demographic structure is having a huge effect on the resources of the society. The latest set of statistics indicated that in 2016 27.3% of the total population was aged 65 or over (Figure 3). The proportion of this age group in the population has increased by 10% in the past 16 years, from 17.36% in 2000. According to a forecast, the ageing trend among the population will continue. The 65+ age group will increase to 31.8% of total population by 2030, and to 40.5% by 2055. If nothing changes in the healthcare structure, in next two decades the spending on healthcare for the elderly will dramatically increase. It is worrisome that this financial burden is definitely going to be worse and that the next generation might have to bear the financial burden.

The country also faces an unusual but significant challenge in formulating major policy changes to its healthcare system. In a 10-year period between 2007 and 2017, the Prime Minister changed seven times. Given the game of Merry-Go-Round the Prime Ministers are engaged in, the government, unsurprisingly, only managed to implement mainly piecemeal reforms in the long-established universal healthcare system.

The history of the current Japanese healthcare system started in 1961, when its population was required to participate in either an employee health insurance program or in the local/regional-based health insurance program. The latter became known as the National Health Insurance scheme, NHI. Effectively, from then Japan started to have a mandatory social health insurance for every employed subject. A national pension system was also set up, specifically for people employed in large corporations. This pension scheme was then extended to people working in small companies and the self-employed, as well as the unemployed between 20 and 60 years. In 1973, a legislation was passed under the Welfare Law specifically for the elderly, so that this segment of the population could have free access to the healthcare service. A comprehensive universal health coverage was thus fully implemented.

At present, there are two main categories of health insurance schemes in Japan (Table 2). The first falls under the category called Company Health Insurance (*Shakai Hoken*) and it covers all the full-time employees in companies that employ more than 500 people. This insurance scheme also covers civil servants, school teachers, as well as all their family members. Their insurance plans are managed by the Japan Health Insurance Association (JHIA), Mutual Aid Association and Association/Union Administered Health Insurance (previously called the Government Managed Health Insurance, GMHI).

The second main category is the National Health Insurance (*KokuminKenko Hoken* – Citizen Health Insurance), which is for those who are self-employed, and for people employed in small companies, part-time or contract workers, as well as those who are working in the fishery and agriculture industries, the unemployed and the elderly. NHI is responsible for managing the health insurance plans for these groups of people.

The health insurance system is financially supported by the contributions from employees and employers, which amount to the equivalent of 48.7% of the total medical ex-

Health Insurance System	Employee based health insurance		Seamen's Insurance	Mutual aid association		
Insurance target	General employees	The insured under Article 3-2 of the Health Insurance Aids		National public employee	Local public employee, etc.	Private school teachers/staff
Insurer	JHIA	Health Insurance Society	JHIA	Mutual aid associations		Corpora-tion
Insurance plan	1	1,409	1	1	20	64	1
Number of subscribers (1,000 persons)	36,392	29,131	19	125	8,836		

Health Insurance System	National Health Insurance (NHI)			Medical care system aged 75+
Insurance target	Farmers, self-employed, etc.		Retired person (under Employee health insurance)	
Insurer	Municipalities	NHI associations	Municipalities	Union for medical care aged 75+
Insurance plan	1,716	164	1,716	47
Number of subscribers (1,000 persons)	35,937			15,767

Table 2. The health insurance system structure. Modified from [MHLW – Annual Health, Labour and Welfare Report 2016]

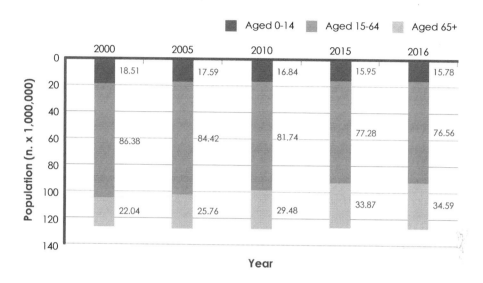

Figure 3. Japan population by age group 2000-2016. Modified from [MHLW – Statistics and Other Data]

penditure in the fiscal year of 2014. In the same year, the government subsidies to low-income and unemployed people and the elderly amounted to the equivalent of 38.8% of the total medical expenditure. Thus, patients' out-of-pocket contributions account for a relatively small portion of the total medical spending. For example, in the same year (2014), it was only the equivalent of 11.7% of the total medical expenditure (Figure 3).

Therefore, the basic principle of the Japanese healthcare services is to ensure that all people have an equal access to medical services and facilities, and are entitled to a nearly uniform benefits package, covering almost all drugs and treatments, except experimental methods. People do not need to choose their insurance scheme, because it is determined by their employment type. This health insurance system has not undergone any major structural changes for the past 50 years. Also, because of this reason, people are well aware of the benefits they are entitled to, and also accustomed to access the medical service at low cost, without many limitations.

Unfortunately, the slow economic growth in the past 20 years accentuated the deficiencies of the system. In effect, it is a system lacking a rigorous system of checks and controls on its services. It is because of this lack of checks and controls that some problems aggravated over time, such as over-prescriptions and the abuse of in-patient services. Japan is known for setting the record of the longest average hospital stays, at 17.2 days, versus the OECD Countries average of 8.1 days in 2013.

The healthcare model that Japan adopted is basically fee-for-service reimbursement, with the patient responsible for 30% of the medical costs, and their insured scheme paying for the remaining 70%. The patients' proportion will decrease to 20% when they reach

70 years of age, and again to a further 10% when they reach 75. Within this co-payment system, the ceiling of the annual treatment cost for the patient is set at a maximum of JPY 600,000 (USD 5,417). The patient's payment ceiling will change to JPY 310,000 (USD 2,827) in 2020. For certain types of special treatments, such as those that require long-term medical care, patients could also leverage other supplementary health insurance programs to relieve their financial burden.

One important consideration within the existing healthcare system has always been waiting to be addressed. It's the current inefficient referral system for treatment. In 2014, 67.4% of the 8,493 hospitals in Japan were run privately, as were 83% of the 100,461 clinics. These private healthcare institutions are very independent, with little information sharing or co-operation between them. In the absence of a central information gathering system, the structure does not promote a condition whereby the optimal allocation of healthcare resources could be achieved. Only in 2015, a medical information network – called Information Communication and Network (ICN) – was implemented by the Japan Medical Associations (JMA).

Since the healthcare demand has risen, due to an increasing number of elderly patients, it becomes evident that, to maintain its quality, the system must have a robust and continuous source of funding. Yet, the Japanese healthcare system does not draw its financial resources from various revenues, but is increasingly relying on the government's budget more than before. An interesting comparison would that with South Korea, where the healthcare system is additionally supported by the taxes on tobacco consumption; and with China, which is additionally supported by the revenues from a national lottery.

So, the increasingly significant drawback in the current system is due to the fact that the financial contributions drawn from the employees' health insurance premium are not directly proportional to the growth. The sluggish economic situation resulted in a shrinking workforce. The problem is then further exacerbated by the fact that a significant proportion of the young people under the National Health Insurance (KokuminKenko Hoken) tends to skip their contribution, since most of them are working part-time or as contract workers. This group of people is most likely to have lower income and less job security per se. To contribute to the healthcare insurance scheme run by the National Health Insurance, they actually have to pay a higher premium than those who are employed full-time and are with the Company Health Insurance scheme (Shakai Hoken).

Since in recent years the Japanese business is dealing with an increasingly fast-changing environment, many companies are no-longer keeping up with the culture of providing life-long employment. Instead, they hire on contract terms. This lead to an increasing number of part-time and contract workers: hence the growing risk of these young people opting not to contribute to their insurance plans; and that, in turn, becomes another causal factor for the diminishing healthcare financial resources.

Without a structural reform of the healthcare system and an improved economic situation, which would generate more revenue for the treasury, the government is struggling to keep up with the brisk pace of healthcare spending. The government tried to control healthcare spending by increasingly tightening the cost control on all pharmaceutical products, including patent protected and non-protected drugs. There is a regular biennial drug price review since 1992. The result of this review has been a median 4-7% reduction in the NHI reimbursement price to both hospital and pharmacies in the last decade.

However, it was only in 2016, when it became once again more stable, that the government could attempt a more comprehensive revision of the healthcare system. It examined the price revision on medical services, the promotion of community-care services, and the review on how to price marketed pharmaceutical products.

In late 2016, the Japanese Central Social Insurance Medical Council (*Chuikyo*) announced a long list of price revision for hospital fees and pharmacies, that they will charge the patients with, under the public health insurance schemes. A surcharge of USD 46 (JYP 5,000) will also be imposed on patients going to a hospital for a consultation without a doctor's referral. The aim is to encourage community based care, by increasing the financial incentive for doctors to treat patients at home rather than at the hospital. By far the most significant policy implemented to reduce the healthcare burden was to renegotiate the prices paid for drugs and to introduce policies to promote the consumption of generics. The updated generic drugs pricing policy involves a reduction in the price from 60% to 50% of the originator product, and a review on the biennial calculation of the drug price. There will be a further discussion on this topic later on in this chapter.

Among all these measures, what caused a lot of concerns among the pharmaceutical industry is the increasing frequency and magnitude of the drug price review. The drug price for the in-line product could be reviewed yearly as of 2018. For the block-buster products, the annual drug sales exceeding a threshold of USD 1.37 billion (JYP 150 billion) might face a cut of up to 50% on their price tag. Ono Pharmaceutical has already been forced to cut down 50% on the price of Opdivo (for cancer treatment) in 2017, and Gilead Pharmaceutical has also reduced 30% of the price of their Hepatitis C treatments in 2016.

Though the immediate effect of limiting the growth of healthcare spending is evident, feedbacks from the pharmaceutical industry are mixed. Some would say that it should discourage pharmaceutical companies to launch a new innovative product in Japan. Against all the odds, the thought of cost containment is likely to remain paramount for the Japanese administrators.

9.3 Structure of Decision Making and Pathways of Market Access

"Medical fee" in Japan refers to all the costs involving medical services, and that includes consultation, diagnosis, treatment and surgery, as well as the cost of medicines, etc. The "medical fee schedule" is in effect a price list containing the official pricing; and reimbursement is the same for the whole country. The formulation and price level of the medical fee is strictly regulated by Ministry of Health, Labor and Welfare (MHLW – *Koseirodosho*), based on the recommendations of the Central Social Insurance Medical Council (*Chuikyo*).

The Medical Council provides the price setting principle, and the price and conditions of the medical fees. They discuss the principle of medical policy and formulate the principles of price revisions on medical fees. The Medical Council has a total 20 nominated members, including seven representatives from payers – i.e. employee-based health insurance scheme and community-based health insurance scheme – seven representatives from healthcare professionals, mainly physicians and pharmacists, and six representatives from the academic world (Figure 4). The overall healthcare budget is determined by the National Diet (*Kokkai*), which is the equivalent of the Parliament.

In principle, once a pharmaceutical product is approved by the Pharmaceutical and Medical Devices Agency (PMDA), it is then included in the NHI reimbursement list for consideration.

In 2011, the government rectified a notorious problem called 'drug lag'. Previously, new therapies would take up to 660 days, or 22 months, to be launched. Patients' access to a new therapy was seriously delayed. To address the issue of 'drug lag', PMDA increased the number of staff from 520 in 2011 to 750 in 2014, and simplified the new drug application process. For new drug applications, the timeline after changes became an average of 60 days, and a maximum of 90 days for them to be approved for reimbursement. At present, it is quicker to introduce a new therapy or new treatment in the Japanese market, than in Europe, where the average is 180 days.

The current guideline on the drug pricing system is based on the announcement of 'Drug Pricing Standard' Notification no. 0210-(1) and no. 0210-(2) made in 2016 by the Economic Affairs Division at Health Policy Bureau, a subsidiary of the Ministry of Health, Labor and Welfare. This included an updated guideline for a regular drug price review process that started in 1992. It was originally developed to narrow the gap between the reimbursed price and the market price of pharmaceutical products sold to hospitals, clinics

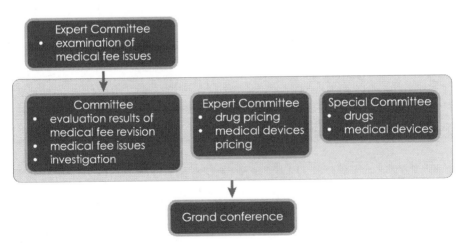

Figure 4. Structure of Central Social Insurance Medical Council (*Chuikyo*) and its committees

and pharmacies. This NHI price review is biennial. Prior to each review, an official survey of market prices was carried out in the fall of the previous year, and the results of this survey constituted a reference for determining any changes in the drug price.

The acceptable gap between the reimbursed price and the market price, known as *yakassa*, has been set at 2% since 2000. If discounts on the product exceed this amount, then the product would be subject to price cuts during the price review. The last price review was carried out in 2016, with reference to the survey conducted in 2015, and that was before the pilot study on cost-effectiveness was conducted, in the same year. It is estimated that only about 22% of the drugs on the market were not affected by those particular discount-based price-cuts.

The Medical Council also provides guidelines on new drug pricing, and they also have the option of adding a price premium for what they consider innovative therapies.

The basic rule for re-pricing the launched products is to calculate the weighted average price of the drug class and then add the consumption tax (8% VAT). The price adjustment for the last few years was 2% (called the R-zone, a price adjustment range). Both the market price and sales volume in hospitals and pharmacies were considered for the calculation of the weighted average price. Table 3 shows the drug price review on long-listed pharmaceutical products in the years 1992-2016.

Year	Year of survey conducted for reference	R-Zone (Price adjustment range %)	Average price cut (%)
1992	June 1991	15	-8.1
1994	June 1993	13	-6.6
1996	June 1995	11	-6.8
1997	September 1996	10 (8% for long-listed products)	-3.0
1998	September 1997	5 (8% for long-listed products)	-9.7
2000	September 1999	Range adjusted 2	-7.0
2002	September 2001	Range adjusted 2	-6.3
2004	September 2003	Range adjusted 2	-4.2
2006	September 2005	Range adjusted 2	-6.7
2008	September 2007	Range adjusted 2	-5.2
2010	September 2009	Range adjusted 2	-6.3
2012	September 2011	Range adjusted 2	-6.3
2014	September 2013	Range adjusted 2	n. a
2016	September 2015	Range adjusted 2	n. a.

Table 3. Drug price review on long-listed pharmaceutical products for the years 1992-2016 [IMS Market Prognosis 2012; JPMA, 2017]

Special Price Adjustment in the 2016 Drug Price Review

The special price adjustment in the fiscal year 2016 was specifically targeted on drugs that have been on the reimbursement list for a long time. If these products have a generics version launched at least five years before, but the generic penetration remains less than 70% (previously set at 60% in the 2014 drug price review), an additional price revision is triggered (Table 4). This latest guideline has increased the pressure on reducing the price for those drugs that have been on the reimbursement list for a long time, but are able to remain in the market with low generic penetrations.

Another feature newly added to the 2016 price review was to impose an additional price cut when the product is achieving very high annual drug sales. This policy change was made with special reference to those drugs with sales substantially greater than the predicted ones. The special price adjustment in price review, initiated in 1996, was made to monitor those products that have exceeded their predicted sales, and the products with added indications after the original listing for the NHI reimbursement. The level of sales foreseen is very important, since it is used to determine the price of the drug during the negotiation for reimbursement (Table 5 and Table 6).

Drug Price Review 2014		Drug Price Review 2016	
Generic penetration (%)	Price reduction (%)	Generic penetration (%)	Price reduction (%)
< 20	-2.0	< 30	-2.0
20-40	-1.75	30-50	-1.75
40-60	-1.5	50-70	-1.5

Table 4. Special price adjustment for long-listed products with low generic penetration in 2016 [2016 HIRA International Symposium]

Drug Price Review 2014		Drug Price Review 2016	
Level of predicted sales	Price reduction (%)		Price reduction (%)
≥ 2-times of predicted annual sales and/or annual sales > JPY 15 billion (USD136.6 million)	-17	≥ 1.5-times of predicted annual sales and/ or annual sales > JPY 100-150 billion (USD 910 million-1.37 billion)	Maximum reduction 25
≥ 10-times of predicted annual sales and/or annual sales > JPY 10 billion (USD 91 million)	-17	≥ 1.3-times of predicted annual sales and/ or annual sales > JPY 150 billion (USD 1.37 billion)	Maximum reduction 50

Table 5. Recalculation the price of drugs with very high annual sales in Drug Price Review 2014 and 2016 [2016 HIRA International Symposium]

	Product	Market Authorization Holder	Predicted sales	Price before reduction	Price after reduction
Method 1	Avastin	CHUGAI Pharmaceutical	• JPY 30. 1 billion • (USD 274.6 million) • 18,000 patients	JYP 180,000 (USD 1,648)	JYP 160,000 (USD 1,465)
	Plavix	Sanofi	• JPY 53. 4 billion • (USD 488.8 million) • 670,000 patients	JYP 280 (USD 2.56)	JYP 200 (USD 1.83)
Method 2	Sovaldi	Gilead Sciences	• JYP 98. 7 billion • (USD 903.4 million) • 19,000 patients	JYP 62,000 (USD 567.5)	JYP 42,000 (USD 384.4)

Table 6. Examples of price reduction on drugs with very high annual sales in 2016 [2016 HIRA International Symposium]

Note.

Method 1: ≥ 1.5-times of predicted annual sales and/or annual sales > JPY 100-150 billion (> USD 910 million-1.37 billion)

Method 2: ≥ 1.3-times of predicted annual sales and/ or annual sales > JPY 150 billion (> USD 1.37 billion)

Previously, if there was a large discrepancy between the predicted sales and the actual ones, these companies would be asked to cut their product prices during the following drug price revision. In the new pricing system introduced in 2016, an *ad hoc* drug price reduction will be put into effect immediately, rather than waiting until the next regular biennial drug price review.

However, it is interesting to point out that the drug price review 2016 was not introduced solely for the purpose of cost containment. On the contrary, a premium up to a maximum of 5.41% of the drug price could be added for product considered innovative. This specifically referred to products that had been on the NHI listing for less than 15 years, and without a generic version available on the market. In addition, these products will not be subject to price adjustment. This was specifically aimed to support innovative products and to eliminate the issue of off-label use.

Cost-effectiveness Assessment in the 2016 Drug Price Review

In April 2016, in the same year as the drug price review, a pilot project of cost-effectiveness assessment for pharmaceutical products and medical devices was introduced. The pilot was significant for the country because it had been the first review of this nature for drug pricing in at least 50 years, and was only possible for a relatively long period of three years of political stability.

This reform started with a pilot scheme of 13 products, of which 7 were pharmaceutical products and 6 medical devices. Treatments for hemophilia, HIV and rare intractable diseases were excluded from this cost-effectiveness assessment, as with new products that were rejected for reimbursement. The re-pricing of these products should be completed by end of the fiscal year 2017. However, as the fiscal year in Japan actually starts in April, it means that the actual implementation will be in April of the following year, 2018. Given that the Japanese business practice is known for its opaque nature, the scheme proposed could be considered as a relatively bold move for the future development of the access to the pharmaceutical market in the country.

The aim of this trial of cost-effectiveness analysis was to use the results for the re-pricing of drugs and devices in the NHI list at the end of the fiscal year 2017. This re-pricing will be done after applying all the pricing rules of the 2016 biennial drug price review. This exercise might help MHLW to show that the final updated price is reasonable and should be acceptable, since it is based on a form of economic analysis. As yet, details of how to integrate the results of the cost-effectiveness assessment in price revision are not yet specified, but a discussion on the topic is planned in the next drug price review in the fiscal year 2018.

Based on the selection criteria developed by the Special Committee set up under the Central Social Insurance Medical Council – *Chuikyo* in 2012 on cost-effectiveness, both new drugs and medical devices listed between 2012 and 2015 could be chosen in the pilot project. The selection was that of the products that had received the approval for reimbursement with the highest rate of premium, with a sales record which also had reached the highest level of predicted peak sales. These were then compared with products which had received a 10% premium approval on their price.

The companies, once their drugs were selected for the pilot project, were requested to submit data on their degree of cost-effectiveness, as well as their projection regarding the highest level of sales. In the same application, they also have the option of asking for an additional premium that is ≥10% of the government reimbursement price. It is interesting to note that while MHLW believed that it was very important to have the assessment result as reference materials, the Special Committee did not take them into consideration in their calculation of the official pricing.

Looking from the historical perspective, pharmaceutical companies in Japan could submit economic evaluation data in their application for listing as early as 1992. However, in the absence of clear guidelines on precisely what types of information or data were required, and also to what extent the information would influence the decision on the level of price and reimbursement, out of 256 applications for reimbursement between 2006 and 2011, only eight were new drugs that had submitted economic evaluation data for review.

Then, it was only twenty years later, in 2012, that a committee on cost-effectiveness assessment was formally set up under the Medical Council (*Chuikyo*). It became the Special Committee on Cost-Effectiveness. It drew its members from health insurance, healthcare providers, pharmaceutical industry, public sector and experts in health economic assessment. The function of this committee was to take cost-effectiveness as an important reference in the decision making process for price and reimbursement. Yet, the committee took four years to arrive at the common ground of using Quality-Adjusted Life Years (QALY) as the basic measurement outcome. But they have not yet agreed on how to translate QALY into financial units. On the other hand, the committee said to be willing to accept to consider other types of outcome measurement in their assessment, if they were considered by NHI to be appropriate to the related disease area and medical technology.

Strictly speaking, Japan could be considered as a pioneer in Asia in the use of economic assessment in the reimbursement process for drugs and medical devices, although Australia was the first country to conduct mandatory economic appraisal in the reimbursement process in 1993. Yet after 25 years, the related policy in Japan still has a lot of rooms for improvement in the use of the economic perspective in pricing and reimbursement.

The one significant progress that needs to be acknowledged is the confirmation on the selection criteria of products eligible in the pilot project (Table 7). This pilot project started in 2016, and is expected to be completed by 2017. Despite a delay of two years from the original schedule, it remains the first formal step for the government to apply an economic assessment in the pricing and reimbursement process.

At present, Japan does not have the equivalent of a formal HTA agency to support the assessment, such as NICE in the UK or IQWIG in Germany. In the pilot project, the coordination with pharmaceutical companies and the academic representative is done through the National Institute of Public Health (NIPH). The economic assessment data covered a period of two years from the fiscal year 2016 to 2017. After the initial data submission, NIPH will then send the data to the academic group, composed of clinical epidemiologists and health economists, for approval. The data were again sent to a sub-committee under the Special Committee on Cost Effectiveness, called Expert Committee of

For the listed drugs whose reimbursement decision were made in fiscal years 2012 2015	
Products using similar efficacy comparison method	• Received the highest premium rate, or • ≥10% premium and the highest sales (or price)
Products using cost calculation method	• Received the highest premium rate, or • ≥10% premium and the highest sales (or price)
For the new drugs whose reimbursement listing was done after October 2016	
Products using similar efficacy comparison method	• Predicted highest sales JYP 50 billion (USD 45.5 million) for drugs • Predicted highest sales JYP 5 billion (USD 4.5 million) for medical devices
Products using cost calculation method	• Predicted highest sales JYP 10 billion (USD 9.1 million) for drugs • Predicted highest sales JYP 1 billion (USD 0.9 million) for medical devices

Table 7. Selection criteria for products participating in the pilot projects [Shiroiwa, 2017]

	Pharmaceutical products		Medical devices
	Generic name	Brand name	
Similar efficacy comparison method	Sofosbuvir	Sovaldi	KawasumiNajuta Thoracic Stent Graft System
	Combination of LedipasvirAcetonate/ Sofosbuvir	Harvoni	Activa RC
	Combination of Ombitasvir Hydrate/Paritaprevir Hydrate/Ritonavir	Viekirax	Vercise DBS System
	Daclatasvir Hydrochloride	Daklinza	Brio Dual 8 neurostimulator
	Asunaprevir	Sunvepra	
Cost calculation method	Nivolumab	Opdivo	J-tec Autologous Cultured Cartilage (JACC)
	Trastuzumab/Emtansine	Kadcyla	Sapien XT

Table 8. Pharmaceutical products and medical devices selected for the cost-effectiveness assessment in the pilot project [Takashi, 2014]

cost effectiveness for review and assessment. Members of this Expert Committee remained anonymous to the public, and they decided whether they considered the medical technology in application cost-effective. After the review, there will be a close-meeting between the Special Committee on Cost-Effectiveness and the company, as the Market Authorization holder, with a draft of the written result for assessment. The final decision on price and reimbursement rests with the Medical Council (*Chuikyo*). Table 8 reports the pharmaceutical products and medical devices selected for the cost-effectiveness assessment in the pilot project.

"Basic Drug" in the 2016 Drug Price Review

The pilot study of price adjustment based on a cost-effectiveness assessment was one of the measures for an *ad hoc* price cut in Japan. From the biennial drug price review between 2008 and 2012, there were a total of three instances of special adjustments of drug price and an average price cut of 4-6 % on long-listed products. So far, the rules for these drug pricing remained blurred and diffused. While the objective of the Japanese government is to control the rising expenditure on pharmaceutical products, it remained equally important that an excessive discounting would not affect or discourage the launch of innovative therapies, since the cost control measure should also not hamper the development of the pharmaceutical industry. For that reason, to counter the pressure to lower

> **Box 1. Definition of "basic drug" [JPMA, 2017]**
>
> 1. The drug has an established position in the clinical settings and has been clearly shown to be widely used in clinical practice.
> 2. The basic drug may have similar products with same ingredients and dosage form; it is required that at least one product has been listed on NHI reimbursement for 25 years or longer.
> 3. The basic drug may have similar products with same ingredients and dosage form; the average price differences between the NHI reimbursement price and the current market price of these similar products (including basic drug) cannot exceed that of all the listed reimbursement products.

the prices, there was also an upward special price adjustment for innovative therapies which would put on a price premium protection as of 2011.

On top of all these various considerations, another pricing measure on basic drugs was announced in 2015 to ensure a stable supply of essential drugs (Box 1). It was the 'Comprehensive Strategy to Strengthen the Pharmaceutical Industry', which was published by the Ministry of Health, Labor and Welfare. It stated that "if a drug has been listed in the drug price list for a long period of time, and has successfully undergone a drug price revisions, but its supply is difficult to discontinue due to the demand in the clinical prac-

Category	Number of ingredients (products)	Products (example)	Indications
Pathogenic organism	51 (169)	• Amolin fine granules • Ebutol tablets • Retrovir capusles • Arasena-AIV drip	• Various infectious diseases • Pulmonary tuberculosis • HIV infection • Herpes simplex • Encephalitis, etc.
Narcotics	6 (15)	• MS Contin tablets • Morphine hydrochloride injection	• Pain relief for various cancers • Pain relief/sedation for severe pain
Unprofitable	77 (264)	• Phenytoin powder • Thyradin powder • Endoxan bulk powder (oral use) • Pam IV injection • Soldem 3 transfusion	• Convulsive seizure • Congenital hypothyroidism • Multiple myeloma • Organophosphate poisoning • Hydration when oral intake is impossible

Table 9. Examples of "basic drug" in the drug pricing system reform of fiscal year 2016 [2016 HIRA International Symposium]

tice, it is necessary to ensure its continuous and stable supply to the market". The aim was to ensure that even the minimum NHI reimbursement price set in the price recalculation would still generate enough financial incentive for the company. From the 2016 drug price review there was a total of 134 active ingredients and 439 products falling into this category (Table 9).

Pricing Rules for New Drugs

There are two methods used for assessing the pricing of new drugs. The first method is comparing similar products. This is feasible when a reasonable comparator therapy can be identified. Basically, the requirement is that the comparator is a branded drug launched within 10 years, without any generic present on the NHI reimbursement list. This comparison method is designed for pricing a new product based on the cost per day of the comparator therapy. For the new product two different ways of comparison can be chosen within this method; i) with an innovative product or ii) with a me-too product which refers to a product with little novelty. The differences between these two comparison methods are on the following price adjustment. New products priced using the second way of comparison, me-too products, will not be awarded a price premium. On the other hand, the products will have to adjust their price downwards if their price is set at 1.25 times or higher than the average foreign market price, which refers to the average market price in the US, Germany, France and the UK.

The second method is cost calculation when no comparator is identified. It measures the level of profit for the product. This method takes into account the cost of raw materials, labor cost, manufacturing expenses, manufacturing cost, marketing, as well as R&D cost, distribution cost, consumption tax and operating profit. The calculation of operat-

	Premium applied	Characteristics
Innovative Premium	70-120%	• New mechanism of action • High efficacy or safety • Significant improvement in treatment
Value Premium	5-60%	• High efficacy or safety • Significant improvement in treatment
Marketability Premium	5% or 10-20%	• Orphan drugs, etc.
Pediatrics Premium	5-20%	• Pediatric indication • Dosage • Administration, etc.
SAKIGAKE Premium	10-20%	• The new listing drug designated as a reference model for promoting local R&D in Japan (SAKIGAKE designation)

Table 10. Premium applied on new innovative drug in the drug pricing system reform of fiscal year 2016 [2016 HIRA International Symposium]

ing profit is obtained from a combined figure with a ratio on marketing cost and administration cost, as well as a ratio on expenses and labor cost. The derived figure on operating profit will be multiplied by a coefficient factor based on the average figure collected from the pharmaceutical industry in the last 3 years. Depending on the novelty, safety and efficacy of the new drug, the figure of the target for its operating profit could be revised upwards by up to 100%, or revised downwards by as much as 50%. The unit cost of labor is referenced to the average figure from the monthly labor survey in Japan, conducted by MHLW. The cost of distribution is in reference to the average figure released

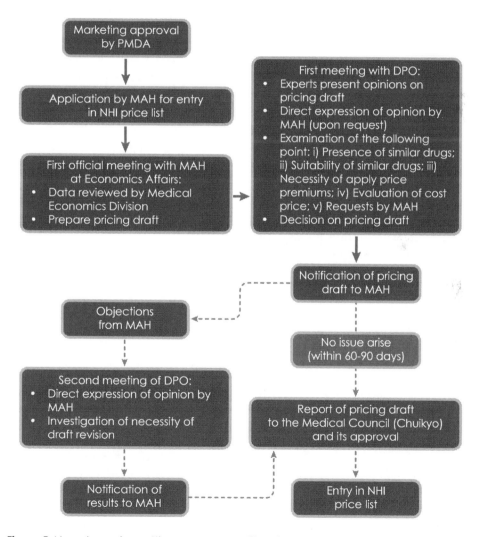

Figure 5. New drug price setting process. Modified from [JPMA, 2017]

on 'Current Report of Pharmaceutical Industry', carried out by MHLW. For the 2016 drug price review, these reference figures were derived from the average of the years 2012 to 2014.

If a new product is rated as innovative, a premium rate can be added, regardless the method used in new drug pricing. This is an incentive program started in 2010 to encourage the development of innovative drugs. Since the regular price review eroded the drug price, this premium pricing system provides a buffer for subsequent price cuts on the new drug (Table 10).

At this point, the new drug receives a temporary price. In the next step, this temporary price will be compared with the new product average market price listed in several foreign Countries. There are four Countries chosen for this adjustment process: the US, Germany, France and the UK. The temporary price may need to be adjusted if it meets one of the following conditions: i) if the temporary price is 1.25 (or more) times the average foreign price, the price of the new drug will be adjusted downwards; ii) if the temporary price is 0.75 (or more) times the average foreign price, the price of the new drug will be adjusted upwards. Figure 5 reports the new drug price setting process.

Pricing Rules for Generics

The Japanese government believes that one of the effective solutions to cut down the spending on pharmaceutical products is promoting the use of generics. In 2007, the Japanese government set a prescription goal on national generics equal to 30% by volume by 2012. In 2016, the government adjusted the target of generic prescription to 70% by the middle of 2017. This target was again revised to 80% or more by the end of 2020. Though the government encourages the prescription of generics, their penetration is expected to be still low by international standard. For example, the use of generics in Germany and the UK are both around 70%. In 2015, according to the IMS sales data, the generics volume share was 33.5% of the total of the dispensed pharmaceutical products. Based on the research findings from MHLW, the generics share is 56.2%. The calculation of generic penetration only looks at off-patent originator medicine as the denominator.

As of 2008, new generics drugs have the opportunity to enter the NHI reimbursement list twice a year. In addition, pharmacies also receive financial incentives from the government to dispense generics. The 2016 drug price review changed the minimum generics dispensing quota. Financial incentives will be given when the pharmacy uses over 65%of generics per prescription. If the physicians do not want to use generics, they are now required to specifically note that down next to the medicine, on the prescription. If not specified, it is possible to substitute the product with its generic at the dispensary. But the most impactful measure on the promotion of the use of generics remains the direct price control. In the past, the reimbursement price on generics was 70% of the originator's price for the first generic drug. In 2016, a reduction in starting prices for new generics takes it down to 50% of the current price of the original drug, and might go down to 40% if 10 or more similar products are listed simultaneously.

9.4 **Challenges**

Examining the "Basic Policy on Economic and Fiscal Management and Reform 2017", if one were to predict the possible future development of the drug price system, Japan is likely to continue the direction of cost-effectiveness based on drug use, and it will encourage the development of innovative therapies. Fiscal deficits are unlikely to deter the government to shy away from the principle of universal healthcare coverage. Rather, the pressure on reducing the budget is likely to continue, and to concentrate on 'me-too' products and products that have been on the reimbursement list for a long time. It has been announced that the biennial Drug Price Review will now be changed to an annual one as of 2018. Considering these changes, it seems that only the highly rated innovative products could successfully apply to add a premium on their price. In order to successfully contain the acceleration of price increase, an evidence-based drug pricing system is likely to be the solution for the government in assessing the 'innovativeness' and 'usefulness' of the new medical technologies. If the details of a review system could be finalized by the end of the fiscal year 2017, then perhaps there will be a realistic chance of successfully introducing Health Technology Assessment (HTA).

The real question regards the extent to which the updated policies could so far accommodate two key objectives: a 'sustainable universal healthcare system' and the 'promotion of innovation'. If the government does succeed with the present pilot study, then it might be even able to relieve the growing financial burden on healthcare spending, while maintaining the remarkable quality of the people's health.

So far, to stimulate once again the economic growth in the country, the current government has strongly focused on the 'Japan Revitalization Strategy'. The core essence of a part of this strategy is to encourage the industry to invest more back in the country. Pharmaceutical companies are an important sector of the industry, especially with their research and product development. On the other hand, the government also faces the dilemma of reducing the spending on pharmaceutical products. So there is a very delicate balance of the economic interest. With the latest updates and pilot schemes of the drug pricing system, the pharmaceutical industry might not find Japan such a profitable market. An example is the government strategy on the promotion of biosimilars.

The pathway for the access of biosimilar into the country market was introduced in 2009, and it was mostly aligned with the guideline of the European Medicine Agency (EMA). The price of biosimilars is set as 70% of the reference product. On top of that, biosimilars can add a 10% premium to their price, based on the level of investment in clinical development. With the premium, the maximum price of a biosimilar could therefore be 77% of the reference product. All biosimilar products are priced the same, regardless of the sequence they enter the market in, and are not subject to price erosion depending on their date of market entry.

Currently, biosimilars could enter the NHI list either in May or in November. The May application should be approved by January, and the November application should be approved by July of the following year. Once the product is included in the reimbursement list, it could gain access quickly to hospitals or the retail market, and be available for prescriptions almost right away. Patients can have a 70% reimbursement of the treatment cost when using biosimilar product. Furthermore, a financial incentive is offered to hospitals if they meet the minimal biosimilar dispensing quota, which is 22% of their total dispensations. The market access of biosimilars is quite clear and straightforward in this sense.

Table 11 reports the list of biosimilars launched in Japan in the years 2009-2017 . By April 2017, a total of 11 biosimilar products from 5 different biologics were launched in Japan. This is less than the products launched in West-Europe Countries. Even though Japan offered a favorable price and premium, the biosimilar penetration is limited. In Germany, in the period between 2007 and 2017, 18 biosimilar products were launched, using a free-pricing system. The price of biosimilars can retain 75% of the reference product in the market, with an additional 25-30% on rebate contract.

In Japan, not all listed biosimilar could actually reach their ceiling price of 70% of their reference product. In addition, it is rare to see a premium added to a pricing for biosimilars. Out of the 11 biosimilar products listed, so far there is only one product which can receive the 10% price premium: it is the biosimilar of epoetin alfa, by Kissei Pharmaceutical/JCR.

Biosimilars are also in the program of biennial drug price review with other products on the reimbursement list. Biosimilar products have undergone an average of 2% price cut during the last few re-pricing review. Since the biennial drug price review will switch

Biosimilar	Marketer	Reference product	Approval Date
Somatropin BS SC Sandoz	Sandoz/Nipro	Genotropin (somatropin)	September 2009
Epoetin Alfa BS Syringe JCR	Nippon Kayaku	Espo (epoetin alfa)	May 2010
Filgrastim BS Syringe NK	Nippon Kayaku	Gran (filgrastim)	May 2013
Filgrastim BS Syringe Mochida	Mochida	Gran (filgrastim)	May 2013
Filgrastim BS Syringe F	Fuji Pharma	Gran (filgrastim)	May 2013
Filgrastim BS Syringe Teva	Teva	Gran (filgrastim)	May 2013
Filgrastim BS Syringe Sandoz	Sandoz/ Sawai	Gran (filgrastim)	November 2014
Infliximab BS IV Infusion CTH	Celltrion	Remicade (infliximab)	November 2014
Infliximab BS IV Infusion NK	Nippon Kayaku	Remicade (infliximab)	November 2014
Insulin Glargine BS Cartiridge Lilly	Eli Lilly	Lantus (insulin glargine)	August 2015
Insulin Glargine BS Injection Kit (FFP)	Fujifilm Pharma Co.	Lantus (insulin glargine)	July 2016

Table 11. List of the biosimilars launched in Japan in 2009-2017

to yearly from 2018, this might even encourage physicians and patients not to switch to biosimilars, or even generics. The relatively low co-payment amount for the originator or reference product will certainly be a factor affecting the use of biosimilar. This implies that there is a hidden challenge to market access in Japan.

Health Technology Assessments help policy-makers and the pharmaceutical industry to make a scientific calculation of a drug's value and price. But several elements are required to make the assessment meaningful and impactful.

Firstly, an accurate and transparent framework for the cost-effectiveness analysis in the drug pricing system is fundamental. After four years of discussion, the Special Committee on Cost Effectiveness only arrived at an alignment of using QALY as the base unit to measure the performance of medical technology, but it has not yet reached a consensus on the cost of QALY. There is always the question of whether it should be at a fixed cost, or if it should be kept flexible with the assessment criteria. Until the completion of the pilot project, at the end of the fiscal year 2017, the extent of the economic evaluation of the pilot study on the impending drug pricing system cannot be known.

Another concern about the market access environment in Japan is the fact that the decision-making process generally takes a long time. Take, for example, the decision of introducing HTA in pricing and reimbursement. It would have taken a total of 4 years, from the establishment of the first special committee in 2012, to finalizing the details of the policy on HTA in 2018 – if, that is, it could finally take place by the end of fiscal year 2017. It will not be a surprise if the Japanese government fails to conclude the assessment in a timely manner during the introduction of the HTA.

With the attempt of introducing the health technology assessment, Japan has not yet designated a formal institution to manage the policy. At present, the National Institute of Public Health is responsible for coordinating the pharmaceutical companies with the Special Committee on Cost-Effectiveness, which was set up in 2012. Members of the Special Committee could be on a three 2-consecutive-year term, or a maximum service term of 6 years. The service duration of the committee members is especially interesting, because the time expiration of their maximum term also almost coincides with the completion of the very first pilot project on cost-effectiveness assessment for re-pricing. Whether these members could transfer their learning, derived from the pilot project, to policy formulation before they finish their term of service, it remains an interesting question. A successful continuity of the HTA development in the drug pricing system will only be feasible when the knowledge can be transferred and integrated.

Apart from the issue of continuity, the market also faces another challenge in the absence of local HTA experts and experienced executives to support the assessment process. It is believed that many members of the Special Committee on Cost Effectiveness had very little knowledge on HTA when they joined the committee itself. Experience in the industry, useful to help carry out the assessment, was also limited. The collection of patients and clinical data for economic assessment is an important preparation step in the implementation of an economic analysis, but it takes time.

If one takes the HTA development in South Korea as a reference, the latter encountered a bottleneck in 2006, when the government started to implement HTA within the

Section	Content
Perspective	'Public healthcare payer's perspective' is considered standard. Other perspectives could be applied, if necessary
Target population (patient group)	Patients who meet the indication of the medical technology at the time of the analysis
Comparator	Medical Technology, reimbursed by public health insurance (NHI), widely used in clinical practice and expected to be used to a larger extent.
Additional benefit	The additional benefit in terms of effectiveness, safety, and/or other attributes of the medical technology should have a systematic review
Method of analysis	Cost-effectiveness analysis (CEA); Cost-utility analysis (CUA) should also be used
Subgroup analysis	Applicable if it is necessary
Time period	The length of time should be sufficient to evaluate the value of medical technology
Outcome	Quality-Adjusted Life Year (QALY) as the base unit of the outcome
Methods to calculate the QoL score	Preference-based instruments with scoring algorithms developed in Japan
Mapping	Yes
Clinical data (source of information)	Systematic review
Indirect comparison	Yes (if a comparator does not exist)
Cost calculation	All costs paid by public insurers (NHI, central and local governments), patients, productivity loss (applicable, depends on the perspective)
Cost (source of information)	Medical fee schedule and NHI drug price list
Estimation of productivity loss	Human capital method
Discount rate	2% (sensitivity analysis 0-4%)
Modeling	Yes
Sensitivity analysis	Deterministic and probabilistic sensitivity analysis
Reporting	Standard format is set; Result of the analysis should be open to public access

Table 12. Summary of the Guideline for Economic Evaluation of Drugs and Medical Devices in Japan [Shiroiwa, 2017]

price and reimbursement process. The lack of experience and the volume of applications overwhelmed the system. Consequently, it took two years to resolve the problems associated with the processing of the applications with the new system. The same problem is likely to occur when Japan starts to formally introduce HTA in 2018.

Moving to a new approach concerning reimbursement, the industry will also need to adapt and prepare itself for the new data requirement, including epidemiological data and cost data in the assessment of new medicines. In this case, an agreement between the government and the industry on the methodology used in the analysis is critical. The first draft on the guideline of Economic Evaluation of Drugs and Medical Device was officially approved by the Medical Council in February 2016 (Table 12). This guideline contains 15 sections, and it has an overview of how the economic assessment should be made. Perhaps this will provide the common platform for a fruitful dialogue between the industry and the government to successfully adopt the new approach.

9.5 Look-out for Near Future

Japan is the third biggest economy in the world, but its slow growth is unlikely to improve, at least in the next 3 years. The government announced that the primary budget deficit will increase to JPY 8.3 trillion (USD 83 billion) for the fiscal year 2020. This government budget deficit projection will be a substantial increase from the previous projection of JPY 5.5 trillion (USD 50 billion), announced in 2016. It means that the government continues to expect that the growth of tax revenue will be slower than expected. Due to its huge unpopularity, the plan to increase consumption tax from the current 8% to 10% has been delayed to 2019. The government spending will certainly outpace revenue in the next few years.

Under the budget pressure, the government should be very cautious in allocating its resources, and that includes the healthcare services sector. The overall objective seems that to prioritize the healthcare benefits for the elderly and the children. This is reflected in the proposed 'Comprehensive Reform of Social Security and Tax', which has been submitted to the National Parliament (DIET) for approval in 2018. The resources will be in the form of creating home care/long-term care within the community. The current administration has also promised to increase the benefit coverage and pension for low-income people and part-time workers. Should these policies be executed, the government would need additional financial resources.

So far, there is no indication that the government will increase the patients' co-payment or add new healthcare funding. Health-technology assessment is the major attempt by the government to justify the price of new medical technologies. Otherwise, it is expected that further cost-containment measures applied to pharmaceutical products will be the way for the government to solve the issue of the increase in healthcare spending.

In fact, the frequency and magnitude of the special price adjustment have increased in the last few years. New pricing rules were announced and implemented at short notice. These changes are becoming too frequent and are affecting long-term planning for the industry. Changes always work better if they are applied progressively, rather than sporadically.

If the government truly believes the principle of universal health coverage and maintenance of low co-payment, for its long-term success, then a review and overhaul of the whole system would be far more effective than any fragmentary change.

The use of cost-effectiveness assessments could be an improved method to support pricing decisions. Since the Medical Council (*Chuikyo*) plans to transfer the lessons learned from the pilot project to the actual implementation of HTA in 2018, the market access pathway will change. However, in order for the new system to be effectively run, it is certainly desirable to have collaborations and good communications between the payers, the new HTA organization, the patients and the pharmaceutical industry. It is not unusual to encounter practical problems in moving from one system to another – and some of them have already been mentioned before, such as incomplete local epidemiological data, insufficient number or knowledge on the part of HTA experts to assist the analysis, pharmaceutical companies which also need to train their own market access executives, potential delay for patients in accessing the new technologies, etc. It is important for the government to prepare the mitigation plan and keep the industry informed. This will allow the industry to implement a timely management of the issues and prepare itself for the launch plan. Patients could then benefit from the medical technology, with the resources provided by the government. It is but a common goal for both the government and the pharmaceutical industry to work for the interest of the patients. However, there is one last consideration that is vital for the government, in order to achieve a reasonable drug price at an efficient cost-benefit: the system must be backed up by a good data infrastructure, and an efficient data sharing system. Only then it could generate the evidence needed to facilitate an accurate value assessment.

Lastly – and this is especially relevant to this country – Japan desperately needs the continuation of a stable political climate. At last the Prime Minister office has been held for a few years, after a long period of frequent changes: now it would be detrimental to all parties concerned if such office were to frequently rotate once again.

9.6 **Bibliography**

- Basic Policy on Economic and Fiscal Management and Reform 2017. Cabinet-published draft. Social Security, 2017: 33-35. Available at http://www.jga.gr.jp/library/old/www.jga.gr.jp/common/img/eng/pdf/bp2017.pdf (last accessed July 2017)
- Brasor P, Tsubuku M. Japan' s health care is far from free, and ballooning costs could mean higher premiums. The Japan Times, 11th August, 2017. Available at thttps://www.japantimes.co.jp/news/2017/08/11/business/japans-health-care-far-free-ballooning-costs-mean-higher-premiums/#.Wa5djbIjGUk (last accessed July 2017)

- Central Intelligence Agency. The World Factbook. Available at https://www.cia.gov/library/publications/the-world-factbook/ (last accessed June 2017)
- DRG - Decision Resources Group. Market Access Challenges in 2017: Impacts of Japan's drug pricing policy reforms. The Decision Resources Group blog, 10th March, 2017. Available at https://decisionresourcesgroup.com/drg-blog/market-access-challenges-2017-impacts-japans-drug-pricing-policy-reforms/ (last accessed July 2017)
- Health Insurance Review & Assessment Service (HIRA), Korea. 2016 HIRA International Symposium Publications, Japan's Medical System and Drug price Standard.
- IMS Market Prognosis 2012-2016 –Asia/ Australia Japan, 2012
- Japan drug-pricing reform to get blueprint by year-end. Nikkei Asian Review, 26th November, 2016. Available at https://asia.nikkei.com/Politics-Economy/Policy-Politics/Japan-drug-pricing-reform-to-get-blueprint-by-year-end (last accessed July 2017)
- Japan Generics Medicines Association. Available at http://www.jga.gr.jp/english/country-overview/ (last accessed July 2017)
- Japan Pharmaceutical Manufacturing Association. Health insurance programs and drug pricing in Japan. Pharmaceutical Administration and Regulations in Japan. 2017.
- Available at http://www.jpma.or.jp/english/parj/individual.html (last accessed July 2017)
- Japan to miss FY2018 deficit-cutting target on tax hike delay. Reuters Business News, 22nd July, 2016
- Japan's fiscal 2020 primary budget deficit put at ¥8.3 trillion. The Japan Times, 25th January, 2017. Available at https://www.japantimes.co.jp/news/2017/01/25/business/economy-business/japans-fiscal-2020-primary-budget-deficit-put-¥8-3-trillion (last accessed July 2017)
- Medicine for Europe, Country Specific Market Access Policies 2017, Available at http://www.medicinesforeurope.com (last accessed August 2017)
- Ministry of Health, Labour and Welfare (MHLW). The Comprehensive Reform of Social Security and Tax. Available at http://www.mhlw.go.jp/english/social_security/kaikaku.html (last accessed June 2017)
- Ministry of Health, Labour, and Welfare (MHLW) website. Available at http://www.mhlw.go.jp/english/ (last accessed July 2017)
- Ministry of Health, Labour, and Welfare (MHLW). Annual Health, Labour and Welfare Report 2016. Available at http://www.mhlw.go.jp/english/wp/wp-hw10/index.html (last accessed July 2017)
- Ministry of Health, Labour, and Welfare (MHLW). Changing social security system. Available at http://www.mhlw.go.jp/english/social_security/dl/social_security6-f.pdf (last accessed September 2017)
- Ministry of Health, Labour, and Welfare (MHLW). National Institute of Population and Social Security Research, Population Projections for Japan

(December 2006). Available at http://www.mhlw.go.jp/english/social_security/dl/social_security6-g.pdf (last accessed July 2017)

- Ministry of Health, Labour, and Welfare (MHLW). Statistics and Other Data. Available at http://www.mhlw.go.jp/english/database/report.html (last accessed July 2017)
- Ministry of Internal Affairs & Communications. Statistic Bureau, Results of Population Estimate. Available at http://www.stat.go.jp/english/data/jinsui/index.htm (last accessed July 2017)
- Organisation for Economic Co-operation and Development. Health Statistics 2017. Available at http://www.oecd.org/els/health-systems/health-data.htm (last accessed June 2017)
- OECD. Health at a Glance 2015: OECD Indicators. Paris: OECD Publishing, 2015. Available at http://dx.doi.org/10.1787/health_glance-2015-en (last accessed June 2017)
- Shiroiwa T, Fukuda T, Ikeda S, et al, Development of an Official Guideline for the Economic Evaluation of Drugs and Medical Devices in Japan. *Value in Health* 2017; 20: 372-8
- Shiroiwa T, Fukuda T, Ikeda S, et al. New decision-making for the pricing of health technologies in Japan: the FY 2016/2017 pilot phase for the introduction of economic evaluations. *Health Policy* 2017; 121: 836-41
- Takashi F. HTA Development in Japan. Health Technology Assessment and Health Policy: Recent developments across Asia. ISPOR 7th Asia-Pacific Conference. 3-6 September, Singapore
- Yokokura Y. Policy Address. *JMAJ* 2016; 59: 141-4

https://doi.org/10.7175/747.ch10

10. Market Access in Australia

Zafer Çalişkan[1]

[1] *Department of Economics, Hacettepe Universtiy, Ankara, Turkey*

10.1 Background

Australia became an independent nation on 1 January 1901, when the British Parliament allowed the six Australian colonies to govern in their own right as part of the Commonwealth of Australia. The Commonwealth of Australia was established as a constitutional monarchy, because was established with a written constitution and because the head of state was Queen Victoria. The national language is English, but the most common other languages are Mandarin, Italian, Arabic, Cantonese, and Greek. The Australian estimated resident population in 2016 was 24.7 million, spread over 7,741,000 sq. km. Australia is divided into six states and two territories (Figure 1), the most populous states being New South Wales and Victoria.

Figure 1. Australian Administrative Division

The World Bank national account data indicated that Australia's is the world's thirteenth largest economy. In 2016 the Gross Domestic Product (GDP) was worth 1,129 trillion US dollars Purchasing Power Parity (PPP) while the GDP per capita was last recorded at 46,789 US dollars (PPP). This prosperity translates into a higher life expectancy, lower mortality, and better quality of life. Life expectancy has been continually increasing in Australia, as in other OECD (Organization for Economic Co-operation and Development) countries.

In 2014 the average life expectancy was 82.4. The average life expectancy for females increased from 73.9 years in 1960 to 84.4 in 2014. For males, it increased from 67.9 years to 80.3. Between 1970 and 2014, the percentage of Australians aged 65 and over increased from around 8.3% to around 14.7%.

However, as in other countries, the extent of the national health spending in Australia is determined by several factors, such as the structure of the healthcare system, the aging of the population, changing diseases, healthcare demand, macroeconomic level, etc. In nearly all the OECD countries, the public sector is the main source of healthcare financing, representing 72.9% of the total health expenditure. However, Australia shows a lower average share of public spending of the GDP (69.2% in 2015). In addition, Australia's per capita health spending was 4,420 US dollars (PPP) in 2015, and healthcare cost amounted to 9.3% of GDP, quite similar to the OECD average of 9% of GDP.

In terms of burden of disease, as in the other developing countries, chronic diseases such as cardiovascular diseases, cancers, COPD, and diabetes, are the leading cause of illness, disability, and death. In Australia in 2013 they accounted for 90% of all deaths. The disease groups contributing the most to the burden were cancer (19%), cardiovascular diseases (15%), mental disorders and drug abuse (12%), musculoskeletal conditions (12%) and injuries (9%). Together, they accounted for around two-thirds of the disease burden.

Due to the increasing prevalence of such non-communicable diseases (NCDs) after inpatient and outpatient care, the pharmaceutical expenditure represents the most important healthcare expenditure item in Australia.

Although the spending on pharmaceuticals is slightly lower than in some OECD countries, such as Germany, Switzerland, Canada, and Japan, the per capita pharmaceutical bill in Australia was around 656 US dollars (PPP) in 2015. In addition, the share of Over-the-Counter (OTC) drugs is relatively high, accounting for half of the pharmaceutical spending.

10.2 The Healthcare System

Compared with other countries, the Australian healthcare system is considered sufficient to bring full coverage and optimal outcomes for the whole population in terms of life expectancy, infant mortality and better life (according to the OECD Better Life Index).

As in other developed countries, the purchasers of healthcare services are separated from the providers. Such a structure led to expectations which increase the effective use of healthcare services through the competition among providers, but also reinforce primary care and the development of health outcomes.

Historically, until the middle of the twentieth century, individuals had to pay for their own healthcare, or take out an insurance. Private practitioners and hospitals provided health services, and some degree of free treatment was provided by the public hospitals handled by the States and by charitable institutions.

From the late nineteenth century to the mid-1940s, the friendly society movement was a driving force behind the healthcare system, offering members a range of benefits, including unemployment benefits and sick pay; furthermore, it purchased medical services from doctors on behalf of its members. Box 1 shows the major healthcare reforms and policy measures since 1946 (Box 1).

Currently the Australian healthcare system is based on an universal health coverage. The financing and delivering of the system are funded mainly by taxes, with the support of statutory insurance levy and private healthcare expenditures.n Australia, the Australian Government (or Commonwealth), and the state and territory governments are responsible for the provision and funding of healthcare services, as well as population health programs, community health services, health and medical research, and Aboriginal and Torres Strait Islander health services (Figure 2).

Box 1. Major healthcare reforms and policy measures in Australia [Healy, 2006]

- 1946: Hospital Benefits Act (Commonwealth subsidies for State-run public hospitals)
- 1950: Pharmaceutical Benefits Act (Commonwealth subsidies for pharmaceuticals)
- 1953: National Health Act (Commonwealth subsidies for medical services)
- 1975-1984: Health Legislation Amendment Act 1983 (Introduction of universal health insurance)
- 1985: Home and Community Care Act
- 1986: Disability Services Act
- 1989: Therapeutic Goods Act
- 1990s: Pay-for-performance element in primary care payments
- 1994: Health Legislation Amendment Act
- 1996: Medicare provider number legislation (Section 19AA of the Health Insurance Act 1973)
- 1997: Aged Care Act
- 1997: Private Health Insurance Incentives Act
- 1999: Introduction of the private health insurance rebate, and Lifetime Health Cover 2000
- 2004: Medicare Plus funding changes and safety net provisions for out-of-pocket

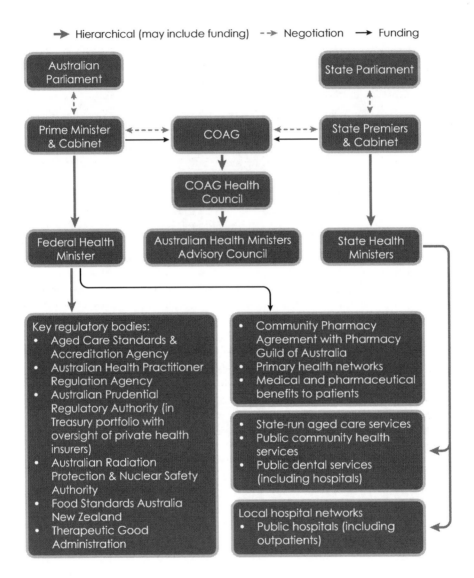

Figure 2. Organization of the healthcare system in Australia. Modified from [Mossialos, 2016]

COAG = Council of Australian Governments

The Australian Government funds three major schemes: Medicare Benefits Scheme (MBS), Pharmaceutical Benefits Scheme (PBS) and the private health insurance rebate. In addition, community (non-hospital) services are directly funded by the Australian Government on a fee-for-service basis. State and territory governments are responsible for public hospital services (largely funded by the Australian government under a federal/ state cost-sharing arrangement), community health services, and mental healthcare.

Australian taxpayers pay 2% of their income as Medicare levy. If their income exceeds AUS$ 90,000 per year, and they do not have a private health insurance, there is an additional Medicare Levy Surcharge (MLS) of 1 to 1.5%. Therefore, a large proportion of the population takes out optional private health insurance for hospital and some ancillary services. MLS is designed to encourage individuals to take out private hospital cover and, where possible, to use the private hospital system to reduce the demand on the public Medicare system. To make the private health insurance more affordable, the Australian Government offers rebates for private health insurance premiums. Private Health Insurance provides access to the private hospital system or to the doctor of choice within public hospitals.

The Australian Government spends a relatively large amount on medical services provided by general practitioners (un-referred) and specialists (referred), and benefit-paid medications, with the balance coming from the non-government sector. On the other hand, community health services are funded by the state and territory governments, which share most of the expenditure on public hospital services, while non-government sources account for large portions of the expenditure on dental services, private hospitals, aids and appliances, all other medications (medications for which no government benefit has been paid) and other health practitioners' services.

Australia's 2016 health report shows that, during 2013-2014, the Australian Government and state and territory governments paid, respectively, 41% and 27% of the total healthcare expenditure. The remaining was shared among individuals, through out-of-pocket expenses (18%), private health insurers (8.1%) and through accident compensation schemes (5.9%). The contribution from the Australian Government, state and territory governments and the non-government sector varies, depending on the types of health goods and services being provided.

Despite the fact that both Australian Government and state and territory governments contribute much to the healthcare service, private health insurance is considered a parallel financing mechanism and therefore it is an important part of the Australian healthcare system. There are two types of private health insurance in Australia: hospital policies, that covers hospital expenses, and general treatment (also known as ancillary or extras cover), that covers dental, physiotherapy or ophthalmic treatments. They can be obtained separately or in combination.

According to a recent report of the Australian Prudential Regulation Authority, although private health insurance is optional, in 2017 55% of the population had general treatment cover, while about 46% had hospital treatment cover by private health insurances. Due to the popularity of the private health insurance, over the years the non-government expenditure including private health expenditure has been increasing.

In 2014-15, the share of private health insurance funds provided 8.7% of total expenditure. Between 2004-2014 private healthcare spending increased by 7.5%, while public health spending grew a little faster than the private (7.8%). These funds originate both from individuals who pay premiums to private health insurance funds and from subsi-

> **Box 2. Mechanisms for rebates on health insurance premiums**
> 1. Insurers offer members a reduced premium and then insurers claim reimbursement from the Government.
> 2. Members pay the full premium and claim the rebate through their income-tax return, at the end of the financial year.
>
> Both mechanisms of rebates are considered subsidies allocated by the Australian Government for the services that were partially funded through benefits paid by the health insurance funds.

dies allocated by the Australian Government. The Australian Government provides a rebate to reduce the burden of insurance costs for eligible people, and maintains the private health insurance cover (Box 2). To determine the rebate, a level income test is performed.

The Australian Government also sets the national healthcare policies. Figure 3 provides a picture of the main services, funding responsibilities and providers in Australia.

10.3 **Medicare**

Medicare is a universal public health insurance scheme funded by the Australian Government; it was introduced in 1984 to provide free or subsidized access to public hospital services and treatment by health professionals. The Medicare Benefits Schedule (MBS) is the list of Medicare services subsidized by the Australian Government.

The Medicare system has three parts: hospital, medical and pharmaceutical. Hospitals are an important component of the Australian healthcare system and have a significant share of healthcare expenditure. In 2016, in Australia there were 1,322 hospitals, of which 624 were private. Australian Government and the state and territory governments fund about 90% of the healthcare in public hospitals and 32% of that in private hospitals, while the remainder of the funding is provided by individuals, and the Department of Veterans' Affairs. Private hospitals are mainly funded by private health insurances and out-of-pocket payments by patients. Medicare offers fee-free treatment to a public patient in a public hospital, by a doctor appointed by the hospital, and it covers 75% of the MBS fee for the services and procedures for private patients in a public or private hospital.

10.4 **Pathways of Market Access (Regulation, Pricing, and Reimbursement)**

The growing demand for pharmaceuticals and medical devices in Australia resulted in an increase in the healthcare expenditure. Like other developed countries, Australia in-

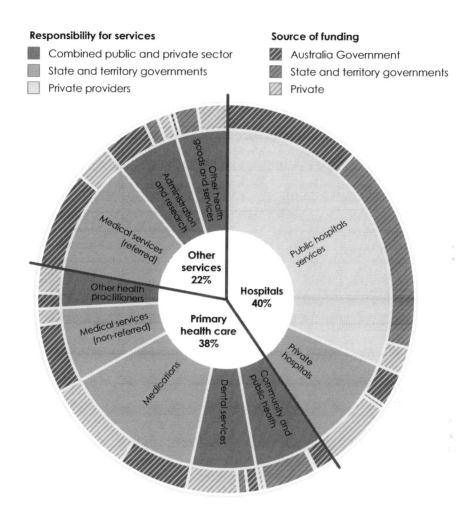

Figure 3. Health service funding and responsibilities (2013-2014). Modified from [Australia's health series no. 15, 2016]

Note. The inner segments indicate the relative size of the expenditure in each of the three main sectors of the health system. The middle ring indicates the relative expenditure on each service in the sector, and who is responsible for providing the service. The outer ring indicates the relative amount of the funding and the funding source for the different services.

troduced price control mechanisms and pathways to manage the pharmaceutical expenditure.

The Australian regulatory framework of pharmaceuticals and medical devices mainly relies on four different agencies, that are responsible for conducting pharmaceutical regulation, pricing and reimbursement: the Therapeutic Goods Administration (TGA), the Pharmaceutical Benefits Advisory Committee (PBAC), and the Pharmaceutical Benefits

Scheme (PBS). The Australian National Medicines Policy is designed by these four agencies. Regulatory procedures have been established to ensure the quality, safety and efficacy of the therapeutic goods available in Australia. The supply of drugs is controlled through three main processes:

- Pre-market evaluation and approval of products to be supplied;
- Licensing of manufacturers;
- Post-market surveillance.

In this structure, PBS has undertaken a key role in the safe and timely access of Australians to medicines. The Australian Government funds pharmaceuticals through the PBS. Initially, the selection of the medicines to be listed within the PBS was based only on clinical needs, largely irrespectively of the cost. However, since 1988 medicines being considered for inclusion in the PBS are evaluated for comparative effectiveness and cost-effectiveness, with a mandatory economic evaluation since 1993.

Market Authorization

To be supplied in Australia, a new drug must gain an approval under the requirements of the Therapeutic Goods Act 1989, thereby proving its safety, quality, and effectiveness. Approval is also required to extend the indications of an established drug. Applications are managed by the TGA that has seven statutory expert committees it may call upon to obtain independent advice on scientific and technical matters. For prescription drugs, advice is sought from the Advisory Committee on Prescription Medicines (ACPM).

The TGA regulates therapeutic goods through pre-market assessments, post-market monitoring and enforcement of compliance with standards, and licensing of the Australian manufacturers and the assessment of the compliance by foreign manufacturers with the same standards of their Australian counterparts. The TGA adopts a risk management approach to regulate the therapeutic goods.

Coverage, Pricing and Reimbursement

Once a prescription drug is approved for marketing, the company usually applies to have the drug listed in the PBS. Once the PBAC has recommended a drug for listing in the PBS, the Department of Health negotiates the price with the company. After an agreement is reached, the Australian Government considers the advice of the PBAC and decides whether the drug will be listed in the PBS.

Drugs included in the PBS are listed in two formularies:

- Formulary One (F1) contains drugs that i) have only one brand for each form and strength listed in the PBS; and ii) are not interchangeable at the patient level with a drug that has multiple brands listed in the PBS.
- Formulary 2 (F2) contains all the drugs that do not meet the criteria for F1, excluding single-brand combination drugs (i.e. multi-branded pharmaceutical items, drugs included in therapeutic groups, because they are interchangeable with other drugs that have multiple brands).

Drugs in F1 are moved to F2 when the first additional brand is listed in the PBS. In 2016, although only 14.8% of the medications were in F1, the cost to the government was 53.1% of the total cost. Drugs in F2 account for 78.5% of the volume, and 33.5% of the cost. According to the 2014-15 Health Department Annual Report of the Australian Government, in June 2015, the PBS included 793 medicines in 2,066 forms and dosages, sold as over 5,300 differently branded items. In 2015-2016, there were 370 new and amended PBS listings, including the high-cost medicines for the treatment of cancers, such as trastuzumab, pertuzumab and trastuzumab emtansine for the treatment of metastatic breast cancer, and pembrolizumab and trametinib for the treatment of melanoma.

In addition to the drugs and medicinal products available under normal PBS arrangements, a number of drugs are also available as pharmaceutical benefits, but are distributed under alternative arrangements which are specified under "Section 100" of the National Health Act 1953. Several programs exist for the provision of drugs as pharmaceutical benefits in this way, and this section lists those drugs which are available under the highly specialized drugs program, the efficient funding of chemotherapy, the botulinum toxin program, the human growth hormone program, the IVF program, and the opiate dependence treatment program.

According to the PBS Expenditure and Prescriptions report 2015-2016, the total PBS government expenditure on an accrual accounting basis for the 2015-2016 financial year was AUD 10,838 million, compared with AUD 9072.1 million for the previous year. This is a 19.5% increase. Total PBS prescription volumes decreased by 1.9% to a total of 208 million for 2015-16, compared to 212.1 million for the previous year. Government expenditure amounted to AUD 7,964.9 million, which was 85.1% of the total cost of the PBS prescriptions. The remainder was patient contributions, that amounted to AUD 1,394.2 million, down from AUD 1,465.9 million in the previous twelve-month period.

The majority of the government expenditure on PBS prescriptions was directed towards concessional cardholders (75.9% of the total). On the other hand, the average dispensed price per prescription of PBS medicines increased to AUD 45.00 in 2015-16 from AUD 40.45 in the previous financial year. The average government cost of these prescriptions was AUD 38.29 for the same period (AUD 33.54 in 2014-15). The five drugs with the highest cost to the government were ledipasvir + sofosbuvir (AUD 357.9 million), adalimumab (AUD 334.7 million), ranibizumab (AUD 217.8 million), sofosbuvir (AUD 213 mil-

---

Box 3. Therapeutic Group Premium Policy

The Therapeutic Group Premium (TGP) Policy was introduced in 1998 and applies to specifically defined groups of drugs which have similar safety and health outcomes. Within these groups, the drugs can be interchanged at the patient level. The Government subsidizes all drugs within a group to the level of the lowest priced drug. The difference in price between the lowest priced drug and the highest priced drugs within the group is called TGP and is paid by the patient. The prices of the items in the therapeutic groups are reviewed annually.

lion) and aflibercept (AUD 213,1 million). The PBS drugs most frequently dispensed were atorvastatin, followed by esomeprazole and rosuvastatin.

In Australia, as in many other countries, to reduce unnecessary pharmaceutical demand consumers pay a co-payment against the cost of each PBS medicine. The amount of co-payment is adjusted on 1 January each year, in line with the Consumer Price Index (CPI). From 1 January 2017, the co-payment for people with eligible concession card (concessional beneficiaries) is AUD 6.30; for the rest of the population (general beneficiaries) is AUD 38.80. The Australian Government pays the remaining cost. From January

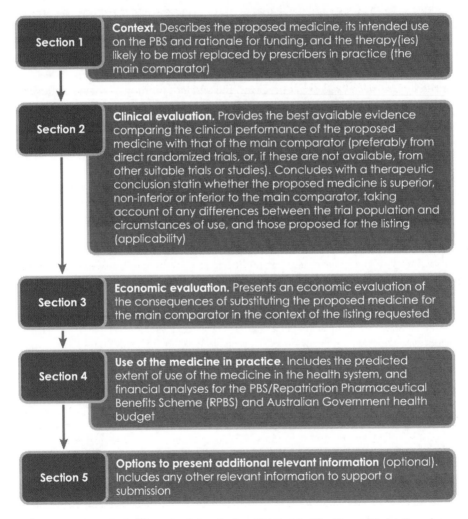

Figure 4. Structure of a major submission to the PBAC. Modified from [Guidelines for preparing submissions to the PBAC]

2016, pharmacists may discount the PBS patient co-payment by up to AUD 1.00; this is not mandatory and the pharmacist may choose whether or not to provide it (this option does not apply for prescriptions which are an early supply of a specified medicine). On the other hand, PBS provides a safety net for limiting the amount spent on medicines by individuals or families. On 1 June 2017, the safety net thresholds was AUD 378.00 for concession card holders, and AUD 1,494.90 for all other patients.

Apart from the assessment of new medicines, the PBAC is also responsible for the listing in PBS of the vaccines funded under the National Immunization Program (NIP), the already listed drugs, and the assessment of new medicinal products. During three annual meetings, the PBAC considers submissions from pharmaceutical companies, medical bodies, health professionals, and private individuals and their representatives. The PBAC has two sub-committees:

- The Economics Sub-Committee (ESC), that advises on cost-effectiveness policies and evaluates cost-effectiveness aspects of major submissions to the PBAC.
- The Drug Utilization Sub-Committee (DUSC), that monitors the patterns and trends of drug use and makes utilization data available publicly.

The PBAC has not a unique decision rule, but rather weighs a range of relevant factors in its considerations, such as the place in therapy, the overall effectiveness, cost, and cost-effectiveness of a proposed pharmaceutical compared with other pharmaceuticals listed for the same or similar indications, the potential cost to government health budgets, the "rule of rescue" listing in PBS. The submission procedure to the PBAC for a new medicine is shown in Figure 4. The PBAC differentiates submissions in "major submissions" and "minor submissions". In the case of the listing of a new medicine or vaccine or substantial changes in a "restricted listing", major submission should be made, including an economic evaluation. Minor submissions generally relate to requests to change existing listings that do not change the population or the cost-effectiveness ratio of the treatment.

10.5 Mapping and Structure of Decision Makers

The national drug policy in Australia is complex and undergoes periodic reforms, as can be seen in Box 1. These reforms mainly focus on price control, cost containment and management of the expenditure, while considering equality and quality. As discussed above, in Australia before a drug can be sold, it must be first approved for safety, quality and effectiveness by the TGA, and then deemed cost-effective by the PBAC for listing in the PBS. The final decision on whether and how pharmaceuticals should be listed in the PBS is made by Minister for Health (Figure 5).

In the Australian pharmaceutical pricing and reimbursement system, between the Australian Government and the beneficiaries there are many layers, including TGA, Australian Register of Therapeutic Goods (ARTG), PBAC, and PBS.

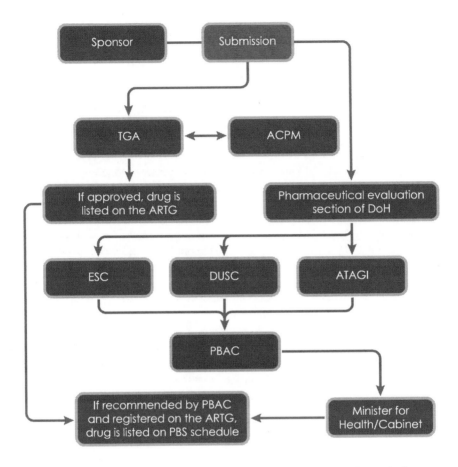

Figure 5. Decision-makers and the process of listing in PBS schedule in Australia. Modified from [CHERE, 2013]

ACPM = Advisory Committee on Prescription Medicines; ARTG = Australian Register of Therapeutic Goods; ATAGI = Australian Technical Advisory Group on Immunization; DoH = Department of Health; DUSC = Drug Utilization Sub-Committee; ESC = Economics Sub-Committee; PBAC = Pharmaceutical Benefits Advisory Committee; PBPA = Pharmaceutical Benefits Pricing Authority; PBS = Pharmaceutical Benefits Scheme; TGA = Therapeutic Goods Administration

Therapeutic Good Administration (TGA)

In Australia, before a medicine can be listed in the PBS, a pharmaceutical company must apply to the TGA to have the medicine included in the ARTG, so that it can be sold. For the marketing, the pharmaceutical company must provide evidence that the medicine meets the required standards of quality, safety, and effectiveness for the intended use.

Australian Register of Therapeutic Goods (ARTG)

In Australia, if a therapeutic good is not entered in the ARTG, it cannot be dispensed. Thus, the ARTG provides information on all therapeutic goods. In April 2016 there were approximately 86,896 products in the ARTG.

The Pharmaceutical Benefits Advisory Committee (PBAC)

The PBAC is a statutory committee established under the National Health Act of 1953. Committee members are general and specialist practitioners, pharmacists, and a representative of consumers. PBAC's evaluations and decisions are based on its two sub-committees: the Economics Sub-Committee (ESC) and the Drug Utilization Sub-Committee (DUSC). The ESC evaluates a drug based on a pharmacoeconomic perspective for major submission to the PBAC. The DUSC assesses the projected usage and financial cost of drugs. The additional collection of data on the actual use and its analysis are also provided by DUSC.

PBAC is tasked with making recommendations to the Minister for Health about which drugs and medicinal preparations should be listed for subsidy. The primary role of PBAC is to consider the value for money of new drugs. Besides regularly reviewing the list of PBS items since 2006, the PBAC also recommends vaccines for funding under the National Immunization Program (NIP). The PBAC meets three times a year, usually in March, July, and November.

The PBAC has 17 members who are appointed by the Minister for Health, including medical practitioners, pharmacists, consumers, and health economists. The PBAC considers submissions for new listings or changes to existing listings from industry sponsors, medical bodies, health professionals, private individuals, and their representatives. Since January 2010, the sponsor is also required to pay a cost-recovery fee to the PBS for the evaluation and listing of medicines and vaccines in the PBS and NIP. Each submission must comply with the PBAC guidelines that specify the clinical and economic data that must be submitted. All major submissions must provide an economic analysis undertaken by the sponsor, while submissions of new forms of previously listed products, or changes to the conditions of use, are considered as minor and they do not require the presentation of an economic evaluation.

Pharmaceutical Benefits Scheme (PBS)

The origin of PBS date back to 1919, when a program was established to provide subsidized medicines to World War I veterans and their families. Formally, in 1948 PBS was established to create lists for all the medicines. All the medicines in the PBS schedule are dispensed to patients at a Government-subsidized price. The cost of most prescription drugs is covered by PBS, which is available to all Australian residents who hold a current Medicare card. Foreign visitors from countries with which Australia has a Reciprocal Health Care Agreement (i.e. the UK, Ireland, New Zealand, Malta, Italy, Sweden, the Netherlands, Finland, Norway, Belgium, and Slovenia) are also eligible to the PBS.

Medicines listed in the PBS schedule can fall into three broad categories:

- Unrestricted benefits, for medicines with no restrictions on therapeutic use;
- Restricted benefits, for medicines that can only be prescribed for specific therapeutic uses;
- Authority-approved benefits, for medicines that require prior approval from the Department of Health.

10.6 Challenges and Catalyzers for Market Access

The Australian government has maintained a strong focus on the regulatory and funding processes, in order to control expenditure as well as ensuring the safety, quality, and effectiveness of drugs. According to many analyses of the Australian pharmaceutical expenditure, drug prices are many times higher than in other developed countries. The prices of generic medicines in particular are too high compared to other countries.

Challenges

According to public discussion, the key challenges are the regulation of the pricing and reimbursement system as well as getting the value for money, funding innovative medicines and the treatment of rare diseases. Because of these reasons, there is growing concern about PBS expenditure, its budget affordability by the community, and the out-of-pocket costs for each individual patients. The National Commission of Audit stated that PBS spending is projected to grow by 5.4% per year from 2013-14 to 2023-24.

Despite recent cost containment policies aimed at keeping low the cost of medicines in the PBS schedule, there is growing evidence that many Australian patients are struggling to afford their prescribed medicines. According to a study by Kemp et al, Australian patients have faced increased prescription medicines costs over the recent years, and the expenditure on the part of patients is now in the mid to upper range versus the comparable countries.

On the other hand, Australia over the next decade will face serious challenges, that will strongly affect the pharmaceutical budget; in particular the increase in the demand for cancer drugs. According to Karikios et al., PBS expenditure on anticancer (anti-neoplastic) drugs and the average price paid by the PBS for anticancer drugs both increased significantly from 2000 to 2012, with an average annual increase in PBS expenditure on anticancer drugs of 19.1%, compared with 9.0% for all the other drugs combined. Furthermore, the average price paid by the PBS per anticancer drug prescription has increased by 133% between 2011-2012. Delayed funding decisions, or lack of funding for new cancer medicines in the PBS, have also been raised as a major concern by some consumer organizations and the pharmaceutical industry. For example, on 3 December 2014, the Australian Senate tasked the Senate Community Affairs References Committee to report on the availability of new, innovative and specialist cancer drugs in Australia.

In particular, the Committee was charged with focusing on issues related to the timing of access and affordability for patients; how the PBAC and PBS handles these medicines, and the impact of delays in approval on patients; and the impact of the quality of care on cancer patients.

The use of generic medicines in Australia is scarce by international standards, and the Australian generic price reductions are lower than those in many other countries. According to a report by the Grattan Institute, in 2013 Australian paid over $ 1 billion too much per year for generic drugs. In this price scenario, generic drugs gained a lower market share than expected. Due to these high prices, generic drugs captured a smaller share of the market than expected. Nevertheless, the next expiry of a number of patents and the introduction of improved price disclosure arrangements are expected to increase the use of generics and reduce the pharmaceutical spending.

Catalyzers

Australia was the first country to introduce formal economic evidence-based funding of pharmaceuticals in 1993. Although most prescribed drugs are paid by the PBS through community pharmacies, some are distributed under alternative arrangements. A recent study conducted by Chim et al. shows the public preferences regarding the criteria for resource allocation decisions and that should be incorporate into PBCA decision-making processes (the severity of the disease, the diseases for which there is no alternative treatment available in the PBS – unmet need, the diseases that affect patients who are not economically wealthy and lifestyle-unrelated diseases). In line with these circumstances, under Section 100 of the National Health Act, 1953 several alternative programs have been arranged for the provision of some medicines. One of these is the Highly Specialized Drugs (HSDs) program.

HSDs are medicines for the treatment of chronic conditions such as cancer, HIV and organ transplantation. Because of their clinical use or other special features, their supply is commonly restricted through public and private hospitals having access to appropriate specialist facilities. Only the practitioners affiliated with these units can prescribe these drugs as pharmaceutical benefit items. Another arrangement is the "S100 Supply Arrangements for Remote Area Aboriginal Health Services" (AHSs), which improves the access to the PBS for patients in remote areas. Under these arrangements, the customers of

---

Box 4. PBCA criteria for Rule of Rescue (RoR)

When all four factors apply concurrently, RoR can be applied.
1. There are no pharmacological nor non-pharmacological alternatives
2. The medical condition is severe, progressive and expected to lead to premature death
3. The medical applies only to a very small number of patients
4. The proposed medicine provides a worthwhile clinical improvement sufficient to qualify as a rescue from the medical condition

participating AHSs are able to receive PBS medicines directly from the AHS upon consultation, without the need for a normal prescription form, and without charge.

In Australia, the PBAC is not obliged to accept some preferences or alternative opinions in its decision making, in some exceptional conditions such as a rare disease, or to take action for disadvantaged groups, i.e. reverse discrimination, it allows for the consideration of the Rule of Rescue (RoR) criteria as part of its decision-making process (Box 4).

Finally, the Australian Government provides subsidized access to expensive lifesaving drugs for very rare life-threatening conditions through the Life Saving Drugs Program (LSDP). The amount of funding for this program is limited, and determined on a yearly basis. The request for inclusion in the LSDP must be submitted in conjunction with the submission to the PBAC for PBS listing; the Chief Medical Officer can advise the Minister for Health on the drugs to be included in the LSDP.

10.7 Good Examples of Successful Market Access Strategies

In 2010, the Australian Government and the local pharmaceutical industries announced that they had reached an agreement on the establishment of a Managed Entry Scheme (MES) that would attempt to satisfy the needs of the key stakeholders. The basis of the scheme is that a product will be listed at a price commensurate with its cost-effectiveness, based on the evidence existing upon launch. Thereafter, the price of the product will be adjusted (upward or downward) on the basis of cost-effectiveness estimates arising from the generation of further RCT evidence (post-launch). Although MES could implement both non-outcome-based schemes and outcome-based schemes, according to Vitry et al. (2014) most of the managed entry agreements are non-outcome-based. Furthermore, the study of Vitry et al. showed that at February 2013, immune modulating agents (33.8%), nervous system (15.5%), alimentary tract and metabolism (9.8%) and cardiovascular system (7%) medicines were the drugs most represented in the MES. Furthermore, twenty-six (37%) pricing arrangements were applied to medicines restricted to supply through public and private hospitals (Section 100), and three products (abacavir, bosentan and efavirenz) have been listed with special bonus arrangements being agreed with the sponsor, rather than a rebate agreement.

10.8 Look-out for Near Future

The pharmaceutical pricing and reimbursement policy in Australia is quite complex and has been undergoing a series of reforms over many years. Despite the many challenges facing the pharmaceutical industry in Australia, there is an expected growth in this market, since it was valued at $ 22.7 billion in 2013 and is projected to reach $ 32 billion by 2020. In Australia, the PBS budget is uncapped and, although several overall policies have been effective in decreasing drug prices and pharmaceutical expenditure, the current PBS expenditure and the potential for a high growth in the future, cause concerns for the long-term sustainability of the PBS. There are also increasing concern about the timely access to new medicines at affordable prices. The registration of novel chemical entities can be substantially delayed in Australia, where patients must wait several months to have access to some breakthrough medicines. In order to overcome such a challenge, the Government has recently taken steps to fast-track the registration of new drugs, generics, and biosimilars in the Australian market.

10.9 **Bibliography**

- Australian Government. Department of Health. Available at http://www.health.gov.au/ (last accessed June 2017)
- Australian Government. 2014-2015 Department of Health Annual Report. Available at www.health.gov.au/internet/main/publishing.nsf/content/annualreport2014-15 (last accessed June 2017)
- Australian Government. Department of Health and Ageing. Annual report 2012–201. Volume 2. Available at https://www.health.gov.au/internet/main/publishing.nsf/Content/annual-report2012-13/$File/Volume%202.pdf (last accessed June 2017)
- Australian Government. Department of Health. About the PBS. Available at http://www.pbs.gov.au/info/about-the-pbs (last accessed June 2017)
- Australian Government. Department of Health. Guidelines for preparing submissions to the Pharmaceutical Benefits Advisory Committee (PBAC). Available at https://pbac.pbs.gov.au (last accessed June 2017)
- Australian Government. Department of Health. Other supply arrangements outside the Pharmaceutical Benefits Scheme (PBS). Available at http://www.health.gov.au/LSDP (last accessed June 2017)
- Australian Government. Department of Health. The Pharmaceutical Benefits Scheme Available at http://www.pbs.gov.au (last accessed June2017)
- Australian Government. Department of Health. The Therapeutic Goods Administration. Available at https://www.tga.gov.au (last accessed June 2017)
- Australian Government. Federation. Available at http://www.australia.gov.au/about-government/how-government-works/federation (last accessed June 2017)
- Australian Institute of Health and Welfare. Australia's health 2016. Australia's health series no. 15. Canberra: AIHW, 2016
- Australian Institute of Health and Welfare. Australia's hospitals 2014–15 at a glance. Canberra: AIHW, 2016
- Australian Institute of Health and Welfare. Australian Burden of Disease Study: Impact and causes of illness and death in Australia 2011-summary report. Australian Burden of Disease Study series no. 4. Canberra: AIHW, 2016

- Australian Institute of Health and Welfare. Health expenditure Australia 2014-15. Health and welfare expenditure series no. 57. Canberra: AIHW, 2016
- Australian Prudential Regulation Authority – APRA. Annual Report 2017. Available at http://www.apra.gov.au/AboutAPRA/Publications/Documents/Annual_Report_2017.pdf (last accessed June 2017)
- Centre for Health Economics Research and Evaluation – CHERE. Pharmaceutical Policy in Australia. University of Technology, Sydney. Working Paper 2013/01. Available at https://www.uts.edu.au/sites/default/files/wp2013_01.pdf (last accessed June 2017)
- Chim L, Salkeld G, Kelly P, et al. Societal perspective on access to publicly subsidised medicines: A cross sectional survey of 3080 adults in Australia. *PLoS One* 2017; 12: e0172971
- Duckett S, Breadon P. Poor Pricing Progress: Price disclosure isn't the answer to high drug prices. Grattan Institute, 2013. Available at https://grattan.edu.au/report/poor-pricing-progress-price-disclosure-isnt-the-answer-to-high-drug-prices/ (last accessed June 2017)
- Healy J, Sharman E, Lokuge B. Australia: Health system review. *Health Systems in Transition* 2006; 8: 1-158
- ISPOR Global Health Care Systems Road Map. Australia – Pharmaceutical, 2015. Available at https://www.ispor.org/HTARoadMaps/Australia_Pharm.asp#5 (last accessed June 2017)
- Karikios DJ, Schofield D, Salkeld G, et al. Rising cost of anticancer drugs in Australia. *Intern Med J* 2014; 44: 458-63
- Kemp A, Roughead E, Preen D, et al. Determinants of self-reported medicine underuse due to cost: a comparison of seven countries. *J Health Serv Res Policy* 2010; 15: 106-14
- Kuchenreuther MJ, Sackman JE. Market Access Outlook for Australia. BioPharm International 2015; 28: 40-5. Available at http://www.biopharminternational.com/market-access-outlook-australia (last accessed June 2017)
- Lopert R. Evidence-based decision-making within Australia's pharmaceutical benefits scheme. *Issue Brief (Commonw Fund)* 2009; 60: 1-13
- Mabbott V, Storey P. Australian Statistics on Medicines 2014. Commonwealth of Australia 2015. Available at http://www.pbs.gov.au/statistics/asm/2014/australian-statistics-on-medicines-2014.pdf (last accessed June 2017)
- Mossialos E, Wenzl M, Osborn R, et al. 2015 International Profiles of Health Care Systems. The Commonwealth Fund, 2016. Available at http://www.commonwealthfund.org/~/media/files/publications/fund-report/2016/jan/1857_mossialos_intl_profiles_2015_v7.pdf (last accessed July 2017)
- OECD Health Data. Available at https://data.oecd.org/ (last accessed June 2017)
- Paolucci F, García-Goñi M. The Case for Change Towards Universal and Sustainable National Health Insurance & Financing for Australia: Enabling the Transition to a Chronic Condition Focused Health Care System. Australian Health Policy

Collaboration Technical paper No. 2015-07. Melbourne: Australian Health Policy Collaboration, 2015

- PBS Information Management Section Pharmaceutical Policy Branch. Expenditure and Prescriptions Report 2015-2016. Available at http://www.pbs.gov.au/statistics/expenditure-prescriptions/2015-2016/expenditure-prescriptions-report-2015-16.pdf (last accessed June 2017)

- The Senate Community Affairs References Committee. Availability of new, innovative and specialist cancer drugs in Australia. 2015. Available at http://www.aph.gov.au/Parliamentary_Business/Committees/Senate/Community_Affairs/Cancer_Drugs (last accessed June 2017)

- Vitry A, Mintzes B, Lipworth W. Access to new cancer medicines in Australia: dispelling the myths and informing a public debate. *J Pharm Policy Pract* 2016; 9: 13

- Vitry A, Roughead E. Managed entry agreements for pharmaceuticals in Australia. *Health Policy* 2014; 117: 345-52

- Wonder M, Backhouse ME, Sullivan SD. Australian managed entry scheme: a new manageable process for the reimbursement of new medicines? *Value Health* 2012; 15: 586-90

- The World Bank. Data Catalog. Available at https://data.worldbank.org/data-catalog (last accessed July 2017)

https://doi.org/10.7175/747.ch11

11.Market Access in New Zealand

Zafer Çalişkan[1]
[1] *Department of Economics, Hacettepe Universtiy, Ankara, Turkey*

11.1 Background

New Zealand or *Aotearoa* (in Māori: land of the long white cloud) is situated in the South Pacific Ocean, south-east of Australia (Figure 1). The three main islands (North Island, South Island and Stewart Island) cover an area of 264,537 km². In 2016 the population was estimated at 4,790,371. The majority of the people are of European heritage; other ethnic groups are Maori, Pacific Islander, and Asian. New Zealand has three official languages: Te Reo Māori, English and New Zealand Sign Language.

Figure 1. New Zealand Administrative Division

In recent years the economic growth has been faster in New Zealand than in most other OECD (Organization for Economic Co-operation and Development) countries. In 2016 the Gross Domestic Product (GDP) was worth 174.8 billion US dollars Purchasing Power Parity (PPP), while the GDP per capita was last recorded at 37,108 US dollars (PPP). According to the report "Health at a Glance 2015" from the OECD, New Zealand spends about 3,590 US dollars (PPP) on healthcare annually. In addition, OECD reports that in 2015 New Zealand's per capita pharmaceutical expenditure was 284 US dollars PPP. In recent years, thanks to high and sustainable economic growth rates, New Zealand's expenditure on health was equivalent to 9.4% of the GDP, well above the OECD average of 9% of the GDP. In comparison with other OECD countries, New Zealand spends less on pharmaceuticals in terms of percentage of total expenditure on health.

Despite the high per capita healthcare expenditure, over the last decade the share of government spending, as a quota of the total spending on health, remained relatively constant (at around 80%), although well above the average for OECD countries (73%). In New Zealand, about 20% of the total health spending is privately funded, mainly through out-of-pocket payments, while the private health insurance market is relatively small.

People living in the countries with the highest health spending also tend to have better health outcomes; since New Zealand has one of the highest living standards among OECD countries, the higher spending is accompanied by better health outcomes. Since the early 1980s, New Zealand accomplished remarkable improvements in terms of health status, and recent OECD Health Statistics indicate that major health indicators – such as infant mortality rate, life expectancy and maternal mortality – have improved considerably. New Zealand's life expectancy figures are similar to those for most western European nations.

During the last decades, the population experienced a shift from high mortality/high fertility to low mortality/low fertility. According to the OECD Health Statistics, life expectancy in 2015 was 81.7 years overall, with a low gap between the genders, since life expectancy at birth was 79.9 and 83.4 years for men and women, respectively, both above the average for OECD countries. With regard to the health standards of the population, the average health expectancy for females increased from 68.1 years in 1990 to 71.8 in 2015; for males, it increased from 64.3 years to 69.9. Between 2006 and 2016, the percentage of New Zealanders aged 65 years and over increased from around 12% to around 15%; therefore, New Zealand is one of the four leading countries, with more than 85% of people reporting to be in good health, like Canada, the United States, and Australia.

Although in the past four decades there have been improvements in the health status, the changing demographic structure influenced the epidemiological transition, with a shift from communicable to non-communicable diseases, and to the conditions associated with an aging population (heart disease, diabetes and mental health conditions), and issues such as obesity, that lead to long-term health problems. A large proportion of the health loss New Zealanders experience comes from long-term conditions, such as cancer and diabetes. According to the most recent mortality data (2016) all cancers, ischemic heart disease, cerebrovascular disease and diabetes mellitus seem to be the major cause of death.

11.2 **The Healthcare System**

New Zealand Public Health and Disability Act 2000 (the NZPHD Act) stated that the ultimate objectives of the health care system are to provide equal, accessible and high-quality health care services to the whole population. New Zealand has been one of the countries with universal health coverage to finance and deliver healthcare to all its citizens, where healthcare is mostly covered by the public structures, with support from private and also non-governmental organizations. The Ministry of Health (the Ministry) is the main agency responsible for the provision of healthcare services; it has a range of roles in the system, in addition to being the key advisor and support to the Minister, and it funds a series of national services, including disability support and public health services.

Historically, the development of health care services in New Zealand was initiated by the New Zealand Social Security Act 1938. According to this setting, New Zealand set up a predominantly tax-funded healthcare system that made most services freely available at the point of delivery, with a mix of public and private provision which marked the introduction of the universal right to tax-financed and comprehensive healthcare.

The New Zealand health and disability system's statutory framework is made up of over 20 pieces of legislation, among which the most significant are:
- Health Act 1956;
- New Zealand Public Health and Disability Act 2000 (the NZPHD Act);
- Crown Entities Act 2004.

The Health Act 1956 sets out the roles and responsibilities of key participants to safeguard public health (the Minister of Health, the Director of Public Health, and the designated public health officers. It contains provisions for environmental health, infectious diseases, health emergencies, and the National Cervical Screening Programme.

The NZPHD Act i) establishes the structure underlying the public sector funding and the organization of health and disability services; ii) establishes the District Health Boards; iii) sets out the duties and roles of key participants (the Minister of Health, the Ministerial committees, and the health sector organizations); and iii) sets the strategic direction and goals for the New Zealand health system.

Many of the organizations that provide health services in New Zealand are Crown Entities. The Crown Entities Act provides the statutory framework for the establishment, governance, and operation of the Crown entities, and clarifies accountability relationships and report requirements between the Crown entities, their board members, the responsible Ministers, and the House of Representatives.

The New Zealand healthcare system underwent some changes after the Social Security Act 1938. A number of developments also occurred in terms of social security from the 1940s to the 1990s. In 1993 a new model called 'purchaser/provider' market-oriented system was introduced. With the 1993 Health and Disability Services Act, four Regional Health Authorities were established, and each was allocated a budget to purchase, from both public and private providers, health and disability services for its own regional populations; many disability services were previously the responsibility of the social welfare sector. The provider arms of the previously 14 Area Health Boards were converted into 23 Crown Health Enterprises, which had to function as commercial entities, run hospital, community, and public health services; and return a surplus to be reinvested in health.

The current system was implemented through the NZPHD Act 2000, which created 20 District Health Boards (DHBs) and was a fundamental step in the transition to a population-based health system. The DHBs cover geographically defined populations and may either deliver services themselves or fund other providers to do it. They are crown entities (statutory corporations) and must report to the Minister of Health for setting strategic direction, appointing the chief executive, and their own performance.

The Ministry of Health is primarily responsible for ensuring the efficiency of the health and disability system that in New Zealand is mainly funded by general taxation into central government (Vote Health). Box 1 outlines the main responsibilities of the Ministry of Health.

Other policy-making bodies include The Ministry of Social Development, the Ministry of Māori Development, the Ministry of Pacific Island Affairs, the Office for Disability Issues and the Accident Compensation Corporation. There are also twenty DHBs, which operate on local level and are responsible for providing and funding healthcare in their areas and are monitored by the National Health Board, within the Ministry of Health.

The Ministry's role in the funding of health services remained relatively stable over the last three decade. The health reforms occurred in the 1980s and the 1990s were not of the same magnitude as the changes occurred during the middle of the 20th century. Over the past 30 years, the percentage of total current funding from public sources gradually decreased from 88% to the 77-83% range, which has persisted since 1992. Of this public funding source, the Government's direct health funding through the Ministry is the largest contributor to the total health and disability funding (approximately 72.5% in 2009/2010 compared with 69.6% in 1999/2000).

The New Zealand health system's funding comes mainly from Vote Health, which in 2016/2017 amounted to just over $16.142 billion. Other significant funding sources include the Accident Compensation Corporation (ACC), other government agencies, local

---

Box 1. Responsibilities of the Ministry of Health [NZ Health System. Ministry of Health website]

- Providing policy advice on improving health outcomes, reducing inequalities, and increasing participation.
- Implementing, administering, and enforcing relevant legislation and regulations.
- Monitoring the performance of DHBs and other Crown entities in the health sector.
- Acting as the Minister's agent
- Providing health information and processing payments.
- Facilitating the collaboration and coordination within and across sectors.
- Planning and maintaining the service frameworks nationwide.
- Planning and funding public health services, disability support services and other service areas that are retained centrally.

governments, and private sources (private health insurance premiums and a small contribution from non-profit organizations) and out-of-pocket payments. The Ministry of Health allocates more than three-quarters of the public funds to manages DHBs through Vote Health. DHBs use this funding to plan, purchase and provide health services, including public hospitals and the majority of public health services, within their areas.

11.3 **Pathways of Market Access (Regulation, Pricing, and Reimbursement**

The demand for pharmaceuticals and medical devices in New Zealand is growing, along with the government expenditure in this sector; on the other hand, the supply side of the New Zealand pharmaceutical market has been defined an oligopolistic structure. Since the local manufacturing base is small and production is insufficient, many pharmaceuticals are imported from European, Australian and North American manufacturers. There are three agencies that are responsible for pharmaceutical regulation, pricing and reimbursement in New Zealand: the New Zealand Medicines and Medical Devices Safety Authority (Medsafe), the Pharmaceutical Management Agency (PHARMAC) and the Pharmacology and Therapeutics Advisory Committee (PTAC). PHARMAC decides which medicines receive public funding, following advice from PTAC (Figure 2).

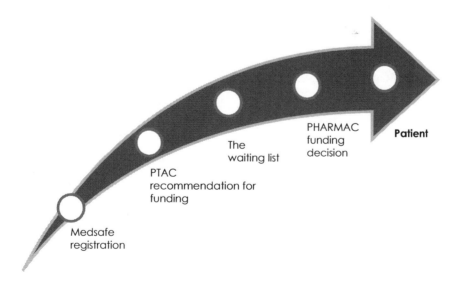

Figure 2. The funding process of prescription medicines in New Zealand
Medsafe = New Zealand Medicines and Medical Devices Safety Authority;
PHARMAC = Pharmaceutical Management Agency; PTAC = Pharmacology and Therapeutics Advisory Committee

Market Authorization

Medsafe is a business unit of the Ministry of Health and is the authority responsible for the regulation of therapeutic products in New Zealand. Medsafe determines which medicines and medical devices can be marketed and sold in New Zealand, and regulates the products used for therapeutic purposes, including medicines, related products, medical devices and controlled drugs used as medicines. Medsafe is responsible for ensuring the safety, efficacy and quality of medicines through pre-marketing approval, that must be obtained for new and changed medicines, and post-marketing surveillance. New medicines cannot be marketed in New Zealand without the consent of the Minister of Health, while medicines to which changes have been made cannot be marketed without the consent of the Director-General of Health. Post-marketing surveillance monitors the safety of medicines and medical devices in use. Products shown to be unsafe are removed from use, and prescribers are advised about the new safety information.

Coverage, Pricing and Reimbursement

PHARMAC is a single purchasing entity that manages the determination and purchase of pharmaceuticals on behalf of the DHBs, following their registration by Medsafe. PHARMAC has a predetermined fixed budget and, in order to provide the medicines considered necessary, employs therapeutic and economic analyses to guide its decisions. PHARMAC develops and maintains the New Zealand Pharmaceutical Schedule (the

---

Box 2. PHARMAC's activity 2015/2016 [PHARMAC Annual Report 2015/16]

Combined Pharmaceutical Budget
- **$ 800 million:** DHBs' combined pharmaceutical expenditure (on budget)
- **44.4 million:** number of funded prescription items filled (3% increase)
- **3.5 million:** number of New Zealanders receiving funded medicines
- **$ 79 million:** amount of savings achieved
- **15:** number of medicines funded
- **6:** number of medicines with access widened
- **38,478:** estimated number of additional patients benefiting from decisions

Hospital Medicines
- **$ 6.69 million:** full-year savings for DHB hospitals from hospital medicines decisions
- **$ 1.178 million:** cost of new investments in hospital medicines
- **$ 25.37 million:** savings for Vote Health over five years after the costs of the new investments
- **13:** number of new hospital medicines funded

Hospital Devices
- **2,084:** additional line items in the Pharmaceuticals Schedule under national contracts
- **$ 9.15 million:** net saving over five years from contracts during the year
- **$ 22.35 million:** savings over five years from all contracting to date

---

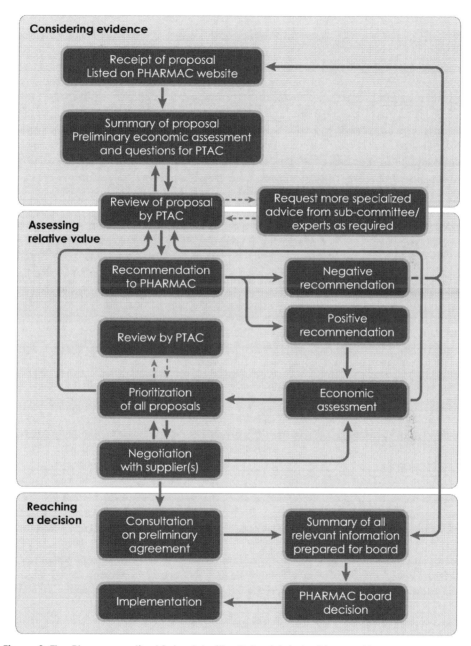

Figure 3. The Pharmaceutical Schedule (the Schedule) decision-making process. Modified from [PHARMAC Annual Report 2014-2015]

PHARMAC = Pharmaceutical Management Agency; PTAC = Pharmacology and Therapeutics Advisory Committee

Schedule), in which all funding decisions are listed. If a clinically effective product is offered at a price that reflects comparative value-for-money in the New Zealand context, it is listed on the Pharmaceutical Schedule.

In 2016, approximately 2000 prescription medicines and therapeutic products that can be prescribed by a medical doctor, dentist, registered midwife, designated nurse practitioner or optometrist, are listed in the Schedule. It is partly or fully subsidized from a national pharmaceutical budget. The Schedule is published three times a year and updated monthly on the PHARMAC website. PHARMAC negotiates the prices of inpatient and outpatient medicines, vaccines, and medical devices, and manages a capped national budget for outpatient and cancer medicines (Box 2). The mechanism used by PHARMAC to obtain lower prices include competitive tendering, sole supply contracts, reference pricing, bundling deals, risk-sharing agreements and the promotion of the use of generics.

PHARMAC generally undertakes or reviews two forms of economic analysis: a cost-utility analysis (CUA) and a budget-impact analysis (BIA). Therefore, if PHARMAC believes that clinical advice on the application is required, the first step in the assessment process will be a review of the Application by the PTAC or one of the specialized sub-committees (Figure 3).

PHARMAC is currently a Crown Entity and, while its corporate status has changed over the years, it has always remained accountable to the public (by way of the District Health Boards and/or the Minister of Health). In order to meet the budgetary goals, PHARMAC employs a variety of formulary-based expenditure management tools on behalf of the District Health Boards. In this way, the price is established by negotiation (a process which parallels standard commercial negotiations) and savings are derived from the stimulation of the competition, by listing new product and by reviewing the terms and conditions of products already listed in the Schedule.

According to the OECD Report on Competition and Regulation Issues in the Pharmaceutical Industry, there are also some key strategies for the efficient definition of subsidies and prices:

- **Reference pricing** is the primary way by which PHARMAC stimulates price competition. Reference pricing establishes a common subsidy for drugs that have the same or similar therapeutic effect.
- **Market caps** establish limits for the expenditure on a particular drug. These limited maximum annual contracts require PHARMAC to pay a fixed annual maximum amount to a supplier, regardless of the amount prescribed, dispensed or consumed.
- A **tendering** process is used to enhance the level of price competition in the generic markets. This involves selecting one off-patent drug to be the sole brand listed in the Schedule. This technique enables generic suppliers to achieve a greater market share and overcomes the tendency of physicians to prescribe by brand name.
- **Targeting.** There are restrictions on the access to a subsidy for a limited amount of drugs in the Schedule. The purposes of these restrictions are: targeting the subsidy for the drug to those patients for whom it will provide the best value (mainly for the more expensive drugs); taking into account the specific features of the drug (e.g. the

> **Box 3. Nine criteria for funding decision [PHARMAC website]**
>
> 1. Health needs of all the eligible population.
> 2. Particular health needs of Maori and Pacific peoples.
> 3. Availability and sustainability of existing medicines, therapeutic medical devices, and related products.
> 4. Clinical benefits and risks.
> 5. Cost-effectiveness of meeting the health needs by funding the drug rather than using other publicly funded health and disability support services.
> 6. Budget impact of any changes to the schedule.
> 7. Direct cost to health service users.
> 8. Government's priorities for health funding.
> 9. Any other criteria PHARMAC might consider fit (after appropriate consultation).

need to be prescribed by a specialist); helping manage the expenditure; and providing a bargaining tool for the pharmaceutical companies.

In the decision process, the committee also takes into account nine decision criteria (Box 3).

PTAC is PHARMAC's primary clinical advisory committee. It recommends to PHARMAC which medicines to fund, and with what priority.

PTAC and its sub-committees perform a critical review of the application, leading to a confidential statement of the value of a product, in terms of recommendation for funding at a given level of priority (i.e., high, medium, low, or cost neutral), deferment pending further information, or decline. The interested parties, including consumers, are excluded from any direct involvement at this stage.

11.4 Mapping and Structure of Decision Makers

As shown in Figure 4, the healthcare organization in New Zealand is characterized by a mix of public and private ownership, and the Ministry of Health has a range of roles in the system. In terms of financing, most services are universal and the government funding derives from general taxes. This funding contributes to almost 80% of the total healthcare expenditure.

In addition to the Minister of Health, the system includes PHARMAC, DHBs, Primary Health Organizations (PHOs), Public Health Units (PHUs), private non-governmental providers, Māori and Pacific providers and independent general practitioners (GPs). There are also many consumer bodies and Non-Governmental Organizations (NGOs) that provide services and advocate the interests of the various groups, as well as formal advocacy and inquiry boards, committees and entities. The role of the private sector is more organized in terms of supply than financing. Private insurance companies represent a very small segment of the total healthcare expenditure.

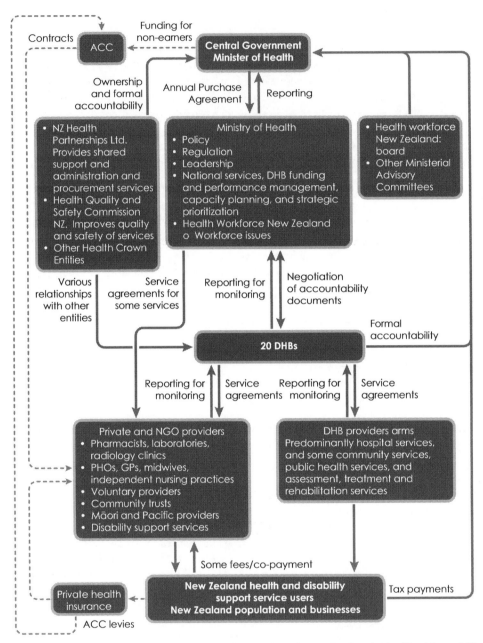

Figure 4. Structure of the health and disability sector of New Zealand. Modified from [NZ Health System. Ministry of Health website]

ACC = Accident Compensation Corporation; DHB = District Health Boards GP = General Practitioner; NGO = Non-Governmental Organization; PHO = Primary Health Organization

The Pharmaceutical Management Agency (PHARMAC)

As previously reported, PHARMAC is a cornerstone agency for the management of pharmaceuticals in the New Zealand healthcare system. PHARMAC was established in June 1993 with the objective of ensuring the best health outcomes from drug treatment, within the amount of the available funding. PHARMAC is governed by a government-appointed but independent board, which refers to the Minister of Health; it acts on behalf of New Zealand's 20 geographically based DHBs, and plans, purchases, and provides health services. PHARMAC plays a crucial role in ensuring the efficiency and effectiveness in New Zealand tendering and negotiations with the pharmaceutical companies, to ensure the best deals.

Over the years, PHARMAC's role has been expanded, and now it ensures the optimal use of medicines, negotiates prices and supply terms for some hospital medicines, manages the basket of essential cancer drugs, and manages special schemes that supply drug funding for people with rare conditions, in addition to manage the community drug budget.

PTAC's members (including senior health practitioners, with expertise in critical appraisal and broad experience and knowledge of pharmaceuticals and their therapeutic uses) are appointed by the Director-General of Health, in consultation with the PHARMAC Board. There are also several PTAC sub-committees, made up of experts in specialist clinical fields such as cardiology and oncology.

District Health Boards (DHBs)

DHBs are responsible for planning and purchasing the full range of services for their respective local populations, including primary and disability support services and hospital care (mainly in public hospitals). Private hospitals provide mainly elective procedures, occasionally under contract with the public system. Government-owned hospitals provide accident and emergency, inpatient, outpatient, and community care for free. Primary health care services such as general practitioner, pharmacy, and diagnostic services are delivered through privately owned, small independent businesses, funded by government fee-for-service subsidies. Patients must pay for GP service except for maternity care, and GP services for children <13. The DHBs allocate resources to improve, promote, and protect the health of the population within their district, and to promote the independence of people with disabilities. DHBs are expected to cooperate with the adjoining districts in delivering services, particularly where there are cross-border issues, and where specialist services draw patients from a larger region, rather than a single district.

Primary Health Organizations (PHOs)

Primary Health Organizations (PHOs) were designed to coordinate ongoing patient care, plan population healthcare needs and reduce the financial and other primary care access barriers, especially for the most disadvantaged. Created between 2002 and 2006, and based on WHO Alma Ata principles of 'comprehensive primary care', PHOs are no-profit, multidisciplinary organizations serving the registered population. PHO funding is capitation-based by DHBs although many continue to reimburse GPs on a fee-for-service basis. A PHO provides services either directly by employing staff, or through its provider members. Additional PHO funding is available for developing Care Plus programs for the management of chronic disease patients, for 'services to improve access', and for the promotion of health.

11.5 Challenges and Catalyzers for Market Access

In essence, New Zealand provides accessible, affordable and universal health care through tax funding. As for the cost of pharmaceuticals, it can be argued that the New Zealand reimbursement system aims to achieve the lowest possible prices. However, as stated by Morgan et al. (2010), PHARMAC's approach to expenditure management is considered aggressive by some, and critics have questioned whether this approach requires a trade-off between expenditure management and patient access to drugs.

Challenges

New Zealand reimbursement model has controlled the rising cost of pharmaceuticals, using containment measures as a budget cap and tender procedure. On the other hand, the impact of these strategies has been very controversial, due to the lower number of new drugs available in New Zealand, compared to other countries. For example, in the period 2000-2009, the New Zealand patient population had access to less than half of the new medicines that were reimbursed in Australia. Furthermore, in New Zealand, the new drugs registration occurred on average 9.0 months later and listing occurred 32.7 months later, giving a 23.7-month difference in the interval between registration and listing. Sixteen of the new medicines listed in both countries (27%) were registered first in New Zealand, but only three of these (ursodeoxycholic acid, dorzolamide and ezetimibe) were listed first in New Zealand. The main reason is that PHARMAC is too focused on cost-containment rather than improving health outcomes.

Another example, reported by Metcalfe et al., is the funding of medicines for particular indications, such as trastuzumab for early-stage HER2+ breast cancer. In 2006 PHARMAC decided against funding a 12-month trastuzumab (Herceptin) program for women with the HER2+ form of breast cancer, which would have an estimated cost of $ 25-30 million/year. Instead, as reported by Cumming et al. (2010), it funded a 9-week course, at an estimated cost of $ 5 million, with a further $ 3.2 million to participate in an international trial of a short versus long course of concurrent treatment. Finally in 2008, the National Party-led government allowed the funding of the 12-month course of trastuzumab for HER2+ breast cancer, bypassing PHARMAC.

In recent years, a separate comparison of New Zealand and 17 other countries showed that New Zealand's drug prices were in the lowest quartile in five cases, and ranked low-

est in four cases (abacavir, escitalopram generic version, mycophenolatemofetil originator, and pioglitazone generic), whereas they were in the highest quartile in seven cases,
and ranked highest in one case (prasugrel). The six other medicines in the highest quartile were darunavir ethanolate, indinavir, insulin lispro, sunitinib, and venlafaxine (being
the originator and the generic).

Catalyzers

The New Zealand pharmaceutical market is dominated by its public health system, so
the public funding system may be attractive for the pharmaceutical industry. On the other hand, with a relatively small population, and a weak purchasing power, a single purchasing organization is considered the best option to protect the healthcare interests of
New Zealand consumers. Here, a variety of techniques such as competitive tendering,
reference pricing, generic substitution and bundling agreements are key objectives.

Good Examples from Successful Market Access Strategies

In Box 5 are reported the major investments of PHARMAC in 2016.

Box 5. Major investments in 2016 [PHARMAC Annual Report 2015-16]

- **Six new respiratory treatments:** five new treatments were funded for people
  with Chronic Obstructive Pulmonary Disease, one new once-daily treatment
  for asthma, and access was widened for two others. These changes cover $
  61 million in gross expenditure, provide savings of approximately $ 27 million
  over five years, and will benefit over 23,000 New Zealanders.
- **Valaciclovir:** access was widened to this treatment for infections caused by
  the herpes virus. Nearly 34,000 more people will now be able to access this
  funded treatment.
- **New treatments for multiple sclerosis:** dimethyl fumarate and teriflunomide
  were funded, bringing the number of funded MS treatments to seven.
- **New medicines for rare disorders:** during the year, PHARMAC managed its
  pilot initiative for the funding of medicines for rare disorders. Four medicines for
  the treatment of rare disorders were funded, with an estimated $ 8.2 million of
  gross expenditure in the first full year:
  - Icatibant is used to treat severe attacks of hereditary angioedema and can be
    administered at home, which benefits the person and their whānau, and DHBs.
  - Siltuximab is a treatment for HIV-negative, HHV-8 negative multicentric
    Castleman's disease.
  - Galsulfase is a treatment for people with the rare enzyme deficiency
    condition Maroteaux-Lamy Syndrome (mucopolysaccharidosis VI). It is
    usually diagnosed in children and can cause damage to bones, joints, eyes,
    heart valves and the nervous system.
  - Bedaquiline is used to treat extensively drug-resistant tuberculosis, a rare
    form caused by bacteria resistant to some usual tuberculosis treatments.

Promoting Generics

New Zealand has one of the highest proportions of generic medicines by volume (third out of 26 OECD countries). PHARMAC encourages the development of generics, calling for competitive tenders for the exclusive supply right, for a limited period, after the patent expires. According to the PHARMAC Annual Report, in 2014/15, the combined pharmaceutical expenditure was $ 795 million. Nevethless, the estimated spending without the savings achieved since 2004, would have been almost $ 2 billion.

11.6 **Look-out for Near Future**

New Zealanders have a very good coverage of their healthcare needs, through public health services. In the past, there were some barriers, such as high co-payments to access healthcare services and pharmaceuticals. Today, cost is no longer a barrier, but the access to new medicines is ongoing in some countries, although the reimbursement and price of pharmaceuticals are assessed and decided on the national level in New Zealand and the major concern is the waiting list for innovative pharmaceuticals.

Since the introduction of the use of generic drugs instead of their originators is an effective way to rationalize healthcare, generic pharmaceutical industry will be an important part of the drug policy in New Zealand in the near future.

Overall, New Zealanders appear satisfied with their healthcare system, with the hope that any changes will bring more equity and sustainability.

11.7 **Bibliography**

- Ashton T. Health care systems in transition: New Zealand Part I: An overview of New Zealand's health care system. *J Public Health Med* 1996; 18: 269-73
- Babar ZU, Francis S. Identifying priority medicines policy issues for New Zealand: a general inductive study. *BMJ Open* 2014; 4: e004415
- Beatty PA, Laking GR. Oncology Pharmaceutical Funding in New Zealand: A Different Approach and a Proposal. *J Oncol Pract* 2015; 11: 249-51
- Cumming J, Mays N, Daubé J. How New Zealand has contained expenditure on drugs. *BMJ* 2010; 340: c2441
- Cumming J, McDonald J, Barr C, et al. New Zealand Health System Review. *Health Systems in Transition* 2014; 4: 1-200. Available at http://iris.wpro.who.int/bitstream/handle/10665.1/10420/9789290616504_eng.pdf (last accessed May 2017)
- Duckett SJ, Breadon P, Ginnivan L, et al. Australia's bad drug deal: high pharmaceutical prices. Melbourne, Grattan Institute: 2013. Available at https://grattan.edu.au/wp-content/uploads/2014/04/Australias_Bad_Drug_Deal_FINAL.pdf (last accessed June 2017)

- International Monetary Fund – IMF. IMF Country Report No. 16/40, 2016. Washington, D.C.: International Monetary Fund, 2016. Available at https://www.imf.org/external/pubs/ft/scr/2016/cr1640.pdf (last accessed June 2017)
- Karikios D, Schofield D, Salkeld G, et al. The rising cost of anti-cancer drugs in Australia. *Asia Pac J Clin Oncol* 2013; 9: 100
- Keene L, Bagshaw P, Nicholls MG. Funding New Zealand's public healthcare system: time for an honest appraisal and public debate. *N Z Med J* 2016; 129: 10-20
- Medsafe – New Zealand Medicines and Medical Devices Safety Authority. Available at http://www.medsafe.govt.nz/index.asp (last accessed June 2017)
- Metcalfe S, Evans J, Priest G. PHARMAC funding of 9-week concurrent trastuzumab (Herceptin) for HER2-positive early breast cancer. NZMJ 2007; 120
- Ministry of Health. Health and Independence Report 2016. The Director-General of Health's Annual Report on the State of Public Health. Wellington: Ministry of Health, 2017. Available at https://www.health.govt.nz/system/files/documents/publications/health-independence-report-2016-apr17.pdf (last accessed June 2017)
- Ministry of Health. Health Expenditure Trends in New Zealand 2000-2010. Wellington: Ministry of Health, 2012. Available at https://www.health.govt.nz/system/files/documents/publications/health-expenditure-trends-in-new-zealand-2000-2010.pdf (last accessed June 2017)
- Ministry of Health. The New Zealand Health and Disability System: Organisations and Responsibilities: Briefing to the Minister of Health. Wellington: Ministry of Health, 2014. Available at https://www.health.govt.nz/system/files/documents/publications/new-zealand-health-and-disability-system-organisations-responsibilities-dec14-v2.pdf (last accessed May 2017)
- Minister of Health. New Zealand Health Strategy: Future direction. Wellington: Ministry of Health, 2016. Available at https://www.health.govt.nz/system/files/documents/publications/new-zealand-health-strategy-futuredirection-2016-apr16.pdf (last accessed June 2017)
- Ministry of Health. New Zealand Health System. Available at https://www.health.govt.nz/new-zealand-health-system (last accessed June 2017)
- Ministry of Health. New Zealand Health System. Funding. Available at https://www.health.govt.nz/new-zealand-health-system/overview-health-system/funding (last accessed June 2017)
- Ministry of Health. New Zealand Health System. Statutory framework. Available at https://www.health.govt.nz/new-zealand-health-system/overview-health-system/statutory-framework (last accessed June 2017
- Morgan S, Boothe K. Prescription drug subsidies in Australia and New Zealand. *Aust Prescr* 2010; 33: 2-4
- Morgan S, Hanley G, McMahon M, et al. Influencing drug prices through formulary-based policies: Lessons from New Zealand. *Healthc Policy* 2007; 3: e121-40
- OECD. Competition and Regulation Issues in the Pharmaceutical Industry. OECD Journal: Competition Law and Policy, 2000. Available at http://www.oecd.org/regreform/sectors/1920540.pdf (last accessed June 2017)

- OECD. Health at a Glance 2015: OECD Indicators. Paris: OECD Publishing, 2015. Available at http://dx.doi.org/10.1787/health_glance-2015-en (last accessed June 2017)
- OECD. How does health spending in New Zealand compare? OECD Health Statistics 2015. Available at http://search.oecd.org/els/health-systems/Country-Note-NEW%20ZEALAND-OECD-Health-Statistics-2015.pdf (last accessed June 2017)
- PHARMAC – the Pharmaceutical Management Agency. Available at https://www.pharmac.govt.nz/ (last accessed June 2017)
- Pharmaceutical Management Agency – PHARMAC Annual Report 2014/15. Available at https://www.pharmac.govt.nz/assets/annual-report-2014-2015.pdf (last accessed June 2017)
- Pharmaceutical Management Agency – PHARMAC Annual Report 2015/16. Available at https://www.pharmac.govt.nz/assets/annual-report-2015-2016.pdf (last accessed June 2017)
- Ragupathy R, Kilpatrick K. Pharmaceutical pricing in New Zealand. In: Pharmaceutical Prices in the 21st Century. Springer International Publishing, 2015
- Vogler S, Kilpatrick K, Babar ZU. Analysis of medicine prices in New Zealand and 16 European countries. *Value Health* 2015;18: 484-92
- Wonder M, Milne R. Access to new medicines in New Zealand compared to Australia. *N Z Med J* 2011; 124: 12-28

https://doi.org/10.7175/747.ch12

12. Pharmaceutical Market in the U.S: a Brief Treatise

Barry A. Bleidt [1]

[1] *Professor, Sociobehavioral and Administrative Pharmacy. College of Pharmacy Nova Southeastern University, Fort Lauderdale, FL, USA*

12.1 Introduction

Pharmaceutical manufacturing in the United States of America (U.S.) is and has been one of the most profitable industries overall during the past several decades. One reason for this fact may be that the U.S. is one of the few countries that do not have price controls on prescription drugs. Products are brought to market through a lengthy, expensive, clinical research process after approval by the FDA. The development, manufacture, and marketing of medications is now a trillion-dollar industry worldwide. Annual global revenues generated by the pharmaceutical industry exceeded one trillion U.S. dollars for the first time in 2014. The industry's revenues grew from approximately $ 390 billion dollars in 2001. This translates into a 250 percent growth over the past thirteen years [1]. The U.S. is the largest pharmaceutical market in the world with revenues valued at over $ 339.7 billion. This volume is more than 3.5 times larger than the second marketplace, Japan, at about $ 94 billion in annual revenue. America accounts for over 30 percent of the worldwide consumption of pharmaceutical products in terms of dollars [2].

The overall purpose of this work is to discuss pharmaceutical market access for the U.S. First, this chapter provides a brief history of the pharmaceutical industry in the U.S. Second, the structure of the highly successful American marketplace is explained along with how our capitalistic model of marketing has fostered the eminence growth of the pharmaceutical industry here. Third, unique characteristics of the well-developed marketing schema by the leading research-intensive manufacturers in the American market are described.

12.2 History and Development of the Pharmaceutical Industry Market in the U. S.

In the early 1900s, the American pharmaceutical was evolving from medicines prepared *secundum artem* on site by the pharmacist to a largely industrialized, technological operation. Ethical, responsible companies utilized botanists and other scientists to identify adulterated or impure crude products. Pharmaceutical research here was primarily limited to studying production problems. In 1912, Josiah K. Lilly, Sr, President of Eli

Lilly and Company, prophetically said that synthetic, active ingredients and biologicals would replace natural, crude products. "Punishing the stomach with large, frequent and nauseous doses is bound to give way where possible to more refined and direct methods. Medicine will become less empirical and more and more rigid demands will be made upon the manufacturer [...]" [3].

By the beginning of World War I, Germany dominated the pharmaceutical and fine chemical industries using a research-based model that helped propel the country's economic growth and industrialization. It was able to export complex, organic chemical intermediates as "raw materials" to the U.S. duty-free, thus inhibiting the American production of synthetic chemicals at a time where their importance was growing internationally and domestically. German-owned patents and German-owned companies controlled much of what was manufactured here. For the most part, the American pharmaceutical manufacturers were merely part of the producer-goods industry.

One hundred years ago, during the summer of 1917 (just a few months after the U.S. declared war on Germany), the Council on National Defense deliberated with 250 American Manufacturers regarding how to put the pharmaceutical industry, among others, on wartime footing. The Federal Trade Commission sanctioned the issuing of non-inclusive licenses to domestic companies to manufacture medicines formerly protected by German-owned patents. The most important after-effects of these events were that the American pharmaceutical manufacturers were able to commandeer economic power and control over their own science and technology [4].

Post World War II, the American pharmaceutical industry began to invest seriously in research and development and to produce highly differentiated consumer goods that were exclusively distributed via community and institutional pharmacies. By the 1960s, drugs had become «social goods [...] goods that are so important in the contemporary social milieu that they lose much of their private commercial character and become closely integrated within the public, and thereby, political sector» [4]. The 1962 Kefauver-Harris Amendment to the Federal Food Drug and Cosmetic Act was enacted, in part, to expand Federal regulation of medical experimentation on humans. The law also required that manufacturers prove drug effectiveness as a condition of gaining marketing approval, as well as requiring promotional activities to disclose accurate side-effect information [5].

Two dynamics have been mostly responsible for fueling the incredible growth of the American pharmaceutical industry. First, Research & Development has evolved into a highly sophisticated spectrum of processes and specialties, including molecular modeling, pharmacogenomics, proteinomics, clinical applications, biologic preparation, pharmacogenetics, packaging, marketing, to name a few. All of which have contributed to unique types of medicines, dosage forms, and distribution systems available in the marketplace. In 2015, the U.S. Food and Drug Administration approved forty-five New Chemical Entities (NCEs) for marketing. Thirty-nine percent (39%) of these approvals were for biologic agents, which were up from twenty-two percent in 2013 (a 77% increase). By 2016, the percentage of approved NCEs that are considered as biologics rose to 59%; thus, signaling a huge shift in the origins of products which are being approved. Effectively, we now have shifted from the synthetic chemical era of medicines to the new epoch of biologic-based drug products [6].

The second parameter that has fueled the pharmaceutical industry tremendous growth is marketing, which has become increasingly more sophisticated, cutting-edge, targeted, and successful. This topic is the subject matter for the rest of the chapter. Marketing processes are very important to the overall economy. They are even more critical to the high degree of success enjoyed by the research-intensive pharmaceutical industry and the considerable profits gleaned by it.

Overall, this chapter highlights the evolution of marketing and promotion and explains the current position of the pharmaceutical marketplace, from the manufacturer's vantage point and, to a lesser degree, the practical standpoint. In the next section, marketing basics as they relate to the U.S. pharmaceutical manufacturing industry and to the practice of pharmacy will be discussed, followed by a focus on the current practices of promotional activities for prescription drug products.

12.3 Pharmaceutical Market Structure

Pharmaceutical marketing is defined as "the sum of all the activities that facilitate the flow of prescription drug products (goods, services, or information) from their origination point (manufacturer, importer, service provider, or information source) to the ultimate consumer (patient)". Marketing processes include shipping systems, channels of

---

Box 1. Universality of Marketing Functions. Modified from [7]

Assembling functions
- Marshalling sufficient raw materials
- Functioning distribution networks
- Selecting appropriate product mix (including different strengths and dosage forms, where applicable)
- Managing resources
- Gathering production and distribution information

Distribution functions
- Setting and following production schedules
- Timing logistics
- Transportation (among all three function types)
- Storage of material and products

Administrative functions
- Risk bearing (for everything throughout all operations)
- Quality control (continuous quality improvement)
- Financing (who pays for what, when)
- Selling (product must be sold)
- Buying (product must be purchased)
- Marketing research on end users and operations

distribution, product and consumer research (economic, social, and behavioral), quality control, merchandising considerations, product promotional practices, pricing strategies, financial risk bearing, planning and logistics, among other things [7].

In a normal marketplace, the market for the producers (sellers) is usually the prospective ultimate user (patients). The prescription drug market is not a normal one; it is a directed market where prescribers direct the purchase by the patient. Either way, it is the marketer's job to persuade consumers to buy or utilize their products. Whomever the producer (supplier) is, numerous operations (tasks) must be executed for the product to be able to reach the correct person in a timely manner. These collective tasks are known as the Universality of Marketing Functions (Box 1); all operations must be performed for the marketing process to work efficiently. A failure of any of these operations leads to problems at the patient end of the supply chain such as wrong item, poor-quality, insufficient quantity, or too many products being delivered. When any part of this system of marketing functions fails, numerous problems arise. The American system excels in all marketing function aspects; these operations are the key to the excellence it enjoys as a leader in marketing pharmaceuticals. If a supplier cannot meet the demand needs of the end-user, then the producer will go out of business (even if it is a government). These facts also apply to health care delivery systems.

Levels of Distribution

In the pharmaceutical/healthcare marketplace, there are many distinct categories of end-users. As a result, there are various levels of distribution (Table 1). Each type of product has similar, yet unique levels. In complex economies, this hierarchy may not be an exact representation and there may be interfaces among the horizontal planes. In the U.S., there is usually a wholesale level (for prescription drugs) or a central office (for service providers) that functions as an intermediary between producer and the place where the patient either purchases or receives their product. This middleman in the marketing process places a critical role in terms of efficiency.

Intrinsic role of the middleman

It is important to note that for each marketing tier, value must be added to the product. If value is not added, then that level will cease to function in an efficient marketplace. "There is a value added to the overall distribution process using wholesalers characterized

Prescription drugs (good)	Health care services	Information
Manufacturer	Health care service originator	Information creator
Wholesaler	Health care service Distributor	Information distributor
Pharmacy	Health care Provider	Information provider
Consumer	Patient	Client

Table 1. Distribution levels for prescription drugs and related products. Modified from [7]

through the concepts of appropriate order quantity, utility of time, place and access. This type of operation is even more important in the efficient and effective distribution system for pharmaceutical products than for general consumer goods" [8].

A wholesaler is defined as "an entity that purchases manufacturers' goods, resells them to others, and that operates one or more facilities where these goods are received, stored and reshipped" [8]. The question is "Why not cut out the wholesaler intermediary and save money by removing a level of marketing?" Certain benefits (such as the minimum number of transactions, sorting, and proximity) accrue to society because of the unique role of the middleman. A discussion of these advantages follows.

Minimum Number of Transactions. The first benefit that accrues to the marketing system and society is that the overall total of monthly exchanges/transactions is minimized. Without pharmaceutical wholesalers, each pharmacy would have to order from the different manufacturers. Below is an example of what the overall number of monthly transactions would be in this scenario (numbers used are not an exact representation):

50,000	x	250	x	4	=	50,000,000
(pharmacies)		(manufacturers)		(weekly orders)		(monthly transactions)

According to this estimation, if each of the 50,000 pharmacies in the U.S. ordered weekly (which would be a low estimate) from each of the 250 manufacturers, the total would be about 50 million transactions monthly. On the other hand, the current system uses the pharmaceutical wholesaler, thereby radically reducing the calculated number of monthly transactions.

250	x	50	x	4	=	50,000
(manufacturers)		(wholesalers)		(orders/month)		

50	x	1,000	x	22	=	1,100,000
(wholesalers)		(pharmacies per wholesaler)		(order days per month)		

				Grand total	=	1,150,000

In the above, closer-to-what-really-happens scenario, each pharmacy (estimating 1,000 pharmacies per wholesaler) receives twenty-two (22) deliveries per month from their wholesaler and each wholesaler orders four times monthly from the manufacturers. When these two calculations are added, the sum is 1,150,000 transactions. This 97.7% reduction in the total number of transactions is accompanied with a similar, large decrease in ordering, shipping, packing, invoicing and other affiliate costs (e.g., holding and interest), as well as the greatly diminished likelihood of errors being committed. Thereby, adding significant value to the overall marketing process.

The overall advantages illustrated above with the current distribution network are further supplemented by the other services offered by most wholesalers to manufacturers and pharmacies. This well-structured, strategic system is responsible for the economic, precise, efficient, and resource-sparing delivery of prescription drugs to their intended end-point of distribution.

Sorting. The second accrued benefit is essentially the definition of what a pharmaceutical wholesaler does. As a marketing concept, sorting has two discrete, but related actions – concentration and dispersion. Concentration – the wholesaler buys from many manufacturers in much larger quantities than an individual retail could, earning substantial discounts typical of such purchases. Consequently, the per-unit and overall total costs are lower. Dispersion – a specific product is shipped simultaneously to a pharmacy after an order has been placed and it is combined with products for that outlet and with requests from other outlets nearby. This process economizes the overall cost of distribution; a key component of marketing.

Proximity. In general, wholesalers are closer to the final marketplace than manufactures. As a result, distributions that are more frequent can be made, sometimes multiple times per day. The idea is "providing the right good at the right time to the right person at the right place" [9].

12.4 Accessing the American Pharmaceutical Market

Gaining access to the pharmaceutical marketplace in the United States requires expensive and highly sophisticated strategies and tactics. However, it can be a very lucrative proposition for those who succeed. This section of the chapter will describe some of the approaches used by current leaders in the industry. Figure 1 depicts many of the methods the pharmaceutical industry uses to build and protect their product's place in the market.

Sampling

A successful tactic used to increase product demand is the use of samples (actual product available in a patient-convenient package). Sampling, as a strategy, is designed to permit prescribers to "test drive" the product in order to learn more about the effectiveness and safety profile of the product at no expense to the patient. Samples are also used as "starter packages" so that patients can initiate their therapy immediately. The professional sales representative furnishes these items to the clinician upon the written request of a prescriber to the manufacturer. These samples are also used to provide medication to those patients who cannot afford to pay for their therapy. Samples can be in the form of an actual product or as a coupon. These vouchers are then presented to the pharmacist to be dispensed. The pharmacist submits these forms to the manufacturer or an intermediary for reimbursement.

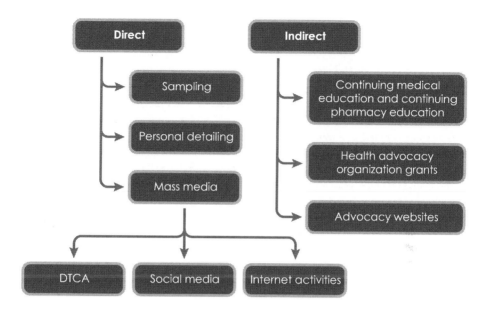

Figure 1. Types of pharmaceutical marketing
DTCA = Direct-To-Consumer Advertising

Personal Detailing

Pharmaceutical companies still engage in in-person visits to prescribers. This high-labor cost strategy is effective in reaching practitioners. Creative methods for accessing hard-to-reach physicians are used by professional representatives such as spicy food catering and ice cream parlor service in-office. These imaginative strategies are successful in promoting prescription products to those who are responsible for their use. Personal detailing has evolved over the years as a lucrative means to grow market share. Due to the high-labor costs, this approach is decreasing as a percentage of the overall promotional effort and is being supplanted by direct-to-consumer advertising (discussed later).

Continuing Professional Education

Pharmaceutical Research and Manufacturers of America (PhRMA) is the organization that represents the leading biomedical research companies in this country. PhRMA established guidelines on engagement with health professionals. These rules include specifics such as the maximum value of gifts and meals that can be provided to prescribers and pharmacists. It also established rules regarding the content and conduct of Continuing Medical Education and Continuing Pharmacy Education programs. In order to circumvent these policies, companies contract with third-party vendors to offer a non-accredited "information session" on a specific product featuring a physician testimonial at a high-end restaurant that would draw the desired audience.

Direct-to-Consumer Advertising (DTCA)

Historically, the preponderance of prescription drug marketing information was targeted directly towards prescribers. In 1981, an advertisement appeared in *Reader's Digest* magazine, a publication for the general public, for Pneumovax® (pneumococcal polysaccharide vaccine) from Merck & Co., Inc. Soon thereafter, print ads in other magazines also ran for Zovirax® (acyclovir) by Burroughs Wellcome & Company (now GlaxoSmithKline). These commercial messages were created to inform the laity that specific prescription medications were available and suggested that they seek advice from physicians about whether this product would work for them. The first broadcast advertisement of a prescription drug to the masses was aired on television May 19, 1983. A commercial was shown for Rufen® (ibuprofen) manufactured by Boots Pharmaceuticals was shown on a major network in Florida [10].

New Zealand and the United States are currently the only two countries that permit direct-to-consumer advertising for prescription drugs. The use of DTCA is controversial; this is why there are so few countries that permit it. Among the advantages of DTCA are that the public has an increased awareness of and is better informed about available treatments, and, therefore, empowers them to be a better partner in their own healthcare. Another advantage is that patients could benefit from having more than one information source about pharmaceuticals and treatment regimens. Additionally, the ads encourage a patient to contact their primary care clinician and promote a more-informed dialogue

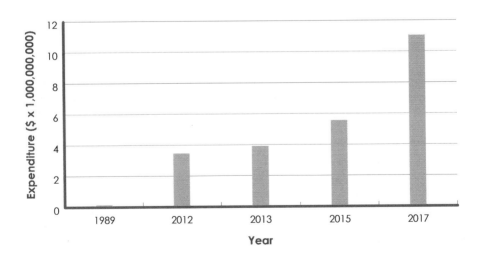

Figure 2. DTCA expenditures in the U.S. [13,14]

between patient and practitioner. Possibly the best public health benefit is that these ads may reduce the stigma associated with the conditions the promoted drugs treat. Research has consistently shown that customers who request a prescription from their practitioner after viewing a DTCA were among the most adherent outpatients [11].

Some of the arguments in opposition to DTCA are:
- the ads may misinform by omitting key information;
- patients lack the analytical skills to assess the provided information;
- the ads rarely focus on non-therapeutic options such as diet, exercise, and other lifestyle changes; and
- they may encourage patients to take too many drugs and will favor the more heavily advertised products.

These ads also promote new products before a comprehensive safety profile can be ascertained in the general population [11]. The American Medical Association adopted a policy in 2015 that calls for a ban on DTCA because of «concerns that a growing proliferation of ads is driving demand for expensive treatments despite the clinical effectiveness of less costly alternatives» [12].

DTCA is now the most prominent mode of health communication that is encountered by the American public [11]. Figure 2 presents the amount expended on DTCA in the U.S. for select years.

Figure 2 presents a vivid picture of the rapid growth of this promotional strategy. DTCA spending has increased from $ 12 million in 1989 to a projected $ 11 billion in 2017 [13,14]. This massive, approximately 916% increase in expenditures on DTCA demonstrates the necessity of engaging in this stratagem to stay competitive. Over 69% of

Type of advertisement	Description	Brief listing of requirements
Product claim	Only type that uses a drug name, its uses, and presents its risks and benefits using understandable language	Specific items must be in the main part of the ad: • Generic and brand name • An FDA-approved indication • Most significant risks via audio
Reminder	Mentions the drug name and maybe its cost, but not its indications Ads not permitted to be used for drugs classified as having serious risks (black boxed warnings)	Cannot imply in audio or visual about drug's uses or safety profile
Help-seeking	Ads that promote a disease or condition and suggest that patients talk with their doctor or pharmacist about it, but do not recommend a specific product	May include the pharmaceutical manufacturer's name

Table 2. FDA regulatory requirements for different types of direct-to-consumer TV ads [17]

the overall spending on DTCA was devoted to television ads in 2016 [15]. The products that had the most money spent on them in 2016 were Lyrica® (pregabalin) at $ 313 million, Humira® (adalimumab) at $ 303 million, and Eliquis® (apixaban) at $ 186 million [16].

The U.S. Food and Drug Administration regulates the content of DTCA. Table 2 presents a brief description of the basic guidelines for the different categories of these ads. These "fair and balance" rules make it more imperative that DTCA be visually mesmerizing to smother the warnings.

Companies have also experimented with DTCA ads shown on social media. In August 2015, the FDA reprimanded Duchesnay USA for a paid message presented on Instagram. Kim Kardashian West, a high-profile celebrity who had just given birth, was a compensated spokesperson. As such, she posted a testimonial about the effectiveness of this **antinauseant** drug and picture of herself holding a bottle Diclegis® (doxylamine succinate and pyridoxine hydrochloride delayed release). This experiment was highly successful in that over 40 million people had access to the ad and 464,000 people "liked it" [18].

12.5 **In Summary**

Many and significant changes have occurred in the American prescription drug marketplace since 2000. Previously "unthinkable" therapeutic categories, new research methods and capabilities, high-tech dosage forms, robotic biomedical and point-of-care diagnostic devices, innovative practice approaches, big data analysis, and persuasive promotional campaigns are among the transformations that have transpired. The fundamental tenets of the industry are transforming due to marketplace, financial, and regulatory forces.

Understanding the magnitude of the many, dynamic forces impacting access to the prescription drug marketplace in the United States is impossible without first comprehending the critical part that promotion by the industry plays. It is highly sophisticated and has evolved to be successful in maintaining or increasing market position. The U.S. pharmaceutical industry has been and still is very clever and creative. «Pharmaceutical manufacturers can be thought of as compounders of various marketing parameters that are concocted skillfully and dispensed to form the company's unique (at least from the business' point-of-view) offerings in the marketplace» [10]. For prescription drugs, the market place in the U. S. is significantly different from for other traditional consumer products in that patients (the end-users) do not have direct access to purchase these items. From a marketing point-of-view, this "directed market" has the distinct advantage that a limited number of prescribers control access to a large end-user patient population exceeding 350,000,000. This scenario provides a dream opportunity to focus marketing efforts on a limited number of people and gain widespread return on investment.

The American pharmaceutical marketplace, because of its high-level of profitability, is able to experiment with unique and innovative promotional ideas that other markets just could not sustain. As a result, many endeavors are tried to promote specific products or to improve (or maintain) market share or an image. It is possible to concentrate marketing efforts on a few to receive widespread benefits.

In the future, I expect more ingenuity and inventiveness in how companies position their products and themselves. High drug prices are a volatile, emotion, and political issue right now. The high cost of marketing is thought to add to the high price charged for prescription drugs. Other significant issues of growing concern within the U.S. are drug shortages (due to limited production facilities, raw material shortages, etc.), drug importation, and counterfeit products. Addressing some or all of these concerns as part of a push to enter or expand a company's market position would be met with an enthusiastic acceptance.

12.6 **References**

1. Statista: The Statistics Portal. Leading countries in global pharmaceutical mergers and acquisitions. Available at https://www.statista.com/statistics/398229/leading-countries-by-pharmaceutical-industry-mergers-and-acquisitions/ (last accessed August 2017)

2. WorldAtlas. Biggest Pharmaceutical Markets in the World by Country. http://www.worldatlas.com/articles/countries-with-the-biggest-global-pharmaceutical-markets-in-the-world.html (last accessed August 2017)

3. Lilly JK. The Pharmaceutical Era. 1912; 45: 449-52; 513-7

4. Vogt DD, Montagne M. The process of drug development: I. Historical interplay of political economics, research and regulation. *Clin Res Pr Drug Regul Aff* 1983; 1: 1-18

5. Drug Amendments Act of 1962. An act to protect the public health by amending the Federal Food, Drug, and Cosmetic Act to assure the safety, effectiveness, and reliability of drugs, authorize standardization of drug names, and clarify and strengthen existing inspection authority; and for other purposes. Public Law 87-781, 76 STAT 780. Available at http://uscode.house.gov/statutes/pl/87/781.pdf (last accessed August 2017)

6. U.S. Food and Drug Administration. Novel Drug Approvals for 2016. Available at https://www.fda.gov/Drugs/DevelopmentApprovalProcess/DrugInnovation/ucm483775.htm (last accessed August 2017)

7. Bleidt B. Marketing activities: The keystone of capitalism, increasing the availability of prescription drugs through pharmaceutical promotion. *J Drug Issues* 1992; 22

8. Bleidt B, Clouse E, Nichols A. How to Develop a Successful Retail Pharmacy Marketing Mix. In: NARD, AACP, NACDS, Glaxo (eds.). Retail Pharmacy Practice Management. Chapel Hill, North Carolina: Health Sciences Consortium, 1990

9. Smith HA. Principles and Methods of Pharmacy Management. Philadelphia, Pennsylvania: Lea & Febiger: 1986

10. PharmaVOICE. How 5/19 changed the industry forever. Available at http://www.pharmavoice.com/article/1232/ (last accessed August 2017)

11. Ventola CL. Direct-to-consumer pharmaceutical advertising: therapeutic or toxic? *P T* 2011; 36: 669-84

12. American Medical Association. AMA calls for ban on DTC ads of prescription drugs and medical devices. Press Release 17 November 2015. Available at https://www.ama-assn.org/content/ama-calls-ban-direct-consumer-advertising-prescription-drugs-and-medical-devices (last accessed August 2017)

13. Millman J. It's True: Drug Companies Are Bombarding Your TV with More Ads than Ever. The Washington Post. March 23, 2015. Available at https://www.washingtonpost.com/news/wonk/wp/2015/03/23/yes-drug-companies-are-bombarding-your-tv-with-more-ads-than-ever/?utm_term=.769b7d135e7b (last accessed August 2017)

14. Global Industry Analysts, Inc. The US Direct-to-Consumer (DTC) Advertising in Pharmaceuticals to Reach US$11.4 Billion by 2017. Available at http://www.prweb.com/releases/direct_to_consumer_dtc/pharma_advertising/prweb8831454.htm (last accessed August 2017)

15. Pharmalive: The Pulse of Pharmaceutical Industry. DTC Ad Spend by Media Type in 2015. Available at http://www.pharmalive.com/dtc-ad-spend-by-media-type-in-2015/ (last accessed August 2017)

16. Horovitz B, Appleby J. Prescription drug costs are up; so are TV ads promoting them. USA Today. March 16, 2017. Available at https://www.usatoday.com/story/money/2017/03/16/prescription-drug-costs-up-tv-ads/99203878 (last accessed August 2017)

17. U.S. Food and Drug Administration. Basics of Drug Ads. Available at https://www.fda.gov/Drugs/ResourcesForYou/Consumers/PrescriptionDrugAdvertising/ucm072077.htm (last accessed August 2017)

18. Kroll D. FDA admonishes drug maker over Kim Kardashian Instagram endorsement. Forbes August 11, 2015. Available at https://www.forbes.com/sites/davidkroll/2015/08/11/fda-spanks-drug-maker-over-kim-kardashian-instagram-endorsement/#526dbfa3587b (accessed 15 August 2017)

19. Bleidt B. Recent issues and concerns about pharmaceutical industry promotional efforts. *Journal of Drug Issues J Drug Issues* 1992; 22

https://doi.org/10.7175/747.ch13

13. Pharmaceutical Market in Canada: a Brief Treatise

Barry A. Bleidt[1], Annette Vidal[2]

[1] *Professor, Sociobehavioral and Administrative Pharmacy. College of Pharmacy Nova Southeastern University, Fort Lauderdale, FL, USA*
[2] *Pharm.D. Candidate, Class of 2019. College of Pharmacy Nova Southeastern University, Fort Lauderdale, FL, USA*

13.1 Introduction

Canada is the largest country in North America in area and the second largest in the world. It is classified as a federal parliamentary democracy/constitutional monarchy having Queen Elizabeth II of the United Kingdom as its head of state. With a population of nearly 37 million, it is the 38th largest country and has the 10th largest Gross Domestic Product (GDP) of 1.5 trillion dollars (U.S.). Canada has the fourth highest per capita expenditure on pharmaceuticals [1].

The purpose of this chapter is to discuss the Canadian pharmaceutical market. First, this chapter will discuss the overall healthcare system in Canada. Then, a more specific description of the Canadian Drug Market will follow. Next, there will be an account of the drug approval process and prescription drug pricing. The Chapter will conclude with a brief treatise of the prescription drug promotion in Canada.

13.2 Canadian Healthcare System

Canada's publicly funded healthcare system was enacted by the Canadian Health Act of 1984 and is informally known as Medicare. Under established federal guidelines, the healthcare system is locally administered by ten provincial and three territorial governments. Therefore, there are thirteen different health insurance plans across the country rather than just one national plan. All Canadian citizens are entitled to reasonable access to preventive care and medically necessary medical treatments from physicians with no out-of-pocket expense [2]. They are also entitled to hospital services, dental surgery, and other medical services with few exceptions regardless of personal income or medical history.

Canada is the only country in the world that has universal health care, but no universal drug coverage. As a result, Canadian patented drug prices are among the highest in the world. Provinces and Territories have established programs of varying comprehensiveness for senior patients (those over 65) and the poor. Around two-thirds of Canadians pay for and have private health insurance to cover items exempted from public reimbursement, such as prescription drugs [2].

13.3 Canadian Drug Market

Most of the Canadian health expenditures (60%) are paid to hospitals, physicians, and pharmaceuticals. Drugs are the second largest component of overall healthcare costs, accounting for 16% of the total. Overall sales of pharmaceutical are now about $25 billion (in Canadian dollars). Canada is the 10th largest pharmaceutical market place in the world and accounts for 2% of the worldwide market. Branded products make-up 77% of the overall sales (in dollars) and generic drugs comprise 66% of the total prescription volume with 87.5% of the sales taking place in community pharmacies. Private prescription drug insurance and individuals account for 58% of all drug expenditures with the federal, provincial, and territorial governments paying for 42% [3]. The annual pharmaceutical manufacturing production domestically was approximately $9.8 billion. Over 50% of all Canadian pharmaceutical production is exported, with the United States being the largest importer. Over two-thirds of the Canadian drug market is imported, mostly from the United States and secondarily from the European Union [3]. Four of the provinces, Alberta, British Columbia, Ontario, and Québec, account for nearly 85% of all expenditures on drugs. Canadian pharmaceutical manufacturers are concentrated in the country's three largest metropolitan areas of Vancouver, Montreal, and Toronto [3].

13.4 Drug Approval Process

Canada has its own unique regulatory approval procedures for prescription drugs, which includes multiple phases and involves several federal government agencies [4]. Pharmaceutical products cannot be sold in Canada until they have successfully navigated the drug review and approval process. The Health Products and Food Branch (HPFB) of Health Canada assesses the safety and efficacy of drug products as well as their quality parameters. HPFB is the federal agency that is responsible for the regulation and evaluation of diagnostic and therapeutic products sold in Canada. In procedures similar to the United States Food and Drug Administration's assessment of a New Drug Application, Health Canada reviews a drug for its quality, safety, and efficacy profiles [5]. The process includes:
- Evaluating the results of submitted preclinical and clinical studies;
- Reviewing manufacturing and production details and guidelines for Good Manufacturing Practices;
- Revising packaging and labeling;

- Examining efficacy and safety claims; and
- Assessing all information pertinent to the drug.

Regulatory approval is granted in the form of a Notice of Compliance (NOC). On average, it takes approximately 12 years from the initial laboratory work.

Once a NOC is issued for a product, the next step is a review by the Patented Medicine Prices Review Board (PMPRB). A manufacturer can establish a price for its drug as it is launched. If the product is patented, however, the amount charged to patients must be within the range fixed by the PMPRB. If the launch price exceeds the limits set, PMPRB has options to reign in the manufacturer's price [6]. It is the PMPRB's function to protect Canadians by safeguarding them from excessive prices on patented medicines. Thirty-seven New Active Substances were approved in 2016 [7] and 37 in 2015 [8].

The final step in the new drug review process is the Common Drug Review performed by the Canadian Agency for Drugs and Technologies in Health. These health technology assessments evaluate the cost-effectiveness and clinical efficacy of new drugs in order to make a recommendation as to whether the drug should be publicly funded [7].

Canadian regulation of pharmaceutical products continues even after a drug is being sold to the public. Manufacturers are accountable for monitoring the safety and quality of their products under the Canadian Food and Drugs Act. They must report all new data collected on serious side effects, including product failures to work as indicated [9].

13.5 Prescription Drug Pricing

Even with the PMPRB review process, Canadian's pay the third highest prices in the world for patented medicines. Among the 35 member countries of the Organization for Economic Co-operation and Development, only citizens of Mexico and the United States pay more. There are millions of self-employed Canadians who do not have workplace drug coverage.

It is estimated that one in ten Canadians (about 3.6 million people) cannot afford their prescription drugs. Additionally, all payers in Canada are struggling with the dramatic increase in the number of high-cost new drugs on the market [10].

13.6 Prescription Drug Promotion

Pharmaceutical promotion in Canada has many similarities to those undertaken in the United States [5]. One key difference is that Canada does not permit direct-to-consumer advertising (DTCA) of prescription drugs. While Canada is a very large country in area, nearly 90% of the population lives within 100 miles of the border with the U.S. There is a significant broadcast, cable, and print media "bleeding" of DTCA across the Canadian border.

As a result, over 50% of Canadians believe that DTCA is legal in Canada. This spill-over effect mitigates the Canadian government's efforts to protect Canadians from these ads. It also provides an opportunity for pro-DTCA forces to criticize Canadian restrictions as ineffective. DTCA from the United States are not pre-cleared by the U. S. FDA, so these unregulated commercials reach Canadians through cable television. The primary objections to DTCA revolve around harm and costs. Many DTCAs promote products with health warnings that are severe and several of the products have been removed from the market for causing health problems. There appears to be a direct correlation between volumes of costly TV ads and drug costs [11].

13.7 **In Summary**

Unimaginable, worldwide influences are causing significant disruption to the healthcare systems. As with other pharmaceutical markets, the Canadian marketplace is undergoing rapid and remarkable changes. The high prices of new biologic products are putting tremendous pressure on both the public and private system of financing prescription drugs.

In Canada, as well as elsewhere, high drug prices are an emotional, volatile, and political issue. Solutions to this situation are yet to be found and could pose a hurdle to market access. Canada has a complex health system, which has variances from Province to Province (and territory to territory). These differences could possibly create barriers to market access as well.

13.8 **References**

1. Oyedele A. One chart shows how much Americans are spending on drugs compared to the rest of the world. Business Insiders. November 4, 2015. Available at http://www.businessinsider.com/pharmaceutical-spending-by-country-2015-11 (last accessed October 2017)
2. Government of Canada. Canada's Health Care System. Available at https://www.canada.ca/en/health-canada/services/canada-health-care-system.html (last accessed October 2017)
3. Government of Canada. Pharmaceutical Industry Profile. Available at http://www.ic.gc.ca/eic/site/lsg-pdsv.nsf/eng/h_hn01703.html (last accessed October 2017)
4. Government of Canada. How Drugs Are Reviewed in Canada. Available at https://www.canada.ca/en/health-canada/services/drugs-health-products/drug-products/fact-sheets/drugs-reviewed-canada.html (last accessed October 2017)
5. Bleidt BA. Pharmaceutical Market in the U.S.: A Brief Treatise. In Kockaya G, Wertheimer A (Eds). Pharmaceutical Market Access in Developed Market. Turin: SEEd Medical Publishers, 2018

6. Government of Canada. Patented Medicine Prices Review Board. Available at http://www.pmprb-cepmb.gc.ca/home (last accessed October 2017)
7. Health Canada. New Drug Authorizations: 2016 Highlights. Available at https://www.canada.ca/content/dam/hc-sc/documents/services/publications/drugs-health-products/health-canada-new-drug-authorizations-2016-highlights-eng.pdf (last accessed October 2017)
8. Health Canada. New Drug Authorizations: 2015 Highlights. https://www.canada.ca/content/dam/canada/health-canada/migration/healthy-canadians/publications/drugs-products-medicaments-produits/2015-highlights-faitssaillants/alt/2015-highlights-faitssaillants-eng.pdf (last accessed October 2017)
9. Health Canada. Health Products and Food Branch. Access to Therapeutic Products: The Regulatory Process in Canada. Available at http://publications.gc.ca/collections/collection_2007/hc-sc/H164-9-2006E.pdf (last accessed October 2017)
10. Government of Canada. Protecting Canadians from Excessive Drug Prices: Consulting on Proposed Amendments to the Patented Medicines Regulations. Available at https://www.canada.ca/content/dam/hc-sc/documents/programs/consultation-regulations-patented-medicine-document/con1-eng.pdf (last accessed October 2017)
11. Chow EC. Direct-to-Consumer Advertising of Pharmaceuticals on Television: A Charter Challenge. *Canadian Journal of Law and Technology* 2011; 9: 73-91

https://doi.org/10.7175/747.ch14

14. Market Access Hurdles in Developed Countries

Mete Şaylan[1], Özge Dokuyucu[2]
[1] MACS Director, Bayer, Istanbul, Turkey
[2] Amgen, Istanbul, Turkey

14.1 Introduction

In most countries, the current and future healthcare challenges are set against concerns over healthcare budget growth, due to the aging population, an increased incidence of chronic diseases, and an easier access to a large repository of health information. On the other side, the rapid pace of therapeutic innovation (advanced therapies, personalized medicines, gene therapies, tissue engineering) and the rising costs of innovation in healthcare (the ever-growing complexity and cost of clinical trials, companion diagnostics, genomic profiling, the requirements for post-launch observational studies) make the prices of medicinal products inevitably higher. Rising healthcare costs represent an unsustainable trajectory for payers in the developed markets, which created additional hurdles for Pharma companies in ensuring access to new medicines. Until a few decades ago, only safety and efficacy guided the decisions about the reimbursement of medicines,

Delaying access and controlling demand	Increasing negotiation power for better pricing
• Prioritization in GMP audits • Long review processes • Forced localization • Cost-benefit assessment for smaller patient groups • Additional real-life data requirements • Outcomes-based MEA • Regional/hospital HTA • Local/National reimbursement guidelines • Import license renewals/limits	• Joint procurement/central tendering • Hospital formularies • Financial-based MEA • Efficiency analysis • Cost-effectiveness and budget impact analysis • Unofficial price data sharing • Therapeutic equivalence class • Reference pricing

Figure 1. Categorization of Market Access Hurdles
GMP = Good Manufacturing Practice; MEA = Managed Entry Agreement

whereas today decisions are made based on cost-containment rationales. As a result of these challenges, market access hurdles for medicinal products have become more diversified in the last two decades, and they can be categorized into two major types (Figure 1), based on the payers' needs and capabilities:

1. Delaying access (long review processes, real-life data requirements, cost-benefit assessment for smaller patient groups, prioritization in Good Manufacturing Practice audits before registration submissions, unscheduled Review Committee Meetings, regional/hospital reviews, outcome-based managed entry agreements) and controlling demand (local reimbursement guidelines, import license renewals/limits, forced localization).

2. Increasing negotiation power for better pricing (cost-effectiveness and budget impact analysis, joint procurement, central tendering, separate budgeting, hospital formularies, efficiency analysis, therapeutic equivalence class, joint Health Technology Assessment initiatives, unofficial price data sharing, reference pricing, financially based managed entry agreements).

Delaying Access and Controlling Demand

Before the 1990s, efficacy, safety, and quality were the key parameters when deciding the reimbursement of new therapies. Once a drug was registered in a country, it was automatically reimbursed and became available to patients, as per its label. Hospital formulary listing was the only barrier for budget holders considering the price of the new drug, which was influenced by prescribing physicians convinced of its clinical benefit. Starting

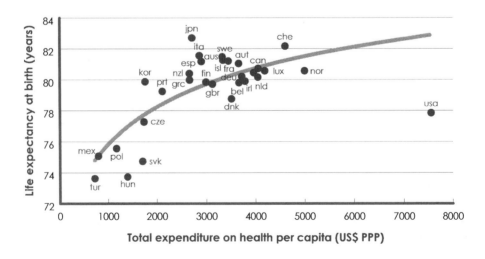

Figure 2. Differences in life expectancy and healthcare spending across OECD countries. Modified from [OECD 2010]

from the 1990s, efficiency became more important: with the increase in healthcare expenditure, the improvement of effectiveness in the use of limited resources, in order to find the best way to support a high quality of care, gained more importance for policymakers. Multiple perspectives were developed to avoid any overuse/misuse, and waste of resources, and the three new data requirements for the evaluation of new products became cost-effectiveness, budget impact, and quality of life. Since 2010, value has become the key factor, so value-based healthcare has become an emerging new paradigm to control costs while ensuring the quality of care. It is fundamental to boost innovation on the part of the suppliers, in order to create value for patients and improve their outcomes.

The concept of value obtained by reducing inefficiencies without compromising the access to quality has emerged as a patient-centric approach, and gained even more importance. Achieving value for money in the healthcare sector is an important objective in developed countries. OECD estimated that the average life expectancy could increase by about two years for the OECD as a whole, if resources were used more efficiently. It was reported that countries that spend the most are not necessarily the ones that fare best in terms of healthcare outcomes. Policy reforms able to increase value for money, in order to increase efficiency, have become one of the top priorities.

One of the most common mechanisms used by payers is to delay access to the market for new and expensive treatments and reduce the volume by trying to control their consumptions. Because of these efforts, a paradigm change occurred, evolving from the traditional payment model based on fee-for-service to value-based healthcare. The traditional system provides incentives for the volume of service performed: this gave rise to concerns about increasing costs and poor performance on quality indicators. Therefore, hospital administrators, private insurance schemes, and public care providers started a transition towards value-based payment models in order to improve healthcare outcomes. New funding and distribution mechanisms for high-cost medicines (i.e., managed entry agreements) have become a tool to provide certainty about the performance of a new treatment for clinical outcomes and the patient health status, including physiologic and mortality measures. Many Pharma companies and medical device manufacturers started using these innovative agreements, which vary across many forms of deal, including shared risk, bundled payments, and volume capitation, in order to overcome the access challenges.

With the introduction of the new funding mechanisms, developing evidence and demonstrating outcomes in real-world studies gained increasingly more importance, because of the possibility to show both the clinical and economic superiority of the new technology vs. the existing alternatives. Furthermore, hospital-level HTA has emerged to improve productivity gains by focusing on the efforts to understand, quantify and improve the efficiency and value in the delivery of healthcare services, taking into account not only drugs and devices but also personal time, supplies and interventions. Many quality and efficiency measures have been introduced in hospitals, ranging from internal quality improvement measures, pay-for-performance incentive schemes, and physician treatment guidelines, including reimbursement guidelines, especially for new technologies. While these tools and measures have increased value gained from technologies, the time needed for assessment has delayed access to innovation. In order to reduce market access delays, drug manufacturers should work on data generation, setting value-based criteria for reimbursement, conducting health economics models with payers at different levels.

Increasing Negotiation Power for Better Pricing

Despite the efforts implemented by the European Commission to expedite the pricing and reimbursement procedures among European Union member countries, the opposition from national governments and members of the European Parliament steadily increased the average delays and time gaps among the countries. In 2002, the EU Commission and the Health Council (consisting of the Health Ministers from the EU Member States) actively supported cross-border collaboration in health technology assessment, which could partly accelerate market access and decrease the gaps between the countries. Finally, in 2004, the European Commission and the Council of Ministers positioned Health Technology Assessment (HTA) as a political priority and urged the establishment of a sustainable European network on HTA. In 2005, 35 organizations throughout Europe answered the European Commission's call and the EUnetHTA Project initial activities started. EUnetHTA Project aims to support the collaboration between European HTA organizations and bring added value to healthcare systems at European, national and regional level. Throughout its activities, this project developed alliances and cooperation among HTA organizations. A report adopted by European Parliament in March 2017 once again highlighted the delays between Marketing Authorization and the subsequent decisions on pricing and reimbursement, the unavailability of products due to budget constraints and the high prices of new technologies and the inequalities of access among countries and regions.

Although there are strategic actions for improving the quality and timing of the technologic review process, pricing and affordability remain the most important reasons behind the real barriers to access. Alternative pricing methods were developed to overcome the payers' concerns at product launch and issues with the international reference pricing. Besides, EU explicitly stated the need for the new approaches to control the increasing financial pressure of new high-priced medicines, to improve patients' access to medicines and to promote innovation. The report "Study on enhanced cross-country coordination in the area of pharmaceutical product pricing", published by the European Commission in December 2015, focused on the international reference pricing, and proposed solutions based on sharing net prices, EU coordination mechanism and mechanism for differential prices. Experts recognized the difficulties in implementing the proposed mechanism (such as political will, legal constraints, agreements between the Member States) and the ineffectiveness of these measures in improving the access to medicines. Again, they came up with the proposal of implementing new pricing policies, such as joint procurement initiatives, which were not within the scope of the EU report. Joint procurement proposals were also mentioned by other international organizations and by politicians: in January 2016, OECD claimed pharmaceutical companies have excessive power in price negotiations, and recommended new approaches to fight the upward trend of launch prices. In March 2016, at the G7 meeting, France proposed other price-control solutions for innovative medicines, and other European ministers explicitly supported the idea by forming new collaborations and bilateral agreements (Benelux and Austria collaboration, Central and Eastern European collaboration, Mediterranean Countries collaboration, Nordic collaboration, Portugal and Spain bilateral agreement for sharing experience and data). Joint procurement discussions, aimed at strengthening the purchasing power of payers, spread out quickly in other regions of the world (Latin America, Eurasia). The Joint procurement related price control mechanism increased the concerns of the life science companies about the payers' deliberate efforts to decelerate the access to new expensive medicines by creating another hurdle, along with the national and regional ones.

14.2 Regional Access Hurdles

In the last decade, with the political empowerment of the regions and the trends for shifting central fiscal discipline to the regions (10 provinces in Canada, 6 states in Australia, 16 lander in Germany, 21 regions in Italy, 17 regions in Spain, 12 regions in Netherland, 21 counties in Sweden) for a more effective control of the health spending, regionalization in healthcare funding became more prominent even in highly centralized countries. However, initial price negotiations remained in the hand of the national authorities, and additional price and volume control mechanism are used by regional payers according to their capabilities and purchasing powers. The growth of regional payers may not be only a simple replication of the national decisions, and regional payers may use different methods to evaluate health technologies, by focusing on other components of market access (i.e., cost-effectiveness for nationwide decision vs. budget impact in the regions. The variety of the decisional analysis tools used by regional payers and their negotiating power require companies to develop different pricing and reimbursement approaches and data types. While payers at national level can decide on issues such as initial Marketing Authorization, prices and reimbursed population, payers at regional level can effect entry date, local marketing activities, restrictions to prescriptions, local recommendations for physicians, physician-company interactions for promotional activities, creation of therapeutic areas. Decision-makers, influencers, and content of data requirements also vary among regions, making market access processes more complex. From the patient's perspective, there is a growing risk of access inequalities due to different efforts by central governments to control regional budgets.

Hospital-Based HTA

Hospital-based HTA is a relatively new concept, which was developed after a nationwide discussion on the impact on end users of large-scale HTAs. It basically consists of the implementation of processes and methods of HTA at hospital level. Although it's generally performed with the resources of the hospitals, it can also be outsourced to independent HTA bodies. It is developed to answer the questions by hospital managers or budget holders relating to the implementation of new technologies and the efficient use of existing technologies in their hospitals. The main objective of the hospitals is the critical appraisal of health technologies on effectiveness, tolerability and reducing overall costs and

Pros	Cons
• List prices to remain at launch price and **minimized risks of international reference pricing**. • Risks on the payer's side are minimized by **reducing the element of uncertainty** of product performance. • Generate evidence in the real-world setting. • Gain market access **without compromising on the launch price** of the drug. • Pay-for-performance schemes **foster price negotiations by reinforcing value messages**. • Conditional reimbursement based on **registry enrolment reduces inappropriate/off-label use**. • Price-volume agreements provide more **stable pricing and reimbursement environment** and offer payers a **budget impact predictability**. • Price-volume agreements can be used as a cost containment tools, together with **prescribing control mechanisms**. • Performance schemes associated with patient responses may influence the **earlier uptake by physicians**. • Patient-based caps encourage the **adherence to label**, to produce maximum response. • Investments in **innovation are boosted**. • Payers have the **flexibility to limit the impact of the introduction of new drugs**, together with horizon scanning activities and price revisions based on post-marketing surveillance.	• **Additional resources and investment** needed to monitor patients or to comply with the agreement conditions by manufacturer, provider, and payer. • **Additional costs** are incurred in managing the schemes. • Manufacturer may be responsible for the **loss of non-responding patients**. • Payers may propose to use data management systems set to monitor patients' clinical progress as **cost management tool**. • Negotiations with payers start at a higher price level at launch, if manufacturers foresee the **risk of price cuts based on the outcomes**. • Price-volume agreements may not ensure an **on-label or appropriate use**. • Schemes do not remove **all financial uncertainties of use** (high demand, resulting in greater-than-anticipated long-term costs). • Schemes may restrict patient access to products, due to the **administrative hurdles in real-life**. • Not **all schemes are useful for patient access** (e.g. limited access if budget cap is reached). • Difficulty to set **stopping rules for agreement or for the withdrawal of the product** when unsuccessful. • **Duplicated and fragmented data collection** efforts for multiple countr Countries.

Table 1. Summary of the pros & cons of performance/outcomes-based managed entry agreements

ensuring the rational use of their resources. Joint decisions made by hospital groups also involve a decrease in the geographical variation in the availability and access to health technologies. There are many reasons for the emergence of hospital-based HTA: global/national recommendations of existing HTA agencies may not answer precise local questions, long assessment periods for national decisions delay the access to expensive new technologies at large research hospitals, all technologies are not evaluated at national level, but they can be medically or economically critical at hospital level. Unfortunately, the lack of transferability of the results in hospital-based HTA causes the duplication of work, with several medical institutions evaluating the same technology. Despite the increasing use of hospital-based HTA, there is limited know-how about its practice and impact. HTA at this level can also be considered as a threat to restrict the clinicians' independence in decision-making. Because of the slow assessment process, when considering critical health results of new technologies, clinicians are not willing to wait for months for a decision. A more frequent use of hospital-based HTA and its wider implementation could help national HTA agencies benefit from their work and observe the results of nationwide decisions at patient level. It should be supported by a political and managerial willingness to smooth out implementation issues and by a reformist approach to the local decision-making processes. Nevertheless, hospital-based HTA practices are progressively increasing, therefore experts in the area already noticed the need for guiding principles and organizational models .

Managed Entry Agreements

Managed Entry Agreements (MEAs) are accepted, at least in theory, as an enabler for pharmaceutical companies to gain earlier market access, and as an opportunity for a fast access to innovation by patients. However, in practice, this process can be transformed into a never-ending vicious cycle of negotiation. There are comparable pros and cons for the implementation of MEAs (Table 1). Due to these risks and difficulties, the industry and the payers have become more and more reluctant to use them.

In most countries, MEAs have been implemented upon the manufacturers' request to facilitate the negotiation process. For instance, in Italy there is no specific law regulating the process; rather, it is decided on a case-by-case basis. However, the Italian Medicines Agency (AIFA) implemented different types of MEAs for each newly launched medicine that presents some uncertainty with regard to clinical effectiveness, budget impact, or potentially inappropriate use. In the UK, MEA proposals are the responsibility of the pharmaceutical companies. Companies can propose MEAs either at the time of the initial submission for assessment, or at the end of the evaluation process. There are no well-defined timelines for implementation, and the average duration of the process varies among the countries and depending on the type of MEA. A lengthy process can create a bottleneck for a timely access to innovative medicines. In any case, it has gained more importance, and there has been a steady growth in the number of agreements implemented.

14.3 **The Next Challenges**

The rapid pace of therapeutic innovation and advanced technologies might substantially extend the survival times, and even cure severe chronic diseases. However, delayed access and price pressures are expected to continue as long as the payers' concerns on budget pressure persist. While drug companies are trying to meet the decision-makers' expectation on the demonstration of the value of innovation, they are exploring new ways of doing business with the spread of digitalization and the empowerment of patients to make informed healthcare decisions. Patient-centric approaches are becoming more and more common, to increase the demand for healthcare services despite the demand control mechanism induced by payers. Digital solutions are becoming critical to meet the needs of patients, to ensure adherence to treatment, and to show outcomes that meet the payers' expectation. Thus, Pharma companies are increasing the use of digital technologies to obtain real-world efficacy data.

With the recent evolution of the business model, the importance of the patients' decision in the choice of their treatment is increasing. It also enables payers to implement risk-sharing schemes based on adherence, daily measured criteria, and quality of life. Policy-makers should establish an infrastructure for the management and digitalization of information, and encourage value-based competition. by reducing new entry barriers. Rapid assessments and common databases can also be used to decrease the discrepancy between HTAs carried out by different bodies, to ensure a timely access to medicines on the part of patients.

14.4 **In summary**

- Price pressure will continue to affect budget holders and the business, economic and scientific methods used to increase decision-making efficiency.
- The decision levels will increase and access will be inevitably delayed.
- Equity in access will remain problematic, because of reimbursement filters by different local and regional payers, and across countries.
- The lack of coordination among layers/regions/countries is obvious, but efforts will continue towards harmonization.
- Financial risk will shift more towards Pharma companies, increasing access hurdles.
- Hurdles start before registration in many low affordability markets with other methods of supply restrictions (GMP, import quotas, forced localization).
- After launch, there are continuous barriers: price reviews, reimbursement restrictions, delisting.
- Digitalization will continue to emerge daily, to increase health literacy and the generation of patient-driven demand for informed decision-making.

14.5 **Bibliography**

- Kogels E, Nuijten MJC. The Emerging Hurdles For Reimbursement And Market Access For New Innovative Pharmaceuticals. ISPOR Connections 2009; 15. Available at https://www.ispor.org/news/articles/Sept09/EHFR.asp (last accessed September 2017)
- Porter ME, Olmstead Teisberg E. Redefining Health Care: Creating Value-Based Competition on Results. Boston, MA: Harvard Business School Press, 2006
- OECD. Health care systems: Getting more value for money. OECD Economics Department Policy Notes 2010; 2. Available at https://www.oecd.org/eco/growth/46508904.pdf (last accessed September 2017)
- Charles River Associates. Assessing the wider benefits of the EU's proposal on strengthening cooperation on health technology assessment from the industry perspective. July, 2017. Available at https://www.efpia.eu/media/219813/cra-efpia-european-cooperation-on-hta-impact-assessment-final-report-july-2017-stc.pdf (last accessed September 2017)
- McGregor M, Brophy JM. End-user involvement in health technology assessment (HTA) development: a way to increase impact. *Int J Technol Assess Health Care* 2005; 21: 263-7
- Sampietro-Colom L, Lach K, Pasternack I, et al. Guiding principles for good practices in hospital based health technology assessment units. *Int J Technol Assess Health Care* 2015; 31: 457-65
- European Commission Study on enhanced cross-country coordination in the area of pharmaceutical product pricing. Luxembourg: Publications Office of the European Union, 2015. Available at https://ec.europa.eu/health/sites/health/files/systems_performance_assessment/docs/pharmaproductpricing_frep_en.pdf (last accessed September 2017)

https://doi.org/10.7175/747.ch15

15. Role of Health Technology Assessment in Pharmaceutical Market Access in Developed Countries

Rabia Kahveci[1], **Wija Oortwijn**[2,3], **Brian Godman**[4,5,6], **E. Meltem Koç**[7], **Birol Tibet**[8]

[1] Ministry of Health Ankara Numune Hospital Health Technology Assessment Unit, Ankara, Turkey
[2] Ecorys Nederland, Rotterdam, The Netherlands
[3] Department for Health Evidence, Radboud University Medical Center, Nijmegen, The Netherlands
[4] Strathclyde Institute of Pharmacy and Biomedical Sciences, University of Strathclyde, Glasgow G4 0RE, United Kingdom
[5] Division of Clinical Pharmacology, Karolinska Institute, Karolinska University Hospital Huddinge, SE-141 86, Stockholm, Sweden
[6] Health Economics Centre, University of Liverpool Management School, Liverpool, UK.
[7] Department of Family Medicine, Izmir Katip Celebi University, Izmir, Turkey
[8] Department of Health Economics and Financing Policies, Turkish Institute for Health Policies, Health Institutes of Turkey, Ankara, Turkey

15.1 Introduction

Introduction and use of a health technology in a health care setting has clinical, economic, as well as organizational, social-cultural, legal and ethical impacts. Health Technology Assessment (HTA) is a multidisciplinary field that addresses these impacts, considering the healthcare context as well as available alternatives. HTA mainly aims to inform policy and clinical decision making. While systematically evaluating the effects of the health technology, HTA addresses direct and intended effects as well as the indirect and unintended effects. It is a multidisciplinary field with well-developed systematic processes and methods [1,2].

A health technology is defined as an intervention that may be used to promote health, to prevent, diagnose or treat acute or chronic disease, or for rehabilitation. Health technologies include pharmaceuticals, devices, diagnostics, procedures and other clinical, public health and organizational interventions [1,2].

Before a health technology is provided to the right patient, who could benefit from it at an affordable price, traditionally several hurdles are faced: the efficacy and safety of a health technology need to be proven; and must be produced with a high quality. These three are necessary for marketing authorization. The fourth hurdle, being assessed for cost-effectiveness, is often a payer's requirement for reimbursement. HTA is mostly done or requested by relevant authorities to assess how the new product compares with the current alternatives and whether it adds value. Perhaps a decade ago, the distinction was more straightforward and the fourth hurdle was separated from the first three. But today the processes are more integrated and redesigned to provide earlier access to valuable technologies.

Health authorities across countries, including western countries, are finding it increasingly difficult to fund all new premium priced medicines [3]. The situation is exacerbated by changing demographics, increasing prevalence of chronic diseases especially non-communicable diseases, the continued launch of new premium priced medicines to address existing unmet need adding to therapeutic complexities, alongside population fragmentation with increasing knowledge of pharmacogenomics, as well as rising patient expectations [4-6].

In this chapter, we aim to explore HTA's role in market access with specific examples from different countries. In line with the scope of the book, we will focus on the pharmaceuticals and developed markets only. We will outline how HTA might lead to different outcomes in different settings and cover new possibilities and challenges to be addressed.

15.2 History of HTA

A healthy society plays a key role in the development of a country and this makes health services one of the most important indicators of a countries' development level [7,8]. The fundamental purpose of healthcare services is to provide the public with equal access to high quality and timely services at a sustainable cost [4,8]. The organization of healthcare and funding systems differ according to the socioeconomic conditions and political context of the relevant country [5,9].

As countries develop economically, health technologies advance rapidly. Rapid developments increase the demand for health care services, and consequently health expenditure dynamics increase [9].

The rapid diffusion of health technologies challenges governments to provide high quality, equal and accessible care for the citizens while managing the health care budgets effectively. Questions about the effectiveness of experimental technologies, as well as increased health care expenditures and restricted health care budgets, led to the development of HTA [10].

Health Technology Assessment became a concept in 1976; it initially spread from the United States (U.S.) to Western Europe and in recent years HTA is rapidly developing worldwide. In 1967, HTA was first used as a term in United States Congress [11]. In 1972, the U.S. Congressional Office of Technology Assessment (OTA) was established and OTA initiated a health program in 1974. During this program OTA published eighty different HTA reports [12], especially focusing on efficacy, safety, and cost-effectiveness [13]. The early products of OTA and evidence based reviews derived by the Cochrane Collaboration displayed the most important roles on shaping the field of HTA.

Inspired by the reports of OTA, The Swedish Council on Technology Assessment in Health Care (SBU) started HTA development in Europe [13]. This first period of synthesizing the available evidence with efficacy and cost-effectiveness supported policy-makers in national health programmes with regard to evidence-informed decision-making [11] After 1985, HTA has gradually spread to nearly all western and southern European countries, then to Central Europe, Latin America, and Asia. International organizations such as the World Bank, World Health Organization (WHO), International Society of Technology Assessment in Health Care (ISTAHC), its successor Health Technology Assessment International (HTAi), and the International Network of Agencies for Health Technology Assessment (INAHTA) all benefit the development and use of HTA [13].

15.3 **HTA and Market Access**

Market access is defined as "openness of a country's markets to foreign goods and services" [14]. Although this is the basic definition, pharmaceutical market access can be considered as a longer and comprehensive process. This is a challenging process where many stakeholders are involved. Processes such as HTA, pricing and reimbursement; industry processes such as R&D, registration, marketing authorization and launch might impact the access process [15]. Furthermore, although there are common frameworks to demonstrate the quality, safety and efficacy of a product, there remains fragmentation regarding marketing authorization applications across the countries in Europe [5].

Due to financial crisis or economic concerns, governments face difficult times and priorities need increasingly to be set given the extent of unmet need that still exists [4,16]. Especially, the last decade has witnessed cost-cuts and increased price negotiations and in this context, HTA has been increasingly recognized to meet policymakers' needs by providing them information on the costs and benefits of drugs. Although the focus lies on providing value for money, it has been quite hard to measure value, interpret it and have data on the appropriate impact on the outcome [17].

HTA serves the purpose of providing policymakers with reliable assessments of the pharmaceuticals that would reflect the real world, but also will aid the manufacturers to prove the value of the drugs they have produced. HTA might highlight the drugs that are expensive compared to their benefits, or might outline the indications and patient groups that would have additional value. Unsafe and ineffective drugs will also be discovered during these processes, leading to active dissemination [18-20].

15.4 HTA, Regulation, Pricing and Reimbursement of Pharmaceuticals

It is relatively easier to harmonize regulatory processes across countries, while pricing and reimbursement decisions on pharmaceuticals depend more on the local context [4,5,21]. For example, it is very difficult to translate cost-effectiveness from one setting to another. Furthermore, the political and health care context, national/regional priorities and social values differ across countries, making it more complex to transfer the outcomes of HTA evaluations. This is quite challenging for the manufacturers as they need to understand expectations of HTA organizations which may vary from country to country. To address this, for instance European countries are seeking to collaborate on HTA assessments (EUnetHTA – discussed later) as well as trying to find ways to collaborate on methodology development and approaches regarding earlier access to medicines including adaptive pathways, and several stakeholders are involved in this collaboration. The approaches will further be explored later in this chapter.

In many countries, pricing and reimbursement decisions are taken at the national level. The manufacturer needs to submit a dossier for this purpose after obtaining marketing authorization; i.e. a license issued by a medicines agency approving a medicine for market use based on a determination by authorities that the medicine meets agreed requirements of quality, safety and efficacy for human use in therapeutic treatment [5]. Many countries use HTA to subsequently guide or inform the pricing and reimbursement processes by assessing the drug's benefits compared to its alternatives alongside cost considerations [21]. In addition to clinical and economic aspects, increasingly other aspects related to the use of a particular medicine are considered. In certain cases, such as life-threatening conditions or orphan diseases, the assessment might find limited evidence or low cost-effectiveness, but the (unmet) need might be high as there are limited therapeutic alternatives. In this case, HTA can be used as a tool to support prioritization ensuring a more rational investment of funds, based on social needs and policy priorities [22]. HTA seems to be the preferred strategy as it addresses both price and appropriate indications for the use of the medicine and the relation between additional value and additional costs [4,22,23].

HTA might inform policymakers about different options and scenarios where there is more flexibility on pricing and reimbursement policies. Rather than an absolute yes or no to reimbursement, companies might need to bring in more evidence to showing benefit on certain conditions. The increasing number of high-priced drugs has started to challenge even wealthier countries to develop policies on how to improve access to medicines in an affordable way. Europe, for example, has set this issue high on their agenda [4,24]. This led to innovative ways of pricing and reimbursing pharmaceuticals, such as value based pricing or managed entry agreements [4,5,25]. These approaches, especially managed entry agreements, were created to enable access to (coverage/reimbursement of) a product subject to specified conditions, such as price negotiations. While this is a way to provide access to the drug, it risks transparency and transferability at the global level [4,25]. We will discuss this further in this chapter.

The European Commission has financially supported several HTA projects to promote the collaboration between Member States (MS) in the European Union (EU) since 1993 [4]. The European Commission and Council of Ministers designated HTA as "a political priority" in 2004, recognizing «[...] an urgent need for establishing a sustainable European network on HTA» [26]. EUnetHTA has coordinated these activities since 2006. EUnetHTA is defined as a «network of government appointed organizations [from EU MS, EU-accession countries, plus European Economic Area (EEA) and European Free Trade Association (EFTA) countries] and a large number of relevant regional agencies and non-for-profit organizations that produce or contribute to HTA in Europe». The collaboration has already resulted in methodological guidelines and tools such as the HTA Core Model – a methodological framework for shared production and use of HTA information in the era of diagnostic technologies, medical and surgical interventions, drugs and screening technologies. The purpose is «to enable production of high quality HTA information in a structured format to support the production of local (national or regional) HTAs and re-use of existing information». HTA organizations use this model as the value framework when assessing technologies within the EU [27].

Since 2009, EUnetHTA collaborated with the European Union and the European Commission partners to administer joint assessments and implement the results. EUnetHTA has finished 20 joint assessments until 2015. This cooperation on HTA projects has the potential to increase the quality of HTA. An assessment can be done in two different ways; a rapid Relative Effectiveness Assessment (REA) and a full HTA. We can evaluate the incremental therapeutic value of technologies with a rapid REA; however, a full HTA has a broader perspective. A rapid REA covers the following domains: health problem and current use of technology, description and technical characteristics, safety and clinical effectiveness; furthermore, a full HTA also includes the following domains: costs and economic evaluation, ethical analysis, organizational aspects, patient and social aspects, and legal aspects [27].

Relative effectiveness is defined as «the extent to which an intervention does more good than harm compared with one or more alternative interventions under the usual circumstances of healthcare practice». Especially payers are more interested in evaluating the relative effectiveness of new healthcare technologies compared to standard care or other technologies, and have documented their preferred comparators [21]. This interest in relative effectiveness information in Europe is due to the early information need for guiding reimbursement and funding decisions about new health technologies [3-5,28].

EUnetHTA published a review about REA in 2011. According to this report, most countries surveyed use REA to support national reimbursement decisions of drugs, but the subject and methodology vary across countries due to the health system, reimbursement processes, the socio-cultural structure and the level of GDP per capita of the country [27].

15.5 **How HTA Differs from One Setting to Another**

The scope and methods of HTA may be adapted to the needs of a particular health system, but it is known that each country has its own priorities, sources and unique decision-making processes. Below we will give four country examples on how HTA structures change from setting to setting and discuss how they compare with regard to the decisions made with certain pharmaceuticals.

HTA in France

In France, HTA is governed and organized officially based on the legislations of the government and the SHI (Statutory Health Insurance or *Assurance Maladie* in French) [29]. The French government established the main French HTA organization, called HAS (French National Health Authority or *Haute Autorité de Santé* in French) in August 2004 [29,30]. The main goal of the HAS was determined as being the single organization which covers many activities aiming to improve the quality of health care and ensure equity within the health system [30]. In order to achieve this goal, this organization assesses drugs, reagents, tests, medical devices, practices and procedures as well as health programmes; develops guidelines; provides training and information about quality; accreditates health care providers and certifies physicians [29,30]. As an independent (non-governmental) public institution, HAS has financial autonomy and collaborates with several partners such as governmental health agencies, national health insurance funds, research centres, societies of healthcare professionals and patients [30].

HAS has extensive in-house scientific expertise, nevertheless it is also authorized to undertake commissions external experts (e.g. academicians, professionals, other experts) [29,30]. HTA is done by the HAS before inclusion of new medicines on the positive list for reimbursement can occur [29]. After a health technology receives the regulatory approval from EMA (European Medicines Agency) or AFSSAPS (French Health Products Safety Agency or *Agence Française de Sécurité Sanitaire des Produits de Santé* in French), an HTA report is an obligation in order to be considered for pricing and reimbursement by French decision makers [29,30]. Necessary HTA is conducted by two specific commissions within the HAS [29]. The Transparency Commission (*Commission de la Transparence* in French) evaluates drugs, while CNEDIMTS (National Commission for the Evaluation of Medical Devices or *Commission nationale d'évaluation des dispositifs médicaux et des technologies de santé* in French) evaluates medical devices and procedures [29]. Obligatory HTAs, which are done for all new health technologies by the aforementioned commissions based on the documents presented by the manufacturers before the market launch, have a direct influence on the reimbursement rate of SHI and a less direct influence on the price (statutory tariff) [29,30]. Two reviewers evaluate and criticize each HTA study, before it is discussed by the relevant commission. The HTA procedure in France may be classified into two steps [29,30]:

- First step is the assessment of the product's medical benefit or therapeutic value which is called SMR *(Service Medical Rendu* in French) [21,29,30]. This assessment is done in absolute terms for all different types of use of the product, based on its clinical efficacy and safety, its importance within the therapeutic strategy, existence or absence of its alternatives, severity of disease which is indicated to treat, type of the treatment (preventive, curative or symptomatic) and its impact on public health which reflects epidemiological issues and quality of life [29,30]. The SMR level of the health technologies (e.g. major or considerable, important, moderate, low or weak but justifying reimbursement, insufficient) play an important role with reimbursement decisions and the reimbursement rate (from 0 to 100%) decisions [29,30].
- The second step is the assessment of the product's relative medical benefit compared to similar alternatives which is called ASMR (Improvement in the Relative Medical Benefit or *Amélioration du Service Medical Rendu* in French) for drugs or ASA (Improvement in Expected Benefit or *Amelioration du Service Attendu* in French) for medical devices and procedures [21,29,30]. This assessment is done and a grade, based on the improvement in medical effectiveness over similar alternatives, is given by the Transparency Commission for drugs and CNEDIMTS for medical devices and procedures [29]. ASMR or ASA grades of the health technologies (e.g. 1 for "major improvement" or "life-saving health technology", 2 for "important improvement", 3 for "significant or moderate improvement", 4 for "minor improvement", 5 for "no improvement") affect the decisions on pricing explicitly [21,29,30]. Therefore, this step of the assessment incentivizes the manufacturers to provide sufficient data about their products [29].

The HAS commissions examine the documents of the manufacturers, reviews the existing literature systematically and eventually updates all previous decisions about existing health technologies once every five years [29].

Since 2013, another HAS commission called CEESP (Commission for Economic Evaluation and Public Health or *Commission d'Évaluation Économique et de Santé Publique* in French) conducts an economic assessment under specific conditions such as; having a health technology which is considered as ASMR/ASA grade 1, 2 or 3 and may influence SHI expenditure significantly by its price and/or its effect on health care services' organization, medical practices or coverage conditions of patients or having a health technology which have or is expected to have a 20 million Euros or higher turnover after two years on the market [29].

The Ministry of Health is the responsible body to commission the assessment of other technologies such as the necessary equipment for a procedure [29]. Waiting until any additional information becomes available, or asking for surveys or observational research, are possible advices which follow the HTA reports [29]. It is usual that the manufacturers finance the research [29]. However, the researchers should be independent from the financiers [29].

There are multiple criteria used in the appraisal process that is done by the Transparency Commission. The most important criteria for the opinion are actual benefit, improvement in actual benefit, and target population. There is a formal appeal process of 90 days in which companies get the chance to appeal and contest the decision. The HAS makes a recommendation to UNCAM (National Union of Health Insurance Funds or *Union Nationale des Caisses d'Assurance Maladie* in French), which provides the Ministry of Health with a final recommendation about inclusion in the SHI [31].

HTA in the Netherlands

The health system of the Netherlands includes a social health insurance system in which public insurance is compulsory. Citizens older than 18 years pay a flat premium per year for the basic insurance, while people with low incomes are financially compensated. In addition, complementary (voluntary) insurance exists. Through the Health Insurance Act, citizens are entitled to a basic benefit package, although for some entitlements co-payments exist. Health insurers play an important role in implementing the Health Insurance Act, and they are obliged to accept each citizen that wants to pursue a health insurance with them [32].

In 2016, around 10% of GDP was spent on health care, while this was around 9% in 2007. The Health Insurance Act governs curative care, including primary care and hospital care. Around 60% of the health care budget (700 million Euros in 2016) is allocated to this part of health care [32,33].

The Ministry of Health, Welfare and Sports (VWS) is responsible for the content of the benefit package, which comprises essential medical care, medical aids as well as pharmaceuticals. The National Health Care Institute (ZIN) also plays an important role – it has a legal advisory task with regard to the benefit package; its Appraisal Committee (ACP) has an advisory role in coverage-decision-making, while the Ministry of Health makes the final decision.

HTA has been introduced in the Netherlands in the early 1980s. At that time, the Health Insurance Council (now ZIN) and the Ministry of Health became concerned about the rapid developments in health technology (e.g. transplantations, and IVF) and their impact on health care and society, especially in terms of cost. During the 1980s and the 1990s, a series of policy-oriented reports were published that either focused on HTA or included HTA as part of future policy in the Netherlands. All these reports recommended a strong program of HTA as part of Dutch health care. An important impetus for HTA in the Netherlands was the launch of a national HTA research program in 1988 [34]. The Ministry of Health funds the program, which is currently running for the years 2016-2018 and 2019-2021 [35]. The program has evolved over the years, from being a more academic program, towards a program that is addressing the needs of health care professionals, patients and decision-makers [36]. In 1991, the Committee on Choices in Health Care (*Commissie Dunning*) suggested to use HTA for coverage decision-making using four criteria: necessity, effectiveness, efficiency and whether or not the interventions can financial borne by the individual (affordability) [34]. Since 2006, the main role of ZIN is managing the benefit package of health care, and one of its tasks is to advice the Minister of Health about coverage decision-making. ZIN currently makes use of four criteria, clearly inspired by those set out by the Dunning Committee: necessity, effectiveness, cost-effectiveness and feasibility. Franken et al [37] questions whether economic evaluation play an important role in the Dutch system as actual cases (e.g. orphan drugs for Pompe and Fabry disease) [6] showed that it seems rather difficult to put restrictions even though the economic evidence is clear. This situation might prove different in the near future as ZIN is in the process of further optimizing the current (appraisal) system, by further operationalizing the criteria necessity and cost-effectiveness, as well as using deliberative processes based on Daniels and Sabin's Accountability for Reasonableness framework [38].

HTA in Germany

Germany was relatively late compared to other European countries to engaging in HTA activities [39]. In the early years, HTA was mainly conducted by individual researchers. HTA has now become an official necessity in decision-making with regard to which health technology should be covered through *SHIs (Statutory Health Insurance)*, as a result of the SHI Modernization Act, which was announced in 2014 [39,40].

Currently, the main organizations involved in HTA are IQWiG (Institute for Quality and Efficiency in Health Care or *Institut für Qualität und Wirtschaftlichkeit im Gesundheitswesen* in German) for assessment and G-BA (Federal Joint Committee or *Gemeinsamer Bundesausschuss* in German) for the appraisal [39,40]. The G-BA has a department which can provide scientific advice for assessment, but they almost never produce HTA reports.

The G-BA is a multisectoral committee, which consists of dentists, physicians and representatives of hospitals, (non-voting) patients and SHIs [40]. It has a responsibility to control coverage and limitations on prescribing in order to ensure efficiency in the system [40]. Therefore, it evaluates new examination and treatment methods, assesses new medicines, categorizes them into reference price groups and publishes clinical guidelines, which need to be presented to the Federal Ministry of Health for approval [40]. The G-BA decisions based on the level of additional benefit may be appealed based on evidence and legislation [40]. Additional benefit is determined by assessing mortality, morbidity and health related quality of life of the new medicine versus current standards, similar to France [41]. The G-BA makes the final decision publicly available. Most HTAs are conducted by IQWiG.

IQWiG is an independent institute, which was founded in 2004, to assess medical efficiency, quality and effectiveness [40]. Since the new Competition Enhancement Act was announced in 2008, formal cost-effectiveness analyses have become an indispensable part of the German system and IQWiG is authorized to assess cost-benefit ratios of medicines in Germany [40]. It prepares HTA reports either at G-BA requests or self-initialized (for non-pharmaceutical products) [40]. It does not have any decision-making powers and its advice to the G-BA (e.g. including or excluding health technologies into the SHI coverage) are not binding [39,40]. The most important criteria used in the assessment phase are patient relevant outcomes, including mortality, morbidity and health related quality of life as opposed to surrogate measures. Context and implementation issues are partly taken into account (e.g. prescribing restrictions for certain pharmaceutical products are investigated). IQWiG is forced by law to make the evidence report of the assessment publicly available [31]. IQWiG has an informal collaboration with HAS (French National Health Authority) and NICE (National Institute for Health and Care Excellence), which provides bilateral sharing of basic information and scientific evidence with France and the England (in the United Kingdom) [40].

HTA in England/Wales, UK (United Kingdom)

HTA processes are usually aimed to evaluate value for money and eventually inform health policy-making at the national level in the UK [42]. NICE (National Institute for Health and Care Excellence), which is an independent public body founded as a Special Health Authority in 1999, is the main organization which is responsible for providing national guidance on the promotion of good health and the prevention and treatment of ill health [42]. Therefore, it supplies national guidance on specific health technologies (e.g. drugs and medical devices) through its HTA processes and on clinical practice through its clinical guideline development processes based on existing evidence [42,43]. However, in course of time after its foundation, it has taken up further duties in the field of public health as well [42].

Purchasers in the UK have local freedom to choose which health technologies they will buy and they are not obliged to purchase only cost-effective health technologies [43]. In other words health technologies, which are not found cost-effective, may also be covered locally [43]. The NHS (National Health Service) organizations in England and Wales are obliged to finance drugs and therapies approved by NICE based on HTA reports since 2002 [42]. It is also an obligation for NHS organizations to revise their clinical management procedures when NICE clinical guidelines are published [42].

NICE is responsible with both the assessment and the appraisal. Once a technology is referred to NICE for evaluation, NICE writes a draft assessment report together with the Department of Health, including health outcomes and costs. After stakeholder consultations, the scope of the HTA is finalized and all consultees and others are invited to make a submission. The evidence provided by the manufacturer is then reviewed by an independent academic group [31]. The Appraisal Committee of NICE comprises of 20-25 members from diverse backgrounds and includes lay members. It is the Committee's role to appraise the evidence gathered in the assessment phase, including clinical effectiveness and health-related factors, cost-effectiveness, social value judgements and costs (savings) outside NHS or non-health gains. Additional criteria are taken into account for end of life medicines. The Committee summarizes the key evidence and their own view on the evidence, and provides a preliminary recommendation, which is open for consultation. Comments are considered in a second Appraisal Committee meeting, after which the final recommendation to the NHS follows.

There is evidence showing that NICE guidance may affect the market share of drugs, patient access to medicines, prescription attitudes and clinical practices [42]. Most of the drugs, which exist on the market of the UK, are assessed and relevant guidance is published by NICE [43]. Additionally, Northern Ireland, Scotland and Wales have their own advisory organizations to provide recommendations about clinical effectiveness, cost-effectiveness and prescription of medicines with health care devolved in the United Kingdom [43]. SMC (Scottish Medicines Consortium) takes this responsibility in Scotland, while AWMSG (All Wales Medicines Strategy Group) does it in Wales. NHS boards in Scotland should act in line with SMC recommendations [43]; however, this may not always be possible in view of budgetary issues.

Comparison on HTA and Decision Outcomes in Different Settings

As described above, the way in which HTA bodies/programmes are organized and provide input to decision making differs between health systems. In some countries, the HTA body (e.g. NICE in the UK) or an advisory council (e.g. National Health Care Institute in the Netherlands) develops guidance and/or recommendations concerning reimbursement of health technology. In other countries, there is a strong separation between the assessment and appraisal procedure (e.g. in Germany, IQWiG provides the assessment and the national authority – G-BA, decides on the added benefit of pharmaceutical products). Other models also exist – e.g. in France, where HAS (*Haute Autorité de Santé*) is mainly responsible for providing recommendations regarding the reimbursement of pharmaceuticals. The CEPS (*Comité Économique des Produits de Santé*), also a separate body, is responsible for price negotiations with pharmaceutical companies.

Abbreviated indication	Brand name (generic)	HTA recommendation					
		Germany	The Netherlands	France	England/ Wales	Scotland	Poland
Breast cancer	Eribulin	Equal benefit	Added benefit	Added benefit	Negative	Negative	Negative
Colorectal cancer	Aflibercept	Added benefit	Not assessed	Equal benefit	Negative	Negative	Positive
Gastric cancer	Tegafur/ Gimeracil/ Oteracil	Not assessed	Lesser benefit	Lesser benefit	Not assessed	Positive	Negative
Melanoma	Ipilimumab	Added benefit	Added benefit	Added benefit	Positive	Negative	Positive
Non-small cell lung cancer	Crizotinib	Equal benefit	Not assessed	Added benefit	Negative	Negative	Negative
Prostate cancer	Abiraterone	Added benefit	Equal benefit	Added benefit	Positive	Negative	Positive
Renal cell carcinoma	Axitinib	Added benefit	Not assessed	Added benefit	Positive	Negative	Positive

Table 1. Recommendation regarding (selected) oncology drugs having received marketing authorization (2011-2013) in selected EU countries [27,47]

With regard to the use of HTA in decision making, it can be observed that in addition to the level of clinical benefit and cost-effectiveness, increasingly other aspects are taken into account in the appraisal [44]. For orphan drugs different criteria might apply in either the assessment phase (e.g. France), the appraisal phase (e.g. The Netherlands) or both (e.g. Germany) [45]. The approach taken seems to be correlated with the institutional context and the organization making the recommendation or decision, the financing and governance of the health system, as well as the culture and values of a country [46]. Obviously, this might lead to different decisions. This can also be seen in the Table 1, in which selected countries used the same assessment results based on relative effectiveness (using EUnetHTA Core Model). The diverging results could also be due to the fact that the scope (comparators and cost considerations) and the methodology used vary across countries [47]. Allen et al [48] found similar results in a study on national reimbursement decisions in nine countries for more than 100 new active substances approved by the European Medicines Agency.

15.6 Ongoing Developments Impacting on the Role of HTA to Improve the Managed Entry of New Medicines

There have been particular issues with the funding of new medicines for Hepatitis C given the potential number of patients, the possibility of a cure for this chronic infectious disease, the high launch price in a number of countries with associated potential budget impact, as well as concerns with the high level of profitability in some countries at over 99.9% gross profit at the initial requested prices [49-51]. This has resulted in extensive negotiations for discounts as well as restricted use, including managed entry agreements, which is not in the best interests of patients or health authorities [50-54]. There have also been concerns and issues with increasing prices of new cancer medicines and those for orphan disease despite little evidence that new cancer medicines extend or improve life [4,5,55,57]. The cost of new medicines to treat patients with cancer have risen more than tenfold in the past decade despite the low cost of goods of some new cancer medicines, lower than publicized R&D costs as well as current levels of profitability [58-61]. High reimbursed prices for new cancer medicines has been helped by the emotive nature of the disease area, which has typically translated into greater leeway among payers for granting premium prices even for very modest improvements in patient outcomes [4-6,55,57,61-63]. These concerns have already resulted in requests for price moderation for new cancer medicines for future sustainability [61,64,65]. Health authorities, particularly those providing universal access, are increasingly concerned if prices continue to rise given the appreciable number of new cancer medicines in development [4,5,65-67]. A similar situation is also seen for new medicines for orphan diseases given ever increasing prices [4,5,68], with public pressure resulting in, for instance, new medicines for orphan diseases in the Netherlands funded up to 15 million Euros/QALY [69].

Having said this, independent drug information journals, particularly in Europe, believe very few new medicines are truly innovative; with the vast majority seen as similar in their impact on health, or only marginally better, than existing medicines [5,6,70,71]. Consequently, these new medicines should command lower or similar prices to existing standards; or at best only limited increases versus existing standards based on HTA as well as key pricing and reimbursement considerations [4,5,21,41,72]. However, currently concerns with the definition of innovation and value, as well as issues of priority, unmet need and emotion, cloud such discussions and deliberations [63,73-76]. This is a challenge for the future especially in Europe to maintain the ideals of equitable and comprehensive healthcare.

There have also been concerns with some of the marketing activities of pharmaceutical, especially if this leads to inappropriate prescribing which add to costs and/ or potential patient safety [3,77-83]. This includes issues of 'evergreening' of medicines further adding to costs without necessarily improving patient care [84]. However, there are ongoing moves to address key stakeholder concerns particularly regarding the promotion of new medicines [85-87]. This includes improving the core competencies and standards of pharmaceutical physicians [88,89]. In addition, educating physicians that patients enrolled into clinical trials may be different to those seen in routine clinical care, which can mean additional vigilance [3,90].

There are also concerns among some health authorities regarding risk sharing arrangements, or Managed Entry Agreements (MEAs), to improve the affordability of new medicines and reduce uncertainty [25]. These have to be balanced though against no reimbursement if no agreements are reached. These concerns include potential savings in reality, whether health systems have the ability to monitor patient outcomes in routine clinical practice, and the administrative burden and costs associated with such schemes [3,25,75,91-93]. However not surprisingly given rising prices for new medicines, the number of such arrangements has grown in recent years especially for new anti-cancer medicines, although this is not universal [4,25,94-96]. It is likely these schemes will continue, certainly in the short to medium term, given increasing financial pressures and limited alternatives [96,97]. However, this has to be balanced with the need for health authorities and pharmaceutical companies to publish the outcomes of such schemes against their objectives to guide future decision making. Currently, there is a paucity of such information [4,25].

Alongside this, there are also increasing concerns among payers across Europe regarding issues relating to the potential introduction of adaptive pathways for new medicines to accelerate access to new innovative medicines [98,99]. Key concerns include i) issues of payment, i.e. who will pay for the new medicine during its testing phase among patients and at what price, ii) where does the product liability lie prior to full marketing authorization, pricing and reimbursement, iii) how is innovation and unmet need defined, iv) how long are new medicines in the adaptive pathways process prior to full evaluation, v) whether such schemes are needed in reality with fast-track schemes for new medicines already in existence, vi) whether health authorities currently have the necessary ability to monitor the effectiveness and safety of new medicines in routine clinical care, vii) wheth-

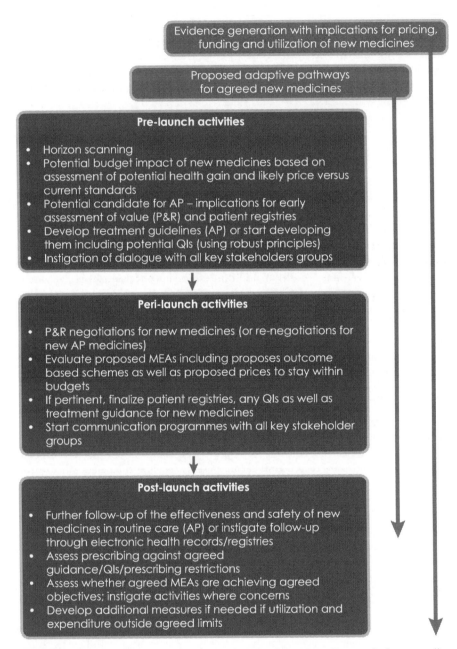

Figure 1. Schematic representation of ongoing models across Europe to improve the managed entry of new medicines. Modified from [3-6,98,108-112]

AP = Adaptive Pathways; MEAs = Managed Entry Agreements; P&R = Pricing and Reimbursement; QIs = Quality Indicators

er payers have the necessary powers to disinvest in new medicines if found not to be cost-effective in reality and manufacturers are reluctant to lower prices. Additionaly, if health authorities do not have the necessary IT systems, who would pay for their subsequent development [99]? However, the use of patient registries post launch have helped address issues of appropriateness and concerns with new medicines such as potentially increasing rates of infection and cancer with the use of biological medicines to treat immunological diseases such as rheumatoid arthritis and psoriasis. Such concerns have not proved to be the case in long term follow-up of these patients [100-106]. Long term follow-up of patients in public healthcare databases have also demonstrated significantly improved long-term graft survival in kidney transplant patients prescribed cyclosporine versus tacrolimus despite current beliefs [107].

These issues and concerns have resulted in the development of new models, especially among European countries, to better manage the entry of new medicines, which also includes potential new models for valuing new medicines for orphan diseases given current concerns [3-6,66,108]. The proposed models include the role of HTA. In addition, HTA activities are increasingly used to guide disinvestment activities, with monies transferred to fund more effective and/or more efficient medicines [18-20]. Discussion of disinvestment activities is outside the scope of this chapter. However as mentioned, there have been published case histories regarding the disinvestment of medicines from a number of countries [18]. More recently, the authorities in Brazil have published a new approach that also includes assessing the effectiveness and safety of potential medicines for disinvestment in the real world, adding robustness to any decisions [19].

New Models to Improve the Managed Entry of New Medicines

A three-stage model has been proposed, and is now being implemented, to improve the managed entry of new medicines especially from a health authority perspective [3-6,66,108,109] (Figure 1). The model begins with pre-launch activities including horizon scanning and forecasting, the potential development of quality indicators for new medicines, as well as including new medicines that could go through the proposed adaptive pathways program especially in Europe [98,109-111]. This will increasingly include in Europe potential new medicines going through the adaptive pathways scheme [98,99].

Peri-launch activities including a fuller assessment of the potential value, requested prices and likely reimbursement, with or without a managed entry agreement, of new medicines versus any preliminary evaluation pre-launch [5,21,66,94]. Post-launch activities include the evaluation of ongoing managed entry agreements including continuing assessment of the effectiveness and safety of new medicines in routine clinical practice as well as the monitoring of prescribing against agreed quality indicators and guidelines.

Pre-launch activities

Pre-launch activities include horizon scanning and budgeting activities [109]. Horizon scanning is seen and defined as «identifying new medicines or new uses of existing medicines that are expected to receive marketing authorization from the Regulatory Author-

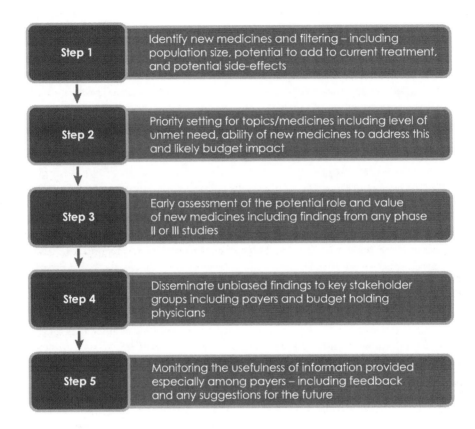

Figure 2. Horizon scanning sequencing activities. Modified from [109,118,121]

ity in the near future and estimating their potential impact on patient care» [113-116]. Since 1999, 18 countries across continents including Europe have been collaborating under the EuroScan project [111,116-118]. Each member agency is unique in its approach; however, they all have a common goal of informing particularly health authorities and hospital managers about new and emerging technologies that could have a significant impact on their health system [104,117,119,120]. Typical activities regarding horizon scanning among leading Western countries, including leading Western European countries, are discussed in Figure 2.

Key filtration and information components of reports in European countries including Austria, Italy, Sweden and the UK are contained in Table 2.

Horizon scanning units can issue different reports as new medicines approach potential marketing authorization to further help heath authorities in their planning [109,111]. This includes Italy (Table 3), with medicines selected based on an agreed filtration process (Table 2).

Criteria	Key considerations
Filtration Criteria	• Current status, e.g. how close to marketing authorization • Likely population size • Severity of the disease area in question/whether a current priority area • Ability to meaningfully improve patient outcomes/address a situation currently associated with appreciable morbidity and mortality – consequently potentially influence treatment guidelines • Potentially innovative way of treating current diseases/level of innovation • Possibility of safety concerns, e.g. dabigatran • Potential budget impact including the potential for savings; part of a new growing class of medicines • Potential for off-label use • Could potentially require reorganization of healthcare services • Likely media/public interest • Likely non-optimal introduction rate following marketing authorization • Potentially legal, ethical or politically interesting considerations
Key components of early assessment reports	• Description of the medicine including disease area and mode of action • Likely clinical need and size of the likely patient population(s) • Current treatment approaches and alternatives; and possible pipeline products • Summary of efficacy in Phase II and III studies (depending on availability and timing of the reports) • Current completed and ongoing studies • Likely budget impact as well as any early pharmacoeconomic assessment • Potential to monitor utilization post-launch against agreed guidance • Possible marketing approaches among companies

Table 2. Key filtration criteria and components of horizon scanning reports in Europe. Modified from [3,109,111,116-118]

Enhancing the robustness forecasts concerning the likely utilization and expenditure of new medicines is increasingly essential to improve subsequent planning and resource allocation given ever increasing pressure on resources [3,4]. One example combining a number of factors to improve budget forecasting, which involves multiple expert groups, is from Stockholm County Council in Sweden [110]. Their forecast with expert groups, including physicians, pharmacists and health authority personnel, involves assessing the likely role of new medicines as well as the future utilization of existing medicines. Regression analyses are conducted on aggregate sales data and predicted trends are adjusted for possible changes in the market including possible patent expiries, with implications for appreciably lowering the price of medicines, as well as potential chang-

Reports available 36 months before potential MA for selected medicines	Reports 18 months before potential MA for selected medicines	Report 12 months before potential MA for selected medicines
The report provides data from Phase II trials as well as of ongoing Phase III trials of targeted medicines. These reports help identify areas of research of interest to the Italian NHS which are currently not being met by pharmaceutical companies.	These reports are essentially for internal purposes among regional health authorities in Italy. The reports critically assess available results of completed Phase III trials and their implications. They help identify and prioritize emerging medicines likely to have a clinical and economic impact on the Italian NHS.	These reports critically evaluate available efficacy and safety data on new agreed medicines. The Italian Unit assesses their possible level of innovation, possible place in therapy (target population) as well as the potential economic (budget) and social impact. The reports are seen as particularly useful for national and regional health authorities.

Table 3. Different reports and their timescales from the Italian Horizon Scanning Project (IHSP) prior to potential EMA marketing authorization (MA). Modified from [109,111]

es in the reimbursement status of medicines [109,110,122]. All of these factors are combined into a yearly forecast, which is subsequently monitored to improve future forecasting [109,110,118].

These activities in Europe will grow with the potential introduction of new medicines under the adaptive pathways scheme [98]. Similarly, for any early access schemes where budgetary responsibility is borne by the payers rather than pharmaceutical companies. These potentially include conditional approval schemes to accelerate access to new medicines for serious debilitating or life-threatening conditions; however, there are concerns [123,124]. This is different to fast track schemes, which are already in existence [98].

Whilst proposed adaptive pathways are welcomed by European payers and their advisers to accelerate early access of new medicines, especially those for debilitating diseases and where currently limited or no therapies are available for treatment, there are still considerable concerns. These concerns have been summarized in a number of published papers [98,99,123,125,126], and include the fact that there will still be inequity in the availability of new medicines across Europe depending on potential prices. Payer HTA considerations for assessing potential prices for new medicines going through the adaptive pathways route will also need to evolve to consider how to effectively deal with increased uncertainty, and build this into their negotiations with pharmaceutical companies [99,127].

Peri-launch activities

As already mentioned in previous paragraphs, European countries typically adopt different approaches to the pricing and reimbursement of new medicines, which can potentially be classified into those countries that assess the level of innovation of new medicines against existing standards using HTA principles as part of price negotiations such as Austria, France and Germany [4,5,21,128]. Alternatively, basing reimbursement and funding decisions on economic criteria such as cost/QALY with or without threshold levels [4,5,21,129,130]. Currently, only a minority of countries using economic principles set threshold levels [21]; with suggestions by some that threshold levels should be lowered for long term sustainability [131].

European health authorities are increasingly requesting Budget Impact Analyses (BIA) as part of health economic assessments for reimbursement/funding and formulary approval decisions [4,109]. This will help with future forecasting, building on current initiatives [109,110] as BIAs help estimate the possible financial consequences with the envisaged diffusion of new technologies into healthcare systems [132]. Key components of any budget impact analyses include [109,133]:

- The perspective of the budget holder/payer.
- The defined time horizon (which is typically up to 3 years).
- Clearly defining the setting.
- Expressing the results as undiscounted cost differences between the use of the new medicines and the current situation.
- Taking into account potential trade-offs in terms of healthcare resources taking account of the potential variable effectiveness of the new medicine in different populations, especially if there are likely to be differences in the patient populations in routine clinical care compared with the Phase III trials.

There are concerns though with the majority of published BIAs including issues of bias, which negatively impacts on their current usefulness to health authorities [134].

Peri-launch activities also increasingly include assessing possible managed entry agreements (MEAs), sometimes referred to as risk sharing arrangements or other definitions [25,91,94,95], especially in Europe. However as mentioned, there are increasing concerns with such schemes, whether financial based or outcome based, among health authority personnel [25,91,109]. A key consideration, especially for outcome based schemes, is the availability of IT systems to routinely collect data on the use, effectiveness and safety of new medicines as part of these schemes. The use of individual patient records or registries for each new medicine, as well as any paper based scheme, quickly becomes challenging for clinicians and other healthcare professionals [91]. However, these concerns have to be weighed against the potential benefits of MEAs including [91,94,109]:

- Improving the opportunity for reimbursement, especially if decision making includes economic considerations such as cost/QALY and/or strict pricing criteria for new medicines, and for 'payers' to work within defined budgets.
- Such schemes help limit the 'off label' use of new medicines and/ or indication creep in clinical practice.
- Potential for payers to only fund new medicines that produce the desired health gain and/or help target physician prescribing to those patients where health gain is greatest through for instance biomarkers and other strategies.

- Enhance the ability of health authorities to monitor the safety and effectiveness of new treatments in routine clinical practice, especially where patients may be more elderly and/or more co-morbid than those enrolled into Phase III clinical trials.

In addition, with respect to ultra-orphan medicines, given the complexities of R&D, conditional approval and reimbursement including managed entry schemes may be one way forward to enhance their reimbursement and funding [135]. However, a prerequisite should be the demonstration of a minimum significant clinical benefit within a reasonable time frame, with limited reliance on any surrogate measures [135].

Consequently, there is an urgent need for publications assessing the impact and usefulness of MEAs against agreed criteria to provide future direction.

There are also concerns with current approaches to the pricing of cancer medicines and those for orphan diseases leading to proposed changes. These are summarized in Sections "New Cancer Medicines" and "New Medicines for Orphan Diseases" below. New proposals are also being considered for gene therapies given their likely costs, which include annuity payments [136,137]. Debates regarding the funding of new gene therapies will continue as more are launched.

New cancer medicines

Concerns with increasing prices of new cancer medicines, the limited health gain of an appreciable number of them including potential 'targeted treatments', and the number in development [4,5,55,57,61,62,138], have resulted in suggestions for establishing minimum targets for stating whether new cancer medicines are an advance, or not, for pricing and funding justifications [139,140]. As a result, potentially address concerns that funding of new cancer medicines at high prices, with often limited health gain, has been enhanced by the emotive nature of the disease [63,141]. As a result, negatively impacting on available resources for other patient populations within finite budgets. Similar considerations exist where specific budgets have been assigned to new cancer medicines to the detriment of other disease areas [142]. However, such concerns with the potential impact on raising the bar for licensing and funding considerations are not universal [143,144].

Suggestions for advanced cancers center on minimum increases in additional survival, especially given concerns with surrogate markers such as progression free survival, and overall response, on their impact on overall survival [4,55,139,145-148]. These debates will continue, with HTA analyses playing an increasing role.

Other suggestions to help improve future pricing and reimbursement considerations in challenging areas include multi-stakeholder debates to better align the needs for robust evidence requirements, given concerns with surrogate markers, and a collectively shared definition and acceptance on what are clinically relevant benefits for patients and society across disease areas [149]. As a result, help better shape the concepts of value to improve pricing and reimbursement deliberations in the future and reduce current controversies. This is particularly important in the cancer area given the appreciable number of new cancer medicines in development, and their likely prices, coupled with considerable unmet need [5,16,67].

New medicines for orphan diseases

There is also increasing concern regarding the funding for new orphan medicines given ever increasing prices [4,5], despite potential offsets with risk sharing arrangements [135]. Such concerns are exacerbated by situations where new medicines for orphan diseases have been funded up to 15 million Euros/QALY the non-classic form of Pompe disease [69]. However, this is not always the case with ten (over 50%) of 19 orphan drugs available on the EMA website in November 2013, for which health economic data were available, met a threshold level of 30,000 GB£/QALY [150].

Such deliberations have resulted in the development of multicriteria decision analyses tools involving all key stakeholder groups [4-6,151,152]. Examples include the Transparent Value Framework developed via an EU initiative [6]. It is expected such developments will grow given the number of orphan medicines in development, including very targeted cancer therapies [67,153].

Post-launch activities

Post launch activities are increasing as payers and others wish to assess the effectiveness and value of new medicines in routine clinical care, building on examples in for instance France. This includes any assessment as part of adaptive pathways programmes or MEAs.

As mentioned, this has included assessing rates of infection and cancer with the use of biological medicines to treat immunological diseases such as rheumatoid arthritis and psoriasis [100-106], as well as assessing long-term graft survival in kidney transplant patients prescribed either cyclosporine or tacrolimus [107]. Other examples including assessing the appropriateness of prescribing, as well as the effectiveness and safety of new oral anti-coagulants such as dabigatran given early concerns [3,154-156] as well as the use and potential risks associated with medicines for weight loss [157]. Post launch activities also include risk management plans, which incorporate risk evaluation and mitigation strategies normally required by the EMA and FDA as part of any medicine approval process to help ensure that the benefits of any new medicine outweighs its risks [158,159].

Conclusion and Next Steps

It is likely that the managed entry of new medicines will become more formalized with increasing horizon scanning and budget activities before launch, especially with developments such as adaptive pathways. This will require an increasing role for HTA and the development of additional skills dealing with increasing uncertainty.

It is also likely that we will see developments in reimbursement decision making especially for new cancer medicines and those for orphan diseases, as well as new gene therapies. This is essential given their potential budget impact and continuing concern with available resources coupled with continuing unmet need. All key stakeholder groups should be part of such developments in the future.

15.7 **References**

1. HTAi – Health Technology Assessment international. What is HTA? Available at https://www.htai.org/htai/what-is-hta/ (last accessed September 2017)
2. HTA glossay.net. Available at www.htaglossary.net (last accessed September 2017)
3. Malmstrom RE, Godman BB, Diogene E, et al. Dabigatran - a case history demonstrating the need for comprehensive approaches to optimize the use of new drugs. *Front Pharmacol* 2013; 4: 39
4. WHO. Access to new medicines in Europe: technical review of policy initiatives and opportunities for collaboration and research. Available at http://www.euro.who.int/__data/assets/pdf_file/0008/306179/Access-new-medicines-TR-PIO-collaboration-research.pdf?ua=1 (last accessed September 2017)
5. Godman B, Oortwijn W, de Waure C, et al. Links between Pharmaceutical R&D Models and Access to Affordable Medicines. A Study for the ENVI Committee. European Union, 2016. Available at http://www.europarl.europa.eu/RegData/etudes/STUD/2016/587321/IPOL_STU(2016)587321_EN.pdf (last accessed September 2017)
6. Godman B, Malmstrom RE, Diogene E, et al. Are new models needed to optimize the utilization of new medicines to sustain healthcare systems? *Expert Rev Clin Pharmacol* 2015; 8: 77-94
7. Akyurek EC. Global Budget as a Reimbursement Method in Health and Turkey. *Journal of Social Security* 2012; 2: 124-53
8. Tutar F, Kilinc N. Economic Development Potential of the Healthcare Market in Turkey and its Comparison with Examples from Different Countries. *Afyon Kocatepe University IIBF Journal* 2007; 9: 31-54
9. Dastan I, Cetinkaya V. Comparing Health Systems, Health Expenditures and Health Indicators in OECD Countries and Turkey. *Journal of Social Security* 2015; 1: 104-34
10. Oortwijn W, Mathijssen J, Banta D. The role of health technology assessment on pharmaceutical reimbursement in selected middle-income countries. *Health Policy* 2010; 95: 174-84
11. Banta D. The development of health technology assessment. *Health Policy* 2003; 63: 121-32
12. Banta D, Behney CJ. Office of Technology Assessment health program. *Int J Technol Assess Health Care* 2009; 25 Suppl 1: 28-32
13. Banta D, Johnson E. History of HTA: Introduction. *Int J Technol Assess Health Care* 2009; 25 Suppl 1: 1-6
14. BD – Business Dictionary. Available at http://www.businessdictionary.com/definition/market-access.html (last accessed September 2017)
15. PHARMAfield. Market Access in practice: do you have a strategy? Available at https://www.pharmafield.co.uk/features/2008/11/Market-Access-in-practice-do-you-have-a-strategy (last accessed September 2017)

16. Kaplan W, Wirtz V, Mantel-Teeuwisse A, et al. Priority Medicines for Europe and the World. 2013 Update. Available at http://www.who.int/medicines/areas/priority_medicines/MasterDocJune28_FINAL_Web.pdf (last accessed September 2017)

17. Barham L. Market access: The impact of HTAs on strategy. Eye on Pharma 2011. Available at http://social.eyeforpharma.com/commercial/market-access-impact-htas-strategy (last accessed September 2017)

18. Parkinson B, Sermet C, Clement F, et al. Disinvestment and Value-Based Purchasing Strategies for Pharmaceuticals: An International Review. *PharmacoEconomics* 2015; 33: 905-24

19. Guerra-Junior AA, Pires de Lemos LL, Godman B, et al. Health technology performance assessment: real-world evidence for public healthcare sustainability. *Int J Technol Assess Health Care* 2017; 33: 279-87

20. Brett J, Elshaug AG, Bhatia RS, et al. A methodological protocol for selecting and quantifying low-value prescribing practices in routinely collected data: an Australian case study. *Implementation Science* 2017; 12: 58

21. Paris V, Belloni A. Value in Pharmaceutical Pricing. Paris: OECD Publishing, 2013

22. Vogler S, Paris V, Ferrario A, et al. How can pricing and reimbursement policies improve affordable access to medicines? Lessons learned from European countries. *Appl Health Econ Health Policy* 2017; 15: 307-21

23. Drummond M, Jönsson B, Rutten F, et al. Reimbursement of pharmaceuticals: reference pricing versus health technology assessment. *Eur J Health Econ* 2011; 12: 263-71

24. European Commission. Council conclusions on innovation for the benefit of patients (204/C 438/06). Brussels: 6 December 2014

25. Ferrario A, Arāja D, Bochenek T, et al. The implementation of managed entry agreements in Central and Eastern Europe: Findings and implications. *Pharmacoeconomics* 2017; 35: 1271-85

26. The EUnetHTA. Available at http://www.eunethta.eu/about-us/history (last accessed September 2017)

27. Oortwijn W on behalf of the HTAi Policy Forum. From Theory To Action: Developments In Value Frameworks To Inform The Allocation of Health Care Resources. Background Paper 2017 Policy Forum. Available at https://www.htai.org/index.php?eID=tx_nawsecuredl&u=0&g=0&t=1514959761&hash=0e4dd72f37c05587b449805eaf40592edee96efd&file=fileadmin/HTAi_Files/Policy_Forum/HTAi_Policy_Forum_2017_Background_Paper.pdf (last accessed September 2017)

28. Towse A, Jonsson B, McGrath C, et al. Understanding Variations In Relative Effectiveness: A Health Production Approach. *Int J Technol Assess Health Care* 2015; 31: 363-70

29. Chevreul K, Berg Brigham K, Durand-Zaleski I, et al. France: Health system review. *Health Syst Transit* 2015; 17: 1-218

30. ISPOR Global Health Care Systems Road Map. France Pharmaceuticals, 2009. Available at https://www.ispor.org/HTARoadMaps/France.asp (last accessed September 2017)

31. Oortwijn W, Determann D, Schiffers K, et al. Towards integrated health technology assessment for improving decision-making in selected countries. *Value Health* 2017; 20: 1121-30

32. Ministry of Health, Welfare and Sport. Healthcare in the Netherlands. 2016. Available at https://www.eiseverywhere.com/file_uploads/0f57b7c2d0d94ff457692 69d50876905_P4-HealthcareintheNetherlands.pdf (last accessed September 2017)

33. Schäfer W, Kroneman M, Boerma W, et al. The Netherlands: Health System Review. *Health Syst Transit* 2010; 12: v-xxvii, 1-228

34. Banta HD, Oortwijn W. The history of health technology assessment in the Netherlands. *Int J Technol Assess Health Care* 2009; 25 Suppl. 1: 143-7

35. ZonMw. Program on Health Care Efficiency Research. Available at https://www.zonmw.nl/en/research-and-results/efficiency-studies/programmas/programme-detail/health-care-efficiency-research/ (last accessed September 2017)

36. Van der Wilt GJ, Rovers M, Oortwijn W, et al. Hospital-based HTA at Radboud University Medical Centre in the Netherlands: Welcome to Reality. In: Sampietro-Colom L, Martin J (eds.). Hospital-Based Health Technology Assessment. Switzerland: Springer International Publishing, 2016

37. Franken M, Koopmanschap M, Steenhoek A. Health economic evaluations in reimbursement decision making in the Netherlands: Time to take it seriously? *Z Evid Fortbild Qual Gesundhwes* 2014; 108: 383-9

38. Zorginstituut Nederland. Pakketadvies in de praktijk. Wikken en wegen voor een rechtvaardig packet. Available at https://www.zorginstituutnederland.nl/publicaties/rapport/2017/09/06/rapport-pakketadvies-in-de-praktijk-wikken-en-wegen-voor-een-rechtvaardig-pakket (last accessed September 2017)

39. Busse R, Blümel M. Germany: health system review. *Health Syst Transit* 2014; 16: 1-296

40. ISPOR Global Health Care Systems Road Map. Germany Pharmaceutical, 2009. Available at https://www.ispor.org/HTARoadMaps/Germany.asp (last accessed September 2017)

41. Godman B, Paterson K, Malmstrom RE, et al. Improving the managed entry of new medicines: sharing experiences across Europe. *Expert Rev Pharmacoecon Outcomes Res* 2012; 12: 439-41

42. ISPOR Global Health Care Systems Road Map. United Kingdom (England and Wales) - Reimbursement Process, 2008. Available at https://www.ispor.org/HTARoadMaps/UK.asp (last accessed September 2017)

43. Cylus J, Richardson E, Findley L, et al. United Kingdom: Health system review. *Health Syst Transit* 2015; 17: 1-125

44. Tanios, N, Wagner M, Tony M, et al., and the International Task Force on Decision Criteria. Which criteria are considered in healthcare decisions? Insights from an international survey of policy and clinical decision makers. *Int J Technol Assess Health Care* 2013; 29: 456-65

45. Kawalec P, Sagan A, Pilc A. The correlation between HTA recommendations and reimbursement status in Europe. *Orphanet J Rare Dis* 2016; 11: 122

46. Torbica A, Drummond M, Ferré, F, et al. Economic evaluation and health technology assessment in Europe and USA. A comparative analysis. Executive Summary. MedtecHTA Work Package 4, 2015. Available at http://www.medtechta.eu/wps/wcm/connect/272245ac-ebee-4709-a7b1-35a8a6c9c8bd/ExecutiveSummary_+MedtecHTA+WP4_D4.1.pdf?MOD=AJPERES (last accessed September 2017)

47. Kleijnen S, Lipska I, Leonardo Alves T, et al. Relative effectiveness assessments of oncology medicines for pricing and reimbursement decisions in European countries. Ann Oncol 2016; 27: 1768-75

48. Allen N, Liberti L, Walker SR, et al. A comparison of reimbursement recommendations by European HTA agencies: is there opportunity for further alignment? *Front Pharmacol* 2017; 8: 384

49. Brennan T, Shrank W. New expensive treatments for hepatitis C infection. *JAMA* 2014; 312: 593-4

50. Phelan M, Cook C. A treatment revolution for those who can afford it? Hepatitis C treatment: new medications, profits and patients. *BMC Infect Dis* 2014; 14 Suppl 6: S5

51. de Bruijn W, Ibanez C, Frisk P, et al. Introduction and Utilization of High Priced HCV Medicines across Europe; Implications for the Future. *Front Pharmacol* 2016; 7: 197

52. Andrieux-Meyer I, Cohn J, de Araujo ES, et al. Disparity in market prices for hepatitis C virus direct-acting drugs. *Lancet Glob Health* 2015; 3: e676-7

53. Liao JM, Fischer MA. Restrictions of Hepatitis C Treatment for Substance-Using Medicaid Patients: Cost Versus Ethics. *Am J Public Health* 2017; 107: 893-9

54. Barua S, Greenwald R, Grebely J, et al. Restrictions for Medicaid Reimbursement of Sofosbuvir for the Treatment of Hepatitis C Virus Infection in the United States. *Ann Intern Med* 2015; 163: 215-23

55. Wild C, Grossmann N, Bonanno PV, et al. Utilisation of the ESMO-MCBS in practice of HTA. *Ann Oncol* 2016; 27: 2134-6

56. Godman B, Wild C, Haycox A. Patent expiry and costs for anti-cancer medicines for clinical use. *Generics and Biosimilars Initiative Journal* 2017; 6: 105-6

57. Davis C, Naci H, Gurpinar E, et al. Availability of evidence of benefits on overall survival and quality of life of cancer drugs approved by European Medicines Agency: retrospective cohort study of drug approvals 2009-13. BMJ 2017; 359: j4530

58. Hill A, Redd C, Gotham D, et al. Estimated generic prices of cancer medicines deemed cost-ineffective in England: a cost estimation analysis. *BMJ open* 2017; 7: e011965

59. Kelly RJ, Smith TJ. Delivering maximum clinical benefit at an affordable price: engaging stakeholders in cancer care. *Lancet Oncol* 2014; 15: e112-8

60. Prasad V, Mailankody S. Research and Development Spending to Bring a Single Cancer Drug to Market and Revenues After Approval. *JAMA Intern Med* 2017; 177: 1569-75

61. Experts in Chronic Myeloid Leukemia. The price of drugs for chronic myeloid leukemia (CML) is a reflection of the unsustainable prices of cancer drugs: from the perspective of a large group of CML experts. *Blood* 2013; 121: 4439-42

62. Kantarjian HM, Fojo T, Mathisen M, et al. Cancer drugs in the United States: Justum Pretium--the just price. *J Clin Oncol* 2013; 31: 3600-4

63. Haycox A. Why Cancer? *PharmacoEconomics* 2016; 34: 625-7

64. Tefferi A, Kantarjian H, Rajkumar SV, et al. In Support of a Patient-Driven Initiative and Petition to Lower the High Price of Cancer Drugs. *Mayo Clin Proc* 2015; 90: 996-1000

65. Ghinea H, Kerridge I, Lipworth W. If we don't talk about value, cancer drugs will become terminal for health systems. The Conversation, 2015. Available at http://theconversation.com/if-we-dont-talk-about-value-cancer-drugs-will-become-terminal-for-health-systems-44072 (last accessed September 2017)

66. Matusewicz W, Godman B, Pedersen HB, et al. Improving the managed introduction of new medicines: sharing experiences to aid authorities across Europe. *Expert Rev Pharmacoecon Outcomes Res* 2015; 15: 755-8

67. EFPIA. Health and Wealth. Pharma industry's contribution to health and wealth

68. Cohen JP, Felix A. Are payers treating orphan drugs differently? *J Mark Access Health Policy* 2014; 2: 23513

69. Simoens S, Picavet E, Dooms M, et al. Cost-effectiveness assessment of orphan drugs: a scientific and political conundrum. *Appl Health Econ Health Policy* 2013; 11: 1-3

70. Editorial Staff. New products and new indications in 2016: a system that favours imitation over the pursuit of real progress. *Rev Prescrire* 2017; 37: 132-6

71. Vitry AI, Shin NH, Vitre P. Assessment of the therapeutic value of new medicines marketed in Australia. J Pharm Policy Pract 2013; 6: 2

72. Godman B, Bucsics A, Burkhardt T, et al. Insight into recent reforms and initiatives in Austria: implications for key stakeholders. *Expert Rev Pharmacoecon Outcomes Res* 2008; 8: 357-71

73. Prata WM, Silvestre R, Godman B, et al. A Critical Look at Innovation Profile and Its Relationship with Pharmaceutical Industry. *International Journal of Scientific Research and Management (IJSRM)* 2017; 5: 5934-48

74. Wonder MJ. Assessment of the therapeutic value of new medicines marketed in Australia. *J Pharm Policy Pract* 2013; 6: 7

75. Hollis A. Sustainable Financing of Innovative Therapies: A Review of Approaches. *PharmacoEconomics* 2016; 34: 971-80

76. Antonanzas F, Terkola R, Postma M. The Value of Medicines: A Crucial but Vague Concept. *PharmacoEconomics* 2016; 34: 1227-39

77. Cohen D. Dabigatran: how the drug company withheld important analyses. *BMJ* 2014; 349: g4670

78. Davis C, Abraham J. Is there a cure for corporate crime in the drug industry? *BMJ* 2013; 346: f755

79. Spurling GK, Mansfield PR, Montgomery BD, et al. Information from Pharmaceutical Companies and the Quality, Quantity, and Cost of Physicians' Prescribing: A Systematic Review. *PLoS Medicine* 2010; 7: e1000352

80. Desai T, Dhingra V, Shariff A, et al. Quantifying the Twitter Influence of Third Party Commercial Entities versus Healthcare Providers in Thirteen Medical Conferences from 2011 – 2013. *PloS one* 2016; 11: e0162376

81. Fleischman W, Agrawal S, King M, et al. Association between payments from manufacturers of pharmaceuticals to physicians and regional prescribing: cross sectional ecological study. *BMJ* 2016; 354: i4189

82. Light DW, Lexchin J, Darrow JJ. Institutional corruption of pharmaceuticals and the myth of safe and effective drugs. *J Law Med Ethics* 2013; 41: 590-600

83. Civaner M. Sale strategies of pharmaceutical companies in a "pharmerging" country: the problems will not improve if the gaps remain. *Health policy* 2012; 106: 225-32

84. Vernaz N, Haller G, Girardin F, et al. Patented drug extension strategies on healthcare spending: a cost-evaluation analysis. *PLoS Med* 2013; 10: e1001460

85. Francer J, Izquierdo JZ, Music T, et al. Ethical pharmaceutical promotion and communications worldwide: codes and regulations. *Philos Ethics Humanit Med* 2014; 9: 7

86. Yu SY, Yang BM, Kim JH. New anti-rebate legislation in South Korea. *Appl Health Econ Health Policy* 2013; 11: 311-8

87. Brkicic LS, Godman B, Voncina L, et al. Initiatives to improve prescribing efficiency for drugs to treat Parkinson's disease in Croatia: influence and future directions. *Expert Rev Pharmacoecon Outcomes Res* 2012; 12: 373-84

88. Silva H, Stonier P, Buhler F, et al. Core competencies for pharmaceutical physicians and drug development scientists. *Front Pharmacol* 2013; 4: 105

89. Dubois DJ, Jurczynska A, Kerpel-Fronius S, et al. Fostering Competence in Medicines Development: The IFAPP Perspective. *Front Pharmacol* 2016; 7: 377

90. Joppi R, Cinconze E, Mezzalira L, et al. Hospitalized patients with atrial fibrillation compared to those included in recent trials on novel oral anticoagulants: a population-based study. *Eur J Intern Med* 2013; 24: 318-23

91. Adamski J, Godman B, Ofierska-Sujkowska G, et al. Risk sharing arrangements for pharmaceuticals: potential considerations and recommendations for European payers. *BMC Health Serv Res* 2010; 10: 153

92. Williamson S. Patient access schemes for high-cost cancer medicines. *The Lancet Oncology* 2010; 11: 111-2

93. Toumi M, Jaroslawski S, Sawada T, et al. The Use of Surrogate and Patient-Relevant Endpoints in Outcomes-Based Market Access Agreements : Current Debate. *Appl Health Econ Health Policy* 2017; 15: 5-11

94. Ferrario A, Kanavos P. Managed entry agreements for pharmaceuticals: the European experience. Brussels: EMiNet, 2013. Available at http://eprints.lse.ac.uk/50513 (last accessed September 2017)

95. Ferrario A, Kanavos P. Dealing with uncertainty and high prices of new medicines: a comparative analysis of the use of managed entry agreements in Belgium, England, the Netherlands and Sweden. *Soc Sci Med* 2015; 124: 39-47

96. Carlson JJ, Chen S, Garrison LP, Jr. Performance-Based Risk-Sharing Arrangements: An Updated International Review. *Pharmacoeconomics* 2017; 35: 1063-72

97. Garattini L, Curto A. Performance-Based Agreements in Italy: 'Trendy Outcomes' or Mere Illusions? *PharmacoEconomics* 2016; 34: 967-9

98. Ermisch M, Bucsics A, Vella Bonanno P, et al. Payers' Views of the Changes Arising through the Possible Adoption of Adaptive Pathways. *Front Pharmacol* 2016; 7: 305

99. Vella Bonanno P, Ermisch M, Godman B, et al. Adaptive Pathways: Possible Next Steps for Payers in Preparation for Their Potential Implementation. *Front Pharmacol* 2017; 8: 497

100. Mercer LK, Askling J, Raaschou P, et al. Risk of invasive melanoma in patients with rheumatoid arthritis treated with biologics: results from a collaborative project of 11 European biologic registers. *Ann Rheum Dis* 2017; 76: 386-91

101. Raaschou P, Simard JF, Asker Hagelberg C, et al. Rheumatoid arthritis, anti-tumour necrosis factor treatment, and risk of squamous cell and basal cell skin cancer: cohort study based on nationwide prospectively recorded data from Sweden. *BMJ* 2016; 352: i262

102. Hellgren K, Dreyer L, Arkema EV, et al. Cancer risk in patients with spondyloarthritis treated with TNF inhibitors: a collaborative study from the ARTIS and DANBIO registers. *Ann Rheum Dis* 2017; 76: 105-11

103. Iskandar IY, Ashcroft DM, Warren RB, et al. Comparative effectiveness of biologic therapies on improvements in quality of life in patients with psoriasis. *Br J Dermatol* 2017; 177: 1410-21

104. Garcia-Doval I, Cohen AD, Cazzaniga S, et al. Risk of serious infections, cutaneous bacterial infections, and granulomatous infections in patients with psoriasis treated with anti-tumor necrosis factor agents versus classic therapies: Prospective meta-analysis of Psonet registries. *J Am Acad Dermatol* 2017; 76: 299-308.e16

105. Davila-Seijo P, Garcia-Doval I, Naldi L, et al. Factors Associated with Receiving Biologics or Classic Systemic Therapy for Moderate-to-Severe Psoriasis: Evidence from the PSONET Registries. *Acta Derm Venereol* 2017; 97: 516-8

106. Iannone F, Gremese E, Atzeni F, et al. Longterm retention of tumor necrosis factor-alpha inhibitor therapy in a large Italian cohort of patients with rheumatoid arthritis from the GISEA registry: an appraisal of predictors. *J Rheumatol* 2012; 39: 1179-84

107. Gomes RM, Guerra Junior AA, Lemos LL, et al. Ten-year kidney transplant survival of cyclosporine- or tacrolimus-treated patients in Brazil. *Expert Rev Clin Pharmacol* 2016; 9: 991-9

108. Permanand G, Pedersen H. Managing new premium-priced medicines in Europe. *J Pharm Policy Pract* 2015; 8(Suppl 1): K2

109. Godman B, Joppi R, Bennie M, et al. Managed introduction of new drugs. In Elseviers M, Wettermark B, et al (eds). Drug Utilization Research: Methods and Applications. Chichester: John Wiley & Sons, 2016

110. Wettermark B, Persson ME, Wilking N, et al. Forecasting drug utilization and expenditure in a metropolitan health region. *BMC Health Serv Res* 2010; 10: 128

111. Joppi R, Dematte L, Menti AM, et al. The Italian Horizon Scanning Project. *Eur J Clin Pharmacol* 2009; 65: 775-81

112. Campbell SM, Godman B, Diogene E, et al. Quality indicators as a tool in improving the introduction of new medicines. *Basic Clin Pharmacol Toxicol* 2015; 116: 146-57

113. Wettermark B, Godman B, Eriksson C, van Ganse E, Garattini S, Joppi R, et al. Einführung neuer Arzneimittel in europäische Gesundheitssysteme (Introduction of new medicines into European healthcare systems). *GGW* 2010; 10: 24-34

114. Wild C, Langer T. Emerging health technologies: informing and supporting health policy early. *Health policy* 2008; 87: 160-71

115. Wild C, Simpson S, Douw K, et al. Information service on new and emerging health technologies: identification and prioritization processes for a European union-wide newsletter. *Int J Technol Assess Health Care* 2009; 25 Suppl 2: 48-55

116. Packer C, Fung M, Stevens A. Analyzing 10 years of early awareness and alert activity in the United kingdom. *Int J Technol Assess Health Care* 2012; 28: 308-14

117. Nachtnebel A, Geiger-Gritsch S, Hintringer K, et al. Scanning the horizon: development and implementation of an early awareness system for anticancer drugs in Austria. *Health policy* 2012; 104: 1-11

118. Eriksson E, Wettermark B, Persson M, et al. The Early Awareness and Alert System in Sweden: History and Current Status. *Front Pharmacol* 2017; 8: 674

119. EuroScan International Network, A toolkit for the identification and assessment of new and emerging health technologies. Birmingham: EuroScan International Network, 2014

120. Martino OI, Ward DJ, Packer C, et al. Innovation and the burden of disease: retrospective observational study of new and emerging health technologies reported by the EuroScan Network from 2000 to 2009. *Value Health* 2012; 15: 376-80

121. Nachtnebel A, Breuer J, Willenbacher W, et al. Looking back on 5 years of horizon scanning in oncology. *Int J Technol Assess Health Care* 2016; 32: 54-60

122. Godman B, Wettermark B, Hoffmann M, et al. Multifaceted national and regional drug reforms and initiatives in ambulatory care in Sweden: global relevance. *Expert Rev Pharmacoecon Outcomes Res* 2009; 9: 65-83

123. Davis C, Lexchin J, Jefferson T, et al. Adaptive pathways to drug authorisation: adapting to industry? *BMJ* 2016; 354: i4437

124. Banzi R, Gerardi C, Bertele V, et al. Approvals of drugs with uncertain benefit-risk profiles in Europe. *Eur J Intern Med* 2015; 26: 572-84

125. Joppi R, Gerardi C, Bertele V, et al. Letting post-marketing bridge the evidence gap: the case of orphan drugs. *BMJ* 2016; 353: i2978

126. Hawkes N. Specialists attack drug agency's fast track approval scheme. *BMJ* 2016; 353: i3060

127. Grimm SE, Strong M, Brennan A, et al. The HTA Risk Analysis Chart: Visualising the Need for and Potential Value of Managed Entry Agreements in Health Technology Assessment. *Pharmacoeconomics* 2017; 35: 1287-96

128. Godman B, Campbell S, Suh HS, et al. Ongoing Measures to Enhance Prescribing Efficiency Across Europe: Implications for Other Countries. *J Health Tech Assess* 2013; 1: 27-42

129. Godman B, Gustafsson LL. A new reimbursement system for innovative pharmaceuticals combining value-based and free market pricing. *Appl Health Econ Health Policy* 2013; 11: 79-82

130. Svensson M, Nilsson FO, Arnberg K. Reimbursement Decisions for Pharmaceuticals in Sweden: The Impact of Disease Severity and Cost Effectiveness. *PharmacoEconomics* 2015; 33: 1229-36

131. Raftery JP. NICE's cost-effectiveness range: should it be lowered? *PharmacoEconomics* 2014; 32: 613-5

132. ISPOR. ISPOR Task Force on Good Research Practices. Report of the ISPOR Task Force on Good Research Practices – Budget Impact Analysis. Available at http://www.ispor.org/workpaper/BudgetImpactAnalysis/BIA_TF0906.asp (last accessed September 2017)

133. van de Vooren K, Duranti S, Curto A, et al. A critical systematic review of budget impact analyses on drugs in the EU countries. *Appl Health Econ Health Policy* 2014; 12: 33-40

134. Faleiros DR, Alvares J, Almeida AM, et al. Budget impact analysis of medicines: updated systematic review and implications. *Expert Rev Pharmacoecon Outcomes Res* 2016; 16: 257-66

135. Schlander M, Garattini S, Kolominsky-Rabas P, et al. Determining the value of medical technologies to treat ultra-rare disorders: a consensus statement. *J Mark Access Health Policy* 2016; 4

136. Jorgensen J, Kefalas P. Annuity payments can increase patient access to innovative cell and gene therapies under England's net budget impact test. *J Mark Access Health Policy* 2017; 5: 1355203

137. Marsden G TA, Pearson SD, Dreitlein W, et al. GENE THERAPY: Understanding the Science, Assessing the Evidence, and Paying for Value. Office f Health Economics, 2017. Available at https://www.ohe.org/news/new-publication-gene-therapy-understanding-science-assessing-evidence-and-paying-value (last accessed September 2017)

138. Godman B, Finlayson AE, Cheema PK, et al. Personalizing health care: feasibility and future implications. *BMC medicine* 2013; 11: 179

139. Ferguson JS, Summerhayes M, Masters S, et al. New treatments for advanced cancer: an approach to prioritization. *Br J Cancer* 2000; 83: 1268-73

140. Cherny NI, Sullivan R, Dafni U, et al. A standardised, generic, validated approach to stratify the magnitude of clinical benefit that can be anticipated from anti-

cancer therapies: the European Society for Medical Oncology Magnitude of Clinical Benefit Scale (ESMO-MCBS). *Ann Oncol* 2015; 26: 1547-73

141. Pauwels K, Huys I, Casteels M, et al. Market access of cancer drugs in European countries: improving resource allocation. *Target Oncol* 2014; 9: 95-110

142. [No authors listed]. New 50 million pound cancer fund already intellectually bankrupt. *Lancet* 2010; 376: 389

143. Barron A, Wilsdon T. Challenging Perceptions About Oncology Product Pricing in Breast and Colorectal Cancer. *Pharmaceut Med* 2016; 30: 321-6

144. Sobrero A, Bruzzi P. Incremental advance or seismic shift? The need to raise the bar of efficacy for drug approval. *J Clin Oncol* 2009; 27: 5868-73

145. Henshall C, Samson L, Eichler H-G, et al. Understanding the Role and Evidence Expectations of Health Technology Assessment and Coverage/Payer Bodies: What Are They Looking for, and How and Why Does This Differ From What Regulators Require? *Therapeutic Innovation & Regulatory Science* 2013; 48: 341-6

146. Cortazar P, Zhang L, Untch M, et al. Pathological complete response and long-term clinical benefit in breast cancer: the CTNeoBC pooled analysis. *Lancet* 2014; 384: 164-72

147. Prasad V, Kim C, Burotto M, et al. The Strength of Association Between Surrogate End Points and Survival in Oncology: A Systematic Review of Trial-Level Meta-analyses. *JAMA Intern Med* 2015; 175: 1389-98

148. Svensson S, Menkes DB, Lexchin J. Surrogate outcomes in clinical trials: a cautionary tale. *JAMA Intern Med* 2013; 173: 611-2

149. Kleijnen S, Lipska I, Leonardo Alves T, et al. Relative effectiveness assessments of oncology medicines for pricing and reimbursement decisions in European countries. *Ann Oncol* 2016; 27: 1768-75

150. Picavet E, Cassiman D, Simoens S. What is known about the cost-effectiveness of orphan drugs? Evidence from cost-utility analyses. *J Clin Pharm Ther* 2015; 40: 304-7

151. Hughes-Wilson W, Palma A, Schuurman A, et al. Paying for the Orphan Drug System: break or bend? Is it time for a new evaluation system for payers in Europe to take account of new rare disease treatments? *Orphanet J Rare Dis* 2012; 7: 74

152. Gilabert-Perramon A, Torrent-Farnell J, Catalan A, et al. Drug Evaluation And Decision Making In Catalonia: Development And Validation Of A Methodological Framework Based On Multi-Criteria Decision Analysis (Mcda) For Orphan Drugs. *Int J Technol Assess Health Care* 2017; 33: 111-20

153. Mullard A. 2011 FDA drug approvals. *Nat Rev Drug Discov* 2012; 11: 91-4

154. Godman B, Malmstrom RE, Diogene E, et al. Dabigatran - a continuing exemplar case history demonstrating the need for comprehensive models to optimize the utilization of new drugs. *Front Pharmacol* 2014; 5: 109

155. Larock AS, Mullier F, Sennesael AL, et al. Appropriateness of prescribing dabigatran etexilate and rivaroxaban in patients with nonvalvular atrial fibrillation: a prospective study. *Ann Pharmacother* 2014; 48: 1258-68

156. Troncoso A, Diogene E. Dabigatran and rivaroxaban prescription for atrial fibrillation in Catalonia, Spain: the need to manage the introduction of new drugs. *Eur J Clin Pharmacol* 2014; 70: 249-50

157. Forslund T, Raaschou P, Hjemdahl P, et al. Usage, risk, and benefit of weight-loss drugs in primary care. *J Obes* 2011; 2011: 459263

158. EMA. Guideline on Safety and Efficacy Follow-up - Risk Management of Advanced Therapy Medicinal Products. 2008. Available at http://www.ema.europa.eu/docs/en_GB/document_library/Regulatory_and_procedural_guideline/2009/10/WC500006326.pdf (last accessed September 2017)

159. EMA. CHMP Recommendations for the Pharmacovigilance Plan as part of the Risk Management Plan to be submitted with the Marketing Authorisation Application for a Pandemic Influenza Vaccine. 2009. Available at http://www.ema.europa.eu/docs/en_GB/document_library/Report/2010/01/WC500051739.pdf (last accessed September 2017)

https://doi.org/10.7175/747.ch16

16. Impact of the International Reference Pricing on Pharmaceutical Market Access

Gülpembe Ergin Oğuzhan [1]

[1] Ondokuz Mayıs University, Samsun, Turkey

16.1 Definition of International Reference Pricing (IRP)

International reference pricing (IRP) is a process of cost comparison through external reference or cross-reference, which is used by many multinational pharmaceutical companies located in the States of the European Union. The IRP process has been reinforced through the process of mutual recognition of innovative drugs in 1975, the creation of an internal market in the European Union in 1992, and the institution of the European Medical Agency (EMA) in 1995 [1]. Compared to other models, which are based on the evaluation of costs, profits and effectiveness of drugs (value-based pricing), the IRP is a simple process [2].

16.2 Basic Mechanism of the IRP

The IRP aims to limit the expenditure for the reimbursement of drugs, rather than create a process of price regulation. The IRP mechanism is based on the presence of equivalent drugs on the national market to set a reimbursement price, known as the reference price, and the price of the new drug [3]. Reference pricing rules may differ among biologics, vaccines, and pharmaceuticals [1].

16.3 Use of the IRP in Different Countries

In Europe, the IRP is implemented in 29 countries, including 26 of the EU Member States (except the UK and Sweden), Norway, Iceland, and Switzerland. In Europe, every country has a reference "basket", containing the countries used as reference markets for prices [2]. For example, Luxembourg has one country in its basket, while Hungary and Poland have 31 countries in their basket and France and The Netherlands have four (Italy, Spain, Germany and the UK for France, and Belgium, Germany, France, and the UK for The Netherland). The IRP system was implemented in Canada in the 1990s, following the reforms of the laws relating to patents and pricing [4]. In Canada, the Patented Medicine Price Review Board is responsible for comparing national drug prices for innovative drugs with the external prices of nine other countries [5]. The establishment of the price system led Canada to set prices that are consistently below the consumer price index.

The US does not have a price regulation system in place, and the development, manufacture, and launch of pharmaceuticals are regulated by the Federal Food, Drug, and Cosmetic Act (FFDCA) [6], while the Hatch-Waxman Act promotes the manufacture of generic drugs [7]. In Australia, the Pharmaceutical Benefits Scheme (PBS) has been implemented in order to control drug prices. Australia has a system of reference pricing for generic medicines: the price of a new drug is determined based on the price of other interchangeable drugs [8]. If the selling price is higher than the reference price, the difference must be paid by the patient.

16.4 Impact of the IRP on the Pharmaceutical Industry

Impact on Prices

IRP is the process that most impacts the prices of pharmaceutical drugs, biologics and vaccines [9], and this impact depends on the process and methodology used. It was observed that the reimbursement price set in one country could have both a direct and indirect impact on the reimbursement prices of another country [3]. The direct impact is due to the fact that country A uses the price of country B to set its own prices. The indirect impact is due to the fact that another country (C) is included in the basket of country B; therefore, the prices of country A will be influenced by the prices in country C even if the latter is not in its basket [9].

The revenues of the pharmaceutical companies can be influenced by the markets selected to launch their products. For example, if a company launches its products only in high-income countries, the reference prices would not differ much, thereby providing a good level of revenue [9]. However, the country can lower the cost for a better price limit than the one set by the pharmaceutical company [10]; this can be seen in the case of France, where the country exercises price limits, but also considers the therapeutic effectiveness and the economic contribution. The country does not reimburse beyond a certain limit, and this is a cap for the government expenditure on that drug [6]. This leads the companies to set a moderate price in high-income countries also, and to use that price corridor to get the maximum percentage of revenues.

Impact on Volumes

As discussed above, the IRP led the companies to set a single international price, to commit to create a price corridor and to work towards keeping the price within that bracket, for maximum revenue and profits. The impact of the IRP on the pharmaceutical market, apart from the price, consists is the fact that, due to the possible lowering of price in certain markets, the manufacturers can decide not to launch their product in that particular markets. Since the IRP might not work well with their pricing strategy in different countries, the company's market access and sales team might renounce the launch of a particular product in a market that would lower its price, leading to a lowering of the overall prices in other countries as well [9]. Here, the IRP process leads to a negative impact, since it provides the companies with the possibility to prevent a potentially new, innovative and possibly more effective treatment from entering a market, thus negatively impacting the patient's conditions [11]. This particular instance is more important for lower income or less populated countries, since manufacturers might give up the launch process in those countries and launch the drug instead in larger countries, up to the patent's expiry or until other regulatory changes might impact the lowering of overall prices [11]. This does not impact only the patients – because the IRP leads to several failed drug launches and to the loss of new and innovative treatments – but also the companies, which cannot launch their products in more countries, and therefore suffer a decrease in their sales volumes [3]. It was reported that the IRP has a positive impact on volumes and does not help control the healthcare budget [12].

Impact on Market Access Sequencing

Market sequencing is carried out by a company – including a pharmaceutical company – in order to increase the chances of greater profit and increased revenue. Market access and launch teams promote the launch of products in such a strategic manner that several avenues are explored to provide the best alternatives for the price restricted market, and still produce a high revenue [4]. One of the Market Access Sequencing strategies most commonly implemented by companies occurs through the launch of products in unregulated markets, and then a launch in countries that have these unregulated markets in their reference basket. For example, many pharmaceutical companies launch their products in the UK and Germany first at high price level, these being unregulated markets, and then look for and launch in countries that have these markets in their reference basket, such as Italy, Spain and France. In this process, the only loss is borne by low-income or low economic power countries, which most of the time may remain out of the loop of the market launches of these pharmaceutical products. This is known as the 'now or never' strategy: the companies launch their products in all the countries they want to 'now', and all the other countries fall within the category where the company 'never' wants to launch the product [13]. On the other hand, some strategies are used to introduce these pharmaceutical products in low-income countries. One strategy the companies implement to introduce their pharmaceutical markets in low-income countries is to launch the drug in a package size that is not present in the high-income countries, thereby eliminating the need to reference the product as with the other countries. Another strategy includes the introduction of discounts through various offers in low-income countries, so that the actual price remains inherently the same, but the price at which the product is available in that country is lower than that applied in high-income countries [1].

16.5 **Discussion**

The International Reference Pricing (IRP) has been applied by almost all developed nations, except Sweden and the UK. However, in these countries there are other ways of maintaining prices, such as the value-based pricing, implemented by the United Kingdom. Despite the attractiveness of creating similar price processes through a benchmarking procedure carried out in all the countries in which the pharmaceutical products are sold, there are some inherent processes that might be severely and negatively affected. One of these process is the research and development for new and innovative medicines, which is driven by a percentage of the revenues. The IRP does not optimize the price for the well-being of patients, because through IRP there are many treatments that patients might not ever get access to, while it also might not lead to a loss of opportunities through a loss of well-being due to the lack of differential pricing. Thus, the results can be seen in terms of lesser sales revenue from the company perspective, and of loss of treatment opportunities from the patients' perspective. Also, it negatively obstructs the R&D process of new innovative drugs. We can therefore understand the need to create a common ground between reference pricing and differential pricing, where researchers and policy-makers can strategize and devise various schemes that can evenly balance between companies, patients and payers factors such as risk sharing, price and volume, payback, discounts and the burden of further R&D expenses.

16.6 **References**

1. Houy N, Jelovac I. Drug Launch Timing and International Reference Pricing. *Health Econ* 2015; 24: 978-89
2. Geng D, Saggi K. International effects of national regulations: External reference pricing and price controls. *J Int Econ* 2017; 109: 68-84
3. Nagle TT, Zale J, Hogan JE. The strategy and tactics of pricing : a guide to growing more profitably. Oxford: Routledge, 2016
4. Rémuzat C, Urbinati D, Mzoughi O, et al. Overview of external reference pricing systems in Europe. *J Mark Access Health Policy* 2015; 3
5. Morgan SG, Law M, Daw JR, et al. Estimated cost of universal public coverage of prescription drugs in Canada. *CMAJ* 2015; 187: 491-7
6. Salter M. Reference Pricing: An Effective Model for the U.S. Pharmaceutical Industry? *Nw J Int'l L & Bus* 2015; 35:1-27
7. Boehma G, Yao L, Han L, et al. Development of the generic drug industry in the US after the Hatch-Waxman Act of 1984. *Acta Pharm Sin* B 2013; 3: 297-311
8. Paris V, Belloni A. Value in Pharmaceutical Pricing. Country Profile: Australia. OECD, 2014. Available at https://www.oecd.org/health/Value-in-Pharmaceutical-Pricing-Australia.pdf (last accessed September 2017)

9. Persson U, Jönsson B. The End of the International Reference Pricing System? *Appl Health Econ Health Policy* 2016; 14: 1-8

10. Jelovac I, Houy N. Drug approval decision times, international reference pricing and access to new drugs. 38èmes Journées des Economistes de la Santé Français (JESF). Lyon, December 2016

11. Ando G, Lockwood C, Izmirlieva M. The Expansion of Use of Discounted Prices for International Reference Pricing Purposes. *Value Health* 2015; 18: A519

12. Yılmaz ES, Koçkaya G, Yenilmez FB, Impact of Health Policy Changes on Trends in the Pharmaceutical Market in Turkey. *Value Health Reg Issues* 2016; 10: 48-52

13. Towse A, Pistollato M, Mestre-Ferrandiz J, et al. European Union Pharmaceutical Markets: A Case for Differential Pricing? *International Journal of the Economics of Business* 2015; 22: 263-75

https://doi.org/10.7175/747.ch17

17. General Overview of Value-Based Pricing

Güvenç Koçkaya [1]
[1] *CarthaGenetics, Pully, Switzerland*

17.1 The Value-Based Pricing (VBP) Concept

The main initiative taken by a government to change the drug pricing system was undertaken in the UK in December 2010. The deliberation gave way to a new pricing system, the Value-Based Pricing (VBP), which entered into force by 2014. VBP aimed to replace the existing Pharmaceutical Price Regulation Scheme (PPRS) strategy of price regulation, which is a voluntary agreement between the Department of Health (DH) and the pharmaceutical industry, where pharmaceutical companies negotiate rates of drug sales for profit with the National Health Service (NHS) [1]. This negotiation happens every five years, when price and profit controls are established and implemented. Due to the need for a better way of pricing medicines, VBP emerged from the Office of Fair Trading (OFT), who conducted a report in 2007, and recommended that prices of individual pharmaceutical products should reflect more than the investment in the development of the products themselves. Rather, the price of the product should also reflect the "clinical and therapeutic value to patients and – more broadly – to the NHS" [2].

VBP was introduced in the market with the aim to found drugs pricing and access to new health technologies on sound principles that reflect social values and the budget-constrained context.

The pricing scheme thus requires clarity on the issues related to principles and social values and details regarding the implementation and operation process.

This fundamental change in the pharmaceutical regulation offers an opportunity to align the incentives of manufacturers, the NHS, and the individual prescribers. The principles of VBP might be better described as 'benefit-based pricing': the price at which the health benefits of a new product are non-inferior to the health benefits lost due to the services moved to finance it [3].

17.2 Need for VPB in the Pharmaceutical Industry

The Pharmaceutical Price Regulation Scheme (PPRS), which was replaced by the VPB, had existed since the late 1950s, and throughout this period its fundamental principles remained the same. It attempted to combine the process of delivering value for money for the NHS as a purchaser of branded drugs with the creation of a stable and attractive operating environment for the pharmaceutical industry in the UK. However, this blending of procurement and quality policies was contradictory in its actual essence, since the interests of the industry and the customers' needs were not aligned.

Consequently, the VBP process was necessary to create a better system, in order to align the vision of the NHS and NICE in the UK drug industry.

To realize the profits from the VBP scheme, a careful specification on what defines "value" is needed. The OFT report showed that the main focus regards the role VBP plays in aligning the incentives for investment in R&D with the needs of the NHS [4]. Faced with stagnant healthcare budgets, with the added burden of an ever-growing demand for care, the pharmaceutical companies were subject to severe pressure to provide evidence related to the value of their products. Pharmaceutical companies have been subject to public and political control, and while the world is just recovering from the recession, there has been an increased need to ensure a system that oversees the pricing strategy of these organizations [5]. When clinicians and healthcare professionals have some reservations about the effectiveness of a drug, VBP enables pharmaceutical companies to show their commitment, by demonstrating their confidence in the drug's efficacy in a real-world setting. When the market for the drug is highly competitive, VBP gives pharmaceutical companies an opportunity to differentiate their therapies and gain market share [6].

17.3 Stakeholders

The main stakeholders in the VBP scheme are the government, the pharmaceutical industry, and the consumers.

When implementing a VBP strategy, the government body, which in the case of UK is represented by the NHS and NICE [7], aimed at providing a capped price to innovative and generic drugs, to make drugs affordable for the patients. They also made sure that the industries that developed these drugs get the proper credit for investing in a company that does not have a great success ratio [8]. After the implementation of VBR, the government (NHS) was able to save approximately £ 1.2 billion in terms of drugs expenditure, which is a very important achievement for the pharmaceutical industry [9]. Furthermore, drug prices in the UK decreased by 21%, compared to other European countries [6]. Another important stakeholder is the customer, who requires access to important life-saving drugs at affordable costs. The pricing strategy created by VBR helps stakeholders to afford the drugs that otherwise they would not be able to use, and provides them with an alternative to less effective drugs. The third most important stakeholders are the pharmaceutical companies, which earn their profit through the sale of their drugs and also recover the money they lost on failed drug development operations [10]. VBR put a threshold on the pricing of their drugs, which in some cases can lead to losing some profits. However, the pharmaceutical companies can enhance their image within the NHS,

NICE and the customers by providing value to their drugs through VBP. If the drug has value, the healthcare body is sure to provide a good price, which not only promotes drug sales and profits, but also helps create a sound reputation for the company. If the company is able to define and provide value, to measure effective outcomes, and to effectively manage the costs, it can successfully implement a VBP process.

17.4 Current VBP Practices

VBP is defined as "a programs for which financial incentives or disincentives are overlaid on top of the existing reimbursement mechanism (commonly called pay-for-performance – P4P); or fundamental payment reform, such as bundling payments across settings (ambulatory, hospital, or post-acute) or providers (physicians and institutions), or global capitation payments for a wide array of services" [2]. If appropriately structured, VBP holds the potential to motivate providers to improve clinical quality, reduce adverse events, coordinate care, avoid unnecessary costs, encourage patient-centered care, and invest in information technologies and other tools proven effective in improving quality [8]. To be a viable option in the UK, VBP must deliver efficiency (defined as the value for money) to the NHS and also provide adequate incentives for the pharmaceutical industry to invest in innovation. To do so, the new VBP system must be practical and uphold patient access to therapies, by providing quick access to effective therapies and maintaining supply, as well as being legally defensible [11]. Furthermore, a fine balance between financial stability and flexibility must be found among manufacturers and the government, and, finally, the transparency of the process is fundamental, because it upholds all the other factors presented here. The options for patented therapies are complex, since the reflection of value and incentive for innovation must be more explicit [12]. These points, when addressed properly, provide a good chance of creating a good VBP procedure, that can be followed for an effective implementation of the program's ideas.

17.5 Challenges to VBP implementation

Three basic principles of pricing can be distinguished: cost-based, competition-based, and value-based [12]. VBP leads to higher profits than other principles and, unlike them, VBP tries to assess the willingness to pay and to take maximum advantage of it [4]. Despite the superiority of VBP, in practice, cost- and competition-based pricing are still very common [10]. This apparent paradox is the result of the numerous obstacles that must be overcome to implement VBP [13]. VBP often results in a price structure with higher prices than the reference price for some customers, while allowing a price reduction for other customer groups [14], in this case – when the customers who would be willing to pay more may enjoy unintended price reductions – an effect known as arbitrage could happen.

According to Hinterhuber [10]: "the biggest obstacle to the introduction of VBP lies in estimating the differentiated customer value (i.e. the specific value that a product or service has for a customer) and the associated market research costs". Customers must have a full understanding of the processes in order to assess the extension of the added value one solution can generate, compared with the alternative. VBP requires that the price corresponds to the value perceived by the customer and, theoretically, every customer should have a new price offer, which is rarely feasible. For many companies, the problem is that the traditional principles of segmentation are unsuited to VBP. Therefore, VBP requires a specific type of segmentation – "price segmentation" – which takes into particular consideration the price interest, price knowledge, and price intentions as consumer and segment characteristics [15].

17.6 Factors Responsible for a Successful VBP Implementation

There is very limited published literature on the structural and implementation features associated with successful Pay for Performance programs. The studies that examine the effects of alternative designs in order to assess their impact on the provider's behavior are very rare [16]. Based on the published literature [3,5,7,9,17], there have been mixed findings on the effectiveness of VBP programs in meeting its intended goals to improve quality and to control costs. This may be because VBP programs are still a work in progress and these programs are constantly evolving.

One of the features that seems to influence the success of VBP programs is represented by sizable incentives: larger incentives for companies mean larger impact on performance, and a consequent compensation for the effort required to obtain them [18]. Another factor that can affect the success of VBP programs is the understanding, on the part of providers, what is important, and where that importance can be shown [19]. Apart from measuring the outcomes and gaining incentives, there is also a need to engage the key stakeholders in the implementation of the system design.

Similarly, providing an input on the program design and participating in the choice of the performance measures and targets are also important for a successful implementation [12]. In addition, the methodology that measures and rewards performance by assessing objective targets helps motivate the providers to reach set goals and receive an incentive payment [7]. Finally, the support given to providers to help them improve, through the use of data registries, helps the successful implementation of VBR. It is also to be noted that the best practices for sharing, consultative support, health coaching, and other infrastructure building are important types of support to be made available to the providers participating in VBP [20]. VBR has successfully introduced P4P incentives. However, it is not clear whether the system has provided an opportunity cost, and has reached any level of acceptance. Healthcare reformers in the UK are looking to address changes in the healthcare outcomes of the various companies, and are keen to apply innovative ideas, such as the triple-value framework and the NHS RightCare programme. It can be noted that many changes to the UK system are new; the processes can be implemented for a period of trial and error, so that there is sufficient data to draw better conclusions regarding the ways to improve the health outcomes and reduce the country's health inequalities.

17.7 **Conclusion**

VBP is an innovative tool for the authorities to make the right decision within the reimbursement process. On the other hand, innovative medicines with extremely good clinical results can benefit from this approach by showing their value, not their cost.

17.8 **References**

1. Damberg CL, Sorbero ME, Lovejoy SL, et al. Measuring Success in Health Care Value-Based Purchasing Programs: Findings from an Environmental Scan, Literature Review, and Expert Panel Discussions. *Rand Health Q* 2014; 4: 9
2. McHugh M, Joshi M. Improving evaluations of value-based purchasing programs. *Health Serv Res* 2010; 45: 1559-69
3. Kanavos P, Manning J, Taylor D, et al. Implementing value-based pricing for pharmaceuticals in the UK. London: 2020health, 2010
4. Hughes D. Value-based pricing: incentive for innovation or zero net benefit? *Pharmacoeconomics* 2011; 29: 731-5
5. Claxton K, Briggs A, Buxton MJ, et al. Value based pricing for NHS drugs: an opportunity not to be missed? *BMJ* 2008; 336: 251-4
6. Towse A. Value based pricing, research and development, and patient access schemes. Will the United Kingdom get it right or wrong? *Br J Clin Pharmacol* 2010; 70: 360-6
7. Webb D. Value-based medicine pricing: NICE work? *Lancet* 2011; 377: 1552-3
8. Willis M, Persson U, Zoellner Y, et al. Reducing uncertainty in value-based pricing using evidence development agreements. *Appl Health Econ Health Policy* 2010; 8: 377-86
9. Sussex J, Towse A, Devlin N. Operationalizing value-based pricing of medicines. *Pharmacoeconomics* 2013; 31: 1-10
10. Hinterhuber A. Customer value-based pricing strategies: why companies resist. *Journal of business strategy* 2008: 29: 41-50
11. Persson U, Svensson J, Pettersson B, et al. A new reimbursement system for innovative pharmaceuticals combining value-based and free market pricing. *Appl Health Econ Health Policy* 2012; 10: 217-25
12. Danzon P, Towse A, Mestre-Ferrandiz J. Value-Based Differential Pricing: Efficient Prices for Drugs in a Global Context. *Health Econ* 2015; 24: 294-301

13. Cavusgil ST, Calantone RJ, Zhao Y. Tacit knowledge transfer and firm innovation capability. *Journal of Business & Industrial Marketing* 2003; 18: 6-21

14. Avlonitis GJ, Indounas KA. Pricing practices of service organizations. *Journal of Services Marketing* 2006; 20: 346-56

15. Diller H. Price fairness. *Journal of Product & Brand Management* 2008; 17: 353-35

16. Liozu S, Hinterhuber A, Perelli S, et al. Mindful pricing: transforming organizations through value-based pricing. *Journal of Strategic Marketing* 2012; 20: 197-209

17. Raftery J. Value based pricing: can it work? *BMJ* 2013; 347: f5941

18. Jayadev A, Stiglitz J. Two ideas to increase innovation and reduce pharmaceutical costs and prices. *Health Aff (Millwood)* 2009; 28: w165-8

19. Liozu S, Hinterhuber A, Boland R, et al. The conceptualization of value-based pricing in industrial firms. *Journal of Revenue and Pricing Management* 2012; 11: 12-34

20. McGuire, A., Raikou, M. & Kanavos, P., 2010. Pricing pharmaceuticals: Value based pricing in what sense? Eurohealth, 14(3).

21. Mcguire A, Raikou M, Kanavos P. Pricing pharmaceuticals: Value based pricing in what sense? *Eurohealth* 2008; 14: 3-5

https://doi.org/10.7175/747.ch18

18. The Role of Patients in Market Access

Anke-Peggy Holtorf[1], Nigel Cook[2]
[1] *Health Outcomes Strategies GmbH, CH 4055 Basel*
[2] *Head of Decision Support & Insights, Global Patient Access, Novartis Pharma AG, CH4056 Basel*

18.1 Patients are Active Partners

'Meeting the needs of patients' is increasingly important in developed healthcare systems. In this context, active patient involvement should ensure that patient perspectives are considered throughout the research, development, and stakeholder decision-making process. Today, patients rightly expect an active role in managing their disease. Throughout the '90s, some patients started to prepare for the doctor-visit with own research about their symptoms and potential remedies, and even challenged the doctor's recommendations, which before had mostly been accepted without question.

Active patients formed networks and alliances and requested shared decision-making on an individual level. By forming alliances and patient organizations, they also started to demand a voice in decisions about health policies and research. Famous examples are the HIV-community in San Francisco during the '80s, campaigning for the right to participate in decisions that directly affected their lives, or the French Muscular Dystrophy Association, which meanwhile even funds its own research and the development of new therapies [1,2].

Doctors began acknowledging the importance of discussing with their patients the therapeutic options related to their health. Indeed, it became clear that patients often had different views or expressed different needs from those things considered important by healthcare professionals or researchers, justifying a more direct role of patients in developing measures and criteria important in healthcare decisions [3].

Even Patient Reported Outcomes, or PROs, which are supposed to reflect the patient benefits, are sometimes not necessarily considered as *important* or *relevant* by the patients for which the products are intended [4-6]. Many healthcare decision makers now ask for Patient *Relevant* Outcomes and patient experiences when they consider access to new technologies or their reimbursement [7]. A recently released book on 'Patient Involvement in Health Technology Assessment' lays a foundation for more standardized approaches and best practices for including the patient perspective in the evaluation of new therapies [8].

For the practice of medicine, this development has also shaped the newest revision of the "Geneva Physician's Pledge", the modern successor to the Hippocratic Oath for physicians around the world which was approved by the World Medical Association in November 2017 [9]. The new pledge reflects the changing relationship between physicians and their patients. For the first time, the new pledge makes specific reference to respecting the *autonomy* and *dignity* of the patient and to aim for *health* and *well-being* of the patient[1].

18.2 "Nothing About me Without me"

Who decides which criteria or endpoints are relevant to patients? Is it the doctor, with the academic training and the experience of seeing and talking to thousands of patients? Is it the decision-maker charged with ensuring fair and equal access to treatments for all patients? Is it the patient who must live with the disease in her or his specific environment? Or the care person, who sometimes knows best, what is important to the patients they care for and to their life? What about society in general and citizen's (tax payers) view on how the healthcare budget should be spent? While there is no right answer, it has become clear that a multi-stakeholder involvement is needed and that patients and their carers should be heard for the key questions leading to essential decisions on their health or ability to live with a certain quality of life. Indeed, as patient advocates often say: "Nothing about me without me" [10].

18.3 Is Industry Prepared for the Change?

Developers of new health technologies need to be well prepared in order to answer questions about how their new therapeutic intervention provides incremental benefit to those patients for whom they are intended; and also, increasingly, how and to what extent were patients involved in the design of the studies to evaluate the new intervention and its benefits. Before a decision is made on marketing authorization, access or reimbursement, patients will be asked to describe the value from their perspective (see examples of patient considerations in Figure 1) [11-13].

Thus, to ensure that a new technology meets the needs of patients, companies start to more actively involve patients throughout the entire development process and life cycle of the product [14]. This is a new and daunting task for many manufacturers because until now, product development was product or approval centric; direct contact to patients was not systematic nor frequently done. Patient organizations were sponsored and viewed as advocates at the time of decision-making meetings, rather than considered

---

[1] «As a member of the medical profession: i solemnly pledge to dedicate my life to the service of humanity; the health and well-being of my patient will be my first consideration; I will respect the autonomy and dignity of my patient [...]» [9]

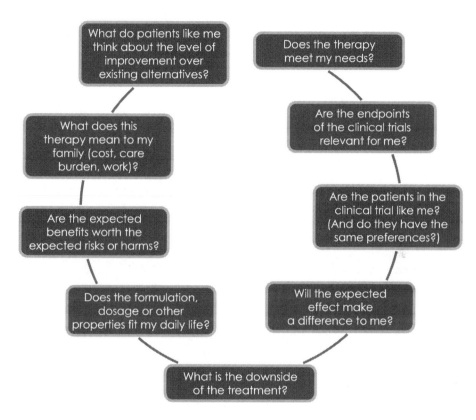

Figure 1. Key questions concerning the differential value of new therapies from the patient perspective

partners with joint interests and inputs to the innovation process [15]. Even for those companies that recognized early on that patients can contribute significantly to a successful development, there was still uncertainty around the 'How', 'What', and 'When' of their involvement [15,16].

A sound and transparent process of involving patients through the product life cycle is therefore essential. At each step of this involvement it should be clearly defined, 1) what the objective of the involvement is, 2) which target audience will be best able to give the required information, 3) which are best (most informative, robust, reliable and fit-for-purpose) methods to elicit the information, 4) what the consequences of the new information would be (how it will inform decisions to be made), and 5) how it will be communicated or disseminated to which target audience, including those in the patient community who contributed. There is no best practice established yet, but there are models emerging, which see patient insights and preferences as important pillars in the development of the evidence-based value proposition of new products [14,16,17].

18.4 Industry Should be Interested: Improved Commercial Attractiveness Through Patient-centric Product Development

Next to meeting expectations of decision makers, solid commercial reasons support the investment in patient (stakeholder) involvement and engagement, as summarized in Figure 2. Aspects such as the optimization of the design of clinical trials and the design of the product itself, increased relevance of the results to patients and decision makers and, potentially, a decrease in the drop-out rate due to better compatibility with patient needs, have been described by other authors [18,19]. If patient representatives or organizations are convinced that the product confers meaningful additional patient benefit, they will support the development and request access to the products.

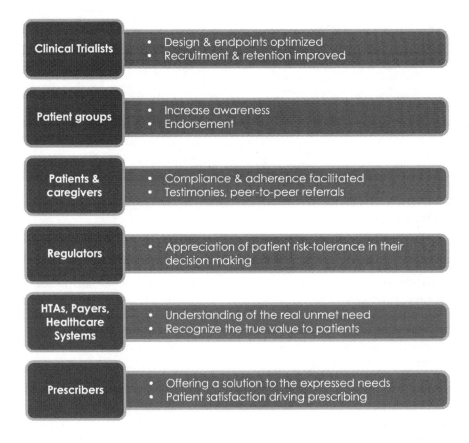

Figure 2. Positive effects of stakeholder involvement throughout the entire product life cycle

Patients may disseminate early information about the technology or upcoming clinical trials or they may explain the evidence from patients' perspective. Regulatory or reimbursement related authorities may better recognize the unmet need and the value of the technology to patients if this information has been elicited from and with patients throughout the development of the product (Figure 2). Prescribers will see that the new technology addresses otherwise unmet patient needs, which will increase the willingness to prescribe it and thus, the uptake of the product.

Levitan et al. estimated the financial value of patient engagement for an oncology program by calculating the expected net present value (ENPV) based on the key business drivers cost, time, revenue, and risk [20]. For a pre-phase-2-program they found a cumulative increase in ENPV of $35 million and for a pre–phase-3 program $75 million and claimed that patient engagement can lead to ENVP increases by more than 500-fold the investment.

18.5 What do Patients Expect from the Engagement Activities?

The values of patients for engaging in quality of life research during product development was recently examined through a world café[2] approach. The participants expressed a strong need for "building genuine, collaborative and deliberative relationships - underpinned by honesty, respect, co-learning and equity". Their motivation was to improve the quality and relevance of the research through their engagement [21]. Patient organizations complained that they saw no reason for being involved only at a late stage of clinical development after study completion. They preferred to see an honest engagement strategy of a company, which allowed them to make an impact on the quality of the data and hence, on the relevance of the product and the underlying evidence. A survey conducted in 2014 among patient organizations identified 6 key expectation categories for engaging in clinical research: 1) relevance to real patients, 2) safety in studies, 3) comprehensible information to study participants, 4) making a contribution to useful therapies 5) making effective therapies accessible, and 6) being part of the team, not just a study object [22]. Therefore, effective patient engagement strategies should build on continuous collaboration and productive relationships between the partners involved. Once more companies engage earlier and throughout development with patients, we can expect a much better alignment of all stakeholders concerning product benefits evaluated and patient unmet needs.

---

[2] World Café workshop: A method allowing each individual in a larger group of participants to actively contribute to the discussion or the development of a theme [Juanita Brown, David Isaacs: The World Café. Shaping Our Futures Through Conversations That Matter, McGraw-Hill Professional]

18.6 **Who is the Patient?**

The term "patient involvement" does not specify which patient is involved and how patient participants are selected. Different types of input can come from patients, carers, patient advocates and patient organizations in different collaborative processes or context. In many situations, the term 'patient' implicitly also includes caregivers (for examples the parents caring for children or the family member caring for elderly patients). In addition to the patients, citizens as representatives of the public may be involved, which is often the case in the context of health technology assessment and reimbursement decisions. It should be noted, that their perspective may differ substantially from that of patients [23]. It is important to understand, which type of involvement is required at each step of product development and which person or organization can best fulfil that requirement. For example, the stage in the patient journey should be considered as well as the purpose of the patients' or organizations' advocacy efforts, which audience they target, and which level of expertise they should have (see Figure 3).

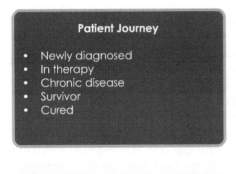

Figure 3. The universe of patient advocates or patient organizations

18.7 Guidance on Involvement in Industry Research, Regulatory Processes, or HTA

Triggered by the Innovative Medicines Initiative (collectively supported by the EU Commission and the European Pharmaceutical Industry), the European Patients' Academy on Therapeutic Innovation Project (EUPATI) was formed as a consortium of patient organizations, academic institutions and pharmaceutical companies under the leadership of the European Patient Forum (EPF) to increase Patient and Public Involvement (PPI) and public awareness of medicines R&D across Europe [15]. EUPATI developed courses to increase the capacity of patient experts for active involvement in medicines R&D, a toolkit for patient advocates to facilitate dissemination of information on medicines R&D to the patients they represent, and an online library of medicines R&D information for the public. Finally, they developed and released after broad consultation a multi-layer guidance on the best approach to interaction of patients with pharmaceutical industry-led medicines R&D, regulatory authorities, ethics committees and HTA agencies [24]. The guidance is targeted to patients and to the respective party involving the patient representatives.

In the USA, the Patient-Centered Outcomes Research Institute (PCORI, http://www.pcori.org) pushes for processes to ensure that researchers work with patients in the design and conduct of a clinical trial. The vision of the institution is that "Patients and the public have information they can use to make decisions that reflect their desired health outcomes". The institute supports involvement of patients and other stakeholder in research through developing guidance, establishing case examples, and building awareness.

Other guidance documents have been developed by various organizations and mostly focused on specific aspects of patient involvement such as legal or ethical issues described by EFPIA [25] or the 'European Medicines Agency (EMA) Framework of Interaction' between the EMA and patients, consumers and their organizations, which outlines the basis for involving patients and consumers in Agency activities [26].

Several groups have produced guidance for various stakeholders such as clinical and outcomes researchers [27], those who develop guidelines [28], or those who evaluate technologies or therapies through formal health technology assessment processes [7]. Relating to health technology assessment, an international multi-stakeholder workgroup (HTAi Patient and Citizen Involvement Special Interest Group) collaborates and advocates since several years to strengthen the exchange of experience and the continuous methodological development in this area [8,29].

Moreover, organizations have started to set up own organization-specific principles and recommendations for engagement. Over time, it can be expected that these diverse but overlapping guidance initiatives will complement each other, converge, and become accepted and adopted more universally. Specifically as a collaborative approach, the Innovative Medicines Initiative 'PREFER' (2016-2021) aims to assess when and how patient preferences on benefits and risks should be incorporated into decisions on medicinal products and to develop methodological guidance for patient involvement in the development, approval, and post-approval of new therapies (see Table in Appendix) [30,31].

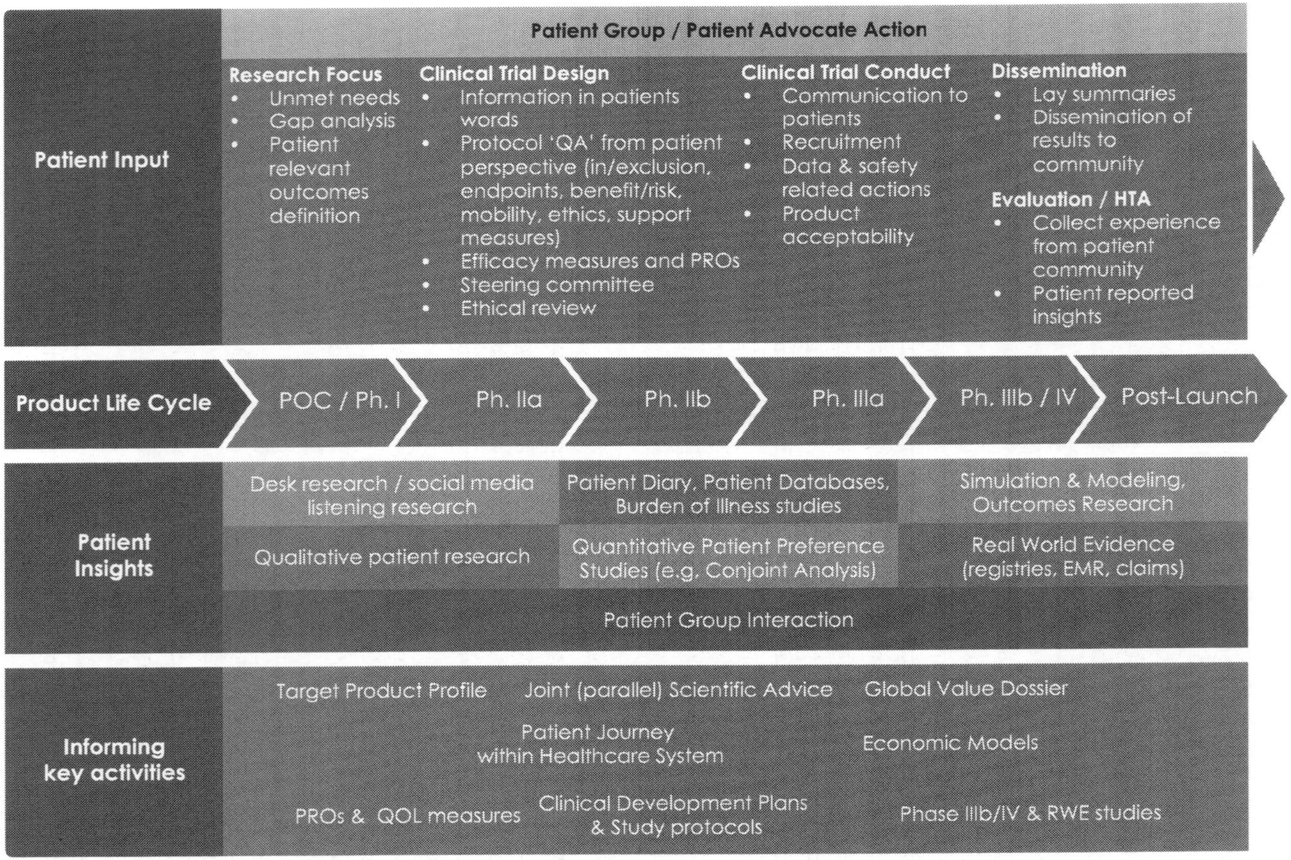

Figure 4. Patient insights and patient input throughout the Product Lifecycle

EMR = Electronic Medical Record; HTA = Health Technology Assessment; Ph. = Phase; POC = Proof of Concept; PRO = Patient Reported Outcomes; QA = Quality Assurance; QoL = (Health Related) Quality of Life

18.8 Activities for Gaining Patient Insights and for Patient Involvement

Gaining patient insights through patient involvement and by collecting information on the *patient perspective* is an ongoing process throughout the entire product lifecycle which starts already in early development phases (phase 1 or pre-clinical). A structured process as outlined in the 'Insights' part of Figure 4 may start with qualitative research on patient behaviors, patient interactions with their environment, and their current choices.

This may be useful for better understanding the disease or condition and its impact on patients, identifying outcomes most important to patients, and understanding benefit-risk trade-offs for treatments. Patient insights can inform the clinical trial protocols or the formulation of specific research questions to quantify certain aspects in the subsequent development steps. After launch, this information can also drive the collection of real life outcomes data on aspects which are beyond the clinical trial context.

The process should be accompanied by patient advisors (patient organizations) with a good knowledge of both the patient perspective and the framework of clinical trial design and medicines development. Their input on various aspects of the clinical studies and their collaboration in the communication to patients as exemplified in the 'Input' part of Figure 4 can help in ensuring that the product-related evidence is important to patients and can facilitate a better uptake and utilization of the product.

Importance of Gaining Patient Insights in Early Development

Better understanding of what the patient values and what their needs are, can inform clinical trial planning including development of educational material about the clinical trials, potential venues for recruitment, convenience to participants, and which terminology is familiar to the patients. There are several observational approaches existing to gather this information. Real life observation of patients or analysis of discussions on social media sites or in bespoke Online Bulletin Boards can reveal valuable information about patient needs or patient values [32,33].

Social media listening is gaining in popularity because it is comparably quick and easy to conduct and can yield a lot of valuable patient and disease information [34,35]. This approach is nice in that it listens to the discussions that are already happening online, in the *words* and through the discourse that patients/caregivers *routinely* use, without in any way influencing those conversations. Hence, without burdening the patients/patient groups with additional surveys, a lot of insights can be gathered on the needs and concerns of patients, to inform drug development and access strategies, as shown in Figure 5.

Online bulletin boards (OBB) are an asynchronous, online tool for qualitative market research, similar to a chat room, that allows invited participants to answer pre-defined questions in a comprehensive manner. The discussion typically runs over 4-5 days,

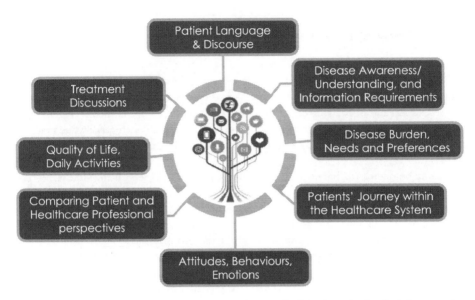

Figure 5. Developing patient insights from social media listening studies to inform early drug development and access strategies

is moderated, structured and allows open answered (free text) answers as well as responses to the posts of the other participants. Typically, 10-12 patients with a specific disease are invited to participate, with the conversation over the course of the study following an outline like that shown in Figure 6. Participants chose nicknames, *providing* anonymity, hence the OBB lends itself very well to uncovering patient insights which might not be revealed in focus groups or telephone interviews, particularly on more sensitive, embarrassing, or emotional issues, that people often have difficulty to talk about openly. The technique *can be used to conduct patient or caregiver research* in highly prevalent conditions as well as extremely rare diseases [36]. Since the online conversation extends over several days, *it also provides the opportunity to go deeper on interesting points that arise, ask for clarification, or explore commonality and differences among participants.*

Patient Preference Studies: building on the insights from qualitative research, patient preference studies can be important as a form of patient-based evidence for highlighting the needs in a quantitative form [37-39]. A task force of the International Society of Pharmacoeconomics and Outcomes Research (ISPOR) has started to define best practices for some of the quantitative methods such as conjoint analysis and discrete choice experiments [40,41] and this is also the subject of the IMI PREFER project [31]. Such studies can be used to show the relative importance to the patient of different treatment attributes for a product in clinical development, i.e. to reveal the value of different product profiles, which is important for informing HTA discussions. Whilst most preference research to date has focused on drugs in late stage development, to show the benefits conferred by the new drug compared to existing ones, increasingly patient preference

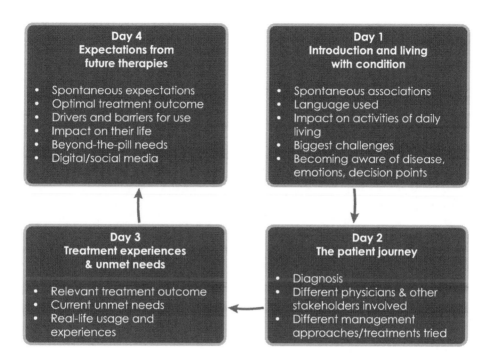

Figure 6. Online bulletin board (OBB) example of typical daily discussion and project flow over 4 days

studies are being conducted much earlier, to highlight the important value drivers from a patient perspective and thereby inform the design of PROs, pivotal clinical trials, and observational studies (Figure 7). The insights and evidence generated through these early development patient preference studies, provide a good foundation for early dialogue/ scientific advice discussions with HTA and regulatory agencies, to align on the importance of patient endpoints and evidence to capture in further development phases. From the regulatory perspective, there is high interest in understanding the benefit/risk profile of new drugs, and whether there are subgroups of patients with different preferences concerning the benefit/risk trade-off [42].

A good example of the use of patient preference studies is Myeloma UK, who have been working with the EMA to explore patient preference for different benefit and risk outcomes in myeloma treatment [43]. A further investigation has since been conducted to understand what myeloma patients want from treatments, to inform further R&D activities in myeloma, inform discussions with stakeholders, and to provide a basis for patient-physician conversations around therapy choices [44]. Myeloma UK are also collaborating with NICE on an exploratory project to enable the development of the quantitative methodology to incorporate patient preferences into HTA.

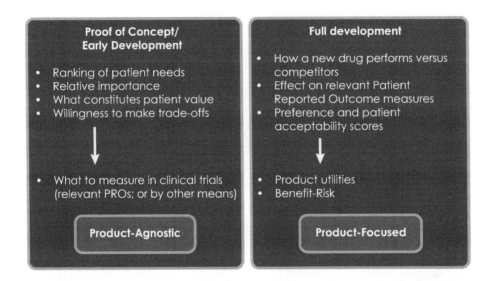

Figure 7. The need for different approaches to address Patient Preferences across the product life cycle. The methodologies may differ depending on the stage of product development and the questions to be answered.

Incorporating Patient Preferences into Health Economic Evaluations. Economic analyses can be conducted from different perspectives such as that of payers, hospitals, the public or the patient. The types of costs and outcomes included in the analysis will be specific to the specific stakeholders' interests (perspective). Currently, not many health economic studies are conducted from the patient perspective. However, both health outcomes and cost will impact the patients' decision on using the therapy and should therefore be more routinely studied [45]. Whilst health economic evaluations have traditionally focused on generic PRO instruments like EQ5D as the basis of the evaluation (e.g., of Quality-Adjusted Life Years), patients often criticize that these generic instruments do not fully capture the aspects that are important to them, and factors beyond Quality of Life are not taken account of in the economic evaluations [6,46]. For example, willingness to pay may be another component of patient preference research, to inform in future the economic evaluations [47].

Addressing patient insights in a stepwise process

Not all options for gaining patient insight may be required for all products and therefore, a patient insight strategy should be developed for each product. Such a strategy is outlined below in Figure 8 and it exemplifies how each step in this process may inform the design of the next step and lead to a more robust clinical trial design and HTA strategy.

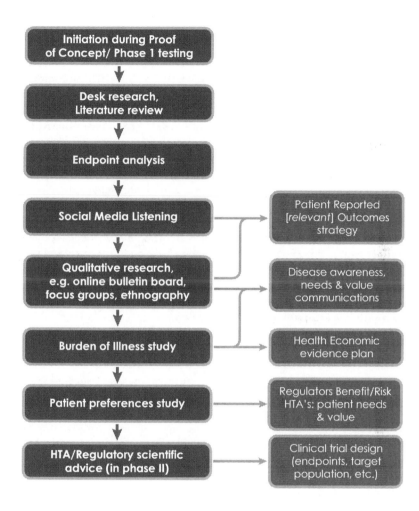

Figure 8. A structured process for patient insight gathering in early drug development

Examples of Patient Input

Patients as Research Partners (PRP): The patient is an equal partner and in direct dialogue with the researcher throughout the design, conduct and evaluation of the research including managerial and oversight roles [48,49].

Patient-Based Evidence: It has been suggested that in addition to clinical and health economic evidence, *patient-based evidence* should be considered in order to achieve high quality healthcare. The term "encompasses the diversity of information that patients provide in evaluating different aspects of care, including patient narratives, data on health-related quality of life and patient experiences survey data" [50]. Several groups have started to work on Patient Experience Frameworks and to define the methodological specifications of such evidence [8,50].

Patient Centered Outcomes Measures (PCOMs): Like Patient-Based Evidence, the concept of PCOMs has emerged in the recent years to overcome the limitation of standardized 'generic' Patient Reported Outcomes instruments. PCOMs include a diverse group of methods which have in common that they are all reported directly by the patients or carers and that they directly quantify the impact of a disease and treatment on health outcomes that matter to patients [6].

Review of patient material: At many stages throughout the product lifecycle, patient advocates may become involved with reviewing activities to ensure the patient relevance and acceptability, and appropriate use of patient-friendly language.

Input on clinical trial protocol: Patient advocacy groups are invited in their specific disease area to look at draft clinical trial protocols. The advocacy groups provide feedback about feasibility, recruitment, retention, outreach, or other important aspects from their viewpoint. The manufacturer will incorporate some of this before the protocol is finalized [3,49]. The input can happen through face to face discussions inside the team or as advisors, web based discussion, through advisory boards, or through other routes of communication [52,52]. An interesting new development is patient-led clinical trials (more specifically coordinated through patient support groups or organizations) which are increasingly gaining in popularity [53]. Whilst full development of a new drug, with all the regulatory and other hurdles to be overcome, is probably a daunting and unrealistic task for most patient organizations to consider, one could envisage an active role in partnering with clinical researchers to initiate and fund projects for the repurposing of already approved drugs in new indications (e.g. in rare cancers) [54].

Patient advocates or organizations as communication channel to patients: Patient advocates may form the bridge to the patient community by ensuring that documentation targeted to patients is understandable to patients or by translating and summarizing information related to clinical research or therapeutic information into patient-friendly language. If patient organizations are involved in the design of clinical studies and support the goals of the study, they may also encourage the patients who fit the inclusion criteria to enroll to the study e.g., through their healthcare provider.

Patient advocates or organizations as contributors to HTA: Healthcare systems are increasingly involving patients in the HTA or decision making processes with varying degree of formal processes [7]. Involvement can happen at any stage from horizon scanning through scoping to the actual assessment report and appraisal committee meeting. In order to learn from and improve the processes for patient involvement, any of the activities should be formally evaluated concerning their impact on decision making and the efficiency and acceptability of the process from both perspectives, the agency and the participating patients [55]. At the International Society for HTA, a multi-stakeholder work group (the Patient and Citizen's Involvement Group; http://www.htai.org/interest-groups/patient-and-citizen-involvement.html) is collaborating in order to improve the methodological, contextual and procedural ground for patient involvement in HTA. This work recently resulted in the publication of a first comprehensive guidance book, including the current status of patient involvement in HTA in numerous countries across the globe [8].

Development of treatment guidelines: It is suggested that patients should be involved in the development of treatment guidelines [56]. A systemativ review by Selva et al. of guidance documents for developing clinical guidelines from 56 institutions revealed that 71.4% of them recommended to include patients in one or several steps of creating the guidance (recommendation, reviewing the final version, formulating clinical questions, scoping, disseminating, implementing) [28]. However, it was not very well defined how this input should be generated. In future, clearer definitions can be expected for patient involvement as relating to the recruitment of the appropriate patients, the routes how patient based evidence or patient insights can be contributed, the acceptance of patient preference studies as appropriate evidence, adapting guidance presentation to highlight patient preference points and guidance on how a guideline can be best used for patient centric and shared decision making [57]. Patient involvement may gain a critical impact on the future adoption of new technologies by guidelines.

Two different groups, ICHOM (International Consortium for Health Outcomes Measurement; http://www.ichom.org) and COMET (Core Outcome Measures in Effectiveness Trials; http://www.comet-initiative.org/ppi/poppie) are engaged in the development of standard sets of outcomes measures for clinical trials and research in key diseases; both organizations actively engage patients to ensure the outcomes that matter to patients are captured and that these measures are adopted internationally. Already certain HTA agencies are referring to these standard outcome sets in their assessments of new drug submissions.

18.9 Up for Discussion

In this chapter, we have laid out the principles and opportunities for patient involvement in order to achieve market access. Whereas patient-focused drug development may once have been considered a 'nice to have', it has since moved on to a point where patient involvement and partnership is now an essential and necessary component of the drug development process, in order to successfully meet the demands of regulatory and reimbursement authorities, and indeed deliver new products which meet the expressed needs of patients for which they are intended.

Activities for gathering patient insights or evidence, as described in the 'Insight' part of Figure 4, can and should now be an integral part of the R&D process of pharmaceutical or medical technology companies. Exactly when to do this, and in which format or with which methodology, is an evolving science with a lot of experimentation happening and efforts to integrate approaches in an efficient, timely and cost effective manner (examples in Figure 4, & Figure 8). Not all of these approaches lend themselves to all stages of development and therefore, it is important to consider at each step what the expected output is, which decisions are to be informed through the patient voice, and which method is best suited to attain it most effectively (see examples in Figure 7).

One limitation is that the needs of the patients may change over time and most likely, also their preferences, e.g. due to changing market environment and availability of new treatments or management strategies. Therefore, the validity of this type of evidence may be short-lived and not be generalizable across healthcare systems and culturally different populations. Nevertheless, those companies will have a competitive advantage who refine their process to allow for sufficient patient insights and involvement and thereby, maximize the fit of their products to the needs of the users. Why would we develop products that are clinically and economically effective but not wanted or needed? Let's invest in a future where new innovative products also address the real needs of patients and provide the therapeutic outcomes they are looking for.

18.10 Appendix: Organizations vested in Patient Involvement

Organization	Focus	Description
ACRES Patient Engagement Initiative (PEI), (USA) http://www.acresglobal.net/about-us/initiatives/patient-engagement-initiative-pei	Clinical Research	ACRES, addresses the need to integrate patient centricity efforts across the research and healthcare environment while also considering the needs and priorities of the other stakeholders within the patient research and care eco-system.
BMJ Partnering with Patients (UK/global) https://involvement-mapping.patientfocusedmedicine.org/initiatives/partnering-with-patients	Research & development	Making medicines more relevant to those people who actually need it. Making sure that we have quality research and support doctors who are our main readers, to become better, more informed doctors. We aim to train doctors to become aware and applicable to patients' needs.
Center for Information and Study on Clinical Research Participation (CISCRP), (USA, global) https://www.ciscrp.org	Clinical research	Engage the public and patients as partners in the clinical research process. CISCRP provides a variety of resources, programs and services that are designed to assist clinical research stakeholders in understanding public and patient attitudes and experiences in research as well as improving volunteer participation experiences and satisfaction.
Center for Medical Technology Policy (CMTP) Real World Evidence, (USA) http://www.cmtpnet.org	Health policy, clinical development	(CMTP) is an independent non-profit organization dedicated to developing a health care system where patients, clinicians, healthcare policymakers, and payers have the evidence they need to make informed health decisions. CMTP focuses on providing methodological guidance, shaping health policy, and transforming clinical research. The work on methodological guidance is conducted under the umbrella of the Green Park Collaborative (GPC), a neutral forum to support dialogue and consensus among stakeholders on methodological standards for clinical research, focusing on real-world effectiveness and value.

Table continues >

> Table continued

Organization	Focus	Description
Community and Patient Preference Research (CaPPRe), (Australia) http://www.cappre.com.au	Policy, patient preferences	An educated consumer voice will help signal to Government, clinicians, and industry the importance of consumer preferences Bringing the two worlds together will help strengthen the PBS for Australia.
Critical Path Institute (C-Path), (USA, UK) https://c-path.org	drug development and regulatory process for medical products	C-Path orchestrates the sharing of data, expertise and knowledge among industry, regulatory authorities, government, patient advocacy groups and academia in the pre-competitive space to generate the evidence needed to improve the drug development pathway.
European Medicines Agency http://www.ema.europa.eu/ema	Regulatory approval	The framework for interaction between EMA and patients and consumers and their organizations outlines the basis for involving patients and consumers in Agency activities.
European Patient Forum (EPF), (Europe) http://www.eu-patient.eu	Health policy, access	Our mission is to ensure that the patients' community drives policies and programs that affect patients' lives to bring changes empowering them to be equal citizens in the EU.
European Patients' Academy on Therapeutic Innovation Project (EUPATI), (Europe) https://www.eupati.eu	Lifecycle of medicines	pan-European project implemented as a public-private partnership by a collaborative multi-stakeholder consortium from the pharmaceutical industry, academia, not-for-profit, and patient organizations with focus on education and training to increase the capacity and capability of patients to understand and contribute to medicines research and development and also improve the availability of objective, reliable, patient-friendly information for the public.
Health Technology Assessment international (HTAi) Interest Group on Patient and Citizen Involvement in HTA (PCIG) http://www.htai.org/interest-groups/patient-and-citizen-involvement/pcig-home.html	Health Technology Assessment	The vision of the HTAi PCIG is "Patient and citizen perspectives improve HTA". Among others, the group has developed resources like 'Values' and various submission templates and hosts a mailing list on the subject [29].
Innovative Medicines Initiative 'PREFER' http://www.imi.europa.eu/content/prefer	Patient Preferences for benefits and risks	A multi-stakeholder collaboration (2016-2021) which aims to assess when and how patient preferences on benefits and risks should be incorporated into decisions on medicinal products. The goal of PREFER will be to provide a set of systematic methodologies and recommendations to assess, engage and include patient perspectives during the development, approval, and post-approval of new therapies.

Table continues >

> Table continued

Organization	Focus	Description
International Children's Advisory Network (ICAN), (global) https://www.icanresearch.org	Children & families	A worldwide consortium of children's advisory groups working together to provide a voice for children and families in health, medicine, research, and innovation through synergy, communication and collaboration.
OMERACT Recommendations for Patient Research Partners Involvement, (Canada) https://www.omeract.org/patient_research_partners.php	Outcomes Measures in Rheumatology	Patient involvement strengthens outcomes research in rheumatology; the contribution of patient research partners to defining important outcome measures, such as minimum clinically important difference, recognizing domains of concern, such as sleep and fatigue, and ensuring feasibility of assessments, such as in the tolerability of MRI scanning times, has been manifest [15,26]
Patient Focused Medicines Development (PFMD), (Belgium/global) http://patientfocusedmedicine.org	Lifecycle of medicines, clinical research	An independent multinational and multi-stakeholder coalition, which aims to bring together initiatives and best practices that integrate the voice of the patient throughout the lifecycle of medicines development, thereby speeding up the creation and implementation of an effective, globally standardized framework.
PatientsLikeMe, (USA / global) http://www.patientslikeme.com	Real life health experience, clinical research, PRO development	PatientsLikeMe is committed to putting patients first. We do this by providing a better, more effective way for you to share your real-world health experiences in order to help yourself, other patients like you and organizations that focus on your conditions.

18.11 **References**

1. Callan M, Turner D. A History of the People With AIDS Self-Empowerment Movement. The Body. The Complete HIV/AIDS Resource, 1997. Available at http://www.thebody.com/content/31074/a-history-of-the-people-with-aids-self-empowerment.html (last accessed July 2017)
2. AFM-Telethon. History of the French Telethon. The French Telethon. Available at http://www.afm-telethon.com/the-telethon/history-of-the-french-telethon.html (last accessed July 2017)
3. Sacristán JA, Aguarón A2 Avendaño-Solá C et al. Patient involvement in clinical research: why, when, and how. *Patient Prefer Adherence* 2016; 10: 631-40
4. de Wit MP, Kvien TK, Gossec L. Patient participation as an integral part of patient-reported outcomes development ensures the representation of the patient voice: a case study from the field of rheumatology. *RMD Open* 2015; 1: e000129

5.   Berglas S, Jutai L, MacKean G et al. Patients' perspectives can be integrated in health technology assessments: an exploratory analysis of CADTH Common Drug Review. *Res Involv Engagem* 2016; 2: 21

6.   Morel T, Cano SJ. Measuring what matters to rare disease patients - reflections on the work by the IRDiRC taskforce on patient-centered outcome measures. *Orphanet J. Rare Dis* 2017; 12: 171

7.   Abelson J, Wagner F, DeJean D, et al. Public And Patient Involvement In Health Technology Assessment: A Framework For Action. *Int J Technol Assess Health Care* 2016; 32: 256-64

8.   Ørtenblad L, Groth Jensen L, Scalzo AL. EUnetHTA: Patients' perspectives in the HTA Core Model. In Facey KM, Ploug Hansen H, Single ANV (eds). Patient Involvement in Health Technology Assessment. Singapore: Springer, 2017

9.   The World Medical Association. The WMA Declaration of Geneva (Physician's Pledge). 2017. Available at https://www.wma.net/policies-post/wma-declaration-of-geneva/ (last accessed July 2017)

10. Puckrein G. Nothing About Me Without Me. Patient Research Exchange 2016) Available at https://www.patientresearchexchange.org/stories/detail/nothing-about-me-without-me (last accessed July 2017)

11. Postmus D, Mavris M, Hillege HL, et al. Incorporating patient preferences into drug development and regulatory decision making: Results from a quantitative pilot study with cancer patients, carers, and regulators. *Clin Pharmacol Ther* 2016; 99 :548-54

12. Klein AV, Hardy S, Lim R, et al. Regulatory Decision Making in Canada-Exploring New Frontiers in Patient Involvement. *Value Health* 2016; 19: 730-3

13. Grainger DL. Patient Involvement in Medicine Development and Assessment. In Facey KM, Ploug Hansen H, Single ANV (eds). Patient Involvement in Health Technology Assessment. Singapore: Springer, 2017

14. Perfetto EM, Burke L, Oehrlein EM, et al. Patient-Focused Drug Development: A New Direction for Collaboration. *Med Care* 2015; 53: 9-17

15. Parsons S, Starling B, Mullan-Jensen C, et al. What do pharmaceutical industry professionals in Europe believe about involving patients and the public in research and development of medicines? A qualitative interview study. *BMJ Open* 2016; 6: e008928

16. Geissler J, Ryll B, Leto di Priolo S. Improving Patient Involvement in Medicines Research and Development. *Therapeutic Innovation & Regulatory Science* 2017; 51: 612-9

17. Low E. Potential for patients and patient-driven organizations to improve evidence for health technology assessment. *Int. J. Technol. Assess. Health Care* 2015; 31: 226-7

18. Pushparajah D, Geissler J, Westergaard N. EUPATI: Collaborating between patients, academia and industry to champion the informed patient in medicines research and development. *J Med Dev Sci* 2015: 1

19. Warner K, See W, Haerry D, et al. Webinar: Guidance on Patient Involvement on Industry-led R&D. EUPATI 2017. Available at https://www.eupati.eu/webinar/webinar-guidance-patient-involvement-industry-led-rd/ (last accessed July 2017)

20. Levitan B, Getz K, Eisenstein EL, et al. Assessing the Financial Value of Patient Engagement: A Quantitative Approach from CTTI's Patient Groups and Clinical Trials Project. *Ther Innov Regul Sci* 2017;1-10

21. Haywood K, Lyddiatt A, Brace-McDonnell SJ, et al. Establishing the values for patient engagement (PE) in health-related quality of life (HRQoL) research: an international, multiple-stakeholder perspective. *Qual Life Res* 2017; 26: 1393-404

22. Holtorf AP. Patient Reported Outcomes. In Pradelli L, Wertheimer A (eds). Pharmacoeconomics. Principles and Practice Torino: SEEd, 2013

23. Fredriksson M, Tritter JQ. Disentangling patient and public involvement in healthcare decisions: why the difference matters. *Sociol Health Illn* 2017; 39: 95-111

24. EUPATI Consortium. Guidance documents on patient involvement in R&D. EUPATI 2016) Available at https://www.eupati.eu/guidance-patient-involvement/ (last accessed July 2017)

25. European Federation of Pharmaceutical Industry Associations (EFPIA). EFPIA Code of Practice on Relationships between the Pharmaceutical Industry and Patient Organisations. EFPIA 2011. Available at https://www.efpia.eu/media/24310/3c_efpia-code-of-practice-on-relationships-pharmapluspt-orgs.pdf (last accessed July 2017)

26. European Medicines Agency. Revised framework on the interaction of the Agency with patients and consumers and their organisations. EMA 2014. Available at http://www.ema.europa.eu/docs/en_GB/document_library/Other/2009/12/WC500018013.pdf (last accessed July 2017)

27. Kirwan JR, de Wit M, Frank L, et al. Emerging Guidelines for Patient Engagement in Research. *Value Health* 2017; 20: 481-6

28. Selva A, Sanabria AJ, Pequeño S, et al. Incorporating patients' views in guideline development: a systematic review of guidance documents. *J Clin Epidemiol* 2017; 88: 102-12

29. Wale JL, Scott AM, Bertelsen N, et al. Strengthening international patient advocacy perspectives on patient involvement in HTA within the HTAi Patient and Citizen Involvement Interest Group – Commentary. *Res Involv Engagem* 2017; 3: 3

30. de Bekker-Grob EW, Berlin C, Levitan B, et al. Giving Patients' Preferences a Voice in Medical Treatment Life Cycle: The PREFER Public-Private Project. *Patient* 2017; 10: 263-66

31. PREFER. IMI - Innovative Medicines Initiative. Available at http://www.imi.europa.eu/ (last accessed August 2017)

32. Tjørnhøj-Thomsen H, Ploug Hansen H. Ethnographic Fieldwork. In Facey KM, Ploug Hansen H, Single ANV (eds.). Patient Involvement in Health Technology Assessment. Singapore: Springer, 2017

33. Street J, Farrell L. Analysis of Social Media. In Facey KM, Ploug Hansen H, Single ANV (eds.). Patient Involvement in Health Technology Assessment. Singapore: Springer, 2017

34. Mullins, A. Generating patient insights in dry eye disease with a social media listening study. *Value Health* 2017; 20: A807

35. Metcalf M, Terkowitz J, Dasgupty N, et al. Learning by Listening, Digitally. *Value Outcomes Spotlight ISPOR* 2017; 3:11-3

36. Cook N. Identification of needs of PVNS patients using online bulletin board. HTAi 2017 Annual Meeting. Rome, June 17-21

37. Ryan M, Scott DA, Reeves C, et al. Eliciting public preferences for healthcare: a systematic review of techniques. *Health Technol Assess* 2001; 5: 1-186

38. Janus SI, Weernink MG, van Til JA, et al. A Systematic Review To Identify the Use of Preference Elicitation Methods in Health Care Decision Making. *Value Health* 2014; 17: A515-6

39. Weernink MGM, Janus SIM, van Til JA, et al. A Systematic Review to Identify the Use of Preference Elicitation Methods in Healthcare Decision Making. *Pharm Med* 2014; 28: 175-85

40. Bridges JF, Hauber AB, Marshall D, et al. Conjoint Analysis Applications in Health?a Checklist: A Report of the ISPOR Good Research Practices for Conjoint Analysis Task Force. *Value Health* 2011; 14: 403-13

41. Reed Johnson F, Lancsar E, Marshall D, et al. Constructing Experimental Designs for Discrete-Choice Experiments: Report of the ISPOR Conjoint Analysis Experimental Design Good Research Practices Task Force. *Value Health* 2013; 16: 3-13

42. Ho MP, Gonzalez JM, Lerner HP, et al. Incorporating patient-preference evidence into regulatory decision making. *Surg Endosc* 2015; 29: 2984-93

43. Postmus D, Richard S, Bere N, et al. Eliciting Individual Patient Preferences on The Benefits and Risks of Cancer Treatments: Results From A Survey Conducted in Myeloma Patients. *Value Health* 2016; 19: A746

44. Myeloma UK. Health Services Research Programme: Understanding what myeloma patients want from treatment - a discrete choice experiment methodological study. Myeloma UK in collaboration with Dr Simon Fifer, Community and Patient Preference Research, Australia. Available at https://www.myeloma.org.uk/what-we-do/research/health-services-research-programme/#1475078129713-e4cbd247-fcd8 (last accessed July 2017)

45. Tai BB, Bae YH, Le QA. A Systematic Review of Health Economic Evaluation Studies Using the Patient's Perspective. *Value Health* 2016; 19: 903-8

46. Holtorf AP, Palacios D, Brixner D. Are patient reported outcomes relevant to patients? Learnings from a patient advocate survey. *Value Health* 2014; 17: A517

47. Tinelli M, Ryan M, Bond C. What, who and when? Incorporating a discrete choice experiment into an economic evaluation. *Health Econ Rev* 2016; 6: 31

48. Wit M, Gossec L. Patients as Collaborative Partners in Clinical Research to Inform HTA. In Facey KM, Ploug Hansen H, Single ANV (eds.). Patient Involvement in Health Technology Assessment. Singapore: Springer, 2017

49. Dudley L, Gamble C, Preston J, et al. What Difference Does Patient and Public Involvement Make and What Are Its Pathways to Impact? Qualitative Study of Patients and Researchers from a Cohort of Randomised Clinical Trials. *PLoS ONE* 2015; 10: e0128817

50. Staniszewska S, Boardman F, Gunn L, et al. The Warwick Patient Experiences Framework: patient-based evidence in clinical guidelines. *Int J Qual Health Care* 2014; 26: 151-7

51. Shklarov S, Marshall DA, Wasylak T, et al. "Part of the Team": Mapping the outcomes of training patients for new roles in health research and planning. *Health Expect* 2017; 20: 1428-36

52. Marlett N, Shklarov S, Marshall D, et al. Building new roles and relationships in research: a model of patient engagement research. *Qual Life Res* 2015; 24: 1057-67

53. Sharma NS. Patient centric approach for clinical trials: Current trend and new opportunities. *Perspect Clin Res* 2015; 6: 134-8

54. Rare Cancers Australia - Research. Understanding Rare Cancers. Available at https://www.rarecancers.org.au/page/14/research (last accessed August 2017)

55. Weeks L, Polisena J, Scott AM, et al. Evaluation of Patent and Public Involvement in Health Technology Assessment. *IJTAHC* 2017 [accepted]

56. Krahn M, Naglie G. The next step in guideline development: incorporating patient preferences. *JAMA* 2008; 300: 436-8

57. Rashid A, Thomas V, Shaw T, et al. Patient and Public Involvement in the Development of Healthcare Guidance: An Overview of Current Methods and Future Challenges. *Patient* 2017; 10: 277-282

https://doi.org/10.7175/747.ch19

19. The Challenges and Future of Advanced Therapies

Selcen Öztürk [1]

[1] *Hacettepe University, Department of Economics, Ankara, Turkey*

19.1 Introduction

Globally, we observe that diagnostic and treatment methods are rapidly changing and evolving, due to epidemiologic and demographic transitions. In this context, personalized medicine is increasingly emerging, because of the recent technological advances in health care service provision. Several definitions have been proposed to define "personalized medicine" (Box 1). A formal definition can be as follows: "Providing the right treatment, to the right patient, at the right time, with the help of new biomarker-based diagnostic tests". Such tests help identify patients at high risk, or patients for whom conventional therapies are less effective, or ineffective – i.e. "stratification" [1].

Patients with the same diagnosis respond differently to the same therapy, due to their different genetic and biological endowments. Personalized medicine evaluates these differences on a molecular basis, and develops advanced therapies which depend on the patient's specific needs. This new field, which is arising from advanced pharmacology and genomics, is defined as pharmacogenomics [2]. Pharmacogenomics focuses on patients for whom pharmaceuticals are ineffective (Box 2). Personalized medicine and advanced therapies are more utilized in genetic and metabolic illnesses, such as cancer or rare genetic diseases. The most recent studies proved the existence of a significant relationship

---

Box 1. Different Definitions of Personalized Medicine

- "The use of new methods of molecular analysis to better manage a patient's disease or predisposition to disease" – *Personalized Medicine Coalition*
- "Providing the right treatment to the right patient, at the right dose at the right time" – *European Union*
- "The tailoring of medical treatment to the individual characteristics of each patient" – *President's Council of Advisors on Science and Technology*
- "Health care that is informed by each person's unique clinical, genetic, and environmental information" – *American Medical Association*
- "A form of medicine that uses information about a person's genes, proteins, and environment to prevent, diagnose, and treat disease" *National Cancer Institute, NIH*

Box 2. Percentage of Patients for Whom Pharmaceuticals are Ineffective [2]

- Depression: 38%
- Asthma: 40%
- Cardiac Arrhythmias: 40%
- Diabetes: 43%
- Migraine: 48%
- Arthritis: 50%
- Osteoporosis: 52%
- Alzheimer: 70%
- Cancer: 75%

---

with certain cancer markers and genes. Therefore, especially for cancer patients with family history of disease, genetic tests help reveal important information about the prognosis, the risk of metastasis, and sometimes even the possible success of the treatment. In this way, genetic tests help prevent unnecessary treatments and their associated costs. Personalized medicine helps identify key molecules in cell proteins. Advanced therapies can be designed to intervene with these key molecules, rather than others, and therefore can be more effective. Thanks to technological advances, the possibility to identify, in the near future, with genetic testing, the metabolic structure of individuals seems plausible; each patient will therefore be treated at the right time and with the right dosage of the right medicine. Advance therapies are expected to develop efficient and successful treatments for many severe, orphan diseases and chronic illnesses, such as cancer. Furthermore, the advances in personalized medicine extend beyond individuals that are already ill, and can offer early risk identification and preventive measures for the entire population [3-5]. For example, many pharmaceuticals used in neurologic and psychiatric treatments are metabolized by an enzyme called cytochrome P450. Cytochrome P450 class includes more than 50 enzymes that are responsible for metabolizing over 90% of pharmaceuticals. The genetic variability of these enzymes creates differences in the patients' responses to several pharmaceuticals. Therefore, gaining information about the genetic structure of the P450 enzymatic class is of great importance in the treatments of several severe and chronic illnesses [6].

19.2 Recent Developments in Advanced Therapies

In 2014, after a 14-year discovery process, the European Commission authorized the first gene therapy, Glybera® (alipogene tiparvovec), for the treatment of lipoprotein lipase deficiency (LPLD, type 1 hyperlipidemia). LPLD is a very rare disease, found in 1-2 individuals in 10 million [7]. The initial application process for the gene therapy for such ultra-rare disease started in December 2009, and the European Authorities rejected the

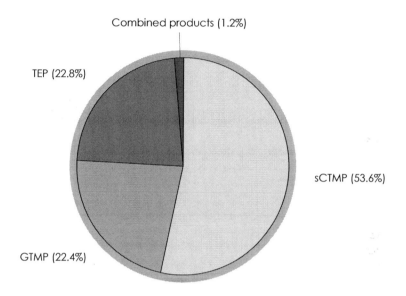

Figure 1. Advanced therapy drugs classification. Modified from [8]
GTMP = Gene Therapy Medicinal Products; sCTMP = somatic Cell Therapy Medicinal Products;
TEP = Tissue Engineered Products

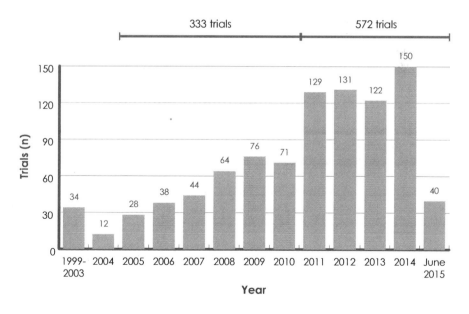

Figure 2. Number of registered trials from 1999 to 2015. Modified from [8]

application twice, due to the lack of wide-ranged efficacy tests. After a final re-examination in 2012, alipogene tiparvovec was approved and authorized for the marketing in the EU. However, five years after the approval, Glybera® was withdrawn from the market, not because of effectiveness or safety issues, but because of its high costs and limited use. In August 2017, the FDA announced the approval of Kymriah® (tisagenlecleucel) for children and young adults suffering from acute lymphoblastic leukemia (ALL), thus introducing the first gene therapy into the US market.

Advanced therapy drugs – that have been developed and are currently being tested – mainly target specific, severe and rare diseases, such as cancer and cardiovascular, musculoskeletal, immunological, neurological and hematological conditions. These drugs can be mainly classified as Gene Therapy Medicinal Products (GTMP), somatic Cell Therapy Medicinal Products (sCTMP), Tissue Engineered Products (TEP) and combined products. As shown in Figure 1, the majority of pharmaceuticals are somatic Cell Therapy Products.

The growing attention to personalized medicine can be seen in the significant increase in the number of trials that have been conducted with advanced therapy drugs from 1999 to 2015 (Figure 2).

Even with these high numbers of trials, today (2017) there are only 8 advanced therapy pharmaceuticals available in the EU market, and 15 in the US (Table 1). Therefore, it is possible to argue that the development of advanced therapy pharmaceuticals and personalized medicine are slower than expected. The reasons for this slow progress are three-fold: scientific – the development processes of advanced therapy pharmaceuticals are complex and R&D is intensive; regulatory – there are significant imperfections in the regulation of advanced therapy pharmaceuticals; and economic – there are issues regarding cost-effectiveness analyses, pricing and reimbursement [1]. In addition, it's possible to argue that, due to these imperfections, the incentives for personalized medicine and the innovation of advanced therapy drugs are not aligned [5].

Even considering the clear cost benefits and the social needs, Authorities may be reluctant to pay large, one-time sums for advanced therapies, for several reasons. Firstly, the effectiveness of the therapy might be in question. Since the approval of advanced therapies encounter problems with available data, the one-time payment must concern a "projected" duration of efficacy rather than an "actual" duration. Secondly, with the recent efforts to decrease pharmaceutical spending, such amounts can create arguments and criticism. In addition, especially for rare diseases, patients might not use advanced therapies. Therefore, even considering their proved effectiveness and cost benefits, the reimbursement of advanced therapies might encounter the reluctance on the part of third party payers. The governments' role should also be clarified in the pricing and reimbursement decisions regarding advanced therapies. A thoughtful structuring of the reimbursement system will also help the pharmaceutical companies to increase the level of investment in advanced therapies, which in return will yield higher benefits for society [9]. Advanced therapies pose a dilemma to health policy Authorities in terms of serious health improvements and challenges due to imperfections in cost-effectiveness analyses, market access, and the decisions on pricing and reimbursement.

Name	Classification	Marketing authorization holder	License date
KYMRIAH	Gene Therapy	Novartis Pharmaceuticals	30.08.2017
ZALMOXIS	Somatic cell therapy	MolMed	18.08.2016
NOVOCART INJECT	Tissue Engineered Products	TETEC	27.06.2016
STRIMVELIS	Gene therapy	GlaxoSmithKline	26.05.2016
IMLYGIC	Gene therapy	Amgen Europe	16.12.2015
HOLOCLAR	Tissue Engineered Products	Chiesi Farmaceutici	17.02.2015
NOVOCART 3D	Tissue Engineered Products	TETEC	29.08.2014
ZYTOKIN	Tumor Vaccine	Deutsches Rotes Kreuz Blutspendedienst	13.06.2014
BIOSEED-C	Tissue Engineered Products	BioTissue Technologies	4.06.2014
T2C001	Tissue Engineered Products	t2cure	31.03.2014
DCVAX-L	Tumor Vaccine	Northwest Biotherapeutics	21.02.2014
MUKOCELL	Tissue Engineered Products	UroTiss Europe	23.12.2013
CHONDROSPHERE	Tissue Engineered Products	co.don	12.12.2013
MACI	Tissue Engineered Products	Genzyme Europe	27.06.2013
GLYBERA	Gene therapy	uniQure	25.10.2012
PROVENGE	Gene Therapy	Dendreon	29.04.2010

Table 1. Advanced therapy medicinal products currently on the market

19.3 Cost-Effectiveness Analysis

Cost-effectiveness analysis (CEA) is a widely used tool in health economics and policy. In short, CEA aims to measure the potential success of any intervention comparing the relative costs of different actions aimed to achieve the same outcomes or effects [10]. In order to compare the costs and effectiveness of a course of action, monetary measures of both the outcome and cost must be provided. In terms of health policy, the outcome is usually measured by evaluating the changes in life expectancy or improvements in quality of life. However, measuring these aspects with money is challenging. The first challenge

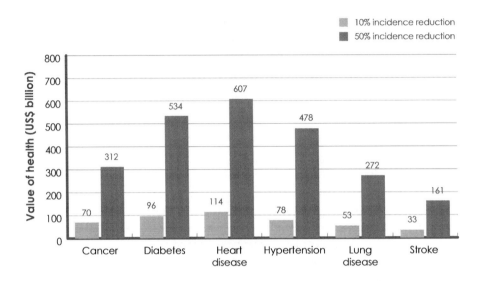

Figure 3. Potential benefits from personalized medicine calculated as cumulative value of additional QALY generated (2012-60, valued at US$ 100,000 each). Modified from [5]

derives from the basic question of microeconomics: "for whose benefit?". We can find different values for the same outcome by considering the perspective of the individual, the society, the payer or the pharmaceutical company. In addition, as reported by Porter (2010) [11], determining the relative outcomes is a complex process in health economics. Porter [11] proposed a "three-tier hierarchy" for outcome evaluation: the first tier includes "survival", or "the degree of health recovery", the second tier contains "time to recovery" and "disutility due to the treatment process", and the third tier embraces "the sustainability of recovery" and "long term consequences of the therapy". In health economics, unfortunately, only the first tier is usually used, and the other two are ignored in terms of outcome evaluation.

Even with only the first tier analysis using survival or the degree of health recovery, the possible individual and social benefits of advanced therapies are undeniable. Dzau et al. [5] use a simulation model to estimate the potential benefits of personalized medicine in early risk detection (Figure 3). With the help of personalized medicine, the individual risk levels for diseases such as cancer, diabetes, heart disease, hypertension, lung disease and stroke can be calculated. With efficient interventions on high-risk individuals, the benefits are reported as a 50-year increase in life expectancy, and $ 100,000/QALY are reported.

Measuring costs can be challenging, due to the uncertainties of the market, difficulties in measuring opportunity cost and external effects [10]. Even considering these major challenges, CEA is widely used in both investment and reimbursement decisions in health economics and policy. The nature of advanced therapies makes it even more difficult to perform a CEA, because it's also important to recognize the risks involved with genetic tests. Furthermore, genetic tests are very expensive, therefore – even though they might provide important information, especially in the early stages of the disease – due to their high costs they are only adopted at a later stage, after the failure of several treatments.

19.4 Market Access

In 1906, the federal US government introduced the Food and Drug Act. In 1962, the amendments to this Act gave the FDA the task to test and approve new pharmaceuticals. The FDA review process – which is lengthy and complicated – has three phases. Including the research and development (R&D) process, a new drug is estimated to take an average of 14 years to be fully developed [10]. Apart from the entry barriers, the intense R&D process and the regulations regarding safety and health technology assessments (HTAs) can limit or delay the market access of new pharmaceuticals. Limited and delayed access is more pronounced with advanced therapies, since they are individual-specific and cannot count on controlled trials with large number of patients.

After the mid-1970s, the FDA introduced new policies to speed up the approval process for "important" pharmaceuticals. According to Philipson et al. [12], the decrease in approval times following the new FDA policies led to significant improvements for patients, due to a faster access to pharmaceuticals. On the other hand, as noted by Olson et al. [13], this rapid access carries risks related to an increase in adverse reactions.

During the last decade, advanced therapies originated a significant debate, because of the rapid technological improvements and the media attention on the subject: therefore, the FDA and the EMA closely monitored and addressed this issue. Within the 21st Century Cures Act, the FDA defined the pharmaceuticals eligible for Regenerative Medicine Advanced Therapy (RMAT). According to section 3033 of the 21st Century Cures Act, a drug is considered RMAT if it involves "cell therapy, therapeutic tissue engineering product, human cell and tissue product or any combination using such therapies or products". Similarly, the EMA defines advanced therapy medicinal products (ATMPs) as "medicines for human use that are based on genes or cells". A Committee for Advanced Therapies (CAT) monitors the safety and efficacy of such pharmaceuticals.

It is important to acknowledge the need for advanced therapies and their potential benefits for the individual's life expectancy and well-being. While R&D efforts continue to increase in this area, it's important to find and suggest solutions to bring advanced therapy pharmaceuticals to the market as soon as possible. In addition, the need for a regulation of such pharmaceuticals in terms of safety, effectiveness and reimbursement is especially important, to get a wider access to these drugs [14]. Finally, in order to avoid delays in market access, regulatory approval processes should be harmonized.

An early market access is important for both pharmaceutical companies and patients; however, the risks associated with an early access should not be ignored. Due to the lack of several efficacy data, such as those from randomized controlled trials, the risks associated with advanced therapies are greater than those of traditional drugs. When it comes to rare, life-threatening diseases, policy-makers should be willing to take higher risks. Acknowledging such need in health policy, both the EMA and the FDA offer a "fast track" option in the case of advanced therapies, stating however that the increased level of risk acceptability is – and must be – temporary. The main problem is that pharmaceutical companies are taking advantage of this earlier access, while regulatory agents are taking the risks. This situation can be considered an example of a principal-agent problem: in health economics it occurs when companies (agents) are acting to maximize their profits, while increasing the risk for patients, especially when regulatory institutions, such as the FDA and the EMA, bear this risk [15,16].

19.5 Pricing and Reimbursement Policies

The increasing importance of advanced therapies also brings to our attention the discussion of the pricing and reimbursement of such therapies. In order to foster investments in advanced therapies, it is estimated that a spending of over $1 million is necessary. However, the potential economic advantages of advanced therapies should also be considered. Brennan and Wilson [9] cite in vivo gene therapy for hemophilia B as an example. The cost of the standard therapy for hemophilia B – which is a rare, severe disease affecting 1 in 20,000 males – is equal to $ 200-300,000 per year, for a total of $ 4-6 million (lifetime treatment), while in vivo gene therapy, which costs just over $ 1 million and requires a one-time treatment, is less expensive.

Most countries experienced a rapid increase in the healthcare expenditures over the last 50 years. Moreover, there is concern that most countries will not be able to finance their healthcare expenditure in the future [17]. Pharmaceutical expenditure consists of approximately 10-15% of health spending. In other words, pharmaceutical expenditure is

Countries	2000	2005	2010	2013	2014	2015
Australia	7.6	8.0	8.5	8.8	9.1	9.4
France	9.5	10.2	10.7	10.9	11.1	11.1
Germany	9.8	10.3	11.0	11.0	11.1	11.2
Japan	7.2	7.8	9.2	10.8	10.8	10.9
Norway	7.7	8.3	8.9	8.9	9.3	10.0
Turkey	4.6	4.9	5.1	4.4	4.3	4.1
United Kingdom	6.0	7.2	8.5	9.9	9.8	9.9
United States	12.5	14.5	16.4	16.3	16.5	16.9

Table 2. Proportion of total health expenditure in GDP for selected OECD countries [OECD Statistics]

Countries	2000	2005	2010	2013	2014	2015
Denmark	9.07	8.58	7.70	6.90	6.76	6.76
Norway	10.21	9.66	7.65	7.59	7.49	7.66
Netherlands	12.29	11.14	9.82	7.76	7.64	7.87
United States	11.37	12.47	11.94	11.38	11.97	12.23
Germany	14.08	15.39	14.97	13.99	14.36	14.31
France	16.90	17.57	16.36	14.99	15.01	14.74
Czech Republic	24.66	25.70	20.42	17.93	17.11	17.32
Australia	15.70	15.22	15.63	14.99	14.39	14.23
Mexico	19.94	35.60	31.50	27.35	27.01	27.20

Table 3. Proportion of pharmaceutical expenditures compared to total health spending for selected OECD countries [OECD Statistics]

a significant driver of the increase in healthcare costs in most countries. Table 2 shows the proportion of total health expenditure in gross domestic product (GDP) for selected OECD countries. It is clear that, for all countries, there is an upward trend, which implies a considerable burden on the budgets. However, it is also important to mention that pharmaceutical expenditures have been found to have significantly positive effects on the patients' life expectancy [18].

Table 3 shows the proportion of pharmaceutical expenditures compared to total health spending for selected OECD countries. In spite of the introduction of new technological pharmaceuticals into the market, there is a surprisingly decreasing trend in the share of drug expenditure with respect to total health spending. This declining trend can be attributed to series of pricing policy interventions and the penetration of generics in most countries.

Despite the cost-reduction trend which occurred in recent decades, pharmaceutical companies experienced rapid growth rates in terms of size and profits. These growth rates attracted the attention of media, society, policy makers and insurance companies and introduced several challenges in terms of expenditure and reimbursement [10].

The delicacy of the issue and the structure of the pharmaceutical market make regulation very important. In a context characterized by monopolistic competition, with a small number of companies, differentiated products, active barriers to entry and high levels of profit, the pharmaceutical companies possess market power, hence they have the ability to increase prices beyond marginal costs and to discriminate prices. As is well known in microeconomics, these issues lead to a decrease in efficiency [19].

Barriers to entry in pharmaceutical industry are of great importance. A barrier to entry is defined as any factor that will restrict the entry of new companies into an existing market [20]. Patents, which are highly utilized in pharmaceutical industry, are the best example of entry barriers [21]. With active barriers to entry, certain companies can have the monopoly power on a specific product and enjoy high levels of profit for a certain period, therefore the social surplus decreases. In pharmaceutical industry, companies actively use patents (with many variations of the product) to impede entry [10]. Because of this, it is possible to argue that the pharmaceutical industry is the most heavily regulated industry worldwide in terms of safety, market access and reimbursement.

Prices in the pharmaceutical industry have long been discussed, due to the high levels of profit for the industry. Pricing strategies depend on the monopoly power of the companies and the monopsony power of the legal Authorities over the pharmaceutical industry, as well as R&D spending, risks involved, price discriminations, regulations and competition levels. In addition to the similar attributes in terms of safety and efficacy issues, pricing and reimbursement strategies differ among countries and health systems. Pricing and reimbursement decisions are key concepts for the market access of drugs. When advanced therapies are considered, pricing and reimbursement are even more controversial, due to the high costs associated with such therapies. On the other hand, early market access is important for advanced therapy pharmaceuticals, since they mostly target severe and chronic illnesses.

According to Lu and Comanor [22], the prices of new pharmaceuticals with significant therapeutic contribution, determined by FDA ratings, are higher at the time of introduction, with premiums ranging from 51 to 79%. The prices of high-ranking pharmaceuticals decline at a slower rate over time, compared to low-ranking pharmaceuticals. A high level of competition from branded rivals negatively affects introductory prices, whereas generic competition has a positive impact. Therefore, Lu and Comanor [22] conclude that the main strategy when introducing a new innovation is the "skimming strategy" – where highest introductory prices are lowered over time – and if the drug is an imitative (generic) product, the pricing strategy is classified as "penetration strategy" – where a lower price is offered for a new product, to lure customers, proving Dean's [23] hypothesis.

Prices in the pharmaceutical industry are also closely related to the associated risk levels. Risks can arise from the chemical property of the drug, as well as the regulations. The perception of high prices and profits – whether justified or not – and increased health expenditures in the pharmaceutical industry leads to heavy regulations and price controls. The main aim of these price controls is to decrease public spending on pharmaceuticals, while increasing social benefits. There are different types of price control used by the Authorities, such as; reference pricing, item-by item negotiation, formula pricing, profit regulation and budgetary controls (line item and global budget) [24].

In the reference pricing system, pharmaceuticals are grouped and compared within their reference groups, and the lowest price is paid within the group [25]. Reference groups can be based on active ingredients – as in the US – or on disease – as in Germany. However, since advanced therapy pharmaceuticals are heavily personalized, a reference group pricing system is not plausible. Many countries, such as Italy and Canada, also use the prices of similar pharmaceuticals in other countries as reference. This drives down the price of drugs of multinational companies, through an increasing international competition. Once again, such strategy is also not possible in the case of advanced therapy pharmaceuticals. Formula pricing is used in Japan, where pharmaceuticals are priced through their formularies. The UK uses the profit regulation system, where companies negotiate with the Authority, are allowed a certain percentage of profit, and set the price accordingly. This leaves big companies with high R&D costs with higher levels of return, since the profits are calculated after R&D and other costs are deducted. Such policy is plausible for advanced therapy pharmaceuticals; however, Authorities will have to face even higher levels of pharmaceutical expenses and increasing level of company profits.

Pricing policies and regulations differ for each country worldwide. Even within the EU, where the drug approval systems are homogeneous, local governments make decisions about pricing and reimbursement

19.6 Discussion and Perspectives

Given the recent developments in technology in the pharmaceutical industry, advanced therapies will be on our agenda in the coming years. Initiatives regarding the legislation, regulation and pricing strategies for advanced therapies must be taken early in the process, for increased social benefits. Unfortunately, the current level of regulations regarding pricing and reimbursement is not promising. Several questions need to be answered, such as: Will governments and/or health insurance companies reimburse advanced therapy pharmaceuticals? How will the reimbursement/insurance policy work in advanced therapy pharmaceuticals? Authorities should commit to eliminate the grey areas in terms of advanced therapy pricing and reimbursement. Apart from the reimbursement decisions, a harmonization of the approval processes of advanced therapy pharmaceuticals seems necessary in order to ensure early market access.

European and US legislations and regulations regarding the testing, manufacturing, marketing and use of advanced therapy products should be harmonized, in order to produce effective results within personalized medicine. Advanced therapy reimbursement options and strategies are very important in personalized medicine, and should urgently be addressed by all countries. Data collection at an early stage is also of great importance for reimbursement decisions. Ideally, pricing and reimbursement issues should be addressed during the phase of discovery of advanced therapy medicinal products. In addition, the costs associated with advanced therapies should be assessed, and decision-makers should consider the possible effects of increased health expenditures [26]. In order to create successful policies, all stakeholders – such as scientists, universities, hospitals, pharmaceutical companies and governments – should be involved in the decision-making process [27].

19.7 Acknowledgements

I am eternally grateful to Dr. Zafer Çalışkan, Dr. Dilek Başar, and Prof. Dr. Güzide Turanlı for their immeasurable help and support in writing this chapter.

19.8 **References**

1. Garrison LP, Towse A. Personalized Medicine: Pricing and Reimbursement Policies as a Potential Barrier to Development and Adoption, Economics of. In: Culyer AJ (ed). Encyclopedia of Health Economics. San Diego: Elsevier, 2014

2. US Food and Drug Administration. Paving the way for personalized medicine: FDA's role in a new era of medical product development. October 2013. Available at https://www.fda.gov/downloads/scienceresearch/specialtopics/personalizedmedicine/ucm372421.pdf (last accessed September 2017)

3. Hamburg MA, Collins FS. The path to personalized medicine. *N Engl J Med* 2010; 363: 301-4

4. Foroutan B. Personalized Medicine: A Review with Regard to Biomarkers. *J Bioequiv Availab* 2015; 7: 244-56

5. Dzau VJ, Ginsburg GS, Van Nuys K, et al. Aligning incentives to fulfil the promise of personalised medicine. *Lancet* 2015; 385: 2118-9

6. Lynch T, Price A. The Effect of Cytochrome P450 Metabolism on Drug Response, Interactions, and Adverse Effects. *Am Fam Physician* 2007; 76: 391-6

7. Burnett JR, Hooper AJ, Hegele RA. Familial lipoprotein lipase deficiency. In: Adam MP, Ardinger HH, Pagon RA, et al. (eds). Seattle (WA): University of Washington, 1993-2018

8. Hanna E, Rémuzat C, Auquier P, et al. Advanced therapy medicinal products: current and future perspectives. *J Mark Access Health Policy* 2016; 4

9. Brennan TA, Wilson JM. The special case of gene therapy pricing. *Nat Biotechnol* 2014; 32: 874-6

10. Folland S, Goodman AC, Stano M. The Economics of Health and Health Care. London: Taylor & Francis Ltd, 2016

11. Porter ME. (2010). What is value in health care? *N Engl J Med* 2010; 363: 2477-81

12. Philipson T, Berndt ER, Gottschalk AH, et al. (2008). Cost-benefit analysis of the FDA: The case of the prescription drug user fee acts. *J Public Econ* 2008; 92: 1306-25

13. Olson MK. The risk we bear: the effects of review speed and industry user fees on new drug safety. *J Health Econ* 2008; 27: 175-200

14. Dunoyer M. Accelerating access to treatments for rare diseases. *Nat Rev Drug Discov* 2011; 10: 475-6

15. Eichler HG1, Pignatti F, Flamion B, et al. Balancing early market access to new drugs with the need for benefit/risk data: a mounting dilemma. *Nat Rev Drug Discov* 2008; 7: 818-26

16. Nguyen H. The principal-agent problems in health care: evidence from prescribing patterns of private providers in Vietnam. *Health Policy Plan* 2011; 26 Suppl 1: i53-62

17. Erixon F, van der Marel E. What is driving the rise in health care expenditures?: An inquiry into the nature and causes of the cost disease. Brussels: European Centre for International Political Economy, 2011

18. Çalışkan Z. The relationship between pharmaceutical expenditure and life expectancy: evidence from 21 OECD countries. *Applied Economics Letters* 2009; 16: 1651-5

19. Carlton DW, Perloff JM. Modern industrial organization. Boston: Pearson, 2015

20. Waldman D, Jensen E. Industrial organization: theory and practice. Oxford: Routledge, 2016

21. Çalışkan Z. Health Economics: A Conceptual Approach. *Hacettepe University Journal of Economics and Administirative Sciences* 2008; 26: 29-50

22. Lu ZJ, Comanor WS. Strategic pricing of new pharmaceuticals. *The Review of Economics and Statistics* 1998; 80: 108-18

23. Dean J. Pricing pioneering products. *The Journal of Industrial Economics* 1969; 17: 165-79

24. Scherer FM. The pharmaceutical industry. In Culyer AJ, Newhouse JP (eds). Handbook of Health Economics, vol. 1. Amsterdam: Elsevier, 2000

25. Çalışkan Z. Reference Pricing and Pharmacutical Market. *Hacettepe Journal of Health Administriation* 2008; 11: 49-75

26. Atilgan E, Kilic D, Ertugrul HM, et al. The dynamic relationship between health expenditure and economic growth: is the health-led growth hypothesis valid for Turkey? *Eur J Health Econ* 2017; 18: 567-74

27. Erben RG, Silva-Lima B, Reischl I, et al. White paper on how to go forward with cell-based advanced therapies in Europe. *Tissue Eng Part A* 2014; 20: 2549-54

List of Main Abbreviations

ABPI	Association of the British Pharmaceutical Industry
ACC	Accident Compensation Corporation (New Zealand)
ACP	Appraisal Committee (The Netherland)
ACPM	Advisory Committee on Prescription Medicines
ADEC	Australian Drug Evaluation Committee
ADSE	*Assistência na Doença aos Servidores Civis do Estado* (Assistance in Disease to Civil Public Servants – Portugal)
AFSSAPS	*Agence Française de Sécurité Sanitaire des Produits de Santé* (French Health Products Safety Agency)
AIC	*Autorizzazione Immissione in Commercio* (marketing authorization)
AIFA	*Agenzia Italiana del Farmaco* (Italian Medicines Agency)
AMNOG	*Arzneimittelmarktneuordnungsgesetz* (Reform of the Market for Medicinal Products – Germany)
AMVSG	*Arzneimittelversorgungsstärkungsgesetz* (Pharmaceutical Care Strengthening Act – Germany)
ANSM	*Agence Nationale de Sécurité du Médicament et des Produits de Santé* (National Agency for Medicines and Health Products Safety – France)
AO	*Azienda Ospedaliera* (Hospital Unit – Italy)
ARRA	American Recovery and Reinvestment Act (US)
ARTG	Australian Register of Therapeutic Goods (Australia)
ASA	*Amelioration du Service Attendu* (Improvement in Expected Benefit – France)
ASL	*Azienda Sanitaria Locale* (Local Health Unit – Italy)
ASMR	*Amélioration du Service Medical Rendu* (Improvement in the Relative Medical Benefit – France)
ATAGI	Australian Technical Advisory Group on Immunisation (Australia)
ATC	Anatomical Therapeutic Chemical
AWMSG	All Wales Medicines Strategy Group
CA	Commercial Agreements
CADIME	*Centro Andaluz de Documentación e Información del Medicamento* (Spain)
CANM	*Comité de Evaluación de Nuevos Medicamentos* (Catalonia, Spain)
CATS	*Comissão de Avaliação de Tecnologias de Saúde* (Health Technology Assessment Commission – Portugal)
CBG	*College ter Beoordeling van Geneesmiddelen* (Medicines Evaluation Board – The Netherlands)
CCG	Clinical Commissioning Groups
CED	Coverage with Evidence Development

CEESP	*Commission d'Évaluation Économique et de Santé Publique* (Commission for Economic Evaluation and Public Health)
CENM	Joint Committee for the Evaluation of New Medicines (Spain)
CEPS	*Comité Economique des Produits de Santé* (Economic Committee on Health Care Products – France)
CFH	*Commissie Farmaceutiche Hulp* (Dutch Pharmaceutical Assistance Committee – The Netherlands)
CFT	Commission of Therapeutic and Pharmacy (Spain)
CHEs	Crown Health Enterprises (New Zealand)
CIPE	Interministerial Committee for Economic Planning
CIPM	*Comisión Interministerial de Precios* (Spain)
CISNS	National Health System Inter-Territorial Council (Spain)
CMS	Centers for Medicare & Medicaid Services
CNEDIMTS	*Commission Nationale d'Evaluation des DIspositifs Médicaux et des Technologies de Santé* (National Commission for the Evaluation of Medical Devices)
CNFT	*Comissão Nacional de Farmácia e Terapêutica* (National Commission on Pharmaceutical Products – Portugal)
COAG	Council of Australian Governments
COMET	Core Outcome Measures in Effectiveness Trials
CPF	*Comité Permanente de Farmacia del Consejo Interterritorial de Salud* (Spain)
CPI	Consumer Price Index
CPR	Prices and Reimbursement Committee
CPRD	Clinical Practice Research Datalink (UK)
CSC	Catalan Health and Social Care Consortium
CSS	*Consiglio Superiore di Sanità* (Italy)
CSU	Commissioning Support Unit (UK)
CTS	Technical-Scientific Committee
DATS	*Direcção de Avaliação das Tecnologias de Saúde* (Health Technology Assessment Direction – Portugal)
DD	*Distribuzione Diretta* (drugs distributed directly through hospital pharmacies – Italy)
DGCBSF	*Dirección General de Cartera Basica y Farmacia* (General Direction of Basic Health Services and Pharmacy – Spain)
DH	Department of Health (UK)
DHBs	District Health Boards (New Zealand)
DIMDI	*Deutsches Institut für Medizinische Dokumentation und Information* (German Institute for Medical Documentation and Information)
DKG	German Hospital Federation
DoHA	Department of Health and Ageing (Australia)
DPC	*Distribuzione Per Conto* (drugs distributed by territorial pharmacies – Italy)

DRG	Diagnosis Related Group
DTCA	Direct-To-Consumer Advertising
DUSC	Drug Utilization Sub-Committee (Australia)
EAMS	Early Access to Medicine Scheme
EAPs	Early Access Programs
EEA	European Economic Area
EFTA	European Free Trade Association
EHCI	Euro Health Consumer Index
EMA	European Medicines Agency
EMR	Electronic Medical Record
EPF	European Patient Forum
ERP	External Reference Pricing
ESC	Economics Sub-Committee (Australia)
EUPATI	European Patients' Academy on Therapeutic Innovation Project
FDA	Food and Drug Administration
FFDCA	Federal Food, Drug, and Cosmetic Act
G-BA	*Gemeinsamer Bundesausschuss* (Federal Joint Committee – Germany)
GCP	Good Clinical Practice
GDP	Gross Domestic Product
GKV	*Gesetzliche Krankenversicherung* (German statutory health insurance)
GKV-SV	GKV-*Spitzenverband* (National Association of Statutory Health Insurance Funds)
GMP	Good Manufacturing Practices
GP	General Practitioner
GTMP	Gene Therapy Medicinal Products
GU	*Gazzetta Ufficiale* (Official Gazette – Italy)
GUEU	*Gazzetta Ufficiale dell'Unione Europea* (European Official Gazette)
GVS	Medicines Reimbursement System (The Netherlands)
HAS	*Haute Autorité de Santé* (French National Health Authority)
HFA	Health Funding Authority (New Zealand)
HPFB	Health Products and Food Branch (Canada)
HSD	Highly Specialized Drug
HST	Highly Specialised Technologies (UK)
HTA	Health Technology Assessment
ICASE	Integrated Care and Support Exchange (UK)
ICD-10-GM	International Classification of Diseases
ICER	Incremental Cost-Effectiveness Ratio
ICF	International Classification of Functioning, Disability and Health
ICHOM	International Consortium for Health Outcomes Measurement
ICN	Information Communication and Network (Japan)
ICS	Catalan Health Institute
INGESA	*Instituto de Gestión Sanitaria* (Spain)

IQWiG	*Institut für Qualität und Wirtschaftlichkeit im Gesundheitswesen* (Institute for Quality and Efficiency in Health Care – Germany)
IRP	International Reference Pricing
ISS	*Istituto Superiore di Sanità* (Italy)
ITR	Relative Therapeutic Index (France)
JHIA	Japan Health Insurance Association
JMA	Japan Medical Associations
KBV	National Association of Statutory Health Insurance Physicians
KZBV	National Association of Statutory Health Insurance Dentists
LEA	*Livelli Essenziali di Assistenza* (essential level of care – Italy)
LSDP	Life Saving Drugs Program (Australia)
MA	Market Access
MA	Marketing Authorization
MAA	Market Access Agreements
MAH	Marketing Authorization Holder
MATCH	Multidisciplinary Assessment of Technology Centre for Healthcare (UK)
MAu	Marketing Authorization
MBS	Medicare Benefits Scheme (Australia)
MEAs	Managed Entry Agreements
Medsafe	New Zealand Medicines and Medical Devices Safety Authority
MES	Managed Entry Scheme (Australia)
MH	Ministry of Health
MHLW	Ministry Health Labour & Welfare (Japan)
MHRA	Medicines and Healthcare products Regulatory Agency (UK)
MLS	Medicare Levy Surcharge (Australia)
MPA	*Läkemedelsverket* (Medical Products Agency – Sweden)
NCE	New Chemical Entity
NHI	National Health Insurance (Japan)
NHS	National Health Service (UK)
NIBSC	National Institute for Biological Standards and Control (UK)
NICE	National Institute for Health and Care Excellence (UK)
NIHR	National Institute of Health Research (UK)
NIP	National Immunization Program
NIPH	National Institute of Public Health (Japan)
NOC	Notice of Compliance
NZPHD Act	New Zealand Public Health and Disability Act
OBB	Online Bulletin Boards
OECD	Organization for Economic Co-operation and Development
OSMED	*OSservatorio sull'impiego dei MEDicinali* (medicines utilization monitoring centre – Italy)
OSP	hospital prescription (Italy)
OFT	Office of Fair Trading (UK)
OTC	Over The Counter

P&R	pricing and reimbursement
P4P	Payment for Performance Agreements
PBAC	Pharmaceutical Benefits Advisory Committee (Australia)
PBPA	Pharmaceutical Benefits Pricing Authority (Australia)
PBS	Pharmaceutical Benefits Scheme (Australia)
PCOM	Patient Centered Outcomes Measures
PCORI	Patient-Centered Outcomes Research Institute (USA)
PCTs	Primary Care Trusts
PFN	*Prontuario Farmaceutico Nazionale* (National Pharmaceutical Handbook – Italy)
PFS	Progression Free Survival
PHARMAC	Pharmaceutical Management Agency (New Zealand)
PHOs	Primary Health Organizations (New Zealand)
PhRMA	Pharmaceutical Research and Manufacturers of America
PH-T	*Prontuario Ospedale Territorio* (Italy)
PHUs	Public Health Units (New Zealand)
PIP	Public Innovative Purchasing
PMCPA	Prescription Medicines Code of Practice Authority (UK)
PMDA	Pharmaceutical and Medical Devices Agency (Japan)
PMPRB	Patented Medicine Prices Review Board (Canada)
PPI	Patient and Public Involvement
PPRS	Pharmaceutical Price Regulation Scheme (UK)
PRO	Patient Reported Outcomes
PRP	Patients as Research Partners
PSN	*Piano Sanitario Nazionale* (national health plan – Italy)
PSR	*Piano Sanitario Regionale* (regional health plan – Italy)
PTAC	Pharmacology and Therapeutics Advisory Committee (New Zealand)
PVH	*Preço de Venda Hospitalar* (Hospital Selling Price – Portugal)
QALY	Quality Adjusted Life Year
RCT	Randomised Clinical Trials
REA	Relative Effectiveness Assessment
RHCA	Reciprocal Health Care Agreement (Australia)
RMAT	Regenerative Medicine Advanced Therapy
RNR	*Ricetta Non Ripetibile* (non-renewable prescription – Italy)
RNRL	non-renewable w/ limitation prescription (Italy)
RoR	Rule of Rescue
RR	*Ricetta Ripetibile* (renewable prescription – Italy)
RRL	renewable w/ limitation prescription (Italy)
SAMS	*Serviços de Assistência Médico Social* (Medic and Social Assistance Services – Portugal)
SBU	*Statens beredning för medicinsk utvärdering* (Council on Technology Assessment in Healthcare – The Netherlands)
sCTMP	somatic Cell Therapy Medicinal Products

SEFH	Spanish Society of Hospitals Pharmacist
SGB	*Sozialgesetzbuch* (German social legal code)
SGB-V	German Social Code, Book Five
SGCMPS	*Subdirección General de Calidad de Medicamentos y Productos Sanitarios* (Spain)
SHI	Statutory Health Insurance
SIATS	*Sistema de Informação para a Avaliação das Tecnologias de Saúde* (Information System for HTA – Portugal)
SiNATS	*Sistema Nacional de Avaliação de Tecnologias de Saúde* (National System for Health Technologies Assessment – Portugal)
SMC	Scottish Medicines Consortium
SMR	*Service Médical Rendu* (France)
SNS	*Serviço Nacional de Saúde* (National Health Service – Portugal)
SOP	*Senza Obbligo di Prescrizione* (without prescription – Italy)
SPC	Summary of Product Characteristics
SSN	*Servizio Sanitario Nazionale* (National Health System – Italy)
T2A	*Tarification à l'Activité* (France)
TC	Transparency Commission (France)
TEP	Tissue Engineered Products
TGA	Therapeutic Goods Act
TGA	Therapeutic Goods Administration
TGP	Therapeutic Group Premium Policy
TLV	*Tandvårds-och läkemedelsförmånsverket* (Dental and Pharmaceutical Benefits Agency –Sweden)
TPC	triple copy prescription (Italy)
U.S.	United States of America
UAF	*Unidades de Atención Farmacéutica* (pharmaceutical care units – Spain)
UNCAM	*Union Nationale des Caisses d'Assurance Maladie* (National Union of Health Insurance Funds)
USPL	used by specialist limitation (Italy)
USSR	Union of Soviet Socialist Republics
VAT	Value-Added Tax
VFA	*Verband forschender Arzneimittel-Hersteller* (Association of Research-based Pharmaceutical Companies – Germany)
VHI	Voluntary private Health Insurance (France)
VWS	Ministry of Health, Welfare and Sport (The Netherlands)
WGP	*Wet Geneesmiddelenprijzen* (Medicine Prices Act – The Netherlands)
Wlz	*Wet Langdurige Zorg* (Long-Term Care Act – The Netherlands)
WTO	World Trade Organization
ZIN	*Zorginstituut Nederland* (National Health Care Institute –The Netherland)
ZVW	*Zorgverzekeringswet* (Health Insurance Act – The Netherlands)

Authors

Haythem Ammar

Haythem Ammar is a PharmD specialized in pricing, reimbursement, and market access as he holds a postgraduate diploma in European Market Access from Université Claude Bernard Lyon I as well as five years' experience in Market Access Consulting for the Pharmaceutical Industry. He holds an MSc from the EM Lyon Business School and a Master of Marketing from East China Normal University in Shanghai. Besides, Haythem has experience in EAP in Europe and strong relationships with key stakeholders at hospital levels and Health Authorities in France. He already participated in the successful launch of orphan drugs into the French market. Haythem's research interests include oncology, hematology, neuromuscular diseases, and rare diseases.

Barry A. Bleidt

Dr. Bleidt is a Professor of Sociobehavioral and Administrative Pharmacy at Nova Southeastern University. He received his BS Pharmacy from the University of Kentucky, PhD in Pharmacy Healthcare Administration from the University of Florida, and his PharmD from Xavier University of Louisiana. Barry has forty years of professional experience in preventing drug problems and substance misuse. Dr. Bleidt served fourteen years as Chair of the Program Committee for the Alcohol, Tobacco, and Other Drugs Section of the American Public Health Association and three years for the Pharmacy SPIG, twenty-three years as the parliamentarian of the American Association of Colleges of Pharmacy, and nineteen years as the Director of Continuing Pharmacy Education for the National Pharmaceutical Association. He currently serves as the Secretary for the NPhA Foundation and as a Delegate to the USP Convention for NPhA. Dr. Bleidt has delivered over 400 presentations and published nearly fifty works. Some of his publications include the books: Clinical Research in Pharmaceutical Development; Multicultural Pharmaceutical Education; and A Guide to the Top 200 Drugs. Dr. Bleidt was inducted as a Fellow into the APhA Academy of Pharmaceutical Research and Science in 2015 and as a Fellow of the National Pharmaceutical Association in 2016. He received the 2013 Chauncey I Cooper Award (the highest honor bestowed by the National Pharmaceutical Association), 2007 Award for Innovative and Exemplary Contributions to the NPhA Foundation, the Ilene B. Stiff Local Association President's Award as the leader of the Virginia Pharmacists Association Local Association of the Year (2001), the James M. Tyson Award (2nd Highest Honor from NPhA (2001);and the American Public Health Association Leadership Award from the Alcohol, Tobacco, and Other Drugs Section (2000). He currently resides in Ft. Lauderdale, Florida.

Zafer Çalışkan

Zafer Çalışkan received his PhD in Economics from Hacettepe University Department of Economics in 2004. He is currently Associate Professor in the Department of Economics at Hacettepe University. From 2014 to 2016 Dr. Çalışkan was Vice Dean of the Faculty of Economics and Administrative Sciences. Dr. Çalışkan is member of Medical and Economic Evaluation Commission of the Social Security Association (SGK) of Turkey. He is also president-elect of ISPOR Turkey Regional Chapter. Dr. Çalışkan has extensive teaching and research experience in microeconomics, health economics, pharmacoeconomics, health technology assessment, hospital economics, and health systems finance. His current research is mainly focused on burden of diseases.

Gülpembe Ergin Oğuzhan

Dr. Gülpembe Ergin Oğuzhan graduated from the Health Administration Department of Faculty of Business Administration at Hacettepe University in 1998. She started to work as a research assistant at Hacettepe University in 2001. She completed her master degree in 2003 and PhD degree in 2009 in Health Administration Management at the Faculty of Health Sciences at Hacettepe University. She started working at Polar Health Economics & Policy as a R&D specialist and business development specialist in 2009, and she worked as a director until 2015. Since 2015, she has worked as an assistant professor at Ondokuz Mayıs University. She has experience as a project manager along with analyses and reporting of the evaluation of healthcare expenditures. She has been the charter member of Association of Health Economics and Policy (SEPD) since 2009. Her field of interests include health services finance, clinical and economic data analysis, health economics and policy, cost accounting and health technology assessment.

Anke-Peggy Holtorf

Anke-Peggy is the founder of the Health Outcomes Strategies. Her areas of expertise are value of healthcare products and policy decisions on healthcare products for the in- and off-patent sector, reimbursement strategies, outcomes research and health economics, health technology assessment processes, payer interactions, product/device/service synergies. In addition, she is engaged in patient involvement initiatives. Anke-Peggy has served as visiting faculty at the University of Utah between 2006 and 2007 and remains adjunct faculty in the Pharmacotherapy Outcomes Research Center at the University of Utah College of Pharmacy, where she in addition to her academic contributions participated as investigator in a variety of outcomes studies. She has published broadly, among others on subjects of evidence-based decision making and quality control in healthcare. As member of the Health Technology Assessment international Association (HTAi) and the International Society of Pharmacoeconomics and Outcomes Research (ISPOR) she is engaged in the workgroups for Patient and Citizen Involvement in HTA, for Precision Medicines Methods and for Health Technology Assessment for pharmaceuticals, medical devices, and diagnostics. Dr. Holtorf has also been appointed as evaluator at the EU-commission on multiple occasions including SME funding programs and serves on the permanent accreditation boards for university programs in Germany. Dr. Holtorf obtained her PhD in natural sciences (Dr.rer.nat) from the University of Marburg (Germany) and her MBA from the University of Birmingham (United Kingdom), and she is certified for work in governing councils/administrative boards (Switzerland). She looks back on over 25 years of experience in the pharmaceutical and chemical industry in research and marketing with global responsibilities. Among others, she was responsible for the global Disease Management strategy and activities of Novartis Pharma, AG. Between 2000 and 2004, Dr. Holtorf managed the biotech business unit of a midsized Swiss chemical company and held a seat in the executive committee. Previously, she was responsible for technical development in the field of products of biologics in mammalian cell culture in the pharmaceutical industry.

Rabia Kahveci

Assoc. Prof. Dr. Rabia Kahveci is currently the Head of Ankara Numune Health Technology Assessment Center in Ankara, Turkey. The Center covers hospital-based HTA, real-world evidence, research and development and innovation. She previously worked in the Turkish Ministry of Health as a member of pharmaceuticals' reimbursement committee, and continues to hold advisory roles around HTA at the national level. She served as the founding President of the Turkish Evidence-Based Medicine Society for eight years. She is a Director of HTAi, Chair of Developing Countries Interest Group of HTAi, and Chair of the Eurasian HTA Initiative. She is a medical doctor, specialized in family medicine, holds a master's degree in HTA, and an associate degree in management of health institutions.

Guvenc Kockaya

Dr. Guvenc Kockaya is a medical doctor and health economist. He received his Master of Science degree in Pharmacoeconomics & Pharmacoepidemiology from the Yeditepe University and his Doctorate degree in Clinical Pharmacology and Medical Pharmacology from the Istanbul University. He completed the European Market Access Diploma Program at Lyon-1 University and studied as a short-term fellow at the Temple University Center for Pharmaceutical Health Services Research. He established the ISPOR Yeditepe University Student Section. In 2011, he became the first Turkish citizen to be awarded the "ISPOR Meeting Travel Scholarship Award". He has several articles and posters that have been published in national and international journals or presented at national and international congresses. He served as the Turkish translation editor of Bootman`s *Principles of Pharmacoeconomics* and WHO`s *Health Technology Assessment in Medical Devices*. He worked for Ministry of Health of Turkey as health economist and was a member of Medical and Economic Evaluation Commission, which evaluates pharmaceutical reimbursement decisions. He also worked as head of market access or health economics department in pharmaceutical & medical device companies for Turkey and Middle East countries. He is the President of the Health Economics and Policy Association (HEPA) and plays an active role in the development of health economics in Turkey; he is a member of scientific advisory board of "Farmeconomia. Health economics and therapeutic pathways". He is the editor of the books titled as "Pharmaceutical Market Access in Emerging Markets" and "Pharmaceutical Market Access in Developed Markets". Currently, he works at CarthaGenetics, a Switzerland based consultant company as market access director for Europe, Turkey, Middle East and North Africa.

Selcen Öztürk

Dr. Öztürk completed her undergraduate education at the Gazi University – Department of Economics in 2006; he received her Master degree from the Hacettepe University – Department of Economics in 2008. Dr. Öztürk completed her PhD education in the field of Economics at the University of Sheffield in 2012. Since 2012, she has worked at Hacettepe University. Her field of interests include microeconometrics, regional economics, labor economics and health economics. Dr. Öztürk has worked as an assistant professor since 2014.

Carme Pinyol

Carme holds MD degree from the Autonomous University of Barcelona, a PhD on Economics from the Castilla-La Mancha University, an MSc in Pharmacoeconomics and Health Economics from the Pompeu Fabra University, an MSc in Health Research from the Castilla-La Mancha University and an Executive Program Degree from the ESADE Business School. She practiced as a Physician until she joined the pharmaceutical industry. She has more over 30 years' experience in the pharmaceutical industry. At Bayer, Carme has held various positions related to clinical research and health economics/market access working in different areas including oncology, cardiovascular, rare diseases, ophthalmology, diabetes, etc. Finally, she was the Head of Market Access for Spain since 2012. For two years she was Principal HEOR at IMS for Spain, Portugal, and Italy. And, after that, she was founder and director of INNOVA-strategic consulting. Currently, she is the Head of Pricing and Market Access for the Southern Europe at Pierre Fabre. She has frequently been invited as a speaker by several Spanish Universities to courses and seminars on clinical research and health economics. She has also authored more than 60 communications in international and national congresses and more than 20 papers in national and international peer-reviewed journals. She is former director of "Revista Española de Economía de la Salud". She is also a reviewer for the journals Gaceta Sanitaria, Value in Health and European Journal of Health Economics. Carme is the President of the ISPOR Regional Spain Chapter and a former member of the Board of the Spanish Association of Health Economics (AES).

Lorenzo Pradelli

Lorenzo Pradelli is medical director at AdRes Health Economics and Outcomes Research srl, Torino, Italy. He is in charge of the design, development and management of pharmacoeconomic researches, with particular reference to the medical and scientific aspects. He is member of the scientific board of *Farmeconomia. Health economics and therapeutic pathways*, published by SEEd. He's author and co-author of more than 30 articles on pharmacoeconomics, including original scientific papers in peer-reviewed journals, oral communications and poster presentations at national and international congresses. Dr. Pradelli is member of the International Society for Pharmacoeconomics and Outcomes Research (ISPOR).

Mete Saylan

Mete Saylan received his medical doctor degree from the Istanbul University Medical Faculty, and he finished his specialization in psychiatry at the Istanbul University Psychiatry Department. He started his academic career with clinical research in neurosciences. In 2001, he joined pharmaceutical industry as clinical research physician, and he worked in medical and market access department of different international pharmaceutical companies. He is currently Market Access Director for Turkey, Iran, and Maghreb countries.

Amir Sharaf

Dr. Sharaf is CarthaGenetics® International Business Development Director. He is a Medical Doctor with six years of medical practice in various settings, and five years' experience in Market Access Consulting for the Pharmaceutical Industry. His research interests include immunology, internal medicine, and oncology. His research focuses on diagnostic value of antibodies in connective tissue diseases, as well as regulatory and economic requirements for the market access of orphan and innovative drugs in the EU. Amir provides targeted methodology approaches for CarthaGenetics® projects, as well as scientific communications to the CarthaGenetics® team, to physicians and health authorities worldwide. Amir speaks English, French, and Arabic, and is based in Carthage, Tunisia.

Nuno Silverio

Nuno Silverio is currently the head of Market Access and Governmental Affairs of Merck in Portugal. With initial training in Pharmaceutical Sciences from the School of Pharmacy of the University of Lisbon, he also has a post-graduation in the economic evaluation of medicines from ISEG and an MBA from AESE/IESE. He has close to 20 years of experience in the pharmaceutical industry, having worked in market access for Wyeth, Pfizer, and Merck, and also at Governmental level at Infarmed. He is an active member of ISPOR, APES (Portuguese Association of Health Economics) and APREFAR (Portuguese Association of Regulatory Affairs Professionals), having led this last organization as its president for a total of 6 years.

Mondher Toumi

Professor Mondher Toumi is M.D. by training, M.Sc. in Biostatistics, and in Biological Sciences (option pharmacology) and Ph.D. in Economic Sciences. Mondher Toumi is Professor of Public Health at Aix-Marseille University. After working for 12 years as Research Manager in the department of pharmacology at the University of Marseille, he joined the Public Health Department in 1993. In 1995 he embraces a carrier in the pharmaceutical industry for 13 years. Mondher Toumi was appointed Global Vice President at Lundbeck A/S in charge of health economics, outcome research, pricing, market access, epidemiology, risk management, governmental affairs and competitive intelligence. In 2008, he founded Creativ-Ceutical, an international consulting firm dedicated to support health industries and authorities in strategic decision-making. In February 2009 he was appointed Professor at Lyon I University in the Department of Decision Sciences and Health Policies. The same year, he was appointed Director of the Chair of Public Health and Market Access. He launched the first European University Diploma of Market Access (EMAUD) an international course already followed by almost 350 students. Additionally, he recently created the Market Access Society to promote education, research, and scientific activities at the interface of market access, HTA, public health and health economic assessment. He is editor in Chief of the Journal of Market Access and Health Policy (JMAHP) which was just granted PubMed indexation. Mondher Toumi is also Visiting Professor at Beijing University (Third Hospital). He is a recognized expert in health economics and an authority on market access and risk management. He authored more than 250 scientific publications and communications and has contributed to several books.

Albert I. Wertheimer

Prof. Albert I. Wertheimer, Ph.D., M.B.A., served as a Director of Lannett Co. Inc. since September 2004 until December 31, 2012. Dr. Wertheimer serves as Member of the Advisory Board of Clinication, Inc. He has a long and distinguished career in various aspects of pharmacy, health care, education and pharmaceutical research. Presently, Dr. Wertheimer is a professor at the School of Pharmacy at NOVA Southeastern University. Dr. Wertheimer also provides consulting services to institutions in the pharmaceutical industry. Dr. Wertheimer's academic experience includes professorships and other faculty and administrative positions at several educational institutions, including the Medical College of Virginia, St. Joseph's University, Philadelphia College of Pharmacy and Science and the University of Minnesota and Temple University. Dr. Wertheimer's previous professional experience includes pharmacy services in commercial and non-profit environments. He is a licensed pharmacist in five states and is a member of several health associations, including the American Pharmacists Association and the American Public Health Association. His academic responsibilities, he is the author of more than 30 books and more than 400 journal articles. Dr. Wertheimer holds a B.S. Degree in Pharmacy from the University of Buffalo, an M.B.A. from the State University of New York at Buffalo, a Ph.D. from Purdue University and a Post-Doctoral Fellowship from the University of London, St. Thomas' Medical School.

Kally Wong

Kally Wong entered consumer and media research early in the career. She specialized in market analysis for the pharmaceutical industry about 15 years ago. She has worked in seven countries span across the Asia Pacific and Europe. Kally is now based in Basel, Switzerland.

Fatma Betul Yenilmez

Fatma Betul Yenilmez has worked as a consultant on market access and health economics both for government and private sector since 2014. Her educational background also includes master degrees and lots of certificates in nursing, market access, and health economics. She published several scientific articles and posters in health economics and market access area.

Made in the USA
Middletown, DE
12 October 2018